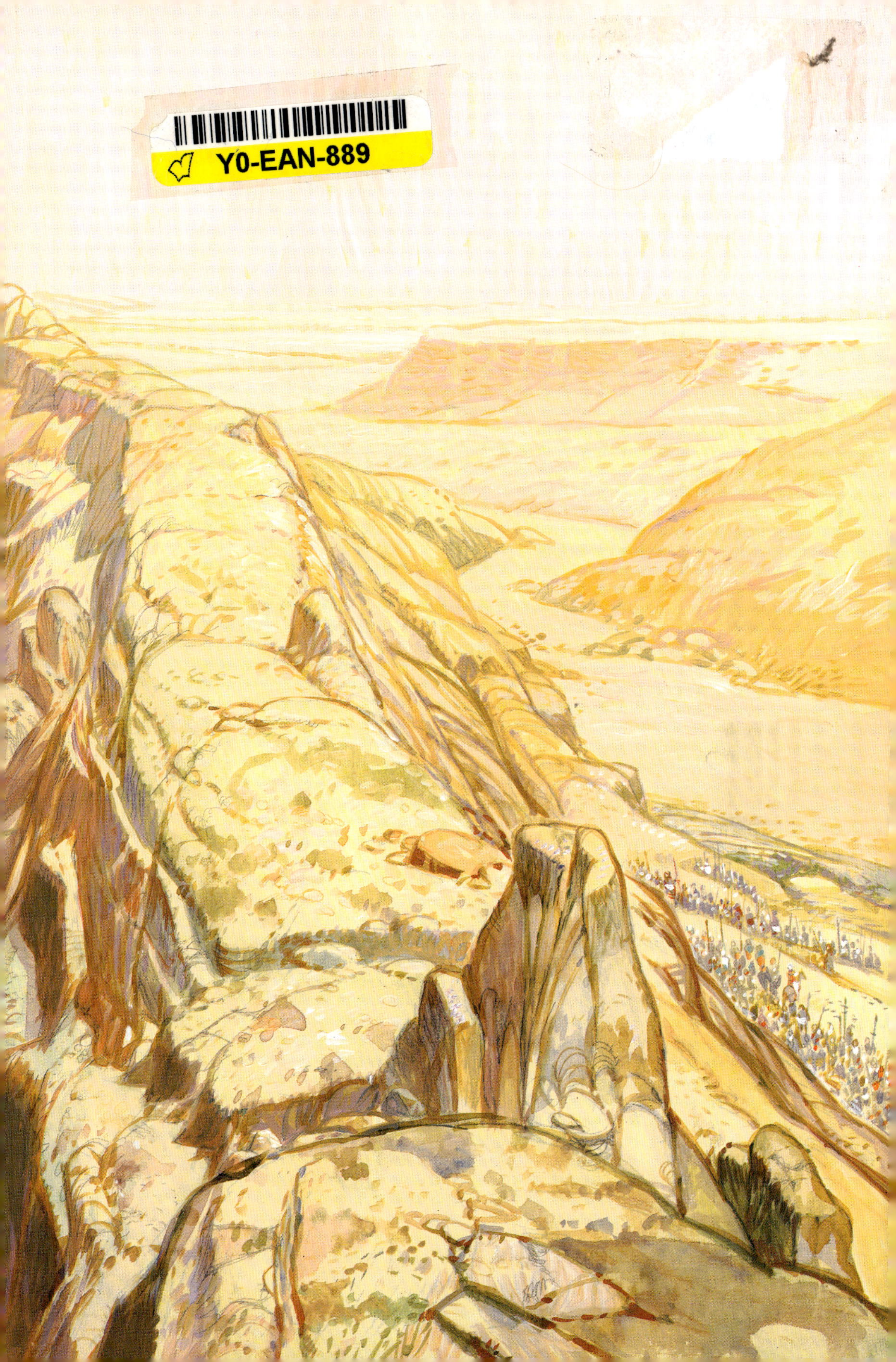

David
From Outlaw to King

Written by Anne de Graaf
Illustrated by José Pérez Montero

Reader's Digest Young Families

David – From Outlaw to King

1 Samuel 21-end; Psalms 52; 59; 34; 142; 57; 23; 60; 2 Samuel 1-10; 1 Chronicles 11-12; 21-22; 2 Chronicles 3

Book 9 – Bible Background 3	

DAVID MUST HIDE

No Food and No Sword 4
The Spy Who Betrayed David 4
David Acts Like a Madman 6
A Cry for Help 6
An Old Friend Returns 9
A Narrow Escape 11
Alone in a Cave 11

DAVID THE WANDERER

A Great Prophet's Death 14
Nabal Is a Fool 14
Abigail 15
David Marries Again 17
David Tricks the Philistines 17

Saul Disobeys Again 18
Everything Is Lost 19
David to the Rescue 21
The Death of Saul and Jonathan 22

KING DAVID

Civil War 22
Making Peace 24
David Is Made King of Judah and Israel 25
Jerusalem 26
The Lord's Covenant Box
Arrives in Jerusalem 27
The Throne Will Last Forever 29
The Lame Prince 30
David Leads His Armies to Victory 30

Other Children's Bible Library Titles . . 32

Book 9 – Bible Background

The Psalms are songs and poems written by David, as well as other musical men of David's time. Because they are about how people feel when they are sad or happy, afraid or alone, the Psalms continue to be read by people, even today.

David was very good at singing and playing instruments. As a boy he taught himself to play the harp while sitting on the hillsides, watching his sheep. After Samuel anointed David, the Holy Spirit helped David sing and play his harp even more beautifully than before.

Each psalm is a poem or song to God. Some of the ones written by David are about how scared he was when Saul was hunting for him, to kill him. In others, David wrote about how much he loved the Lord and about the glory of God.

The books of 2 Samuel and 1 Chronicles continue the story of David. Much of what David did as king is recorded here.

One day the people of Judah and Israel would need to be reminded of Kings like David. At that time they would have spent long years away from their homeland and once again, would want to know how to love God, follow His rules for their lives, and worship the Lord. Then, as now, these stories would have something to teach the people of God.

DAVID MUST HIDE
No Food and No Sword

1 Samuel 21:1-6, 8-9

Saul had been made the first king of Israel by Samuel, a judge who spoke God's words and did what God wanted. At first Saul had been a good king and had also done what God wanted, but then he started to go his own way.

So God told Samuel to anoint a new man as king, and he chose David who was a shepherd boy. At first Saul liked David, not knowing that David was to become king. But as time went on Saul became jealous of David's heroic deeds and angry at his popularity. He tried to kill David, but David escaped from him.

All through the night David continued his escape from Saul. He was a wanted man and he ran for his life. That was the first night of many which he would spend outside, under the stars, listening for the sounds of the men who were chasing him.

By the time the sun rose, David had arrived at the town of Nob, where the Lord's priests lived. He went to the priest Ahimelech and asked for some food.

Ahimelech trembled when he saw David. "Why are you alone?" he asked. He was used to seeing David traveling with his troops.

"I'm on a secret mission which was so urgent, I had to leave without food, weapons, or any of my men. But they will join me later. Now, do you have any food for me?"

Ahimelech said he had only the bread which was placed on the Lord's altar as a special offering. This was the sign of how God always makes sure His people have food. It was against the rules for anyone who was not a priest to eat that bread. But Ahimelech knew it was more important to help a friend in need than to follow rules. So he gave the bread to David.

"And is there a weapon I can use?" David asked.

"There is only the sword of Goliath."

"Ah, yes," David said. "There's no sword like that one. I'll take it with me."

David lost no time and ran out of the town, back toward the wilderness. As he left, he happened to notice one man watching him closely. David was in such a hurry, though, he did not give it much thought. He was on the run again, but this time he had bread and a weapon. "Thank You, Lord. Thank You for these gifts. Now I can fight and live. Protect me, I pray, from my enemies."

The Spy Who Betrayed David

1 Samuel 21:7; 22:6-23; Psalms 52; 59

The man who had seen David leave Nob was the only one besides the priest to know that David had been there. This man had secretly watched as Ahimelech helped David. He was Doeg the Edomite, King Saul's head shepherd. He knew Saul was hunting David.

During the next few days, while David ran from one hiding place to the next, Doeg made his way back to the hill at Gibeah, where Saul had camped with his troops. Saul was just complaining that everyone must be plotting against him since no one seemed to know where David was, when Doeg spoke up. He told Saul everything he had seen while spying in Nob.

Then Saul sent for the priest Ahimelech and accused him of plotting against him. "You are a traitor! Why did you help my enemy?"

"But nobody is as loyal to you as David. He's the captain of your bodyguard. I don't know anything about David's being your enemy. What are you talking about?" Ahimelech said. He did not know how much Saul hated David and was afraid of everyone plotting against him.

Saul shouted in anger, "You will die! You and all your priests! You are traitors!"

But when Saul ordered the guards to kill the priests, the guards refused. They would not harm the priests of the Lord.

So Saul ordered Doeg to kill them. Because Doeg was an Edomite and not a Hebrew, he had no respect for the priests. That day Doeg killed eighty-five priests! Saul also ordered everyone who lived in Nob to be killed – all the men, women, children, and animals.

Only one man escaped, a son of Ahimelech the priest. His name was Abiathar. He managed to run away and find David. When he told David what had happened, David blamed himself for the tragedy. "Oh, I should have known he would tell Saul about me when I saw him watching me in Nob!" David said. "Now that Saul is trying to kill us both, will you stay with me?" he asked Abiathar. Abiathar agreed and stayed under David's protection.

David Acts Like a Madman
1 Samuel 21:10-14; Psalm 34

After David left Nob, he kept running and finally ended up inside the enemy Philistine territory. David went to meet with the Philistine king of Gath, King Achish.

On his way, though, the Philistines recognized him. "Isn't this the Israelite they sing about in their dances? This is the same David from that song, 'Saul has killed his thousands, but David his ten thousands.' Let's make him our prisoner!"

David knew he was in great danger and felt very afraid. The Philistines had been his enemies ever since he had killed their star soldier, Goliath the giant. Now that they had recognized him, they might either kill him or turn him over to Saul, who also wanted him dead.

David said a prayer. He was frightened, and he could do nothing else but turn to the Lord who had saved him from death so many times before.

God showed David what he should do. Whenever King Achish and his men were around, David pretended to be a madman. He rolled his eyes and drooled down his beard. He drew funny pictures on the doors and walls and made strange sounds.

When the king saw him, he shouted at his soldiers, "Don't I have enough madmen around me as it is? Any fool can see this is not General David! Where did you pick up this madman? I don't want him here!"

The Philistines looked at each other. "I could have sworn he was David," one whispered to the other. They shrugged their shoulders, then did what the king had ordered. They brought David to the city gates and dumped him outside the city. David waited until it was dark, then slipped away from the Philistine city. He had tricked the enemy into letting him go free.

A Cry for Help
1 Samuel 22:1-2; 23:1-15; Psalm 142

Everywhere David went, men who did not trust Saul, or who were in trouble, came to David to fight by his side. His brothers, father, friends and strangers, they all joined David's troops. Together, the men moved from cave to cave, hillside to hillside, through the desert and between the cliffs. They were always on the run from Saul's soldiers. But no matter what, David prayed to God to find out when they should leave a place and where they should go next. David knew God protected him, and he trusted the Lord.

One day a messenger came to David. "The Philistines are attacking the Hebrew town of Keilah!" David prayed, asking God if he and his men should go and fight the Philistines.

The Lord answered him, "Go, attack the Philistines and save the people of Keilah."

But David's men were afraid, so David asked the Lord a second time. Again, the Lord said, "Go down to Keilah. I will hand the Philistines over to you." David and his men did as the Lord said. They rescued the town of Keilah and won a great battle against the enemy Philistines.

But afterwards, Saul heard that David was in Keilah and he thought, "Ah, now I have David. Keilah is a city of gates and barred windows, just like a jail. I can trap him inside and there's no way he can escape from me."

When David heard Saul was coming after him with a huge force of men, he asked God, "Will Saul come? And if he does, will the people hand us over to Saul?"

"Yes," God told him. So David and his men fled into the desert. They traveled at night, under cover of darkness and when it was coolest. Day after day Saul searched for him, but God helped David hide in all the right places.

8

An Old Friend Returns

1 Samuel 23:16-18

After days and nights of running from one place to another, David finally stopped and told his men they could rest for a few days. They were camped up on a hillside where there were many caves. David posted lookouts on all sides.

The men had only just started setting up camp, when suddenly, a cry went up from the guard. "Someone is coming!" The men fell silent. Everyone waited. If it was one of Saul's scouts, then Saul was too close and they would have to start running again. Was the visitor a friend or an enemy?

As the stranger came closer, they could see he was alone. David's guards waited a few minutes, then they grabbed the man! But he did not struggle against them. "I'm a friend!" he called out. "Take me to David, he knows who I am!"

The guards brought him into the camp. David came out to see who the stranger was. When he saw the man he cried out loud, "Jonathan! My brother Jonathan!" The two friends fell into each other's arms.

They had not seen each other since the first night David started running from Saul. David hugged Jonathan and cried with joy. "My friend," he gasped, "is there no rest from all this running? Even the towns we save from the Philistines are ready to hand us over to your father. My men don't complain, but there is hardly anything to eat and we almost never have a chance to sleep. I don't know. Sometimes I wonder how we can possibly go on."

Jonathan grabbed his friend's shoulders. David looked dirty and tired, hungry and alone. Jonathan steered his friend into a nearby cave where they could talk alone. As they walked by some of the other men, Jonathan noticed how tired they all looked.

Once in the cave, they sat down and Jonathan looked David straight in the eyes. "Don't be afraid. My father won't lay a hand on you. Someday you will be king over Israel, and I will be second to you. Even Saul knows this."

Jonathan stayed with David and his men for a few days. During that time Jonathan helped David feel better. Yet it would be the last time that David and Jonathan ever saw each other.

When Jonathan left him, David felt sure in his heart that God was still in control and would protect him. David would not give up now.

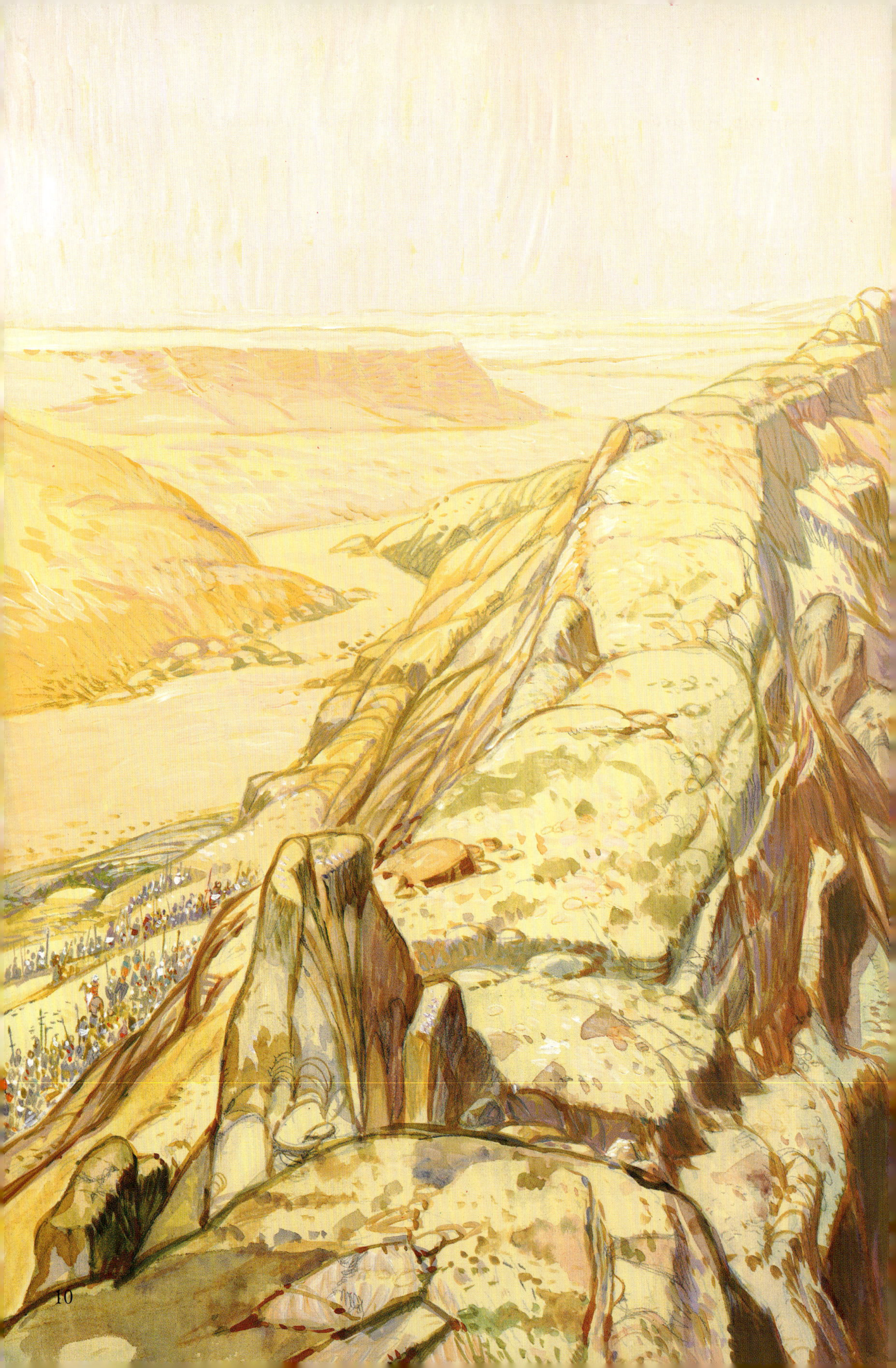

A Narrow Escape
1 Samuel 23:19-28

Over and over again Saul found out where David was hiding. When he did, God protected David. One time, Saul was at Gibeah when people told him that David had camped in the wilderness at Horesh.

Saul tried to catch up with David and his men, who were forced to camp on the side of a mountain. They knew Saul was very close. Saul and his soldiers were on the other side of the same mountain, closing in on David. Soon David and his men would be captured!

Saul started to round the corner on the cliff which would have brought David and his men within sight, when suddenly, he got an important message. The Philistines were attacking again!

David and his men knew Saul was very close behind them. They clung to the cliffs and David prayed to God for protection. They waited and watched for Saul, expecting him to come into view any minute. Saul was so close, they could hear the trumpet blasts from his soldiers.

"Listen!" David told his men. "Did you hear that?" The men held their breath. Yes, it was the trumpet blast from Saul's troops. "It means they're attacking," one man said.

"No, it means Saul is calling off the hunt and retreating. I don't know why," David said. "But Saul is turning around and going home. Praise God!"

Saul had indeed turned around. He needed to go back and fight the Philistines who were attacking the Israelite villages. He had almost caught David, but not quite. So David escaped again, thanks to the Lord's protection.

Alone in a Cave
1 Samuel 24:1-22; Psalm 57

After Saul returned from fighting the Philistines, he sent out spies to ask everyone, "Do you know where David is hiding?" Most people did not know and could not say. But the few who did know, told Saul where David was hiding.

Again, David had moved his men to a part of the country where there were many caves in the hillsides. So Saul took three thousand of his best soldiers and tried to catch David.

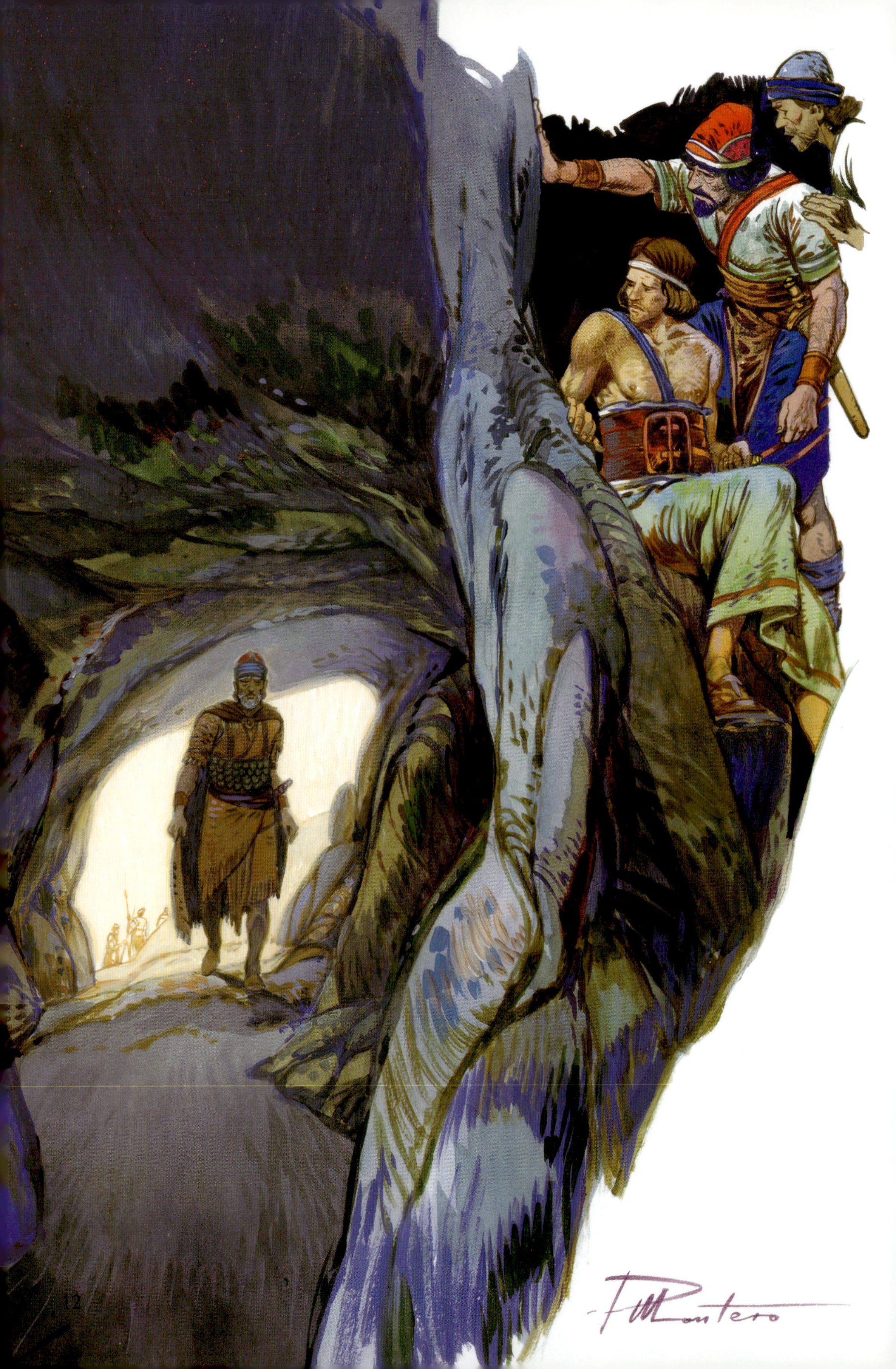

Saul and his soldiers spread out and started climbing cliffs. At one point, when Saul was alone, he looked around for a place where he could relieve himself. He saw a nearby cave and went inside. There was no way he could have known, but hiding deep inside that very same cave were David and his men!

When they saw Saul come into the cave alone, they could not believe their good luck. "Look, David," his men whispered to him. "God has blessed you again. Now is your chance to kill Saul!"

David shook his head and told them that God had chosen Saul to be king. "No one must kill the man God has chosen!"

David crawled down the cave, toward Saul. But instead of killing Saul, very quietly, he cut a corner off Saul's robe. Then he crept back to his hiding place. Saul had not even noticed him. David's men were angry that David had not killed Saul when he had the chance. After all, they had suffered a great deal because of Saul.

The moment he was back with his men, David felt very sorry for what he had done. He had not wanted to harm Saul. "Isn't he the king our Lord God chose?" he told the men who had wanted him to kill Saul. "I should never even have cut off this corner of his robe." Then some of his men offered to kill Saul themselves, but David would not let them.

So Saul got up and left the cave, not even knowing David had saved his life. Once he was outside, though, David came running after him and fell on the ground before him. "My lord the king!" he called out. Saul swirled around in surprise. David held up the cloth. "Look, I cut off this corner of your robe. God gave you into my hands while you were in the cave. But I didn't hurt you! I even kept my own men from hurting you. Now will you believe I'm not your enemy? Why do you chase me like this? I've done nothing wrong!"

Saul saw that David could have killed him if he had wanted to. "A man does not let his enemy escape as easily as you have. I believe you, my son, David. Only promise me you will not hurt my family for what I have done to you."

David agreed and Saul left him and his men in peace.

David was so happy that Saul was going to stop chasing him, he wrote a song of thanks to the Lord. "O God, Your love is so great, it reaches into the heavens. I knew if I trusted in You, You would not betray me. You are always by my side."

It did not take long, though, before Saul went back on his promise. David soon discovered he would only be safe from Saul's dangerous moods if he stayed very, very far out of his reach.

DAVID THE WANDERER
A Great Prophet's Death

1 Samuel 25:1

A short while after Saul told David he would stop chasing him, the great prophet Samuel died. Samuel had grown very old during the years David was on the run. He had never stopped praying for his people. When Samuel died, all of Israel felt sad and huge crowds of people gathered to remember him.

Samuel was the last of Israel's judges. While he lived, Samuel tried to keep peace between the people, reminding them they should stop worshiping the foreign gods of the tribes around them. Some listened to Samuel, but most did not.

Samuel's most important task, though, had been to appoint a king over God's people. Once King Saul stopped obeying God, Samuel became so upset, he cried for days and days. Then, when he anointed David as king, he prayed for David's protection while Saul was chasing him. Samuel did not live long enough, however, to see the day when David become king.

Both David and Saul were at Samuel's funeral. They, as well as all the people who had been touched by God through Samuel's words, cried for the great prophet Samuel.

Nabal Is a Fool

1 Samuel 25:2-13

After Samuel was buried, David and his men moved down to a desert valley where a very rich man called Nabal lived. Whenever this rich man's shepherds brought his sheep to pastures near David's men, they made sure the shepherds were safe and no harm came to the sheep. David and his men protected Nabal's flocks.

When it came time for Nabal to cut the wool from his sheep and sell the wool at market, Nabal held a big party. The people who had worked or helped with the sheep were paid at the party. So David sent some of his men to Nabal with greetings. Because they had helped Nabal's shepherds, Nabal should have given David's men some kind of gift.

But Nabal, was not a very reasonable man. Even worse, he was selfish, proud and often angry. Nabal thought he was better than everyone else. "Who is this David?" he asked David's men when they greeted him. "Why should I give my bread and water and meat to just anyone?" Even when Nabal's shepherds told him how David's men had helped them, he just laughed and drank some more wine.

When David's men told him what Nabal had said, David became angry as well. "Get ready for a fight!" he ordered his men. "We will teach this foolish Nabal a lesson he'll never forget!"

Abigail
1 Samuel 25:14-38

While David and his men were getting ready to punish Nabal for being so greedy and selfish, a servant ran and told Nabal's wife what had happened. Nabal was married to a woman named Abigail. She was very beautiful, but also kind and wise. When she heard what her husband had done, she quickly prepared a great deal of bread, wine, grain, cakes and meat, loaded the food donkeys, and led them to David's camp.

She reached him just as David was saying, "If Nabal wants to repay me with insults, then I'll kill every man in Nabal's house."

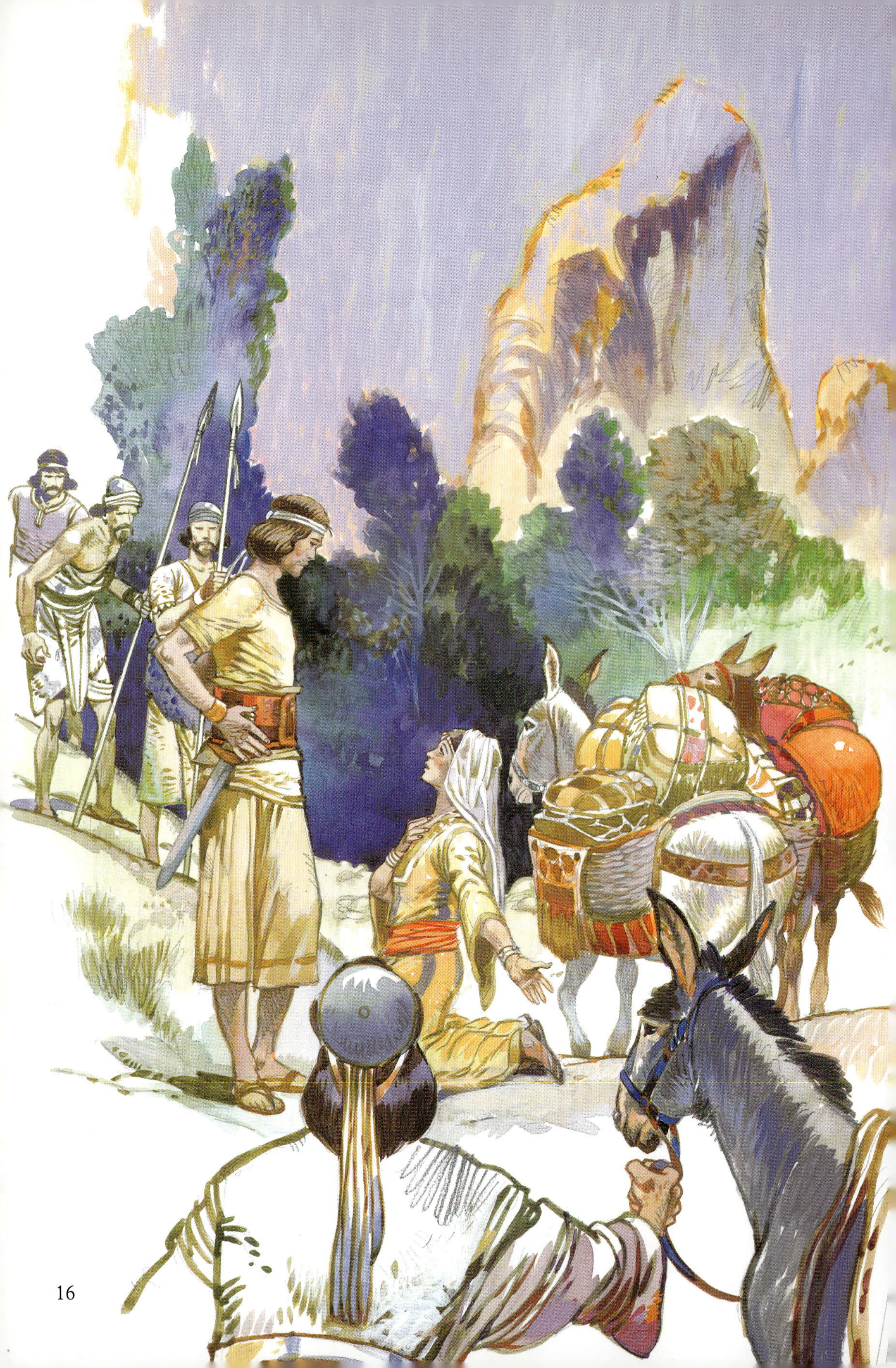

David looked up and saw Abigail coming toward him, followed by donkeys loaded with delicious food. He signaled for his men to stop. Abigail got off her donkey and knelt before David.

"My lord, please pay no attention to my husband Nabal. He is just like his name, which means 'Fool.' Please take these gifts, and let there be no unnecessary killing."

David said to Abigail, "Praise God who has sent you to meet me today. If it weren't for you, I might have killed your husband. Go in peace. We accept your gifts."

When Abigail arrived home, Nabal was still at the big party and very drunk. She waited until the next morning, then told him how close he had come to getting all the men, including himself, killed. When he heard the news, Nabal had a heart attack. He could not move in any way. Ten days later he had a stroke and died.

David Marries Again
1 Samuel 25:39-44

When David heard Nabal was dead, he said, "Praise the Lord. He has kept me from doing wrong and killing for no reason. Now God has punished him, not me."

Then he thought of the lovely Abigail who had had the good sense to meet David with her gifts and prevent many people from being killed. "Send for Abigail," he told his servants. "Ask her to become my wife."

When David's servants gave the message to Abigail, she bowed down with her face to the ground and said, "I would be honored to do what he asks." She would gladly become David's wife. Then she quickly got on a donkey and, together with her five maids, followed David's servants back to his camp. There she became David's wife.

Abigail was David's third wife because he had also married Ahinoam of Jezreel. It was the custom in those days for some men to have more than one wife.

David's first wife, Saul's daughter Michal who had helped David escape, had been taken prisoner by her father. Because Saul had been so afraid of David, he thought he would hurt David by taking away his first love. Saul had found another man to become Michal's husband. Michal and David loved each other very much. He had killed two hundred Philistines for the hand of the king's daughter in marriage. Now they would not see each other again for a very long time.

David Tricks the Philistines
1 Samuel 27:1-12

Saul had broken his promises yet again. He hunted David down, wherever he went. Saul thought David was his enemy, but he was wrong. David only wanted to live in peace with King Saul. Yet he and his men were on the run for months, never knowing whom to trust or where to go.

David had six hundred men with him. It seemed that wherever they hid, Saul always found out about it. "One of these days Saul is bound to catch up with me," David thought to himself. "The best thing to do is go and live with the Philistines. Saul would never dare to cross the border to catch me."

So David went to King Achish and Saul gave up searching for him when he heard he was in enemy territory. The Philistines would never have let King Saul onto their land.

David asked the Philistine king if his men and their families could settle in Gath. King Achish wanted David on his side. He knew Saul was chasing David, so he agreed. "If David's own people, the Israelites, want to kill him, then if I help him, he will become my servant," Achish thought.

But he was wrong. While David and his men lived in the town of Ziklag, where the king had told them they could live, they secretly raided the nearby towns. There, they left no one alive to tell their secret. Every time Achish asked David, "Where have you been today?" David lied. That way, for nearly one and a half years, David and his men killed their enemies while an enemy king protected David from Saul. Once again God gave David a way out of danger as well as a way of protecting the Israelites from their enemies.

Saul Disobeys Again
1 Samuel 28:1-25

The Philistines had threatened to invade all of Israel. Once again they wanted to fight the Israelites. This time, they had gathered all their forces in one place. Unlike the previous smaller battles, this would be a fight to the death. Saul had brought his troops to the battleground and knew it would not be easy to beat the Philistines. He had prayed and prayed, trying to find out who would win the coming battle. But God did not answer Saul's prayers.

When Saul saw how huge the Philistine army was and how much better their weapons were, he was frightened. He badly needed advice about how to fight the battle, so he decided to do something very wrong.

He disguised himself and crept out at night to visit an evil woman. She could talk to the spirits of dead people. Witchcraft was not allowed in Israel. It was against God's Law for people to try and contact spirits of dead people. He wanted the Israelites to believe in Him, not other spirits. When Saul went to this witch, he was breaking God's Law yet one more time.

"What do you want?" she asked him.

"I want you to call up someone who is dead," Saul said.

"But I'm not supposed to do that, You know that's against the Law," the evil woman said. "King Saul said he would kill anyone who does something like that. Are you setting a trap for me?"

"I promise, you won't be punished." So the evil woman called up Samuel from the dead and when she saw him, she turned to Saul and cried out, "You've tricked me! You are Saul!"

But Saul told her not to be afraid. Then Saul saw Samuel's spirit, and he fell down on the ground. He asked him, "Tell me what to do. We fight the Philistines tomorrow and God has turned away from me."

"Why do you bother me? Why ask my advice now, when God has already turned away from you? You didn't obey Him and now it's too late." Samuel said. "Because you have disobeyed the Lord, tomorrow He will hand the Israelite army over to the Philistines. You and your sons are going to die."

When Samuel disappeared, Saul's strength drained away and he fainted in fear. Only after his men begged him to eat something did he have the strength to return to camp. But he had no courage left. He knew the end was near.

Everything Is Lost
1 Samuel 29:1-30:6

While Saul had been gathering his troops and asking the advice of an evil woman, the Philistines had been bringing their troops in from all over the country. Among the leaders was King Achish of Gath, the one who had been protecting David. He asked David and his men to march with him and help fight the Israelites.

Now Achish still thought that while David had lived at Ziklag with the Philistines, he was raiding the Israelites. But actually David had secretly been killing the Israelites' enemies. When the Philistine generals heard Achish had brought David along, they complained.

"No, we don't want David with us during this battle. It would be too dangerous. What if he decides to change sides? If David were to turn against us, Saul might welcome him back home. Why give him the chance he's been waiting for all this time?"

So Achish sent David and his men back to their families. But when David arrived in Ziklag, where he had been living for over a year, he made a terrible discovery.

The town was in flames! While David and his men had been gone, the Amalekites had raided the area! Not one person had been left in Ziklag. They had all been taken prisoner! David and his men cried and wept out loud for their missing wives and children. They were so upset, they became weak from all the crying.

Then David looked around at his men. They were tired, hungry, angry, hurting, and missing their families. David was also filled with a great sadness since he had lost both his wives, Ahinoam of Jezreel and Abigail.

But what made David's grief even worse was that David could hear some of his men blaming him for the bad things that had happened! "David just leads us into trouble. We're tired of all this. Let's get rid of him," they whispered to each other. Some even said they should kill David.

But David found his strength in God. The first thing he did was turn to God for help.

David to the Rescue
1 Samuel 30:7-31

When David saw he was in danger from his own men, he quickly called Abiathar, the son of Ahimelech, who had become a priest. David prayed with him, "Lord God, should I chase the enemy? Will I catch them?"

"Yes, chase them and you will catch them and rescue those you have lost," God replied.

So David rallied his men for action. Six hundred followed him, while two hundred, who were too tired, remained behind to guard the supplies.

All that day, they followed the trail left by the Amalekites. They found an Egyptian slave who had been left behind by the raiders and he promised to lead them to the Amalekite camp.

David and his soldiers crept up on the Amalekites. They were eating and drinking and having a big party. They were so happy with all the loot they had stolen.

Just as dawn broke the next day, David sounded the alarm and his men attacked. They fought long and hard from dawn to sundown. Women and children ran in all directions. As the battle wore on, David and his men became the winners. Only four hundred Amalekites escaped alive, and that only happened because they had camels.

David and his men recovered all their things, as well as their wives and children. They returned to Ziklag, where the two hundred men had stayed behind, protecting the supplies. Some of the men who fought the battle said to those who had not, "You didn't fight, so you don't get any loot."

But David made a new rule that said those who fight must share with those who stay behind and protect supplies. All must share in the takings after a battle. Then David sent gifts of the Amalekite loot to other Israelite towns which had suffered at the hands of the Amalekites.

The Death of Saul and Jonathan
1 Samuel 31:1-13; 2 Samuel 1:1-27;
1 Chronicles 10:1-14; Psalm 23

David was at his home at Ziklag when news of the great battle against Saul's Israelites and the Philistines reached him. This was the battle the Philistine generals had not allowed David to join in.

"It was a terrible battle," the messenger told David. "The Philistines pressed hard after Saul and his sons. They killed his three sons, including Jonathan . . . ." The messenger could say no more for David had fallen to his knees and was tearing at his clothes in grief.

The messenger continued. "The king was surrounded and hit by many arrows. Then he begged his armor bearer to kill him so the Philistines would not capture and torture him. The armor bearer refused. So Saul fell on his own sword, killing himself."

At this, David and his men grieved and wept and did not eat the whole day. The king anointed by God was dead! They grieved for the army of the Lord and the house of Israel. Many Israelite villages had fallen into Philistine hands since the Israelites had lost the great battle. It was a dark day for Israel!

David wrote a sad song about the loss of that battle, and the deaths of Jonathan and Saul.

He wrote, "Israel's glory lies dead on the hills. How the mighty have fallen! Saul and Jonathan — in life they were brave and strong . . . . They were swifter than eagles, they were stronger than lions . . . . I grieve for you, Jonathan my brother. You loved me more than anyone! . . . ."

Later, David wrote one of his most beautiful poems ever. The words describe death as a dark valley. David wrote about how God is there to take your hand and guide you through the darkness, into light. David's words, born out of grief for his friends, continue to comfort people who miss someone they love or must face death, even today.

KING DAVID
Civil War
2 Samuel 2:1-3:5

Some time after Saul's death, David asked God if he should go to Judah. He was wondering what would happen now that Saul was dead and there was no king. The Lord told him to go to Hebron. There, the tribe of Judah anointed David as king!

But meanwhile, the general of Saul's army, a man named Abner, had made one of Saul's sons king over God's people. For the next two years the men of Judah, who followed David, fought against the men from the other Israelite tribes, who followed Saul's son.

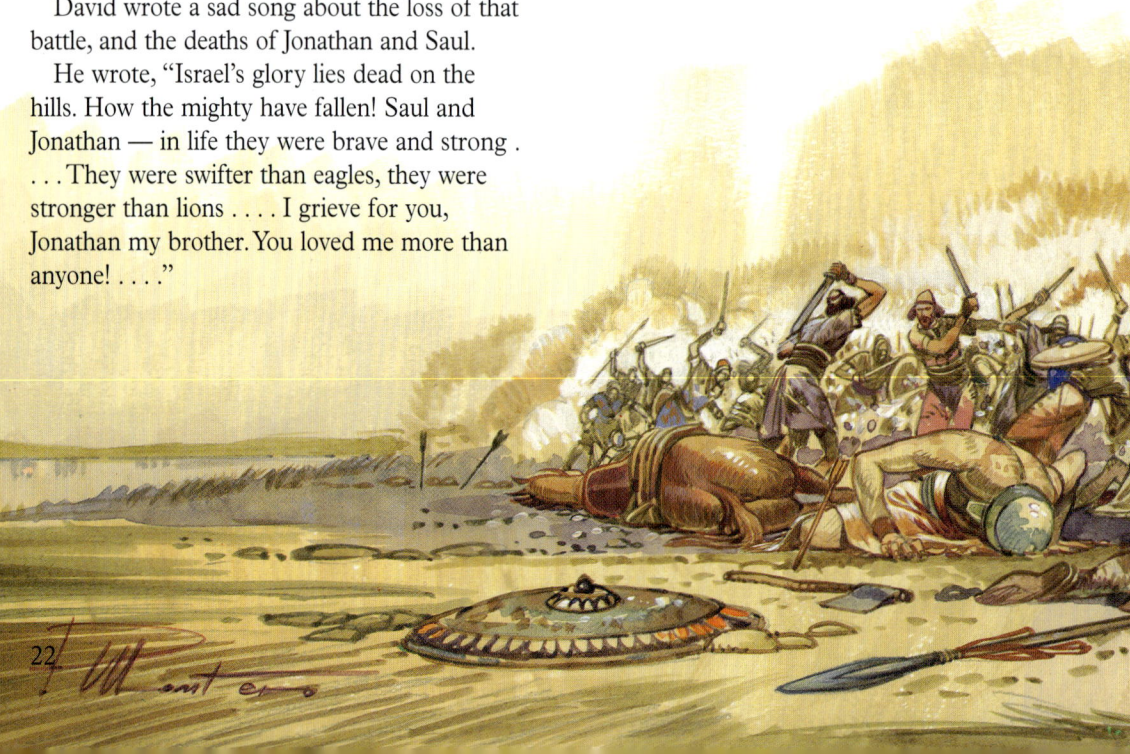

Finally, leaders of the two armies agreed to meet around the lake at Gibeon. Abner's army lined up along one side of the lake, while David's lined up on the other. Abner called out to David's general, Joab. "Choose twelve of your best fighting men and they can fight twelve of mine."

"All right. Let them do it," Joab answered. But when the men fought against each other, not one survived. No one side could be declared the winner.

Then the two armies fought against each other in a fierce battle and David's men won. While only twenty of David's men were missing, 360 of Abner's men had been killed.

The war between Saul's followers and David's followers lasted a long time. David grew stronger and stronger. Saul's army grew weaker and weaker.

Making Peace

2 Samuel 3:6-4:3; 4:5-12

General Abner of Saul's army was a great general. As the war went on, even though his army was losing, Abner fought with great courage and cunning. Despite Abner's being such a great general, there came a time when the son of Saul accused his General Abner of being a traitor. And because of that, Abner, who was popular with the soldiers and people of Israel, decided to go over to David's side.

"This war between brothers has lasted far too long," he thought. "Wasn't David the one anointed by Samuel, after all? I will help David become king over all Israel."

So Abner sent messengers to David, asking to make peace. David agreed and the two men met. The only condition David made of Abner, was that Abner find and return David's first love, Michal, the daughter of Saul, and bring her back to David.

Abner agreed, and he took Michal away from her second husband and brought her to David.

Once Abner had returned Michal to David, Abner met with the leaders of Israel and reminded them of how David has been the Lord's choice of king all along. "Let's make him king now!" Abner said, and the others agreed.

But when Abner was leaving David's home, David's general, Joab, saw him. Joab ran to David and demanded, "That was the enemy Abner! How could you just let him go like that?" Joab thought he had been spying.

David told him about the peace, but Joab was so filled with bitterness because Abner had killed his brother Asahel, he waited for Abner and killed him! When David heard the news he was very angry and told everyone he had had nothing to do with the murder. He made all the men feel sorry about Abner's death.

After Abner's death, the son of Saul whom Abner had put on the throne was murdered. The men who did it came to David with the head of the king, hoping for a reward. But David was furious with them for killing one of Saul's sons, even if he had been an enemy. "For killing a sleeping man on his own bed, I now demand your own deaths!" David said.

David Is Made King of Judah and Israel
2 Samuel 5:1-10, 13-25; 1 Chronicles 14:1-17

Once the son of Saul was dead, all the tribes of Israel went to David and said, "We're all part of the same family. Even while Saul was king, you were the one who led us. We've heard how the Lord told you, 'You will shepherd My people Israel, and you will become their ruler.' " Then all the leaders of all the Israelite tribes made David their king!

When David became king he chose a fortress called Jerusalem to be his city. At that time Jerusalem was just a small village. Even so, it was a well-protected village and would be very hard to capture.

The Jebusites, who lived in Jerusalem, laughed at David. "Ha! You couldn't even fight the blind and crippled of Jerusalem, let alone us!" But David had the blessing of God. When he and his men captured Jerusalem, they made it the royal city of Israel and Judah.

When the Philistines heard that David was king, they called all their troops together so they could attack him. But David asked the Lord what he should do. God told him, "Do not attack right away, but circle around behind them. When you hear the sound of marching in the tops of the trees, move quickly, because that will mean the Lord has gone in front of you to strike down the Philistine army."

It happened just that way and David defeated the Philistines everywhere he went.

David was thirty years old when he was anointed king of Israel and Judah, and became one of the greatest kings the Israelite people ever had. He reigned over both Israel and Judah for forty years in all.

Jerusalem
2 Samuel 5:10-12; 6:1-11; 1 Chronicles 13:1-14:7

When David and his men captured Jerusalem they named it Zion, the City of David. Jerusalem became David's royal city.

The king of Tyre heard David was king and sent his best carpenters and stone masons to build a palace in Jerusalem. When David saw the men building a fine palace of cedar wood and marble, he knew it really was true. He was king! He thanked God and prayed for God's guidance in all that he did.

For David, it was not enough that Jerusalem become known as the City of David. He wanted it to be called the City of God. So David had thirty thousand of his best men go with him to Judah, where the ark of God had been ever since the Philistines returned it. Together they brought it back toward Jerusalem.

But on the way, one of the oxen, who was pulling the cart, stumbled. In order to make sure the ark did not fall out of the cart one of David's men put out a hand to steady the ark. But only the special priests were allowed to touch the ark, so God struck this man dead!

David grew afraid of the power of God and had the men leave the ark at the house of Obed-Edom. Throughout the entire three months the ark was there, that family was richly blessed.

The Lord's Covenant Box Arrives in Jerusalem

2 Samuel 6:12-23; 1 Chronicles 15:1-16:43

When David was told that the ark had brought blessings on the house of Obed-Edom, he decided to try bringing it again to Jerusalem. This time, though, David had his priests carry the Covenant Box on poles, according to the rules God had given Moses about how the ark should be carried.

When the Covenant Box arrived in Jerusalem, the priests put it into a special tent David had made.

Then there was great feasting and dancing. Oh, what a celebration! David had put together a choir and orchestra among the Levite priests. They were to play beautiful music for God and make regular offerings.

28

The people praised and thanked God for all the good things He had done for them. They remembered what God had said to Abraham, Isaac and Jacob. They told the stories of how God rescued them from the cruel Egyptians and helped Moses and Joshua lead them into the promised land where they now lived.

The people danced and sang all day long. David danced the hardest, though. It was as though all the joy and happiness he felt at being God's chosen king, and having the Lord's Covenant Box close by, overflowed into his arms and legs. He bounced around, twisted, turned, did somersaults and sang as loud as he could.

"Let the heavens rejoice, let the earth be glad. Let the sea roar, and all that is in it, let the fields be happy! Then the trees of the forest will sing, they will sing for joy before the Lord!"

David was very happy, but his wife Michal was not. Michal, who was Saul's daughter, watched from the window. "Why is David acting like such a fool?" she thought to herself.

That night when she saw him, she told David she was ashamed of him. Despite their earlier love for each other, because Michal could not join David in being happy before the Lord that day, David and Michal were never close again. And Michal never had any children.

The Throne Will Last Forever
2 Samuel 7:1-29; 1 Chronicles 17:1-27

After David was settled in his palace and had had a time of peace, he said to Nathan the prophet, "Here I am, living in a palace of cedar wood, while the Lord's Covenant Box is still in just a tent."

Nathan said, "Whatever you have in mind, go ahead and do it, for the Lord is with you."

That night, the Lord spoke to Nathan, "Go and tell David, I have no need of a house. I have been moving from place to place with the Israelites. The Covenant Box was always in a tent. But I took David, who was a shepherd, and made him into a king. I promise to build a house for David. The house will be his family.

"I promise David's family will last through the years. His house, which is his family, his kingdom and his throne will be there forever."

God told Nathan that one of David's sons would be the one to build a house for God. "I will love that son and never stop loving him," God said.

When Nathan went to David and told him all that God had said, David was deeply touched. He sat down and prayed, "Who am I that the Lord would do all this for me and my family in the future? I wanted to build a house for You, and now You build the house of a long-lasting family for me. Thank You. I trust You and pray that everything I do would always please You."

David did not know that his family, which God had just promised to protect and love from father to son, would be the same family in which the Messiah would be born. That Messiah would be the King of kings, born in David's hometown of Bethlehem many years later. Jesus would be born into David's family and Jesus would be the King whose kingdom never ends.

The Lame Prince
1 Samuel 20:42; 2 Samuel 4:4; 9:1-13

One day David asked about the family of his best friend Jonathan. "Were they all killed? Isn't there anybody left?" David asked.

Word went out that King David was looking for members of Jonathan's family. One of Saul's old servants was brought to David. This servant was called Ziba. Ziba said, "There is still a son of Jonathan. But he cannot walk, he is crippled in both feet."

"Where is he?" the king asked. The servant told David and the king sent for the boy.

When Mephibosheth, Jonathan's son, came before King David, he was frightened. He knew his father and David had been best of friends. But he also knew his grandfather Saul had tried to kill David.

Mephibosheth had not had an easy life. When his father was killed by the Philistines, Mephibosheth had been only five years old. His nurse had hurried to get the boy to safety once she heard his father and grandfather were dead. There were those among David's soldiers who might have wanted to kill the boy. But in the nurse's hurry, she dropped the boy and he became crippled for the rest of his life.

Because he could not walk, there was no way Mephibosheth could work in the fields. His only way of making a living was to beg.

When Mephibosheth came into the king's throne room, he bowed down. David called out his name, then said, "Don't be afraid. I want to show you kindness because your father and I were such close friends. I give you back all the land that belonged to your grandfather Saul. And you will always be welcome to eat at my table here in the palace." By saying this, David was making him a member of his own family. He was treating Mephibosheth the same as he would any of his sons.

The young man could hardly speak, he was so surprised. He had gone from eating on the streets to eating at the king's table.

"Who am I that you should want to see a dead dog like me?" he asked.

But David's only answer was to call the servant Ziba, who had fifteen sons and twenty servants. He told Ziba he would be in charge of taking care of all the land that Mephibosheth now owned.

Mephibosheth thanked David and from then on, the son of Jonathan lived in Jerusalem and was a rich man with more than enough to eat.

David Leads His Armies to Victory
2 Samuel 8:1-18; 10:1-19; 1 Chronicles 18:1-20:1; Psalm 60

During the years when David was king, Israel and Judah fought against all their old enemies and won. The Lord gave David victory everywhere. Before every battle, David asked the Lord's advice about when and how to attack.

God helped David's men defeat the ferocious Philistines and the murderous Moabites. They beat the Arameans when they attacked David's men the same day the Ammonites attacked from the other side. David's armies captured thousands of charioteers and tens of thousands of enemy soldiers.

David plundered the cities of Edom and Moab, as well as those of the Ammonites, Philistines, and Amalekites. All silver and gold he found, he dedicated to the treasure chests of God. David appointed officials to oversee the treasure and armies and all other parts of his kingdom.

Throughout it all, David was a man of God, a man of prayer. While his armies were winning wars on all fronts, he wrote this prayer to God. "Help us fight the enemy. We can't win the battle on our own strength. We need You. When You are by our side, we always win." David knew all his good fortune came from God and he tried his hardest to please God.

David became famous as the greatest king of Israel. He was a warrior and general. He was king. Most important, though, David was loved by God. That was what his name meant, too, "God's Beloved."

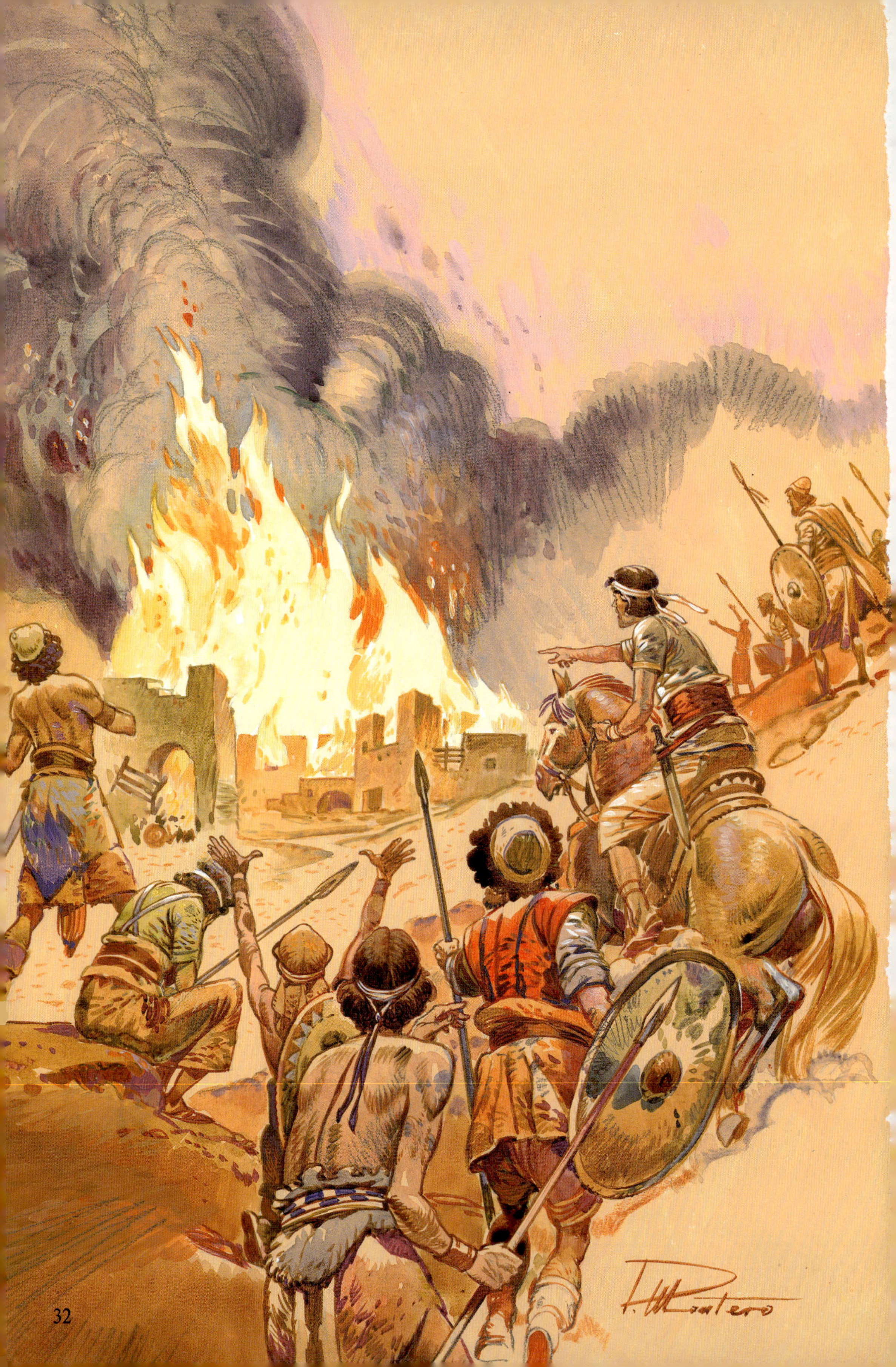

Reader's Digest Young Families
Old Testament

Book 1	Genesis · In the Beginning	
	Genesis 1-22	
Book 2	Israel · God's Chosen People	
	Genesis 23-41	
Book 3	Egypt · From Joseph to Moses	
	Genesis 41-end; Exodus 1-11	
Book 4	Exodus · Moses Leads the People	
	Exodus 12-end; Deuteronomy 1; Leviticus	
Book 5	Desert · The Promised Land	
	Numbers; Deuteronomy; Joshua 1-4	
Book 6	Canaan · Soldiers of the Lord	
	Joshua 5-end; Judges	
Book 7	Faith · Ruth, Job and Hannah	
	Ruth; Job; 1 Samuel 1-2	
Book 8	Samuel · Friends and Enemies	
	1 Samuel 2-20	
Book 9	David · From Outlaw to King	
	1 Samuel 21-end; Psalms 52, 59, 34, 142, 57, 23, 60; 2 Samuel 1-10; 1 Chronicles 11-12, 21-22; 2 Chronicles 3	
Book 10	Kingdom · The Fall of David	
	2 Samuel 11-end; Psalms 32, 51, 3, 63, 18; 1 Kings 2; 1 Chronicles 11- 12, 21-22; 2 Chronicles 3	

Book 11   Solomon · True Wisdom
1 Kings 1-4, 6-12; 1 Chronicles 22, 28-end; 2 Chronicles 1-11; Psalm 72; Proverbs; Song of Solomon; Ecclesiastes

Book 12   Elijah · Working Wonders
1 Kings 13-19, 21-end; 2 Kings 1-2, 9, 17; 2 Chronicles 12-14, 17-20

Book 13   Warnings · Elisha and Isaiah
2 Kings 2, 4-9, 11, 13-14; 2 Chronicles 21-22, 25; 1 Kings 19; Isaiah 28-31; Amos

Book 14   Prophets · Micah, Joel, Jonah & Isaiah
Hosea; Isaiah 1-9, 36-39; Micah; Joel; Jonah; 2 Kings 15-20; 2 Chronicles 26-32; Psalm 46

Book 15   Kings · Israel and Judah
2 Kings 21-24; 2 Chronicles 33-36; Nahum; Zephania; Jeremiah 1-2, 11-20, 26-28, 35-36, 45; Habakkuk; Psalm 73; Ezekiel 1-18

Book 16   Exile · Daniel in Babylon
2 Kings 24-end; 2 Chronicles 36; Jeremiah 24, 30-31, 37-40, 46-end; Ezekiel 24-32; Isaiah 13-24, 40-43; Psalm 137; Lamentations; Obadiah; Danie

Book 17   Freed · The New Jerusalem
Ezekiel 33-37, 40-48; Jeremiah 42-44; Isaiah 44-48; Ezra 1-4; 2 Chronicles 36; Nehemiah 7; Esther

Book 18   Reform · The Last Prophets
Nehemiah 1-10, 12-end; Ezra 4-end; Haggai; Zechariah; Malachi; Isaiah 56-end

Reader's Digest Young Families
New Testament

Book 19   Gospels · The Early Years of Jesus
Isaiah 9, 11-12; Luke 1-5; Matthew 1-4, 14; Psalm 139; Micah 5; Mark 1, 6; John 1-2

Book 20   Miracles · Healing Minds and Bodies
John 2-5; Luke 4-7, 11; Isaiah 53; Mark 1-3, 11; Matthew 5-10, 12

Book 21   Jesus · Following the Messiah
Matthew 8-14; Luke 7-9, 11-13; Mark 3-6

Book 22   Ministry · Jesus Touches People
Matthew 14-18; Mark 6-9; Luke 9; John 6

Book 23   Teaching · The Greatest Commandments
Matthew 18; Luke 9-11, 13-15, 17; John 7-11

Book 24   Stories · Believing the Truth
Luke 15-20; Matthew 19-22, 26; Mark 10-12, 14; John 12

Book 25   Betrayed · In Jerusalem
Matthew 22-26; Mark 12-14; Luke 20-22; John 12-18

INDIAN OCEAN
EQUATOR
AUSTRALIA
Chungking
ASIA
AFRICA
Cairo
Stalingrad
Tokio
JAPAN
PACIFIC OCEAN
EUROPE
ARCTIC OCEAN
ICELAND
GREENLAND
ATLANTIC OCEAN
NORTH AMERICA
Seattle
Boston
New York
Washington
Los Angeles
San Francisco
SOUTH AMERICA
EQUATOR

MOUNT SHASTA

Joseph Muench

Touched by a light that hath no name,
   A glory never sung.
Aloft on sky and mountain wall
   Are God's great pictures hung.

WHITTIER

JOURNEYS THROUGH NORTH AMERICA

A TEXTBOOK IN THE NEW GEOGRAPHY

BY

D<small>E</small> FOREST STULL
TEACHERS COLLEGE, COLUMBIA UNIVERSITY

AND

ROY W. HATCH
STATE TEACHERS COLLEGE, MONTCLAIR, NEW JERSEY

1951

ALLYN AND BACON

BOSTON   NEW YORK   CHICAGO
ATLANTA   SAN FRANCISCO   DALLAS

COPYRIGHT, 1948
BY ALLYN AND BACON

ROD

PRINTED IN THE UNITED STATES OF AMERICA

FOREWORD

This new edition of *Journeys through North America* opens with a journey by air across our country, "As the Airman Sees Our United States." This unit typifies the up-to-date content by which the Stull-Hatch Geographies teach the geography of the Air-Age.

The geography of the Air-Age is truly global in concept, yet it is a geography which even small children appreciate and understand. It is the geography of a new world in which ocean crossings are commonplace and mountain ranges no longer hold back world trade. It is a world of far places and strange faces made familiar by the tales of returned soldiers and their comrades of the air.

This new world of today calls for a clear understanding of its new geography. Old boundaries and old trade routes have yielded to the new world skyways. New social considerations, new political problems, and new economic developments are all part of this evolving new world pattern. Thus, more than ever before, up-to-date instruction in geography embraces the historical and social backgrounds of the peoples and places it seeks to interpret.

Besides being a topic of special interest to children, aviation also offers a stimulating approach to the study of transportation in all of its phases. Clear-cut ideas of geography are especially dependent on understanding the modes and means of travel by which men have moved from place to place on our earth. Modern courses in the social studies recognize the importance of this "journey geography," and the Stull-Hatch books make it a motivating factor throughout the series.

Pupils enjoy traveling to far-off places. "Journey geography" is especially suited to beginners, and in the first volume of the Stull-Hatch Geographies, *Journeys through Many Lands*, the pupil travels by airplane, automobile, boat, train — even by camel — in every continent, beginning with his own country.

This volume, *Journeys through North America* is the second of the series. It gives a detailed study of our country and continues with travels in North America to lands north and south of us. It concludes with brief visits to the West Indies and South America.

The third volume, *Our World Today — Europe and Europe Overseas*, presents old regions of the world to which we trace, primarily, the origins of our own civilization, followed by brief visits to our continental neighbors, north and south. The volume concludes with a visit to the neighboring islands of the Pacific and to South America. The fourth volume, *Our World Today — Asia, Latin America, United States*, introduces the pupil to the Near East, the Far East, the countries south of the Rio Grande and the Panama Canal. Most important, however, is the fact that for the second time in the series, special attention is devoted to a thorough study of our United States. More than half of the book is given to this study.

Certain special features of this volume are worth particular mention.

Objectives. — The leading objectives of *Journeys through North America* are to enlarge the geographical experiences of the children; to enable the child to interpret pictures, maps, and written materials; to help him realize the relation of people's needs to their environment; to develop an appreciation of striking and beautiful scenery; to build up a conception of the earth as a globe; and to create a sympathetic understanding of all peoples no matter how rich or poor their natural environment may be.

Pictures. — No pains have been spared to secure a large number of unusual and appropriate pictures. Thousands of pictures were examined and those selected are placed in close proximity to the written material which they illustrate. Special effort was made to provide colorful and appropriate captions.

Maps. — The maps are many and varied. The journey map gives the pupil a general survey, while the attractive physical-political and population maps fill in the details.

Written Material. — Geography is no mere dull listing of peoples, places, and products. It is alive, rich, and colorful, dealing with real people living on a real earth. The authors have endeavored to communicate this spirit to the pupils by vivid descriptions in simple language, keeping in mind the main objective of all geography work, which is to teach pupils how to see things with geographical eyes and how to think in geographical terms. All new terms are clearly explained.

Integration, Correlation, and Activities. — Geography is treated as one of the social studies which touches all the others. Captain John Smith said, "For as geography without historie seemeth a carkasse without motion, so historie without geography wandereth as a vagrant without a certain habitation." The authors draw upon the field of history, government, or economics whenever it will best help to further the main objective, to show how man adapts himself to his environment. The activities suggested have been drawn from actual classroom practice and are well suited to the various age-levels for which they are intended.

References and Index. — The references are graded for different age-levels and are confined to books likely to be readily available. The table of contents and index enable the pupil to turn quickly to any desired materials. Peoples, places, maps, and pictures are all completely indexed.

Interdependence and International Understanding. — The hope of our world today lies in international understanding, and the entire Series promotes this ideal. Children are never too young to start toward this goal. For this reason in their *Journeys through North America* pupils are given everywhere a sympathetic treatment of the peoples they visit in an effort to lay a foundation at an early age for those friendly relations upon which rest the peace and well-being of the world.

CONTENTS

UNIT		PAGE
I.	As the Airman Sees Our United States	1
	From Boston to Buffalo	3
	From Buffalo to Chicago	6
	From Chicago to Billings	10
	From Billings to Seattle	12
	A Southward Journey	13
	The Trip East	17
	Our Northward Journey	20
II.	Our United States: How Our Country Grew	25
III.	The Pacific States	32
IV.	The Mountain States	54
V.	The West North Central States	78
VI.	The West South Central States	99
VII.	The East South Central States	126
VIII.	The South Atlantic States	147
IX.	The Middle Atlantic States	175
X.	The East North Central States	202
XI.	The New England States	223
XII.	Canada, Our Northern Neighbor	244
XIII.	Newfoundland and Labrador	262
XIV.	Alaska, Our Northern Wonderland	273
XV.	Mexico, Our Southern Neighbor	278
XVI.	The Central American Republics	291
XVII.	The West Indies	297
XVIII.	South America	303
XIX.	Summary of North America	317
Derivations of Names of the States		322
Appendix		323
Statistics		325
References		327
Index		1

MAPS

	PAGE
Journey Map of the United States and Canada	2
United States, Physical-Political	28–29
Sectional Map of the United States	34
The Pacific States, Physical-Political	37
The Pacific States, Population	49
Rainfall Map of the United States	56
The Mountain States, Physical-Political	60
The Mountain States, Population	73
West North Central States, Physical-Political	81
Agricultural Regions of the United States	82
West North Central States, Population	94
West South Central States, Physical-Political	103
West South Central States, Population	119
East South Central States, Physical-Political	131
East South Central States, Population	139
South Atlantic States, Physical-Political	149
South Atlantic States, Population	169
Middle Atlantic States, Physical-Political	177
Middle Atlantic States, Population	191
East North Central States, Physical-Political	205
East North Central States, Population	215
New England States, Physical-Political	225
New England States, Population	238
Canada and Newfoundland, Physical-Political	248–249
Mexico and the Caribbean Lands, Physical-Political	280–281
North America, Physical-Political	319
Supplementary Maps	*following* 322

    North America, Physical-Political
    South America, Physical-Political
    Asia, Physical-Political
    Europe, Physical-Political
    Africa, Physical-Political
    Australasia, Physical-Political

JOURNEYS THROUGH
NORTH AMERICA

BOSTON — OUR STARTING POINT

Courtesy United Air Lines

The magic carpet of the Arabian Nights has turned into a wide-winged silver plane, flying among the clouds.

JOURNEYS THROUGH NORTH AMERICA

I. AS THE AIRMAN SEES OUR UNITED STATES

We need no longer envy the birds. We, too, can fly through the air and look down on the earth below. What better way of seeing our country could there be! We are going to travel in our own special airplane so that we need not depend on the commercial routes.

Our Air Route on the Map. — Let us start from Boston in the northeast, cross to Seattle in the northwest, and then go south to San Diego in the southwest. From there our air route eastward leads across southern United States to the Atlantic coast at Jacksonville, Florida, and then northward to Boston, our starting point. Follow this route on the map on the next page.

Such a journey will take us east and west and north and south across our country and enable us to see how various parts differ. Great cities and smaller towns, farms with their many-shaped fields, forests, plains and mountains, lakes and winding rivers, and man-built roads and railroads crisscrossing the land will all spread out below us as we speed along from one section to another.

The Start from Boston. — All aboard for Buffalo, Cleveland, and Chicago! We climb quickly into the plane and take our seats. The propellers whirl noisily, our plane shoots down the runway, and almost before we know it, the earth is gliding along far below. We are off to see America as the airman sees it!

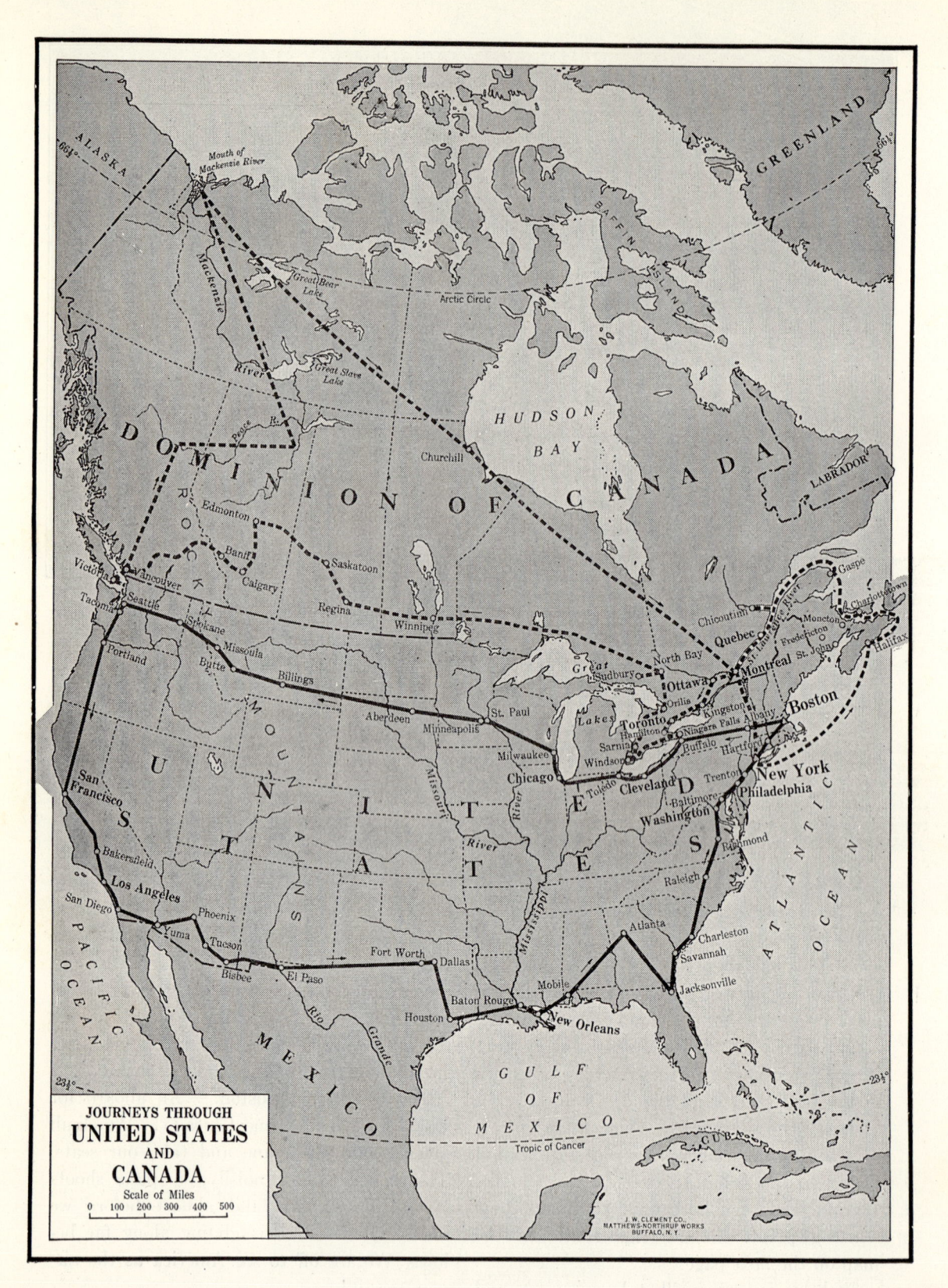

JOURNEYS THROUGH
UNITED STATES
AND
CANADA
Scale of Miles
0 100 200 300 400 500

AS THE AIRMAN SEES OUR UNITED STATES

JOURNEY MAP OF THE UNITED STATES AND CANADA

Map Questions and Activities

This map is to be used at every step in your journey around the United States by airplane. Compare it with the map on pages 28 and 29. It will also be used in connection with your journeys through Canada.

1. Between what two cities is the longest trip? the next to the longest?

2. Taking the distance across the United States as 3000 miles, estimate roughly the total distance flown.

3. How many United States cities are shown on the map?

4. Are you acquainted with any of them? If so, which ones? What can you tell about them?

FROM BOSTON TO BUFFALO

Boston, the "Hub of New England." — As our plane rises higher in the air, we look down over Boston, the industrial center of New England. It lies on peninsulas which border its inner harbor. Long, narrow peninsulas and islands shelter the outer harbor, beyond which stretches the broad Atlantic. Railways, air routes, and steamboat lines radiate from Boston like the spokes of a wheel, making it an important shipping center.

Across Massachusetts. — As Boston fades from view, towns and villages become more scattered, and patches of woods and open fields appear. We pass over Worcester, the second largest city in Massachusetts, lying in a valley surrounded by low hills, and soon reach the broad valley where the Connecticut River, glistening in the sunlight, flows. The different colors of the fields show that various crops are being raised, while large barns and comfortable homes tell us that this is a prosperous farming region. On either side of the river lies Springfield, the third largest city in Massachusetts, where many of the small weapons used by United States soldiers are made. West of the Connecticut Valley we pass over rolling country as we approach the Berkshire Hills in western

Courtesy Springfield Chamber of Commerce
SPRINGFIELD, ON THE BANKS OF THE CONNECTICUT
Half way across the state of Massachusetts, on the flat, fertile plain along the Connecticut River, lies the manufacturing city of Springfield. Here the wheels of industry turn endlessly, as mills and foundries produce paper, knit goods, bicycles, automobile accessories, tools, and electrical appliances.

Massachusetts. Here, nestled in a valley between the ranges is the busy city of Pittsfield, where the east-west and north-south railroads meet.

Over the Empire State. — As we leave Massachusetts, the forested hills give way to an irregular checkerboard of fields divided by a long shining streak which we know is the Hudson River. The city of Albany, capital of New York and an important railroad center, climbs up the west bank of the Hudson and extends out into the country beyond.

From Albany to Buffalo, our route follows the Mohawk Valley and the Erie Canal. The Mohawk Valley cuts across the highlands in the eastern United States, and together with the low plain south of Lake Ontario affords an easy route to the west. The Erie Canal, completed in 1825, made it possible to

BOSTON — WHERE A TEA PARTY MADE HISTORY
© Rovere Scott

Narrow, crooked cow-paths that once knew homespun-clad Puritans have become busy streets and avenues; the church from whose belfry flashed the signal light for Paul Revere has been overshadowed by high office buildings; white-winged clipper ships, with their foreign cargoes, have given way to stately ocean liners.

ALBANY, CAPITAL OF THE EMPIRE STATE
McLaughlin

The little settlement of 1624, called Fort Orange, has grown into an important river-city and has been written into many pages of American history. It was here that the Convention met to propose a union of the colonies.

AS THE AIRMAN SEES OUR UNITED STATES

McLaughlin

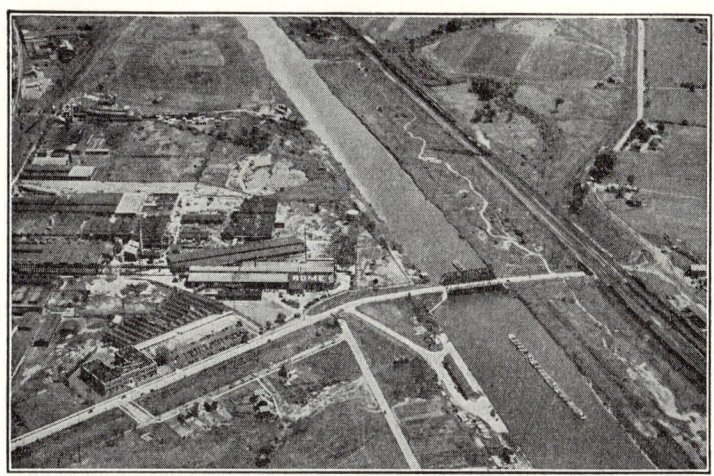

MAN TRAVELS AS HE WILLS

Man has built canals for boat travel; he has laid steel rails for train travel; he has built smooth, concrete roads for automobile travel; and last, and most wonderful, he has built winged ships in which to travel through the air. See how Rome, New York, is here identified for the airman.

go by water from New York City to Buffalo on Lake Erie and thence by way of the Great Lakes into the interior of the country. Pioneers went by the canal to found new homes farther west and sent their products back by this same route. In recent years most of the old Erie Canal has been enlarged to form a part of the New York Barge Canal System. Railroads and good roads now follow this natural highway, which is one of the most traveled parts of our country. As our plane soars along overhead, we look down on the three ways of travel below — by the canal, the railroad, and the automobile highway — and then think of our airplane as the fourth and most wonderful way of all.

Cities and Farms in the Barge Canal Belt. — Many large cities have grown up along this route: Schenectady, noted for electrical goods and locomotives; Utica, with its cotton mills; and Syracuse, with its large chemical plants. Farther west at the falls of the Genesee River is Rochester, noted for its flour mills, kodaks, and optical goods.

Looking down on the plain south of Lake Ontario and the rolling land to the south, we see one of the greatest fruit-producing regions in the United States. Row after row of apple, peach, pear, and plum trees help us to distinguish the orchards from the field crops. Vineyards also are abundant. Cattle grazing in the fields, and large barns with silos tell us that this is a dairying section. The many cities furnish ready markets for large quantities of milk, butter, and cheese.

Courtesy Niagara Falls Chamber of Commerce

THE ROARING, RUSHING WATERS OF NIAGARA FALLS

Who can forget the beauty of these falls, where the tranquil Niagara River suddenly races down the rapids and plunges headlong into the gorge; the rainbow mist, the jeweled drops of spray, the foamy whirlpool of this "thundering water"?

Niagara Falls. — Nearing Buffalo our pilot swings to the north so as to give us a good view of the famous Niagara Falls. These beautiful falls have probably been seen by more people than any other scenic attraction in our country. Beyond the falls lies Canada, and bridges connect the two countries below the falls. Not only do these falls bring pleasure to visitors, but their great power is used to produce electricity in both the United States and Canada. Below the falls, at the foot of the steep sides of the gorge, we see some of the big power houses.

Buffalo. — Buffalo, our first stopping place, lies at the eastern end of Lake Erie. As our plane circles over the city before landing, we get a good view of the harbor with its lake boats, loaded with grain, iron ore, and other products from the central United States. Some of these products are used in the city, others are transferred to trains or canal boats to be shipped east. The large buildings along the lake front which attract our attention are wheat elevators, where wheat is stored. The grain elevators and large flour mills are a striking feature of this city, which is now the leading flour-milling city in the world.

FROM BUFFALO TO CHICAGO

Along Lake Erie. — As we leave Buffalo the tall smokestacks of the steel mills of Lackawanna attract our attention. Iron ore from the Lake Superior region is brought by the ore boats, and railroads from the coal fields farther south bring the coal necessary for this big iron and steel center.

From Buffalo to Toledo, Ohio, our route lies along the shore of Lake Erie. As we fly over the nearly level plain along this lake, we look down upon seemingly endless orchards and vineyards. Winds blowing off the water, which is cooler in summer and warmer in winter than the land, help to modify the temperature and make this one of the greatest fruit-growing regions of our country. Along

Aerial Surveys, Inc.
CLEVELAND — WHERE RAIL AND WATER TRAFFIC MEET
A city noted for its commercial and industrial development, and its civic achievements; a city whose main business street is named for Euclid, Greek father of geometry, and whose residential streets are so lined with trees and shrubs that it is called the Forest City.

the shore are several railroads, many small towns, and some large lake ports. The first we see is Erie, in Pennsylvania, which is not only a shipping center but a manufacturing city. Next come Conneaut and Ashtabula in Ohio, two ports which receive great cargoes of iron ore, which they ship by rail to iron- and steel-manufacturing cities in Ohio and Pennsylvania.

Cleveland and Toledo. — As we approach Cleveland, the largest city in Ohio, the tall tower of the Terminal Building stands out as a landmark for miles around. This city handles more iron ore than any other in the United States. It owes its growth largely

"KODAK AS YOU GO!"
Courtesy Eastman Kodak Company

The slogan of this camera city is well known. Here we see one of the great kodak plants in Rochester, with the little white homes of its workers in straight, prim rows beyond the tall chimneys.

BUFFALO, AT THE END OF THE ERIE CANAL
Fairchild

It has not taken many years for Buffalo to grow from a settlement on the plains where wild animals roamed, to a commercial city of great importance. Burned by the British and Indians in 1813, it is now linked to Canada in friendship by the International Peace Bridge.

CHICAGO, HOME OF TWO WORLD'S FAIRS

Fairchild

Out of a wilderness of marsh and forest, has grown this waterfront city of beautiful civic buildings, wide streets and avenues, lovely parks and playgrounds. Only once has its progress been checked, when the disastrous fire of 1871 destroyed so much of the city. But the undaunted citizens began at once to build a larger, finer city on the ashes of the old. Today, the beautiful outer drive borders the lake front, ending at the outer drive bridge at the mouth of the river.

to its iron and steel mills, for it not only receives and distributes iron ore to many other places, but it uses large quantities in its own manufacturing plants. Here our plane lands to take on gasoline, oil, and provisions. After leaving Cleveland, Lakewood, Lorain, and Sandusky are soon passed and then Toledo lies below us. At the western end of Lake Erie, Toledo has become a leading railroad center; we can see these railroads radiating out from the city in all directions. Naturally, where it is so easy to receive raw materials and send out finished goods, many manufacturing industries have developed.

Across Indiana. — Half an hour after leaving Toledo we are over Indiana. This is a land of prosperous farms, with fertile soil, comfortable homes, large barns, and silos. The numerous villages and towns are connected by roads and railways, which are easily constructed on this level land. The first large city we see is South Bend, situated in a fine farming region and served by several railroads. It is a great manufacturing center where automobiles, farm machinery, railway equipment, and other iron and steel articles of various kinds are made. Soon we find ourselves looking down on Indiana's sand dunes showing white and clear along the shores of Lake Michigan. Before we leave the sand-dune region, tall chimneys rising amid large buildings of various shapes tell us that we are nearing Gary, one of the great steel-manufacturing centers in the United States. Not long ago, its site was an area of sand dunes and marshes. Then the land was drained, streets were laid out, large steel mills erected, and homes for the workers built. To its harbor on Lake Michigan come shiploads of iron ore from the Lake Superior

SOUTH BEND, HOME OF A LARGE AUTOMOBILE COMPANY

When the world moved on from the horse-and-buggy age to the motor age, this factory changed from making fine wagons and carriages to making fine automobiles. Its smoking chimneys proclaim its activity

Chicago Aerial Survey Company

AN INDIANA FARM

From high in the air we can look down on the white crossroads, the whiter house, the big barns and silo, the brown fields, the cattle grazing in the noon-day sun — a toy farm, appearing for an instant and then vanishing behind us.

SAND DUNES

The waters of Lake Michigan lap the sandy shores of the northern point of Indiana, and rolling dunes of wind-swept sand rise and fall away to rise again, hill after hill, like bald spots in a covering of scrub oak and pine.

MILWAUKEE, A TRADING POST THAT BECAME A CITY *Chicago Aerial Survey Company*

This modern commercial city is the focal point of several lines of railroads, many lines of steamers, interurbans and motor buses, and the center of an automobile highway system so famous that it is known as the gateway to vacation land.

mines, while railroads bring the coal and other materials used in making steel.

Chicago. — From Gary to Chicago, the towns are so close together that it looks like one long city. We see many of the railroad lines that make Chicago the greatest railroad center in the world. We pass the suburb of Pullman, where Pullman cars are made, and farther on the famous stockyards, whose products are shipped all over the world. Large buildings, high smokestacks, automobiles, street cars, and trains, — all remind us that Chicago is a great manufacturing center. Flying northward over the city, Lake Michigan lies to our right, or to the east. We see the lake steamers coming and going, the public parks along the lake, and the people enjoying themselves on the beaches. A group of skyscrapers tells us where the business center of the city is located.

Chicago marks the end of the first part of our journey and here we stop and rest for the night.

FROM CHICAGO TO BILLINGS

On to the Northwest! — Flying northward from Chicago, we pass several manufacturing cities before reaching Milwaukee, Wisconsin's largest city. Milwaukee is built around a small bay which gives it an excellent harbor on Lake Michigan. Automobile, machinery, flour, and leather manufacturing, as well as meat packing, are important industries here. Leaving Lake Michigan, we fly across the rolling farm lands of Wisconsin, where herds of cattle, large barns, and silos show that dairying is a leading industry in this state. Soon after crossing the state line between Wisconsin and Minnesota, we come to the "twin cities" of St. Paul and Minneapolis

ST. PAUL, CAPITAL OF MINNESOTA

Courtesy St. Paul Association

On his way to explore the Mississippi River, Zebulon Pike obtained as a grant from the Sioux Indians a piece of land that later became St. Paul. Built along a bend in the Mississippi, it rises in three tiers — the first the railroad terminus, the second the business section, and the third and highest the residential section.

MINNEAPOLIS, GATEWAY TO THE TEN THOUSAND LAKES

Courtesy Minneapolis Chamber of Commerce

It is here, in this modern industrial city, with its skyscrapers, and its mills, and its churches and homes, that the falls of Minnehaha, "the rushing water" of the Dacotah Indians, still "laugh and leap" in the sunlight of the city's loveliest park.

OVER THE ROCKIES

Courtesy Northern Pacific Railway

Drifting along as the clouds drift, we see the Rocky Mountains as white-capped mounds of rock, stretching in every direction, with here and there a valley shot with a thread of silver stream.

situated near each other on either side of the Mississippi River. Both are important railway centers, and both have airports. From above Minneapolis we see right in the midst of the city one of the main reasons for its growth, St. Anthony's Falls. Minneapolis is on the edge of the great northern wheat belt, and these falls were harnessed to turn the mills to grind the wheat into flour.

Lakes and Wheat. — Flying from Minneapolis, we are amazed at the number of lakes, so many that Minnesota is sometimes called the "land of ten thousand lakes." As we leave this district, the scene changes and we look down on a country which appears perfectly flat as far as we can see. Lakes and trees are fewer, and for miles and miles we gaze on fields of waving wheat. This is the great money crop. Farmhouses are scattered and cities are scarce. Our route takes us over Aberdeen, one of the cities of South Dakota, but we see few other cities until we reach Billings, Montana. Halfway across South Dakota, we fly over the Missouri River, west of which stretch the Great Plains, a dry rolling area, on which herds of cattle graze. Farther west, in Montana, we see irrigated areas along streams.

Billings. — The city of Billings, one of our stops, lies near where the Great Plains meet the Rockies. It is situated on the Yellowstone River, which, with its tributaries, provides water for irrigated farming. Billings has grown up as a trading center, and here we spend the night in order to cross the Rockies during the morning hours.

FROM BILLINGS TO SEATTLE

Crossing the Rockies. — As we rise from the field at Billings and head westward, the Rocky Mountains loom up before us. Beneath us are the foothills, with herds of cattle and flocks of sheep. Soon we reach the town of Butte, where copper and silver are both taken from the same mine. A little farther on is Anaconda, marked by its high smokestacks, where much of Butte's copper ore is smelted. What a glorious scene now spreads out before us! North, south, west, — whichever way we look we see nothing but a jumbled mass of high, rugged mountains with evergreens on their lower slopes. Their bare summits and steep, rocky sides give them their name. Most of the people live in the valleys, but sometimes we see a small mining camp higher up the mountains. Passing over Missoula, lying amid beautiful scenery, we cross more high mountains and reach Idaho's great mining district, the Cœur d'Alene. This is one of the richest lead-silver mining centers in the world.

The State of Washington. — Across the Rockies, Spokane, eastern Washington's largest city, comes into view. Soon we are over an open, rolling area, looking down on the huge Grand Coulee Dam piling up the waters of the Columbia River for irrigation, and also generating electric power for many industries. There are almost no trees, but a few wheat fields are seen, while cattle and sheep graze on the bunch-grass lands. At the western edge of this open country, we cross the Columbia River and follow the Wenatchee Valley across the Cascade Mountains, getting glorious views of snow-capped peaks. The western slopes of the Cascades are covered with dense forests of giant trees. All below us looks green, for we are now in a region of heavy rainfall, where the wet west winds from the Pacific Ocean drench the slopes with rain and cause heavy snowfall on the higher peaks. We sight Everett, a port on Puget Sound, and soon reach Seattle, our largest northwestern gateway to the Pacific. With the open sound in front, and a sheltered harbor in the rear, Seattle is well fitted for a seaport. We notice the many docks and ships, the big grain elevators, and the flour and lumber mills. Here at the end of our westward flight, our plane descends and we spend the night.

STATE CAPITOL GROUP AT OLYMPIA, WASHINGTON
Government plays its part in Washington in a setting that has been made very beautiful.

A SOUTHWARD JOURNEY

From Seattle to San Francisco. — Rising from the airport at Seattle, we turn south. Beneath us lies the broad Puget lowland, with the Cascades on one side and the Coast Ranges on the other. We look down on Tacoma, the "lumber capital," and to the southwest catch a glimpse of Olympia, the capital of Washington. To the east we see the glistening snow-covered peak of Mount Rainier, rising nearly three miles above the level of the sound which we have just left behind. It is one of the highest peaks in the United States. Crossing the wide Columbia River, which here separates Washington from Oregon, we land at Portland for a bit of sight seeing. Portland, on the Willamette River near where it joins the Columbia, is the great trading center for this region. The Columbia River not only connects Portland with the Pacific Ocean but gives it a

SEATTLE, SEAPORT OF THE PACIFIC *Publishers' Photo*

We glimpse the white of snow-capped mountains, the green of pines, the blue and green of ocean and lake, as we settle down on the landing field of this city built on hills.

PORTLAND, THE CITY OF ROSES *Publishers' Photo*

Here, at the end of the Oregon Trail, lies the city of Portland. Through its heart flows the Willamette River; at its back rises Mt. Hood, a pinnacle of silver beauty.

Courtesy Tacoma Chamber of Commerce
TACOMA, THE LUMBER CAPITAL OF AMERICA
Beyond the rush and bustle of this seaport city rises the snow-capped peak of Mt. Rainier. Tacoma is the gateway to Mount Rainier National Park.

route eastward through the Cascades into the interior.

South of Portland, we pass over the beautiful farming country of the Willamette Valley, with its fields of grain, fruit orchards, herds of cattle, and flocks of sheep. On both sides wooded hills lead up to the higher mountains, and in the distance towers Mount Hood. Soon we cross the Siskiyou Mountains on the border of Oregon and California, and beyond looms the white summit of Mount Shasta, one of the highest mountains in the United States. After passing Shasta, we descend into the Great Valley of California, and follow the fertile Sacramento River Valley to San Francisco. Flying low, we get a splendid view of this city and its harbor, one of the finest in the world. To the west we gaze on the broad Pacific Ocean through a beautiful channel, called the "Golden Gate" because it gave access to the gold fields in the famous gold rush of 1849.

From San Francisco to San Diego. — From San Francisco we fly southeast through the San Joaquin Valley, looking down on thousands of acres of irrigated vineyards, olive orchards, and orange groves. At the southern end of the valley, we pass over Bakersfield, the center of the oil industry in this part of California. Out of the great valley and over the mountain rim, what a different scene greets our eyes! No orange groves, pastures, or fields of grain, but only great stretches of shrubs and coarse, dry grass! To the east is the Mohave Desert, dreary and uninviting. We are glad when we approach Los Angeles, and the smaller cities near it with their beautiful homes among the hills.

Courtesy United Air Lines
"THE CITY OF OUR LADY THE QUEEN OF THE ANGELS"
As darkness gathers, the myriad lights of Los Angeles glimmer like a spangled coverlet of fallen stars.

THE SACRAMENTO RIVER VALLEY

Publishers' Photo

Under our plane unroll the flat spaces of this fertile river valley, like pieces of some giant picture puzzle, fitted together for all time.

SAN FRANCISCO

© *Gabriel Moulin*

In the curve of an arm of the Pacific lies San Francisco. In and out of its docks steam the ships that sail the seven seas; into its heart arrive the trains and airships that cross a continent. Not content with these ways of transportation, it bridges its "golden gate" with the longest single span in the world — the greatest engineering feat ever attempted.

AS THE AIRMAN SEES OUR UNITED STATES

Los Angeles is now the largest city in the western part of our country. Beautiful mountain scenery nearby and a mild, sunny climate make it an ideal place to live. Its busy harbor at San Pedro has a thriving trade. All about are oil fields and the nearby coast is dotted with resort cities and bathing beaches. In about an hour, we reach the old city of San Diego, our southernmost Pacific port. Before landing, we notice its fine harbor, large enough to hold the whole United States navy and still have plenty of room. San Diego has a delightful climate, and is a popular winter resort. As our plane descends here early in the afternoon, we plan to take a swim in the surf and then spend the rest of the day sight seeing.

THE TRIP EAST

From San Diego to El Paso. — Eastward from San Diego, our airman has to climb high to clear the mountains. There are no dense forests on these mountains and the valleys are dry except where they are irrigated. Beyond them lies the Imperial Valley, a desert that is being transformed into a fruitful farm region by using the waters of the mighty Colorado River for irrigation. Crossing the Colorado, we look down on Yuma, Arizona, the center of another irrigated region much like that of the Imperial Valley. From Yuma to Phoenix, our course lies near the Gila River, with the hot, dry desert on either side. Approaching Phoenix, we look down on the large irrigated valley of the Salt River which joins the Gila not far from Phoenix. Off to the east we see the mountains which are the source of both rivers. The huge Roosevelt Dam stores up the waters of the Salt River, while the Coolidge Dam holds back those of the Gila for power and irrigation.

Leaving Phoenix, we pass Tucson (too-son'), once the capital of Arizona, and we look down on the town of Bisbee, where we see a surface mine, a hill of copper ore. Those tall smokestacks show where the smelters are. About two hours more over this dry country and we reach El Paso, Texas, another of the older cities of the Southwest. El Paso, meaning "The Pass," is on the Rio Grande River where it breaks through the mountains. Across the river in Mexico is the city of Jaurez (hwä'res), connected with

© Scenic Airways, Inc.   Courtesy Arizona Industrial Congress
ROOSEVELT DAM
Under the narrow roadway that joins the rocky shores of Salt River is a circular wall of concrete, 284 feet deep, which provides water for irrigation and power for electricity.

El Paso by a bridge. Street cars which cross the bridge advertise "Go abroad for six cents!" From here to its mouth, the Rio Grande forms the main boundary between Texas and Mexico.

From El Paso to New Orleans. — Somewhere in Texas, our largest state, can be found almost every kind of climate and product in the United States. At first we fly over dry desert with flat-topped plateaus called *mesas*, cones of former volcanoes, and glistening white salt flats. About 100 miles east of El Paso, we cross the Guadalupe Mountains and look down on Guadalupe Peak, the highest in Texas, about 9000 feet high. East of the mountains, we come out over the Great Plains. This is the "cow country," where thousands of white-faced cattle graze, and

SAN DIEGO, CRADLE OF WESTERN AVIATION

Fairchild

In this semi-tropical city, with its air of old Spain, aviation rules supreme. Here, where the United States Army and Navy both maintain air stations, the first non-stop flight across the continent ended; here the famous "Spirit of St. Louis" was made; from here the first air-mail started its flight.

SCIENCE TO THE RESCUE

© *Spence Airplane Photos*

By means of dams, aqueducts, and a purification system, fresh, life-giving water is brought to the Imperial Valley from the Colorado River, turning it from a parched desert into a fruitful garden.

herds of goats feed on the uplands. Many of these are Angora goats, prized for their long, silky wool called *mohair*. As we speed eastward, the land gets lower, and we see more streams, towns, roads, and railroads. This is a "land of cotton." Nearing Fort Worth, we pass over one of the large oil fields of Texas. This state leads all others in cattle, cotton, and oil, all of which have helped the growth of Fort Worth and Dallas, the next two cities we see. From Dallas we fly south over forests, farms, and oil fields to Houston, the largest city in Texas. It is 50 miles inland, but a canal 30 feet deep gives it access to the sea. Many railroads bring in the products of Texas and pipe lines furnish oil for its refineries.

HOUSTON — A SEAPORT FIFTY MILES FROM THE SEA
This one-time capital of the Republic of Texas has become an important city by the unbelievable feat of bringing the ocean to its door.

East of Houston, we see more oil fields and pass within sight of Port Arthur, noted especially for the export of oil. On the lowlands near the coast are rice fields, and farther east, in Louisiana, sugar plantations are seen.

© Airmap Corporation
NEW ORLEANS, THE CRESCENT CITY
The romance of olden days still clings to this famous city — days when the show boats came down the Mississippi River, when the Creoles lived enchanting lives in the quaint houses with over-hung balconies and courtyards, half-hidden behind the gold-knobbed, wrought-iron fences.

From the plane these fields of sugar cane look much like the cornfields we passed over in our westward flight. Again our plane roars over the broad Mississippi, this time over a thousand miles from where we crossed it before. We fly over Baton Rouge, the capital of Louisiana, on the east bank of the Mississippi, where we look down on the tanks and buildings of one of the largest oil refineries in the world. In less than an hour, New Orleans appears, sometimes called the "Crescent City" because it is built in a large bend of the Mississippi. It is the largest port of the southern states, shipping out the products of the great Mississippi Valley, while bananas, coffee, and other products are imported from Central and South America, and from the West Indies.

From New Orleans to Jacksonville. — East of New Orleans we pass along the coast of Mississippi with its attractive resort cities, and soon arrive at Mobile, Alabama's large cotton port. Two rivers, the Alabama and the Tombigbee, unite to form the Mobile River, at the mouth of which the city stands, at the head of Mobile Bay. River steamers and railroads bring Alabama's products here for export. After a brief stop at Mobile, we head for Atlanta, Georgia. Going inland from the coast, we see lumbermen at work, fields of cotton and corn, and orchards of pecans and peaches.

As we near Atlanta, low hills appear; we are passing from the coastal plain to the Piedmont region. We cross the Chattahoochee River, which gives Atlanta its water supply

RALEIGH, CAPITAL OF NORTH CAROLINA   *Ewing Galloway*
We hover for a moment over the business section of this thriving city and catch a glimpse of its lovely homes beyond the tall hotels and the office buildings.

and furnishes it with power to make electricity. Railroads from all directions enter the city, which is one of the greatest railroad centers in the south. Large factories tell us of the manufacturing done here. From Atlanta we head southeast toward Jacksonville. The scenery is much like that which we saw on our way from Mobile to Atlanta. We pass over one of Florida's large swamps, and soon sight Jacksonville, Florida's largest city, some miles from the coast on the St. Johns River. It is Florida's chief railroad and shipping center. Through it pass most of the trains bound for Palm Beach, Miami, and Florida's many other famous winter resorts.

OUR NORTHWARD JOURNEY

From Jacksonville to Washington. — After a night in Jacksonville, we board the plane again for our northward flight. For a while, our route takes us right along the coast, where we notice many resorts with sandy beaches. As far as we can see, the land is low and level and swamps border the rivers. Our first stop is at Savannah, Georgia's leading seaport, and our next at Charleston, South Carolina's largest city and chief port. Both of these cities export much cotton; Charleston, one of our oldest cities, began exporting it in 1734. Here we leave the coast and fly inland over the coastal plain. The land is still low and level; we cross winding rivers, forests and farms, fields of cotton and tobacco, towns and cities, till we come to Raleigh, the capital of North Carolina.

From Raleigh we head north, looking down on field after field of tobacco, the leading money crop in this section. In a little over an hour, we reach the historic city of Richmond, at the falls of the James River where it descends from the Piedmont to the Coastal Plain. Richmond, on the northern border of the "land of tobacco," has many tobacco factories. North of Richmond, we fly over gently rolling country with farms, woods, and open fields, till we sight the tall shaft of the Washington Monument. We see Mount Vernon, the home of George Washington, and, crossing the Potomac, we get a fine view of the Capitol and the White House, where the President lives. Washington is one of the few cities that was carefully planned before any of it was built. Its streets are laid out in a very

ATLANTA

This charming southern city is located near the foothills of the Blue Ridge Mountains. Sixteen miles to the north is the famous Stone Mountain, upon whose smooth and rounded granite sides is carved an everlasting memorial to the heroic struggle of the South during the war between the states.

CHARLESTON, KING CHARLES II'S TOWN

Behind the nine miles of water front, guarded by three forts, is this leisurely southern city of Colonial mansions, with gleaming white columns and gardens heavy with the scent of camellias and roses and jasmine.

regular fashion, while broad avenues named after various states radiate from the Capitol and the White House to different parts of the city.

From Washington to Boston. — Washington is only a few minutes by plane from Baltimore, an important railroad center and seaport on Chesapeake Bay. We see the busy waterfront, the shipyards, factories, and railroad yards which show that this is a city of many industries. From Baltimore to Philadelphia, our route lies over one of the best farming sections in the East, where cattle graze on the level land, through which the many roads and railroads find an easy way. We pass over Wilmington, Delaware's largest city and manufacturing center, and soon sight Philadelphia, our third largest city. As we approach, a group of tall buildings shows where the "downtown" section lies. To the east, we see the broad Delaware River spanned by a long suspension bridge. Piers and shipyards line the waterfront, and large ocean vessels lie at some of the docks. We note how the city is divided into two parts by the Schuylkill River, which here joins the Delaware.

On our way from Philadelphia to New York, we cross the Delaware close enough to Trenton to give us a good view of New Jersey's capital, noted for pottery. Then our route lies across fine farming country, with low hills and numerous cities. Passing over the manufacturing cities of New Brunswick and Elizabeth, we reach Newark, the largest city in New Jersey, where we fly over its well-known airport whose routes radiate in all directions. This was formerly the leading air transport center of the United States. Among the hills to the north lies Paterson, noted for its silk mills. Heading eastward over a low, swampy area toward the Hudson River, we see Jersey City with its factories, Bayonne with its oil refineries, Hoboken with its docks for ocean liners, and the broad Hudson lined on both sides with long piers.

Across the Hudson loom the tall skyscrapers of New York. North of us stretches the graceful George Washington Suspension Bridge, spanning the Hudson, while to the south we see three other large suspension bridges across the East River linking Manhattan and Long Island. Flying eastward over Manhattan Island, we cross the East River, and notice the high railway bridge which runs from the mainland to Long Island. Activity is everywhere: on the water, boats of all kinds; on land, automobiles, street cars, and railways; and in the air all kinds of flying craft. Leaving the bustle of New York, we cross Long Island Sound between Long Island and

Fairchild

PHILADELPHIA, THE CITY OF BROTHERLY LOVE

This Quaker city, founded by the gentle Penn, is steeped in historical memories. Here the young Franklin walked the streets with a loaf of bread under each arm; here Betsy Ross lived; here the Liberty Bell tolled forth the news of Independence; here the Continental Congress met; and here George Washington was inaugurated for his second term as President.

THE CITY BEAUTIFUL

Washington is a city whose chief business is the business of government; a city on whose wide streets and avenues have lived the ambassadors of kings; a city of beautiful buildings like the Supreme Court Building and the Capitol.

GUARDED BY FORT MCHENRY

The harbor of Baltimore, largest city of Maryland and eighth largest in the United States, has a backdrop of towering skyscrapers. From its docks ocean liners leave for all over the world.

Connecticut. We pass over Bridgeport, one of Connecticut's leading manufacturing cities, and a few miles away sight the city of New Haven. Then come the farms of Connecticut with frequent villages and towns, all connected by railroads and good highways. It reminds us of what we saw as we flew west across Massachusetts at the beginning of our air trip. Soon we reach Hartford, the capital and largest city of Connecticut, where we again cross the Connecticut River. More countryside and numerous villages and towns may be seen for nearly an hour and then the familiar glint of the golden dome of the Boston State House greets our eyes once again.

Courtesy Hartford Chamber of Commerce
CAPITAL CITY OF CONNECTICUT

Hartford is famous for two businesses — manufacturing of telephones, typewriters, and other small machines, and for insurance. It is famous also as the home of Mark Twain, and of Harriet Beecher Stowe.

We are back at our starting point, having gone entirely around the United States. We have flown from where we could hear the "dark Atlantic roar" to where the "proud Pacific chafes her strands." We have seen for ourselves how vast our country is, and how different are its various parts. We have seen its high mountains, vast plains, winding rivers, fine farms, and great cities. We would like to spend even more time in some of these sections and learn more about this wonderful land in which we live.

Activities and Questions

1. What were the chief cities we passed over between Boston and Chicago? between Chicago and Seattle?

2. Describe the Rocky Mountains. What are some famous peaks that we saw on our trip along the Pacific Coast?

3. Name the chief rivers and cities on the Pacific slope.

4. Tell the difference between the western and eastern lands that we saw as we were flying east.

5. How many times did we cross the Mississippi River? Where?

6. What cities did we pass on our flight north from Jacksonville to Boston? Which was the most beautiful?

7. About how far did we fly? Measure the distance roughly on the map on page 2.

8. On your airplane journey map and the large map of the United States trace the journey which we have just taken.

9. What part of the trip did you like best? Why?

In covered wagons, drawn by plodding oxen, the pioneers of the East journeyed westward to make a nation.

II. OUR UNITED STATES

HOW OUR COUNTRY GREW

"Our country! 'Tis a glorious land!
With broad arms stretched from shore to shore;
The proud Pacific chafes her strands;
She hears the dark Atlantic roar."

Thus the poet tells us of the broad extent of our country between two mighty oceans. On our airplane trip across the United States and back we had a good first hand picture of its great expanse. It made us want to know more about our country — both its past and present. First, let's see where it started and how it grew.

When the United States first took its place among the nations of the world, it was made up of thirteen states along the Atlantic seaboard containing about 3,000,000 people. Then this young nation began to grow, both in land and in numbers of people. It spread south to the Gulf of Mexico, and west until the Pacific lapped its shores. (See map, pages 28 and 29.)

Vast plains over which *bison* (buffaloes) roamed, snow-capped mountains with waterfalls and rushing streams, deep canyons with brightly colored rock borders, forests of giant trees, — all of these wonders and more were found in the newly added lands. These new sections were divided into territories which were afterward admitted to the Union as states. Now there are forty-eight states with over forty times as many people as there were when the Union was formed.

European Settlers in America. — Europeans were the first to settle on our land,

25

FROM CLAY TO VASES
Pueblo Indian women find time from their household duties to make pottery of many lovely shapes and colors.

coming in groups year after year. To them, America meant opportunity, free land for their homes, and fertile soil to produce food. Here were great forests to furnish lumber, and minerals to make tools and other articles. Best of all, here was freedom to live and worship as they wished.

What the Settlers Found. — Here they found Indians occupying the land, some in homes of bark, others in *wigwams* of animal skins stretched over wooden poles. Many of the Indians raised crops of corn, beans, squash, and tobacco, and later taught the Europeans how to raise these crops.

In the Southwest, some of the Indians made homes in the sides of cliffs to be safe from their enemies. Others built mud or *ado'be* huts, often called *pueblos* (pū-eb'lōz). Many beautiful articles were made by the Indians from their own designs. They were skillful in making pottery, in weaving baskets, and in making leather articles and ornamental designs of beads. Some still continue to make and sell these articles.

The Europeans found in America not a trackless forest, but a land crossed by many paths, the Indian trails. The settlers followed these trails, which later became roads or highways. Where they crossed, traders' cabins were built, and many of these settlements later grew into towns and even cities. Some of the main railroads across the country follow old Indian trails.

Wars with the Indians. — Some of the Indians were friendly, trading with the white people and teaching them how to grow corn and other crops in the Indian way. Treaties were made and often kept for many years on both sides, but sometimes they were broken. As the Indians depended largely on hunting and fishing for a living, they needed large tracts of land, and naturally resented the clearing of the forests and the building of farms and villages by white men. Then, too, some of the settlers looked upon the Indians as savages, and acts of cruelty were committed on both sides before the

EARLY AMERICAN HOMES
Gone are the painted warriors dancing about the fires, gone the war whoops and the tomahawks. Even the smoke-stained wigwams and the feathered headdresses seem unreal.

Europeans succeeded in driving back the Indians and gaining control of the land.

Indian Reservations. — Later the Indians were forced to give up most of the land and move to special areas called Indian reservations. Many of them were transferred to a large tract of land called Indian Territory. This was held for them until 1889, when the United States government purchased a large part of it from the Indians and opened it to white settlement. In 1907 the whole territory was admitted to the Union as Oklahoma.

Some Indians on the reservations still follow their old tribal customs, but others have adopted American ways and live in towns or on farms. They dress and work like other Americans and, except for their dark skins and straight black hair, you probably would not know they were Indians if you met them on the street. The United States has established schools for the Indians and some of them have helped to rule the land which once belonged wholly to their forefathers.

The Central Lowlands Settled. — As the number of people increased, some moved westward into the interior, where there was better farm land and it was easier to make a living. Even before the end of the 18th century, hardy pioneers had crossed the mountains in the East, floated down the Ohio, and begun the hard and dangerous task of turning this land of forest and prairie into farms and villages.

The Westward Movement. — Early in the 19th century, the coming of the steamboat and the building of roads made travel easier. "Go west!" was popular advice, as glowing stories of the richness of these new lands were carried back east. And people went

"TO THE OCEAN WILD WITH FOAM" © *Rovere Scott*
The pioneers spread out over the land like a great sea, washing farther and farther west to meet a great ocean.

PHYSICAL-POLITICAL MAP OF THE UNITED STATES

Map Questions and Activities

1. How many states are there in the United States?
2. How many of these are east of the Mississippi? How many are west of it?
3. Where is the only place in the United States where the boundaries of four states meet? What states are they?
4. Trace the Continental Divide in the Rocky Mountains. What is a divide?
5. How many places on the map have you visited?
6. Which is the largest state? the smallest? the second largest? the second smallest?
7. Which state has the longest coast line?
8. What general difference do you notice between the boundaries of the states in the East and those in the West? Can you think of a reason for this?
9. How are state capitals shown on the map?
10. Use an outline map of the United States and fill in the names of all the states. Compare your map with this one and try again. Keep on trying till you can place the names of all the states in their correct positions.

UNITED STATES
Scale of statute miles
0 50 100 200 300 400
National capitals
State capitals
Railroads
Canals
Divides and watersheds
HEIGHTS IN FEET
Above 10,000
5000 to 10,000
2000 to 5000
1000 to 2000
500 to 1000
Sea level to 500
Land below sea level
DEPTHS IN FATHOMS
Sea level to 100
Below 100
PACIFIC OCEAN
BRITISH COLUMBIA
ALBERTA
SASKATCHEWAN
CANADA
WASHINGTON
OREGON
IDAHO
MONTANA
WYOMING
NORTH DAKOTA
SOUTH DAKOTA
NEBRASKA
KANSAS
COLORADO
UTAH
NEVADA
CALIFORNIA
ARIZONA
NEW MEXICO
TEXAS
OKLA
GREAT BASIN
COLORADO PLATEAU
COLUMBIA PLATEAU
ROCKY MOUNTAINS
GREAT PLAINS
COAST RANGES
SIERRA NEVADA
CASCADE RANGE
BITTERROOT RANGE
WASATCH MTS.
MEXICO
SONORA
CHIHUAHUA
COAHUILA
SINALOA
DURANGO
NUEVO LEON
TAMAULIPAS
LOWER CALIFORNIA
GULF OF CALIFORNIA
SIERRA MADRE OCCIDENTAL
Vancouver
Victoria
Strait of Juan de Fuca
C. Flattery
Mt. Baker
Bellingham
Everett
Seattle
Tacoma
Olympia
Spokane
Mt. Rainier Nat. Park
Mt. St. Helens
Mt. Adams
Astoria
Portland
Columbia R.
Mt. Hood
Pendleton
Salem
Mt. Jefferson
Baker
Eugene
C. Blanco
Mt. Scott
Crater Lake Nat. Park
Mt. Pitt
Warner Lakes
C. Mendocino
Mt. Shasta
Lassen Peak
Sacramento
L. Tahoe
Reno
Carson City
Carson Sink
Humboldt R.
San Francisco
Berkeley
Oakland
San Jose
Yosemite Nat. Park
Fresno
Sequoia Nat. Park
Mt. Whitney
Owens L.
Death Valley
Tulare Basin
Pt. Conception
Santa Barbara Islands
Los Angeles
Long Beach
San Bernardino Mts.
Salton Sea
San Diego
Boise
Salmon R.
Snake R.
Pocatello
Missoula
Anaconda
Butte
Helena
Great Falls
Flathead Lake
Glacier Nat. Park
Kootenai R.
Missouri R.
Milk R.
Billings
Yellowstone R.
Yellowstone Nat. Park
Yellowstone L.
Sheridan
Fremont Peak
Casper
Cheyenne
Great Salt Lake
Ogden
Salt Lake City
Uinta Mts.
Utah L.
Provo
Sevier L.
Green R.
Rocky Mountain Nat. Park
Longs Peak
Boulder
Denver
Pike's Peak
Colorado Springs
Pueblo
Arkansas R.
Trinidad
Mesa Verde Nat. Park
Grand Canyon National Park
San Francisco Mtn.
Phoenix
Tucson
Douglas
Gila R.
Raton
Santa Fe
Albuquerque
Rio Grande
Pecos R.
El Paso
Amarillo
Canadian R.
Red R.
Wichita Falls
Austin
San Antonio
Nueces R.
Colorado R.
Hutchinson
Smoky Hill R.
Republican R.
Platte R.
Niobrara R.
White R.
Cheyenne R.
Black Hills
Pierre
Aberdeen
Bismarck
Minot
Devils L.
Moosejaw
Regina
Lake Winnipegosis
Lake Manitoba
Hermosillo
Guaymas
Chihuahua
Longitude West

GULF OF MEXICO
ATLANTIC OCEAN
ONTARIO
QUEBEC
CANADA
NEW BRUNSWICK
MAINE
N.H.
VT.
MASS.
CONN.
NEW YORK
PENNSYLVANIA
NEW JERSEY
DEL.
OHIO
INDIANA
ILLINOIS
MICHIGAN
WISCONSIN
MINNESOTA
IOWA
MISSOURI
KENTUCKY
WEST VIRGINIA
VIRGINIA
NORTH CAROLINA
SOUTH CAROLINA
TENNESSEE
GEORGIA
ALABAMA
MISSISSIPPI
ARKANSAS
LOUISIANA
FLORIDA
OZARK PLATEAU
APPALACHIAN
PIEDMONT PLATEAU
Cumberland Plateau
LAKE SUPERIOR
LAKE MICHIGAN
LAKE HURON
L. ERIE
L. ONTARIO
Lake Winnipeg
Lake of the Woods
Rainy Lake
Lake Nipigon
Red L.
Georgian Bay
MANITOULIN I.
ISLE ROYAL
L. Okeechobee
The Everglades
Mississippi Delta
Tampa Bay
Apalachee Bay
Delaware Bay
Chesapeake Bay
Albemarle Sd.
Pamlico Sd.
LONG ISLAND
BAHAMA ISLANDS (British)
Florida Strait
C. Cod
C. May
C. Charles
C. Henry
C. Hatteras
C. Lookout
C. Fear
C. Canaveral
C. Sable
Key West
Winnipeg
Duluth
Superior
Marquette
Sault Ste. Marie
Toronto
Hamilton
London
Niagara Falls
Ottawa
Montreal
Quebec
Bangor
Augusta
Portland
Concord
Manchester
Lowell
Boston
Worcester
Providence
New Bedford
Fall River
Hartford
New Haven
Bridgeport
New York
Newark
Jersey City
Trenton
Camden
Atlantic City
Philadelphia
Baltimore
Dover
Washington
Richmond
Norfolk
Portsmouth
Roanoke
Albany
Schenectady
Utica
Syracuse
Rochester
Buffalo
Binghamton
Scranton
Wilkes-Barre
Harrisburg
Altoona
Johnstown
Pittsburgh
Erie
Cleveland
Youngstown
Akron
Canton
Wheeling
Columbus
Dayton
Springfield
Cincinnati
Toledo
Detroit
Flint
Saginaw
Lansing
Port Huron
Grand Rapids
South Bend
Fort Wayne
Gary
Chicago
Rockford
Milwaukee
Madison
Green Bay
Oshkosh
La Crosse
Winona
St. Paul
Minneapolis
Fargo
Grand Forks
Sioux Falls
Sioux City
Dubuque
Cedar Rapids
Davenport
Des Moines
Omaha
Lincoln
Peoria
Springfield
Indianapolis
Terre Haute
Evansville
Louisville
Frankfort
Covington
Huntington
Charleston
St. Joseph
Hannibal
Kansas City
Topeka
St. Louis
E. St. Louis
Jefferson City
Springfield
Joplin
Wichita
Tulsa
Muskogee
Oklahoma City
Fort Smith
Little Rock
Pine Bluff
Texarkana
Shreveport
Fort Worth
Dallas
Waco
Beaumont
Houston
Galveston
Brownsville
Matamoros
Cairo
Memphis
Nashville
Chattanooga
Knoxville
Cumberland Gap
Mt. Mitchell
Asheville
Winston-Salem
Durham
Raleigh
Charlotte
Spartanburg
Greenville
Columbia
Wilmington
Charleston
Atlanta
Augusta
Macon
Columbus
Savannah
Waycross
Birmingham
Montgomery
Mobile
Vicksburg
Jackson
Laurel
Hattiesburg
Natchez
Baton Rouge
New Orleans
Pensacola
Tallahassee
Jacksonville
Tampa
Miami
Adirondack Mts.
Catskill Mts.
Green Mts.
White Mts.
L. Champlain
L. George
Mississippi R.
Missouri R.
Ohio R.
Illinois R.
Wabash R.
Tennessee R.
Cumberland R.
Arkansas R.
Red R.
Sabine R.
Ouachita R.
Tombigbee R.
Alabama R.
Chattahoochee R.
Savannah R.
Pee Dee R.
Cape Fear R.
Roanoke R.
James R.
Potomac R.
Susquehanna R.
Delaware R.
Hudson R.
Connecticut R.
St. Lawrence R.
Ottawa R.
St. Johns R.
Trinity R.
Brazos R.
Kansas R.
Wisconsin R.
St. Clair L.
95°
90°
85°
80°
75°
70°
50
45
40
35
30
25
from Greenwich

west, by the hundreds and thousands, pouring into the Mississippi Valley where good land was cheap. Soon farm buildings dotted the landscape, fields of grain waved in the breeze, and cattle instead of bison grazed on the rich grasses of the prairies and plains.

But all did not stop here. Some pushed on across the Mississippi; some went still farther, selling their farms and belongings to join the westward movement. Trains of covered wagons followed the long trail across the plains and over the mountains, until they came to the "land of promise" in far-off Oregon. Before the middle of the 19th century, some of the best lands in Oregon had been taken up and settlers turned south to seek land in the region acquired from Mexico at the close of our war with that country.

Gold Draws Settlers to California. — About the middle of the 19th century, gold was discovered in California, and there came the famous California "gold rush." Many who failed to find gold stayed and engaged in other work, helping to develop this far western land. Herding cattle and raising food became important industries, so that today the yearly value of California's fruits and vegetables alone is many times that of her gold.

A United Country. — And so people have found homes all over our country. Railroads and fine wide highways now link the East and the West, the North and the South, and swift airplanes carry people, letters, and goods quickly from place to place. The telegraph, the telephone, and the radio enable the people in one section to know instantly what is going on elsewhere. Though far apart, living in many different places, and doing various kinds of work, the people of this vast land are thus united into one great nation.

Activities and Questions

1. Count the number of stars in our flag. For what do these stand? Also count the number of stripes. What do these represent?

2. Canadians often refer to our country as "The States." Europeans commonly call our country "America." Which is right, or are both right? What is the full name of our country? Why is it so named? What abbreviation is used for our country's name?

3. Look through your geography textbook and find pictures of the wonders mentioned on page 1. Watch for others in newspapers and magazines and bring them to class.

4. Look up books about the Indians. Find out how they dressed, what kinds of homes they lived in, and what they had to eat, and report to your class. Different members of your class might tell about Indians in different parts of the country.

5. Why did people in the eastern part of the United States give up their farms and move into the central lowlands? Find out how they traveled.

6. What happened to the Indians, as settlers came and took away their lands? Where are most of the Indians in our country now?

7. Suppose you have a friend living in another part of the United States. Make a list of the ways in which you could communicate with him or her.

8. When something happens in the United States, perhaps hundreds of miles away from where you live, in what different ways may you learn about it?

ALL MANHATTAN WITH ITS POWER AND ITS GLORY LIES BELOW
Fairchild
Crowding every nook and cranny of the strip of land that was bought from the Indians for $24, down to the water's very edge, Manhattan reaches out by bridge, by tunnel, and by ferry to grasp the neighboring shores.

A NEW ENGLAND VILLAGE
McLaughlin
Life can be gently lived in such a village, with its tree-bordered streets, its houses and gardens, and its tall church steeples.

DAFFODILS IN SPRING *Courtesy Tacoma Chamber of Commerce*
"Daffy-down-dilly, just come to town,
In a yellow petticoat and a green gown."

III. THE PACIFIC STATES

STATISTICS OF THE PACIFIC STATES *

STATE	ABBREVI-ATION	AREA SQ. MILES	POPULATION	RANK AREA	RANK POP.	CAPITAL	POPULATION	LARGEST CITY	POPULATION
Washington	Wash.	68,192	1,736,191	19	30	Olympia	13,254	Seattle	368,302
Oregon	Oreg.	96,981	1,089,684	9	34	Salem	30,908	Portland	305,394
California	Calif.	158,693	6,907,387	2	5	Sacramento	105,958	Los Angeles	1,504,277

IMPORTANT PRODUCTS

Washington: — Timber, wheat, fruits (apples), live stock, canned foods
Oregon: — Timber, fruits, live stock, wheat, fish
California: — Petroleum, fruits, vegetables, petroleum products, dairy products

*1940 Census

On our airplane trip probably the most beautiful scenery we saw was in the Pacific states, Washington, Oregon, and California. There were snow-capped mountains, picturesque gorges, great waterfalls, beautiful mountain lakes, and valleys growing nearly every variety of flower, fruit, vegetable, and grain.

Another reason for our interest in these states is that their products are shipped all over our country. Salmon from Oregon, shingles and apples from Washington, and oranges and talkies from California are only a few of the varied articles sent out from these states. How many others can you name?

Mountains and Parks. — Besides the beautiful peaks of Mount Shasta, Mount Rainier, and Mount Hood which we saw from our plane, there are the vast Sierra Nevada

32

LASSEN, MOUNTAIN OF HIDDEN FIRES

White puffs of cloud hover over this volcano as if smoke were issuing from its mouth. Lassen Peak is the only active volcano in the entire United States.

WHERE CRYSTAL WATER FLOWS

From cliffs, seventeen hundred feet high, the Yosemite Falls leap and plunge into a pool of rainbow mist

Ewing Galloway

WIZARD ISLAND

The tree-covered cone of an ancient volcano rises from the clear, deep waters of Crater Lake. This famous lake lies in the steep-sided depression that was formed, long before the human race began, when the top of the original volcanic cone fell in and sank deep into the earth.

AGED MONARCH OF THE FOREST

This giant redwood, with its thick cinnamon-red bark and its green, feather-like leaves, was old when Cyrus the Great ruled Persia.

33

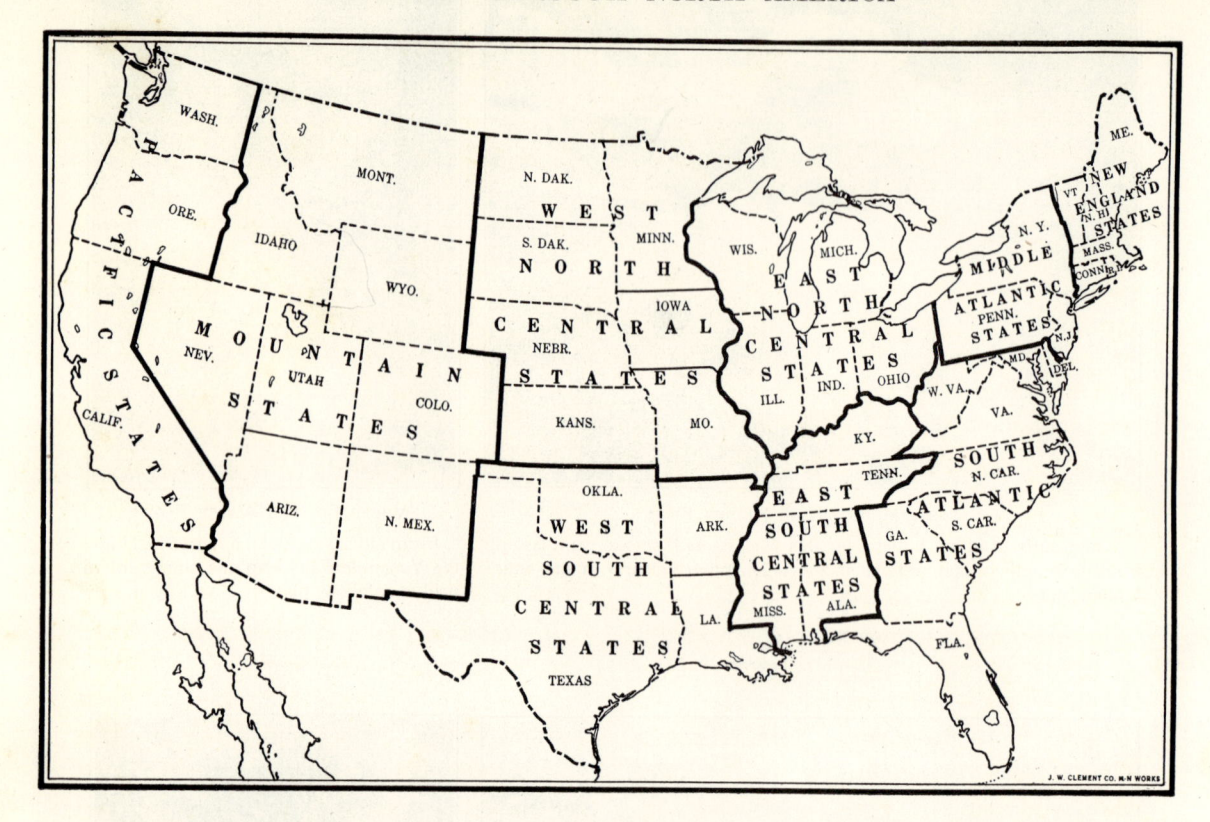

SECTIONAL MAP OF THE UNITED STATES

Map Questions and Activities

This is a map showing by heavy lines the sections of the United States as they are treated in this book. You should refer frequently to this map while studying the various sections.

1. In what group of states do you live?
2. Name the states that border your state on all sides.
3. In what group is each of these bordering states?
4. Which is the largest group? the smallest?

---

and Cascade ranges to the east and the Coastal Ranges near the shore, connected near the boundary of Oregon and California by the Klamath Mountains. These lofty ranges chill the warm, wet winds that blow in from the ocean and the moisture falls as rain or snow. From these mountains many streams rush down to water the valleys below, bringing with them fertile soil and furnishing water power to make electricity with which to light homes, run factories, trolleys, and even railroads.

In these mountains are some of our finest National Parks. The Yosemite is famous for the grandeur of its rock formations and lofty waterfalls. The Sequoia and the General Grant National Parks contain some of California's famous big trees. One of these, the General Sherman tree in Sequoia National Park, is 280 feet high and over 36 feet thick. It is nearly 5000 years old, "the biggest and oldest living thing." The General Grant tree in the General Grant National Park and several others of these big trees are almost as large. Sequoia National Park contains over a million of these trees, thousands of which are over ten feet in diameter.

Mount Rainier in Washington, Mount Lassen in northern California, an active volcano, and Crater Lake in the Cascades are also National Parks. Crater Lake lies in the crater of an old, inactive volcano. It is over 2000 feet deep in places and its deep blue waters are so still that they reflect the steep sides like a mirror.

Lumber. — Years ago the wild animals in the mountain forests yielded quantities of fur. Today lumbering is the chief industry. The beginnings of one of America's most famous fortunes were laid here as early as 1811. John Jacob Astor, a shrewd business man from New York, saw how he could turn fur into gold. He built one of the early fur posts at Astoria near the mouth of the Columbia River. The post grew and he became a very wealthy man. Here fur traders found a country that was peaceful and quiet, where wild animals roamed in abundance.

But as the settlements grew in this area the animals disappeared. Men who had been fur traders became lumberjacks. Today lumbering is the most important industry of this region, and increases in its importance as the lumber supply in other regions of the United States rapidly becomes exhausted. Evergreen trees, spruce, Douglas fir, hemlock, cedar, and pine grow profusely, while there is also the redwood, and in the high Sierras the giant sequoia. A single Douglas fir tree often furnishes enough lumber to build a whole house. Before steamships took the place of sailing vessels, the tall straight trunks of the Douglas fir trees were much prized for making masts.

These same regions grow three other useful lumber trees, western hemlock, western red cedar, and Sitka spruce. Western hemlock makes good flooring and framework of buildings, while the pulp is used to make paper and rayon. Western red cedar is not so strong as the other woods but because of its lasting qualities it is much used for shingles. It contains an oil which helps it resist decay and gives it a pleasing odor. Cedar chests are used for storing woolens and furs to protect them from moths, as insects do not like the smell of cedar. Sitka spruce is a light, strong lumber, much used in making airplanes. The wings of the plane which first carried Colonel Lindbergh across the Atlantic were made of Sitka spruce.

ON THE WAY UP
A group of tourists, on their way to the snow fields on the peak, stop for a moment to rest and admire Mount Rainier.

Publishers' Photo
THE BEGINNINGS OF NEW FORESTS
Ripe cones of the Douglas fir are dried in Washington State and seeds from them are shipped to foresters in various parts of the world for planting new forests.

Note to the Pupil on the Use of Maps

You will find many different kinds of maps in this book. The colored ones show both the physical features of the land and the political divisions. The many black and white maps show where various things like wheat, cattle, fruits, and cotton are produced, and where cities and towns in the United States are located. These all may be used in a variety of ways.

First. — Whenever a geographical place or feature, such as a country or nation, state or province, city, river, or mountain, is mentioned in the text and you are in doubt as to its location, look it up at once on the proper map. Do this faithfully, and it will greatly help your definite locational knowledge.

Second. — Use the scale of miles to judge the distances between places, and the length and breadth of a country, state, or province.

Third. — Pay attention to the key or legend. On the colored maps it tells you what the various colors mean; on the locational maps it shows you roughly the sizes of towns and cities.

Fourth. — Pay attention to the direction marks. On most of the maps, directions are shown by means of parallels and meridians. The parallels of latitude are lines running east and west and measure distances north and south. The meridians of longitude are lines running north and south and measure distances east and west. North means toward the North Pole and south means toward the South Pole. East and west are always at right angles to north and south. Never say "up north" and "down south," because *up* means away from the center of the earth and *down* means towards the earth's center. Read pages 323–324.

Fifth. — When you come to map directions and map questions in this book, try your best to follow the directions and answer the questions. Also, whenever you are asked to refer to a map, do so at once.

MAP OF THE PACIFIC STATES
Map Questions and Activities

1. What is the greatest river flowing through the states of this group? What does it contribute?

2. Explain why most of the large cities are along the ocean. Spokane and Sacramento are exceptions. How do you account for this?

3. It seems that this group of states might have much water power. Can you prove this statement by the map?

4. Name the capital and the largest city in each state. How are the capitals shown on the map?

5. Most of the cities are located in what four valleys or sections? List several reasons why this is true.

6. What is the largest city on our western coast? Give as many reasons as you can for its wonderful growth.

7. Where is the Golden Gate? How important is it? Why is this a good name for this water passage into California?

8. Does our western coast have a broad level coastal plain similar to our Atlantic Coastal Plain? Make comparisons.

9. Name and locate several deserts in this section. Can they be made useful? If so, how?

10. Name and locate several famous peaks and mountains. Tell something about each.

11. Why can these states grow a very great variety of crops?

12. Discuss the advantages and disadvantages which location gives to these three states in the following ways: (*a*) commercial; (*b*) manufacturing; (*c*) agricultural; (*d*) climatic.

13. How far in miles and degrees do these states extend north and south? What would this fact alone tell you?

14. Locate the following cities and give the advantages of the position of each: Olympia, Salem, Seattle, Portland, Sacramento, Tacoma, Long Beach, San Diego.

15. What two rivers drain the Great Valley?

16. The railroads which enter this section from the east seem to come in at about four places. Can you explain this?

Physical - Political
PACIFIC STATES
Scale of Statute Miles
0 50 100 150 200
State Capitals
Railroads
The type used indicates the relative sizes of towns and cities.
HEIGHTS IN FEET
Above 10,000
5,000 to 10,000
2,000 to 5,000
1,000 to 2,000
500 to 1,000
Sea level to 500
Land below sea level
DEPTHS IN FATHOMS
Sea level to 100
Below 100
125°
120°
115°
110°
45°
40°
35°
Longitude West from Greenwich
CANADA
MONT.
WASHINGTON
OREGON
IDAHO
NEVADA
CALIFORNIA
UTAH
ARIZONA
MEXICO
PACIFIC OCEAN
VANCOUVER
Vancouver
Victoria
Strait of Georgia
Strait of Juan de Fuca
C. Flattery
Port Angeles
OLYMPIC MTS.
Mt. Baker 10 750
Bellingham
Anacortes
Port Townsend
Everett
Bremerton
Seattle
Tacoma
Aberdeen
Hoquiam
Olympia
Puyallup
Centralia
Chehalis
Mt. Rainier 14 408
Longview
Kelso
Mt. St. Helens 9 671
Mt. Adams 12 307
Astoria
Vancouver
Camas
Columbia R.
Portland
The Dalles
Oregon City
Mt. Hood
Wenatchee
Columbia
Spokane
Spokane R.
Ellensburg
Yakima
Yakima R.
Snake
Walla Walla
Pendleton
La Grande
Baker
BLUE MTS.
PLATEAU
Salem
Mt. Jefferson 10 523
Albany
Corvallis
Eugene
Willamette R.
Bend
Burns
CEDAR MTS.
Owyhee R.
Snake R.
Boise
North Bend
Coos Bay
Roseburg
CRATER LAKE NAT. PARK
Grants Pass
Medford
Ashland
Upper Klamath Lake
Klamath Falls
Goose L.
Klamath R.
Mt. Shasta 14 181
Pit R.
Eureka
Cape Mendocino
Eel R.
Lassen Peak 10 453
Sacramento R.
Chico
Reno
Carson City
L. Tahoe
Marysville
Sacramento
Santa Rosa
Petaluma
Vallejo
Golden Gate
San Francisco
Oakland
Alameda
Stockton
Modesto
Mono Lake
YOSEMITE NATIONAL PARK
San Jose
Merced R.
Santa Cruz
Watsonville
Monterey
Salinas
San Joaquin R.
Fresno
Hanford
SEQUOIA NAT. PARK
Mt. Whitney 14 496
Owens L.
Owens R.
Death Valley
Tulare Basin
Kern R.
Bakersfield
MOHAVE DESERT
Boulder Dam
San Luis Obispo
Pt. Conception
Santa Barbara
San Buenaventura (Ventura)
Los Angeles
Pasadena
Ontario
Colton
San Bernardino
Redlands
Riverside
SAN BERNARDINO MTS.
COLORADO DESERT
SANTA BARBARA ISLANDS
Long Beach
San Diego
Salton Sea
Brawley
El Centro
Colorado R.
Gila R.
Phoenix
San Rafael
Pittsburg
Richmond
Albany
Berkeley
Piedmont
Oakland
Alameda
San Leandro
San Francisco
San Francisco Bay
Daly City
Burlingame
San Mateo
Redwood City
Palo Alto
San Jose
PACIFIC OCEAN
Burbank
Pasadena
Monrovia
Glendale
S. Pasadena
Beverly Hills
Alhambra
Pomona
Santa Monica
Los Angeles
Huntington Pk.
Bell
Whittier
Inglewood
S. Gate
Compton
Fullerton
Redondo Beach
Anaheim
Long Beach
Orange
Santa Ana
PACIFIC OCEAN

Cutting these big trees and handling the big logs is too heavy work for men with hand tools only, so machines are used for much of the work. After the trunk is sawed through and the tree falls, it is trimmed and sawed into log lengths. Often strong steam engines, called *donkey engines*, "snake" out the logs and load them onto cars to be drawn out of the forest, or perhaps drag them to a waterway down which they may be floated.

Lumbering in these Pacific forests is carried on in a big way. A track is laid into the forest for cars and machinery. Sometimes caterpillar tractors snake the logs near to the track. Then a huge crane, run in on the track, reaches out like a big arm and hand, picks up the logs one by one, swings them around and puts them in place on the cars.

Lumber crews consist of many men, each with special work to do. Regular camps are built for them with garages, laundries, and bath houses. After their work, the men are free to go where they please, or they may remain in camp to read or listen to the radio. Lumbermen working in the open have good appetites, so plenty of wholesome food is provided to keep them strong and healthy. The larger camps are like little towns: cottages are provided for married men and their families, stores furnish supplies, and schools are conducted for the children.

Logging, as this work is called, is only part of the work to be done before the big trees become lumber. The sawmill takes the huge logs and saws them into beams, boards, and strips of lumber for different uses. Some are carefully split into thin sheets for veneer or plywood. Others are made into doors, frames, window sashes, flooring, and shingles. The manufacture of furniture, boxes, barrels, and kegs uses much lumber. The making of wood pulp for paper is another big industry.

Many of the forests in the Pacific states are included in National Forests, where careful watch is kept for fires, cutting of trees is regulated, and young trees are planted wherever this is necessary to take the places of those which have been cut. Lumber companies are also helping in this work of preserving the forests and planting seedlings on the cut-over lands. For even these vast forests will be destroyed in time if trees are simply cut and no effort is made to have others grow in their places. Unlike the mineral treasures, which, once taken out, cannot be replaced, forests will grow again if seed trees are left and given a chance. Even so, we should always remember that fire can destroy in a few minutes a tree that has taken centuries to grow, and we should all help to save the trees as much as possible, especially against forest fires.

Courtesy Douglas Fir Plywood Association
A PLYWOOD PLANT IN WASHINGTON
The continuous sheet of wood unwinds from the giant lathe almost like paper in a newspaper press.

CHRISTMAS GREENS

Publishers' Photo

From the forests of Washington come some of the tall, pungent evergreens that bear the tinsel balls and colored lights of Christmas celebrations, north, east, and south.

SO HAVE THE MIGHTY FALLEN

No fallen tree is too heavy for these "cruisers" to skid to the crane which loads it on cars bound for the mill.

NATURE'S GRANDEST COLONNADES

Ewing Galloway

Beautiful and mighty as these redwoods are, they are being rapidly consumed by the roaring sawmills.

The Inland Empire. — East of the Cascades in Washington and Oregon is a region which produces so many foodstuffs and other products that it is called the "Inland Empire." The winds lose much of their moisture on the western slopes of the mountains, so that this area is drier than most of the Pacific states. But it is a land of ranches and great wheat farms where huge machines glide over the gently rolling land, threshing and harvesting the wheat. Many years ago, layers of lava were poured out over this land and these have helped to make a very rich soil. This means a large crop whenever the rain does not fail. The Grand Coulee Dam across the Columbia River, which was completed in 1941, will store up enough water to irrigate over a million acres of the drier land in this area.

Barley, potatoes, and alfalfa are other crops which are grown here and herds of beef cattle and flocks of sheep graze on the drier areas. These must be fed and sheltered during the winter, but in summer many of them are driven to the mountains and grazed on the mountain pastures, usually in the National Forests. Swine and poultry are also raised.

On the lower eastern slopes of the Cascades are many long, flat-floored valleys with fertile soil. These valleys have been irrigated and turned into fruit orchards and truck gardens. They are noted especially for their fine apples which are carefully packed and shipped all over the country. Some of the best known of these valleys are Hood River, Yakima, Wenatchee, Spokane, and Walla Walla. Besides apples, peaches, plums, pears, cherries, and alfalfa are raised.

Spokane is the leading shipping and manufacturing center of eastern Washington. Falls in the Spokane River furnish electric power to run its flour and lumber mills, its factories, and meat-packing plants. Railroads cross here, making it a center for trade and tourists. Long, white ribbons of road run out through the country in every direction from Spokane, making it easy for townspeople and visitors to enjoy the scenery for which this part of our country is noted. Yakima, Wenatchee, and Walla Walla are other important trading centers in the heart of the Inland Empire.

The Valleys. — The chief valleys of the Pacific States are the Puget Basin in Washington, the Willamette in Oregon, the Great Valley in central California, and the Imperial and Coachella valleys in the south. Here are raised that great variety of products for which the Pacific States are famous.

The Puget Basin. Here the rather cool climate will not allow corn to ripen well, but it is fine for wheat, oats, and barley, and for small fruits and berries. Many of the berries are canned or made into jams and jellies and shipped to other states. Plenty of clear water, green pastures, and mild winters help make this a good region for dairy cattle.

HARVESTING IN EASTERN WASHINGTON
The ripened heads of wheat no longer ripple like waves in the breeze, but lie fallen under the sharp knives of the harvesting machine.

Courtesy Northern Pacific Railway

IRRIGATION

One of the many irrigated vineyards of the Yakima Irrigation Project in central Washington.

Courtesy Spokane Chamber of Commerce

APPLE BLOSSOM TIME

Spring in the Wenatchee Valley means acres of sweet smelling, pink and white blossoms.

Courtesy Portland Chamber of Commerce

IN MOUNTAIN PASTURES

When the warm summer days reach the valleys of the Cascades in Oregon, the sheep are driven to the pastures higher on the mountains to graze where grass is green.

Though dairy products such as condensed milk, cheese, and even butter can be shipped for long distances, usually dairying is carried on near large cities which use most of the dairy products. In the Puget Basin are many cities, among them Seattle, the largest city in the state, Tacoma, Everett, Bellingham, and Olympia, the capital.

BLOSSOM TIME IN OJAI *Josef Muench*
Below the snowy mountain top, the fragrance of almond blossoms fills the air.

The Willamette Valley. This valley is a land of fields and orchards. Although the soil is deep and fertile, there is some irrigation. The climate is so mild that people can work outdoors the year round, and farm animals need very little shelter. People have found this valley so attractive that three-fourths of the population of Oregon now live here.

All kinds of grains, hay, temperate zone tree fruits, berries, nuts, hops, and flax are grown. Prunes are a big crop and loganberries, a cross between raspberries and blackberries, are a favorite among the berries. In hops, Oregon leads all other states. The hops are trained to grow up high trellises or a network of wire to support the vines and when picking time arrives in the fall, whole families often help to gather the crop. Growing flax fiber for making linen is one of the industries here. Moist, cool air during the growing season and dry weather for harvesting favor its growth. The flax plants are pulled by machinery, and linen mills use the fiber to make thread, twine, and linen cloth.

The Willamette Valley is fine for dairying, as good pasture lands are abundant and hay is easily raised. Many goats feed on the cut-over lands. The Angora goats furnish mohair, while milk from herds of milk goats is used to make Roquefort cheese.

Salem, the capital of Oregon, and Eugene, also on the Willamette River, are trading centers for the central and southern parts of the valley. Their canneries, creameries, and mills help to consume many of the farm and forest products.

The Great Valley in California. Central California is a long basin hemmed in by mountains on all sides, broken only by the Golden Gate leading to the Pacific Ocean. Railroads and roads climb over high mountain passes to enter or leave the valley. For many years, rivers have been carrying down and spreading over the floor of this lowland rich soil which is now being used to grow over two hundred different kinds of fruits, grains, and green vegetables. As the mountains shut off most of the rainfall from the valley, irrigated farming is practiced. High in the upper Sacramento River Valley, the Shasta Dam stores up a good supply of water for irrigating the lower lands of the central parts of the valley.

The southern part, drained by the San Joaquin River, is drier than the northern part. It has a climate like that of Mediterranean regions, so olives, grapes, figs, and oranges grow well here. The Spanish mission fathers planted

FORESTS OF FRUIT TREES AT GLENDORA, CALIFORNIA © *Spence*

At the foot of the mountain slopes stretch the orchards, like a great cross-stitch pattern in two shades of green, with a glint of gold or yellow as the oranges and lemons ripen.

Courtesy Los Angeles C. of C.
DATE PALMS IN THE COACHELLA VALLEY

Fan-like the feathery palms spread over the heavy bunches of ripening fruit. Paper bags protect the dates from rain.

Publishers' Photo
SUN-KISSED

Lemons of varying sizes and colors are washed, graded, wrapped, and packed for shipment in this California packing house.

A CALIFORNIA HORSE RANCH
Fairchild
The broad fields of this ranch, level as a ballroom floor, are given over to Spanish Mission barns and paddocks for the horses.

fig and olive orchards, some of which may still be seen. California produces nearly all of the olives grown in the United States. The olives are largely canned as ripe olives or pickles, and the poorer fruit is pressed for oil.

Grapes are grown for various uses in California. Around Fresno, the main crop is raisin grapes. A familiar sight here is the long rows of trays of raisin grapes drying in the sun. In the central part of the valley, grapes are grown especially for table use. These are carefully packed in sawdust and shipped all over the United States. Other grapes are grown for making wine or grape juice and a few are canned. Grapes like those grown in Mediterranean countries do well in California.

Oranges grow on the slopes at the foot of the mountains in the southern part of the San Joaquin Valley. The slopes are better drained, and as the colder air sinks to the bottom of the valley at night, the trees are in less danger of frost.

Wheat growing was once a leading industry in California but now more barley is grown, as it does well in regions where there is little rainfall. Rice is grown in the Sacramento Valley, where the flat land is easily flooded by water from the Sacramento River. It is cultivated and harvested by machinery.

The Coachella and Imperial Valleys. Many years ago, the present Gulf of California extended much farther inland. Then the Colorado River brought down so much rock material that it dammed the valley and shut off the northern end of the gulf. This left an inland sea in such a dry region that most of the water evaporated, leaving only a small body of water now known as the Salton Sea. At the northern end of the Salton Sea is the Coachella Valley and at its southern end, the Imperial Valley. Both of these were once covered by this inland sea, and their soil is very fertile. Here the climate is warm enough so that tropical fruits such as dates can be grown. The water that is needed in the Coachella Valley is furnished by springs

U. S. Department of Agriculture
ORCHARDS AND VINEYARDS
This map shows where most of the following nine fruits are grown: apples, peaches, pears, plums, prunes, grapes, oranges, lemons, grapefruit, and strawberries. Each dot stands for 1000 acres of fruit trees or vines. In some places there are so many acres of fruit that the dots run together. The dark area in Florida stands for citrus fruits; that in Georgia for peaches. Where are most of the fruits in California grown? Locate fruit-growing areas in other states and tell which of the nine fruits are grown there.

WHO CARES FOR A FIG?
The round, ripe, freshly picked fruit will soon dry out under the rays of the warm California sun.

and wells, but the Colorado River is used to irrigate the Imperial Valley. This valley is famous all over the world for its wonderful, rich soil. Oranges, lemons, grapefruit, and green vegetables are raised in these valleys and shipped all over the United States.

Dried Fruit and Canning Industries in California. — The hot, sunny, summer days in California are fine for both ripening and drying fruit. As fruit and vegetables grow so abundantly, it is natural that California should have large dried fruit and canning industries. The fruit dries so quickly that it does not become dark and discolored as it is likely to do where there is more moisture in the air. Immense quantities of canned fruits and vegetables are sent out from this state. The great demand for tin cans has led to the building of factories for the manufacture of these. Thus one industry leads to another.

Along the Coast. — There are five main gateways which carry most of the commerce of the Pacific States. In southern California are the harbors of San Diego and San Pedro. Farther north is the "Golden Gate" where San Francisco with its many docks and piers takes care of the Pacific commerce in that region. Between Oregon and Washington, the Columbia River cuts across the mountain ranges and furnishes an excellent highway from the interior to the Pacific Ocean. Astoria, at its mouth, is an important fishing port and sends out much lumber, but Portland, farther inland on the Willamette River, handles most of the trade. In northwestern Washington is Puget Sound, a large inlet of the Pacific Ocean, with Seattle and Tacoma carrying on most of the commerce.

Fishing. — Fishing is one of the big industries of the Pacific States. Off the coasts of these states, small fish called sardines and large tuna or tunny fish are caught and canned. North from California, salmon, halibut, mackerel, and flounder are found, but salmon are the most important. Though they spend most of their lives in the ocean, they go up rivers to *spawn* (lay their eggs) in fresh water and are easily caught as they swim upstream. Huge seines and fish traps are used to catch them. The Columbia River is famous for its Chinook salmon, one of the finest food fishes known. During World War II the soldiers called the salmon "goldfish." This nickname was not far wrong, when we consider the great wealth the

"I CAUGHT ONE — SO BIG!"
A cast, a nibble, an upward swing, and out of the water rises a fighting-mad tunny, fooled by a bit of bait.

ALL IS NOT GOLD THAT GLITTERS
In the mud and sand and gravel of California's river beds the search for bits of gold still goes on.

salmon industry has brought to the people around the Columbia River.

Most of the salmon are canned. The factories make a practice of canning each day's catch the day it is caught. These canneries along the Columbia and other rivers in the northwest are busy places while the salmon are "running." Astoria, at the mouth of the Columbia, is especially noted for them, but there are many other cities and towns where fish are canned. The preparing and shipping of oysters is an important industry on Puget Sound and the bays along the coast of western Washington.

Mineral Wealth. — California is especially famous for its mineral wealth. In 1848, John Marshall discovered gold while clearing out a mill race at Sutter's Mill near Sacramento. The news spread to the eastern United States and the famous "gold rush" of 1849 began. Clerks left their stores, sailors their ships, laborers their work, and swarmed into the Sacramento Valley. Some people went overland; some by boat around South America; others shipped to the Isthmus of Panama and crossed over to the Pacific Ocean where they then took a boat again for San Francisco. Thousands were soon added to California's population. Even before the year was out there were enough people in this territory to apply for statehood, and the very next year California was admitted to the Union.

In the first three years after the discovery of gold, California produced four times as much gold as had previously been mined in the whole United States. Much of it was obtained from sand and gravel which had been carried down the streams from the mountains where the ore was first formed. The early miners found it quite easy to "wash" the gold-bearing sand and gravel and obtain the particles of heavy gold which readily sank to the bottom.

Gold is also found in the river beds in the California gold district. Much of this has been recovered by dredges which go out on the rivers and scoop up the soft deposits from

Courtesy Los Angeles Chamber of Commerce
OIL, THAT MAKES THE WHEELS GO ROUND
The slender steel shafts proclaim to the world: "Here is Oil, the fuel that keeps thousands of automobiles rolling along."

the bottom. Special machines then separate the gold from these deposits. Since 1850, California has mined over twice as much gold as any other state.

Silver, lead, zinc, and copper are all mined in the Pacific States. The smelting of ores containing these metals, and the manufacture of aluminum and magnesium are important industries in Washington.

In the desert regions of southern California, salt lakes and beds of dried up lakes contain useful minerals, such as salt, soda, and borax. Some contain potash, a valuable fertilizer. Another valuable mineral obtained is tungsten, which is used in making fine steel for tools and tungsten lights.

California is one of our leading oil-producing states. One oil field is centered around Los Angeles, another along the coast northwest of Los Angeles, and the third around Bakersfield in the southern part of the Great Valley.

Most of the oil is refined and converted into gasoline, kerosene, and other products before shipment. Pipe lines carry it from the fields to the refineries, some of which are near the oil fields in the interior and others are at Los Angeles and some of the coastal cities. *Tankers*, vessels built especially to carry oil, come to the port of Los Angeles and other seaports for the petroleum. Much of it is sent to the eastern United States by way of the Panama Canal, and some goes to other countries.

Natural gas is also found in connection with the oil. This is one of the finest fuels for heating and manufacturing purposes.

One can always tell an oil field by the derricks and tanks. To get oil, men drill a deep hole, usually hundreds of feet deep, and then pump out the oil. The derricks are used to support the tools while drilling and afterwards in pumping.

The Deserts of Southern California. — The largest of the deserts in California is known as

ALUMINUM COMBINES LIGHTNESS WITH STRENGTH
An aluminum ingot may be seen on the rollers in the foreground. More than one-third of the aluminum produced in the United States is used in the manufacture of airplanes, automobiles, trucks, buses, ships, and trains. Washington is one of the leading states in the manufacture of this useful metal.

the Mohave Desert. (See map, page 37.) Here are found great stretches of sand dunes covered with sage brush and bunch grass. Railroads cross it in two directions and motor roads also allow people to enter some parts of it and admire the beauty of the spring flowers. Few people live here because water is so scarce that it is hard to make a living.

Northeast of the Mohave Desert lies the famous Death Valley, so called because many people and animals lost their lives trying to cross it on their way to California during the gold rush of 1849. This is the lowest region in our country, being over 250 feet below sea level. It is one of the hottest known regions in the world during the summer months. A little rain, about two or three inches, falls during the winter season. Miles of bare sand dunes, shifting with the wind, form a large part of its surface. Yet there is considerable vegetation and it is said to contain many plants not to be found elsewhere. People have found a use even for this

SAILING HOME FROM SEATTLE

Courtesy Seattle Chamber of Commerce

Behind the sturdy little tug, a big freighter passes through the Lake Washington Canal on her homeward journey.

hot desert. A water hole, which saved the lives of many weary travelers, has become a well pouring out 1000 barrels of water per hour. Here, many feet below sea level, Stovepipe Wells is being developed into a sightseeing and health resort, where artists go to paint the desert scenes.

The Climate of the Pacific Coast. — The Pacific states are noted for their mild climate. This is due to the fact that most of the winds in these states have blown for a long distance over the Pacific Ocean, so they have about the same temperature as the ocean. These winds are not so cold in winter nor so warm in summer as the land. Western Washington, Oregon, and Northern California have one of the most even climates to be found anywhere in the United States. The winters are mild and moist with very little snow on the lowlands, while the summers are clear and comfortable. San Francisco, nearly surrounded by water, has fairly cool summers. But the south has the famous "California climate," so mild and sunny that it has attracted thousands of people from all parts of the United States.

Cities of the Pacific States. — *Seattle* has grown to be the largest of the Puget Sound seaports. For trade with Asiatic countries and Alaska, it has the advantage over San Francisco of being several hundred miles nearer. It has an excellent harbor and a rich land back of it to furnish products for export. Lumber, wheat, flour, canned berries, apples, and canned fish go out, while tin plate, iron and steel articles, shoes, clothing, textiles, glass and electrical supplies come in. Washington and Oregon both trade with California, exchanging such products as lumber, wheat, flour, apples, potatoes, and canned salmon for petroleum products, fruits, and manufactured goods of various kinds.

Tacoma, next to Seattle in size and importance as a seaport, is sometimes called the "lumber capital" because so much lumber is prepared and shipped from here. Large sawmills are also found in *Bellingham*, *Everett*, *Longview*, and *Port Angeles*, all of which ship out lumber. Longview has one of the largest lumber mills in the world.

The city of *Portland* lies on both sides of the Willamette River near where it joins the Columbia. It is the largest city of Oregon, having nearly one-third of the population of

Ewing Galloway

FROM TREE TRUNK TO LUMBER

At Tacoma, the great logs are converted into lumber and then loaded on to steamers to be carried through the Panama Canal to build homes in the East.

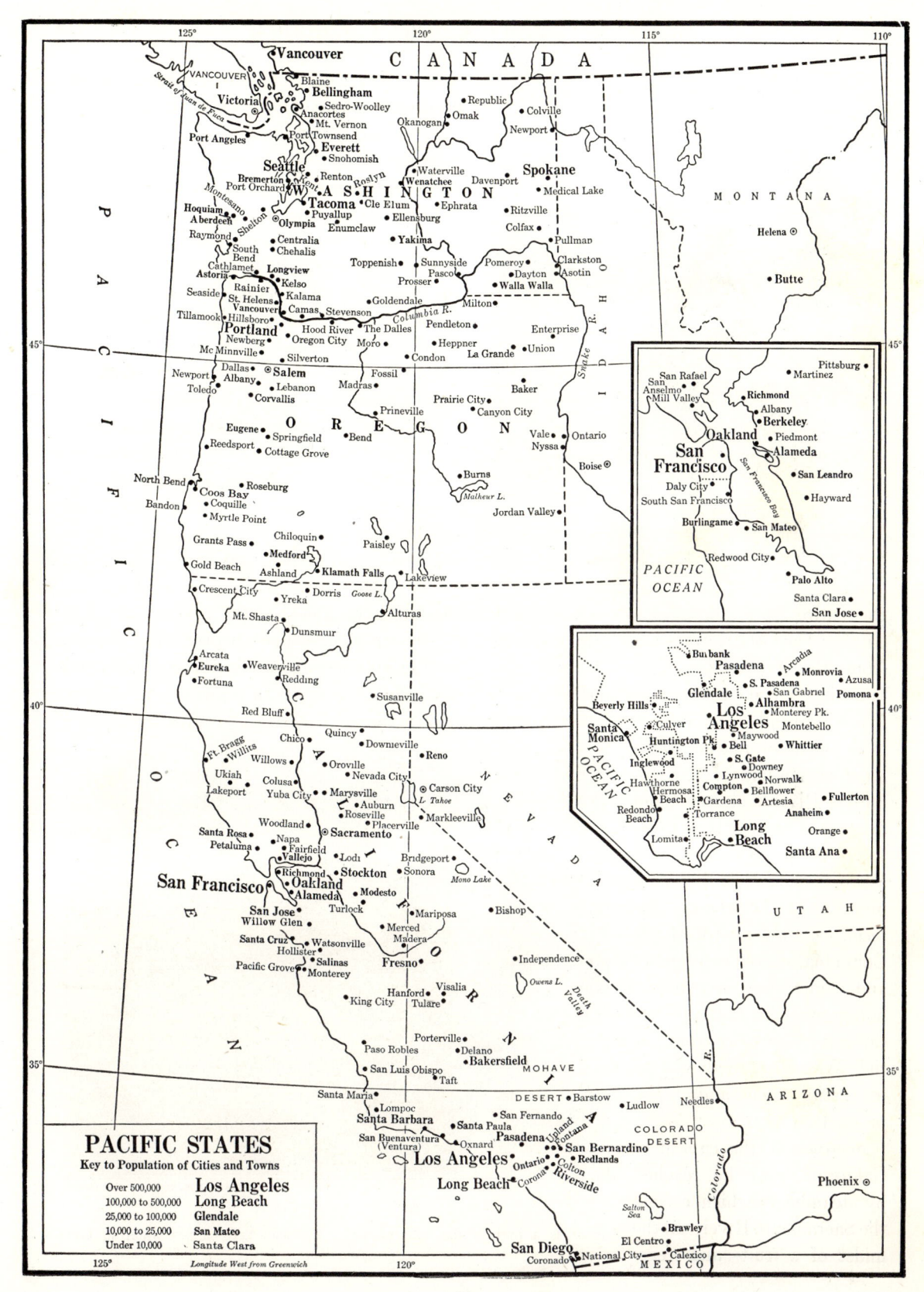

PACIFIC STATES
Key to Population of Cities and Towns

Population	Example
Over 500,000	**Los Angeles**
100,000 to 500,000	**Long Beach**
25,000 to 100,000	**Glendale**
10,000 to 25,000	San Mateo
Under 10,000	Santa Clara

Courtesy Portland Chamber of Commerce
FISHERMEN'S LUCK

Salmon, on the first lap of their journey from open ocean to sealed tin, are caught in great nets, or seines, as they swim upstream in the Columbia River.

the entire state, but *Salem* is the capital. Timber from the forests and farm products from the Willamette Valley furnish raw materials for its many mills and factories. Much furniture is manufactured here, and it is a big wool market, with large woolen mills. The Columbia River is deep enough to allow large vessels to come to the docks, so it is called a seaport, though it is many miles from the coast. *Astoria*, near the mouth of the Columbia, ships much lumber and canned fish, but it has not grown like Portland because it is quite far from the rich Willamette Valley with its many farm and forest products.

Sacramento, the capital of California, may be reached by steamboats which ascend the Sacramento River. In the midst of a fruit- and vegetable-growing district, it has become an important canning center. A large plant which can make many millions of tin cans a day is located here.

San Francisco has one of the finest harbors in the world, connected with the ocean by a strait called the "Golden Gate." From its busy docks the products of the Great Valley are shipped to all parts of the world. In San Francisco's Chinatown, beautiful curios, embroidery and lacquer work are for sale. In 1945, San Francisco was chosen as the meeting place for the United Nations Conference.

Los Angeles, California's largest city, began as a trading station over 150 years ago. Trails followed by the pack trains crossed here. Springs furnished drinking water, and a river gave water for irrigating crops. For about 100 years, the town grew slowly, but recently it has grown so fast that it is now the fifth city in the United States. As Los Angeles grew, its leaders realized that it must have more water to supply the people in the city. So they built an aqueduct to a river among the high Sierra Nevada Mountains,

Courtesy, Dept. of Water and Power
AS THE ROMANS DID IT

Here is a part of the concrete-lined aqueduct that carries water to Los Angeles.

Courtesy San Francisco Chamber of Commerce
CHINATOWN

Here, in the busy city of San Francisco, are the lanterns, the shops, the pagoda roofs, and the sandalwood and teakwood curios of China, far across the sea.

© *Rovere Scott*
THE BAY BRIDGE

This eight-mile bridge, with its double decks, can hold its own with the bridges of the Old World both in beauty and fame.

HAPPY LANDINGS!
Courtesy San Diego Chamber of Commerce

Day after day the shadows of Uncle Sam's fearless birdmen fall on the blue waters of San Diego harbor, and the air is noisy with the hum of army and navy airplane motors.

NOT ALL THE RICE IS IN CHINA *Courtesy California State Chamber of Commerce*
River boats, with their heavy cargoes of rice and barley, are part of the fleet of freight carriers that ply back and forth on the Sacramento River.

240 miles away. Later, they built another long aqueduct to bring water from the Colorado River so they would be sure to have plenty of water in the future.

As Los Angeles is about 20 miles from the sea, the people needed a port from which to ship their products. So at the mouth of the Los Angeles River they dredged a deep harbor at San Pedro and built a long breakwater to protect it. Los Angeles now ranks second among the seaports of the United States in the value of its exports and imports. Many airplanes are now manufactured in this city.

Perhaps no place in the world is better known than Hollywood, home of the "movies." It is part of Los Angeles where the sunny weather, clear air, and variety of scenery nearby make it an ideal place to film pictures. Films made here are not only shown all over our country, but all over the world.

San Diego, California's oldest city, is built on the sloping shores of a bay which gives it a beautiful, large harbor. Here the United States Government has established a naval base. As it never freezes in San Diego, the navy men may have open-air training every day in the year. After the second World War started, many military camps were located nearby. Airplane factories were built to make war planes, and many people moved there to work in these factories.

Activities and Questions

1. Make a list of the chief products of each of the Pacific states. Give reasons for each.

2. Collect pictures of some of the big trees of California.

3. Compare the climate in the northern section of this group of states with that in the south.

THE PACIFIC STATES

4. Name the chief harbors on the Pacific coast. Which has the most commerce? Why?

5. Describe the salmon industry.

6. You are one of the "forty-niners." Tell how you would get to California and what your life there would be like. What caused the "gold rush"?

7. How are the big trees cut and taken to the mill?

8. Measure on the map the length of California and compare it with the distance between New York and Chicago.

9. Name the capitals and largest cities in the Pacific States.

10. What are the main rivers in these states? Which is the largest? What are the rivers used for?

11. Sketch a map of these states, putting in the rivers, chief mountains, and leading cities.

Courtesy U. S. Bureau of Reclamation

THE BIGGEST THING EVER BUILT BY MAN — GRAND COULEE DAM

With steel and concrete, men worked day and night building this huge barrier across the Columbia River, and finished their task two years earlier than was first planned. The mighty force of this great river is now helping to run factories and to light homes and stores in the Pacific Northwest. Grand Coulee Dam, now the largest dam in the world, is 4300 feet long, 560 feet high, and 500 feet thick at the base where it is firmly fastened to the hard rock underneath. It will make possible the irrigation of over a million thirsty acres, just waiting for the magic touch of water and the hand of man to change them from dry, sagebrush land into fertile farms and orchards. Electric power to ease the heavy work in the farm household as well as in the farmyard, and the Columbia River made into a waterway to carry the products to market — all these, once dreams for this little used land, are now becoming real as power houses and canals enable Grand Coulee Dam to do its work.

GREEN PASTURES *J. A. Bogart*

It is as if the pages of history were turned back to the pastoral age of long ago, when shepherds and their flocks roamed the countryside, seeking green pastures.

IV. THE MOUNTAIN STATES

East of the Pacific States is a group which we call the Mountain States. There are eight of them: Idaho, Nevada, and Arizona, bordering the Pacific States; Montana, Wyoming, Colorado, and New Mexico next to the Mississippi Valley; and Utah in the center, surrounded by the others. As their name suggests, these states consist largely of mountains and high plateaus, though they extend over into the great plains on the east. In the high plateaus, streams have cut deep, steep-sided valleys called *canyons*. Some of the valleys are broad, flat, and rimmed with mountains. Here it is usually too dry to grow crops unless water is supplied from streams or wells.

Population. — Though their area is nearly twice that of any other group, the Mountain States have less than half the population of any other region: only a few people to each square mile as compared with the Middle Atlantic States, which have many people to the square mile.

Deserts in the Mountain States. — The Mountain States contain more desert land than any other region in the country. The deserts in these states occur on the lowlands between the mountain ranges in the areas having less than 10 inches annual precipitation. (Precipitation includes rainfall and snowfall. See map, page 56.) In some places, only bare rock, sand, and gravel appear. In others, the soil is too full of salt or alkali for anything to grow. But most of the desert lands contain hardy growths such as sagebrush, or plants such as the cactus, a fleshy, leafless plant with sharp thorns. *Cactus* comes from a word meaning "prickly plant."

Desert soil is usually fertile if water can be supplied. In the southwestern United States, streams from the high mountain ranges furnish

LEANING MOUNTAIN, OGDEN CANYON, UTAH

A white ribbon road winds through the towering peaks of vivid rock, with here and there a few green trees clinging perilously to the thin soil of the canyon's side.

WHAT A CACTUS!

Among the patches of desert shrubs and grasses in Arizona the bristling green stems of the giant cactus reach up sixty feet toward the sky, like a clump of huge tuning forks.

ACROSS THE RIO GRANDE IN NEW MEXICO

Over the Rio Grande and the dull gray mesa beyond, the road goes on to the ancient cliff dwellings of earlier days.

AVERAGE ANNUAL PRECIPITATION

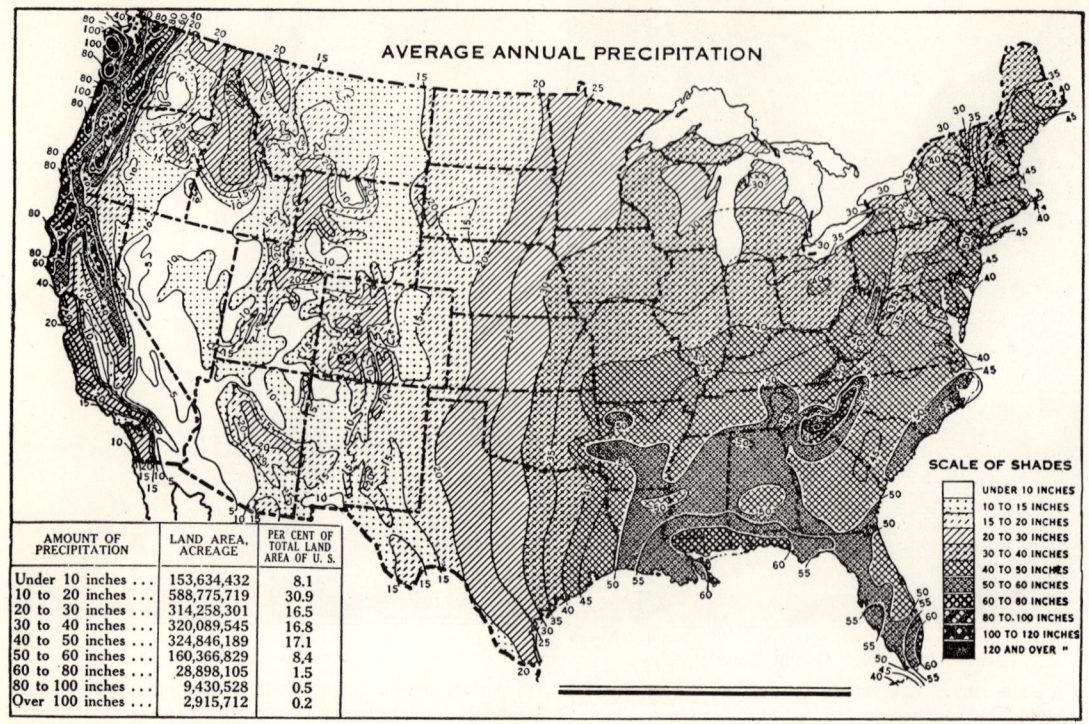

AMOUNT OF PRECIPITATION	LAND AREA, ACREAGE	PER CENT OF TOTAL LAND AREA OF U. S.
Under 10 inches	153,634,432	8.1
10 to 20 inches	588,775,719	30.9
20 to 30 inches	314,258,301	16.5
30 to 40 inches	320,089,545	16.8
40 to 50 inches	324,846,189	17.1
50 to 60 inches	160,366,829	8.4
60 to 80 inches	28,898,105	1.5
80 to 100 inches	9,430,528	0.5
Over 100 inches	2,915,712	0.2

SCALE OF SHADES
UNDER 10 INCHES
10 TO 15 INCHES
15 TO 20 INCHES
20 TO 30 INCHES
30 TO 40 INCHES
40 TO 50 INCHES
50 TO 60 INCHES
60 TO 80 INCHES
80 TO 100 INCHES
100 TO 120 INCHES
120 AND OVER "

U. S. Department of Agriculture

MAP SHOWING AVERAGE RAINFALL IN THE UNITED STATES

This map shows the amount of rain in different parts of the United States for one year. The lines run through places having the same yearly rainfall. For example, the line marked 20 connects places having 20 inches of rainfall during the year. Study the legend or Scale of Shades carefully to learn the amount of rainfall which the different shaded areas represent. In regions having 20 inches or more of rainfall each year, crops can usually be grown without irrigation. Notice the scanty rainfall throughout much of the mountain states area. Only the mountains have much rain. Where do you find areas of very heavy rainfall, 60 inches or more?

Use this map often when you are studying about farming in different parts of the United States. It will help you to locate the rainfall regions and to tell why certain areas have to be irrigated in order to grow crops.

water to irrigate the lower areas between the mountains.

Irrigation in the Mountain States. — The melting snows of the mountains are the source of most of the rivers in the western United States. On the Pacific coast are the Columbia, the Willamette, the Sacramento, and the San Joaquin. The longest river in the country, the Missouri, rises in the Rockies, as do also the Colorado, the Arkansas (Ar′kan-saw), and many smaller streams. Some of these drain fertile valleys, and nearly all are used for irrigation.

Long ago a group of Mormons, a religious sect, went west to find a place where they might settle and be free to follow their religious beliefs and customs as they pleased. They crossed the Rockies and settled in the Salt Lake Valley. Here in this *arid* (dry) region, with water furnished by a river from the nearby mountains, this little band of hard-working men and women started the irrigated farming which has grown today to be one of the biggest and most important industries in the Mountain States.

Irrigated lands are found in all of these states. Colorado leads with over three million acres under irrigation; Idaho has over two million; Montana, Utah, and Wyoming each has over a million; and New Mexico, Arizona, and Nevada have over a half a million each.

THE MOUNTAIN STATES

Statistics of the Mountain States *

State	Abbreviation	Area Sq. Miles	Population	Rank Area	Rank Pop.	Capital	Population	Largest City	Population
Idaho . . .		83,557	524,873	12	43	Boise	26,130	Boise	26,130
Nevada . .	Nev.	110,540	110,247	6	49	Carson City	2,478	Reno	21,317
Arizona . .	Ariz.	113,909	499,261	5	44	Phoenix	65,414	Phoenix	65,414
Montana . .	Mont.	147,138	559,456	3	40	Helena	15,056	Butte	37,081
Wyoming .	Wyo.	97,914	250,742	8	48	Cheyenne	22,474	Cheyenne	22,474
Colorado . .	Colo.	104,247	1,123,296	7	33	Denver	322,412	Denver	322,412
New Mexico .	N. Mex.	121,666	531,818	4	42	Santa Fe	20,325	Albuquerque	35,449
Utah . . .		84,916	550,310	10	41	Salt Lake City	149,934	Salt Lake City	149,934

* 1940 Census

IMPORTANT PRODUCTS

Idaho: — Wheat, live stock, timber, lead, zinc, silver
Nevada: — Live stock, copper, silver, gold, wool
Arizona: — Live stock, copper, cotton, fruits, gold
Montana: — Live stock, wheat, wool, coal, copper
Wyoming: — Live stock, wool, petroleum, refined petroleum, sugar beets
Colorado: — Sugar beets, live stock, grains, silver, coal, vanadium, molybdenum
New Mexico: — Live stock, petroleum, wool, cotton, copper, potash
Utah: — Sheep, sugar beets, silver, lead, wool, gold, copper

In irrigated farming, streams from the mountains furnish the water, and the farms are usually small and the farm homes close together. Crops are large, so the farmer does not need many acres to make a living. Sugar beets, other vegetables, and fruits are commonly grown on irrigated areas, and these require so much labor that a man cannot take care of much land.

Many crops, such as alfalfa and grains, may be grown where there is a light rainfall, but much larger crops are produced on irrigated land so that it pays the farmer to water them. Alfalfa is one of the largest crops grown under irrigation. It is a rich food, especially good for fattening beef cattle and other live stock. Two or three crops can be raised each year on one plot of land. Large quantities are fed to dairy cattle and to beef cattle and sheep pastured on the drier grazing lands.

Sugar beets are an important irrigated crop. They bring good prices, but they require a great amount of hand labor, as the young plants must be thinned out and the weeds pulled by hand. After the beets are pulled, they are "topped" by hand. These tops make good feed for the dairy cattle. After the juice has been squeezed out of the beets in the sugar mill, the pulp which is left is also a fine cattle food.

Irrigation in Arizona. — One of the larger irrigated valleys is that of the Salt River.

THE WASTES OF ARIZONA

Ewing Galloway

In the midst of a desert blossoms an artist colony. Camelback Peak stands a silent sentinel, through the ages.

Back in the mountains, 60 miles away, the Roosevelt Dam holds back the waters of the Salt River, forming Roosevelt Lake. This stores up water for use during the dry season, and helps to prevent floods during periods of heavy rainfall. Thousands of carloads of lettuce, cantaloupes, cotton, and alfalfa are raised here and shipped to other states. Oranges and grapefruit are also raised. This is one of the few regions in the United States where dates will grow, for the warm, sunny weather is much like that of the oases in the African Sahara. A fine grade of cotton with a long fiber is also raised here. It is called Pima cotton, and is similar to the fine Egyptian cotton raised along the Nile in Egypt.

The farmers in the Salt River Valley also get electric power from the Roosevelt and other dams. As the water rushes down from these dams, its power is used to run generators which make electricity. Such a development is called a hydro-electric plant. *Hydro* comes from a Greek word meaning water. The building with the machines which make the electricity is called a hydro-electric plant, and is usually built at the foot of the dam.

Almost south of the Roosevelt Dam is the Coolidge Dam, in the Gila River Valley. In southwestern Arizona, along the Colorado River, near Yuma, is another well-known irrigated area fed by water from the Colorado River. Thus what used to be the "Great American Desert" is coming to produce some of the finest fruit and vegetables in the country.

Hoover Dam. — Across the canyon of the Colorado River, between Nevada and Arizona, the United States Government has built the highest dam in the world. (See map, page 60.) This new dam is known as Hoover Dam and it is over 700 feet high. It furnishes water for irrigating many thousands of acres of land in Nevada, Arizona, and California. A large hydro-electric plant produces electricity to use in the homes and on the farms as well as in factories and mines.

Sites for these big dams have to be carefully chosen by skilled engineers. The dams must be very thick and strong to hold back so much water. The base must rest on solid rock so that the water cannot undermine it, and the rocky sides of the canyon into

Courtesy Bureau of Reclamation
THE WONDERS OF SCIENCE
For centuries the waters of the Colorado River went on their unhindered way. Hoover Dam is now storing their power, and their direction is governed by human skill.

which the ends of the dam are built must also be solid, as the bursting of a dam means a serious flood. Hoover Dam is 650 feet thick at the bottom.

Irrigated Farming in Nevada. — In Nevada, one of the largest irrigated sections is fed by the Truckee-Carson and Humbolt rivers. These rivers, like many others in Nevada, flow into salt lakes which have no outlet. Lack of water is the main reason why Nevada has so few people. Although the sixth largest

DIVERTING THE COLORADO
By means of a diversion canal at Yuma a large stream of water is carried to the Imperial Valley in California.

COOLIDGE DAM, SAN CARLOS, ARIZONA
Three hollow concrete domes hold back the river water for irrigating the land of the Indians.

HOLDING BACK THE MOUNTAIN STREAMS
Even the smallest streams of Colorado are dammed and used for irrigation

FROM WATER POWER TO ELECTRICITY
The power of the water held back by this dam at Great Falls, Montana, generates electric power to run 600 miles of train.

DAMMING THE MIGHTY RIO GRANDE IN NEW MEXICO
Elephant Butte Dam, with its concrete wall a thousand feet long, holds 860,000 million gallons of water.

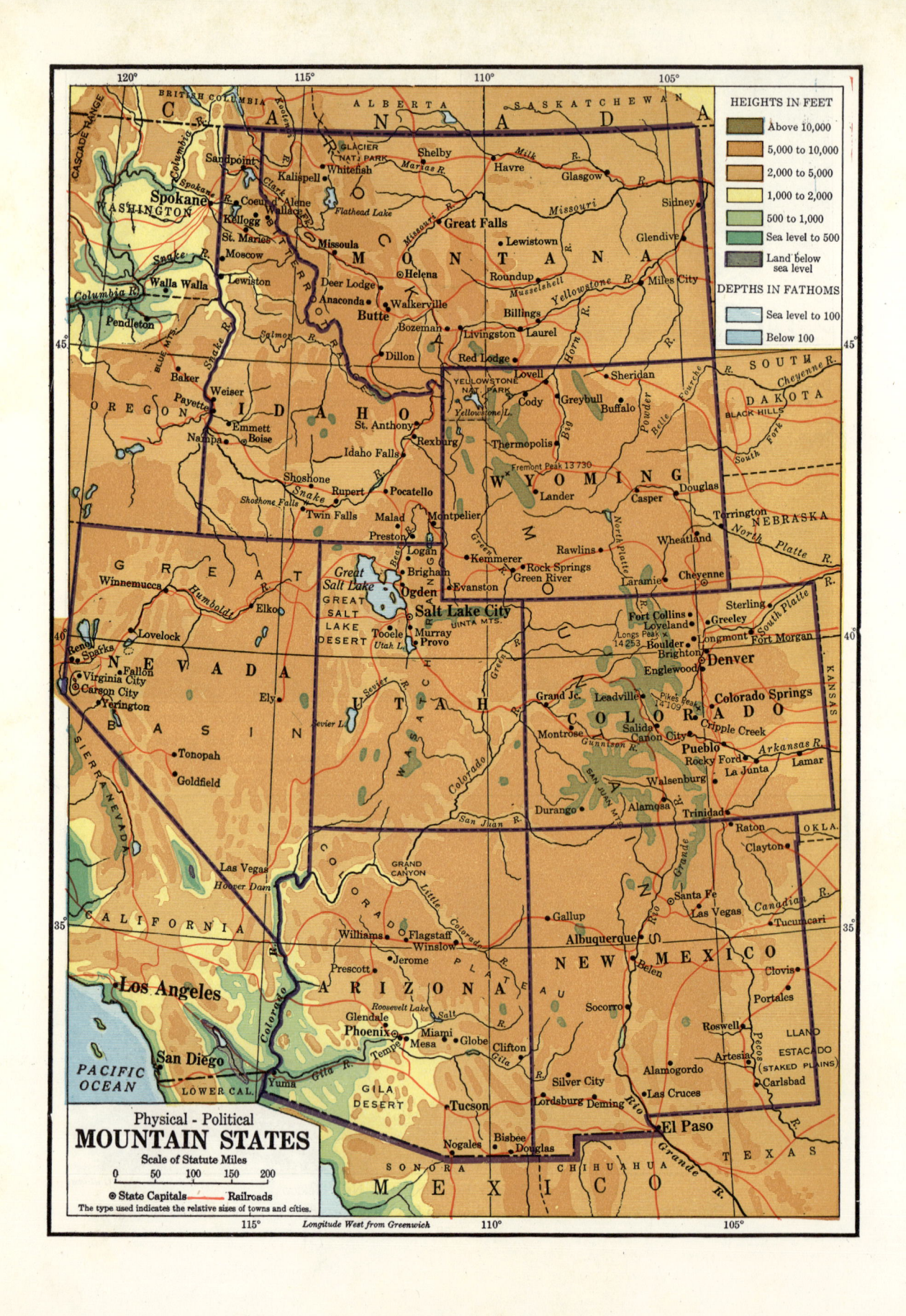

Physical - Political
MOUNTAIN STATES
Scale of Statute Miles
0 50 100 150 200
⊙ State Capitals   — Railroads
The type used indicates the relative sizes of towns and cities.

THE MOUNTAIN STATES

MAP OF THE MOUNTAIN STATES

Map Questions and Activities

1. Name and locate each of the Mountain States. Look at your map and tell why this is a good name for this group of states.

2. Explain from the map why this group of states has about twice as many square miles as any other, yet less than half the population of any other group.

3. Name and locate three other states in the United States each of which has more people than all these eight states. How have climate and surface features helped to cause these differences in population?

4. Do any of these states touch the ocean? How has this influenced their development? What countries lie north and south of this group?

5. What seems to be the average altitude of this section? How does that effect the climate? the products?

6. From a study of the rivers which flow into the Pacific Ocean and into the Atlantic, trace roughly about where you think the continental divide is.

7. Which part seems to have the fewest rivers? Why? What part has rivers which do not flow into the ocean? What is this section called?

8. Indicate on the map several irrigated areas.

9. Is there much water power in these states? Give reasons for your answer.

10. Give some reasons for the growth of Denver and Salt Lake City.

11. From the map would you infer that these states are leading commercial or manufacturing states? Justify your answer.

12. Does this region have many railroads? Why?

13. Why is stock raising the commonest and easiest type of agriculture carried on here?

14. Locate Yellowstone National Park and several famous mountain peaks.

15. Name, locate, and describe the courses of three important rivers which rise in Colorado. Where and how do these rivers reach the ocean?

16. Name and locate the capital and largest city in each state. In which states are they one and the same city?

17. Are there any deserts in this section? Where?

18. Locate the following and tell some interesting things about: Grand Canyon, Great Salt Lake, Colorado Springs, Glacier National Park, Hoover Dam, and Pike's Peak.

---

state in the Union, it has less than 100,000 population. Reno, the largest city, has about 18,000; and the capital, Carson City, fewer than 1600. The largest crops raised in Nevada are alfalfa and hay. The mining towns furnish markets for such irrigated products as fruits and vegetables.

Irrigation in Colorado. — Colorado has many irrigated areas. One of the largest in the western part of the state is the valley of the Grand River, the upper part of the Colorado. East of the Rockies, the largest irrigated district is that of the Arkansas Valley. The Arkansas has its source high in the Rockies and breaks through the front range of the Rockies in a deep, picturesque gorge. From this point eastward across the plains of Colorado, the valley widens into a broad, level area with very rich soil. Here the people have built up one of the largest single irrigated areas in the world. Large quantities of sugar beets are raised and beet sugar is manufactured. In addition to fruits and vegetables, carloads of cantaloupes and watermelons are shipped out each year.

Irrigated Farming in Idaho. — The Snake River and its tributaries furnish water for many irrigated districts in Idaho. The Arrowrock Dam, one of the highest in the world, stores water for irrigated farming and electric plants near Boise, the capital and largest city of the state. Schoolhouses, homes, and other buildings are heated as well as lighted by electricity in some parts of Idaho.

Irrigation in Other Mountain States. — Montana, the "Mountain State," with its many fertile valleys, can raise many crops without irrigation. But by irrigating the land, nearly twice as much can be raised, so the people of Montana have built many dams to store water. Near Helena, the capital, the Missouri River has been dammed and electricity produced here is used to pump water from the river up onto the fields.

HOOVER DAM (FORMERLY BOULDER DAM) © *Spence Air Photos*
Harnessing the great Colorado River and diverting its waters through three miles of tunnel was an engineer's dream before 1933. In 1936 the Boulder Canyon project was complete with dam, spillways, intake towers, outlet works, and power house. Now, floods have been controlled, power is furnished, and plenty of water provided for irrigation and domestic use.

For many years people in Wyoming have been leading water from their rivers over their fields to water their growing crops. They have also built a number of dams so that they may irrigate more land.

In New Mexico, the waters of the Rio Grande are held back behind the huge Elephant Butte Dam, forming one of the largest artificial lakes in the world. Other valleys in New Mexico also have their bordering farm lands fed by the streams.

In Utah large quantities of fruit and vegetables are raised on irrigated land. Some fruits are frozen, packed in ice, and shipped to other states.

Dry Farming in the Mountain States. — Many sections of the drier lands in the Mountain States have too little rainfall to grow most crops and no water for irrigation. Here the farmers grow such crops as wheat, alfalfa, and barley by a method called *dry farming*. Usually a crop is grown one year and then the ground is allowed to lie idle, or *fallow*, for a year. During this idle period, the farmer plows and harrows the ground and does not allow any weeds to grow. This helps to keep the moisture in the ground. Loose surface soil helps to hold the water in the ground whereas weeds take water out of the ground and evaporate it through their leaves. Dry farming is widely practiced in parts of Idaho, Montana, and Wyoming, and to a less extent in Utah and Colorado. Usually such farming is carried on where large machines can be used to prepare the ground, sow the seeds, and harvest the crops. Unlike irrigated areas the farms are large and the houses far apart.

The Great Basin. — Much of Nevada and Utah lie in a region called the Great Basin. It is surrounded by mountains so that no streams flow out of it. It is not level, but has many mountain ranges, with long, flat valleys between. Rain falls on these mountains, feeding rivers and brooks which carry down soil to the valleys. Sometimes the streams disappear in the coarse rock material at the foot of the mountains and then reappear as springs farther down the slope. In the arid regions, streams may flow for a distance and then dry up in the hot, dry sands. The nature of the country is shown by such names as Dry Valley and Cactus Flat.

In many of the lower places of the Great Basin lakes have formed, fed by streams from the mountains. Most of these are salt lakes with no outlets. The hot, dry air carries off much of the water and keeps these lakes about the same size from year to year. But only pure water passes off into the air and the salts contained in the water are left, so after a while the lakes become very salty. The largest lake in the Great Basin is Great Salt Lake in Utah. Excepting the Dead Sea in Palestine, Great Salt Lake is the saltiest body of water in the world. Its waters are over one-fifth salt and you cannot sink in it. Some of the lakes in this arid region dry up in summer. Some former lakes have now dried up and their beds often contain salt, potash, borax, or other useful minerals.

THE WHEAT FIELDS OF MONTANA
Ewing Galloway
The rounded piles of cut wheat dot the hillside like a tufted bedspread laid over the acres of ranch lands.

Minerals in the Mountain States. — Gold, silver, copper, iron, and other metals are found in the Mountain States. The metal is usually mixed with rock material, and the whole is called *ore*. If this ore has a large proportion of gold, it is called gold ore; if it has much iron, it is called iron ore.

The process of treating ores and refining the metals they contain is called *smelting*. Smelting requires coal or some other fuel to produce heat. If water power is plentiful, electricity can be used for this purpose. Sometimes smelting is done near the mines, but often it is cheaper to ship the ore to some place where there is fuel. Smelting is naturally a big industry in the Mountain States where so much mining of metals is carried on.

Gold and Silver. — Gold and silver are produced in paying quantities in all of the Mountain States except Wyoming. Utah and Colorado rank high in the production of gold, while Idaho leads in silver. Generally the ores which contain the gold or silver also yield other metals such as copper, lead, or zinc.

As gold first attracted people to California, so it was the main reason for the first settlements in the Mountain States. Stirred by its discovery in California, men began searching or *prospecting* for gold among the Rockies.

Courtesy Colorado Association
A MILL THAT STAGGERS UP SUNNYSIDE HILL
Hidden in the mountains of Colorado are riches untold — iron, copper, gold, lead, zinc, and silver.

In 1858 and 1859, Colorado had its first "gold rush." In 1860, miners and prospectors established the little town of Leadville high up among the mountains of Colorado about 10,000 feet above the level of the sea. This and Cripple Creek were two of Colorado's most famous mining centers.

Some years before this, gold was discovered on the eastern slope of a mountain in western Nevada. This was the famous Comstock Lode, one of the largest and richest ever found. It was about four miles long, and about 3000 feet wide in its widest part, and one of the shafts was 3500 feet deep. It produced about $600,000,000 worth of gold and silver ore. Ground water running into the shafts and the intense heat in the deeper parts of the mines make it hard and costly to carry on mining.

Where minerals are near the surface, the deposits are usually soon mined and then men search for the *lode,* or vein of ore back in the bedrock from which the deposits came. Digging out the solid ore from the bedrock is called *lode mining.* Most of the gold and silver now mined in the United States is obtained by lode mining. This requires machines both to take out the ore and afterwards to crush it and separate the metals. Sometimes several useful minerals, such as gold, silver, and copper, are all found in one ore, and different ways of separating them must be used.

Copper Mining in the Mountain States. — Gold was the first metal to attract settlers to the Mountain States, but it is no longer the most valuable. Most of the copper now mined in the United States comes from these states and its value is far above that of the gold. Copper wires conduct the electricity which lights our homes, runs our street cars and some of our trains, and makes it possible for us to hear over the telephone and radio. All of the Mountain States except Wyoming produce copper, but Arizona, Montana, and Utah produce the most.

In Montana. Butte, the largest city in Montana, is the state's leading copper-mining center. The large deposits here furnish ore for one of the biggest copper-mining and smelting industries in the country. Smelting plants are found at Anaconda, a few miles away. One of these smelters is said to have the highest smokestack in the world — nearly 600 feet high. This was needed to carry off the sulphurous fumes which come from smelting copper, for these gases kill vegetation. Recently men have discovered a way of confining these deadly fumes and making them into sulphuric acid. This, in turn, is used to make phosphate rock into a valuable fertilizer to make plants grow. Thus the chemist by his knowledge makes harmful products useful.

In Arizona and Utah. Arizona is now our leading state in the production of copper. Of the many places where copper is mined, Globe and Bisbee are best known. Near Bisbee, a hill of copper ore has been stripped and the ore taken out until what was formerly

ON THE TOP OF THE WORLD
Ewing Galloway
Two gray metals, silver and lead, are the rewards of mining in Leadville, Colorado.

WHERE COPPER IS KING

The rocky mountains at Bingham, Utah, are rich in copper ore which is scooped up with steam shovels.

STEADY DOES IT

In this mine at Butte, Montana, a powerful drill bites the rock and ore from out of the mountains where it has lain hidden for centuries.

ORE BY THE CARLOAD IN A MINE AT BUTTE

The loaded cars are on their way to be dumped into the loading bin; the little engine is on its way back for another train.

65

a hill is now a low place known as "The Pit."

In Utah, as in Arizona, both open pit and shaft mining are carried on. One mine is over 4000 feet deep. At Bingham, a large hill of ore is being mined by means of steam shovels which scoop up the ore deposits and empty them into cars to be carried to the smelters. This famous copper mine started as a gold mine in 1866.

Other Minerals in the Mountain States. — Gold, silver, copper, lead, and zinc are the minerals usually thought of in connection with the Mountain States, but in some of these states the value of the other mineral products is greater than that of any of these five metals.

All except Nevada mine coal. Wyoming, Montana, and Colorado produce petroleum. Others mine iron ore. Colorado, with its iron ore and coal, has built up at Pueblo one of the largest iron and steel plants west of Chicago. The coal now mined in Colorado is far more valuable than the gold and silver. Wyoming mines several million tons of coal each year and leads the other Mountain States in the production of petroleum. There are immense quantities of oil shale in Colorado and Wyoming. This is a rock that contains oil. New Mexico has large deposits of potash salts which furnish a valuable fertilizer.

Short Life of Mining Towns. — Mining towns usually grow very rapidly after a valuable mineral is discovered. But as soon as the mineral has all been mined or richer deposits found elsewhere, the miners leave. There are many of these "ghost" mining towns in the Mountain States, where empty houses and deserted streets tell the story of a once thriving center.

Lumbering among the Rockies. — In addition to minerals, the Rocky Mountains have other treasures. One of the greatest of these is timber, which commonly grows on the mountain slopes. Winds blowing over the Mountain States are chilled when they are forced up the mountain sides and drop part of their moisture as rain or snow. This makes it possible for trees and grass to grow here though it may be too dry in the valley below. Thus, there are usually two "timber lines": the lower or dry timber line, and the upper or cold timber line above which it is too cold for trees to grow.

Idaho and Montana have more forests than the states farther south. These are denser and less scattered, so they produce more lumber. In mountainous Idaho, where forests cover about two-thirds of the state, lumbering ranks first among the state's industries. In Montana, over one-fifth of the state is forested, and lumber is among the most valuable products.

After the trees have been cut, various methods are used for getting the logs out of the forest to the railroad which hauls them to the sawmill. Sometimes horses or tractors

OIL FROM WYOMING *Ewing Galloway*
Out of these buttes, great masses of flat, pressed-together rocks, come the oil products of Wyoming.

draw them out with the farther ends dragging. This is called *skidding*. A simpler method is to attach a strong rope or chain to the log and drag it out over the ground. This is called *snaking*. Skidding and snaking are easier when there is snow on the ground. On a steep slope, the logs may be slid down a chute, or a long trough known as a *flume* may be used. Water turned into the flume carries the logs down to the road or track below.

National Forests. — As in the Pacific States many of the forests in the Mountain States belong to the United States Government. These are called National Forests. In them, only a certain number of trees are allowed to be cut each year, and these must be cut and taken out under the direction of government officers. Young trees are planted to take the places of those which have been cut, as well as on other treeless areas where trees should be growing.

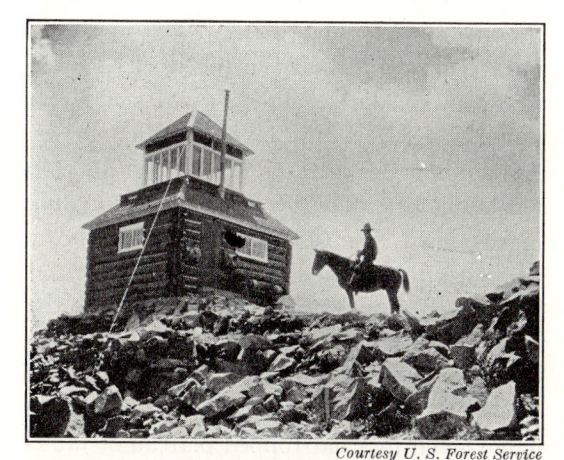

Ewing Galloway
LOGGING IN IDAHO
The tall, bare trunks are loaded by crane on freight cars and hauled to a shipping station.

Men known as *forest rangers* take care of the National Forests. They *patrol*, that is, they go from place to place among these forests and keep careful watch for fires. They also look out for unlawful cutting of trees. Trails and roads have been made through the forests, and watch towers, or lookout stations on high places, have been erected so that the watchers may see for long distances. These stations and the rangers' cabins are connected by telephones. In case the lookout, or man on watch, spots smoke at a distance, he locates the fire by his instruments and then telephones to the nearest rangers.

Following the example of our government, many large lumber companies in the United States are now reforesting cut-over lands, that is, they are planting young trees to take the places of those which have been cut. They also have watchmen to guard against forest fires.

Grazing in the National Forests. — In the National Forests are many open, grassy areas good for grazing animals. By paying a small sum per head, owners are allowed to pasture a limited number of cattle or sheep in the National Forests for a fixed

Courtesy U. S. Forest Service
THE LONE FOREST RANGER
Uncle Sam's guardian of the forests stands silhouetted against the sky at his lookout station on the rocky tip of the mountain.

number of days during the summer season. These areas are carefully fenced and the animals are counted as they go in.

National Parks and Other Attractions. — Some of the most beautiful scenery in the country is found in the Mountain States. Many people visit these states just to view the scenery and enjoy the outdoor life. Others go for their health, for the clear, dry air is a fine cure for diseases such as tuberculosis. Taking care of tourists is a growing business

Ewing Galloway

OLD FAITHFUL AT WORK

In the geyser region of Yellowstone Park the hot core of the earth sends out its underground water in columns of steam like a great boiler that goes on forever.

in the Mountain States as more Americans learn about the wonders here.

To preserve some of these beautiful spots, the United States Government has set aside National Parks and National Monuments. In Montana is Glacier National Park, noted not only for its rugged mountain scenery, its glaciers, mountain lakes, and waterfalls, but for special rock forms carved by the ice in the mountain sides. In northwest Wyoming is Yellowstone National Park, famous for its hot springs, geysers, Yellowstone Lake and Falls, and a deep canyon cut by the Yellowstone River. Here is the most famous geyser in the United States. It is called "Old Faithful," because it erupts, or breaks out, with great regularity every hour. Tourists always want to see "Old Faithful" in action. First they hear a rumble in the ground, then the waters at the top begin to boil and overflow, and then with a great rush the steam and water shoot 125 feet into the air.

The strangest sight of all is the glass mountain and the glass road. This glass is black, not white. It was formed many years ago when a great volcano erupted. The lava from the volcano was so hot that it melted the sand and glass was formed. You probably know that glass is melted sand. Not so long ago builders wished to build a road around this mountain. They used the glass already there. It was melted into blocks and the surface was made smooth. If you go there you will want to ride over this strange glass road.

The state of Arizona has its wonderful Grand Canyon cut deep into the Colorado Plateau by the Colorado River. This is one of the grandest sights anywhere in the world. Utah has Bryce Canyon with its carved rock spires, like the rocks of the Grand Canyon. The Carlsbad Caverns in New Mexico are one of the newly discovered wonders of these western states. Underground water has here produced caverns with all sorts of odd rock shapes forming the walls.

Some of Colorado's most beautiful mountain scenery is included in the Rocky Mountain National Park. Pike's Peak, near Colorado Springs, is an old favorite with tourists. An automobile road now leads to its top where one has a fine view of the surrounding mountains. Near Colorado Springs also is the Garden of the Gods where wind and water have worn down soft rocks and carved the upstanding hard rocks into many peculiar shapes. In southwestern Colorado is Mesa Verde National Park. *Mesa* is a Spanish name given to a flat-topped plateau or tableland standing off by itself. *Verde* means green. It has been given this name because of the green cedar and pinyon trees which

FLOWERS AND MOUNTAINS *Josef Muench*

Lusty sunflowers nod in the breeze; and above them the San Francisco peaks are brushed by the soft summer clouds of Arizona.

Courtesy Glacier National Park
TRICK FALLS, GLACIER NATIONAL PARK

Where the waters of a mountain lake cascade into a silver mist.

© *Hileman*
MT. STANTON

From the snow-field crest of one mountain one looks down to valleys below and up to peaks of Glacier National Park.

MONUMENT VALLEY *Josef Muench*

A stage set of white clouds, towering sandstone cliffs, and odd, dark shadows on the valley floor.

THE ENCHANTED EMPIRE

To the far horizon stretch the terraced rocks and flat-topped mesas of red, purple, white, brown, black, and burnished gold in Grand Canyon National Park.

Courtesy Atchison, Topeka & Santa Fe Railway
TEMPLE OF THE SUN, CARLSBAD CAVERNS, NEW MEXICO

The drip, drip, drip of water has hardened into the crystal curtains and fluted columns which decorate the cavernous depths of this underground palace.

grow upon it. Here in the sides of steep cliffs are the best preserved ruins of the ancient cliff dwellings used by the Indians who lived here long before the discovery of America.

Natural bridges, volcanic mountains with deep lakes in their former craters, and a petrified forest are other wonders of these Mountain States.

Stock Raising in the Mountain States. — The raising of cattle and sheep is another way in which many people of the Mountain States earn a living. Much of the lower land in these states is too dry for raising crops, but enough grass grows to feed animals. The Mountain States raise more sheep than any other group. These are raised mainly on the semi-arid regions among the mountain ranges and on the drier portions of the great plains east of the Rockies. Large flocks of sheep are a common sight in Idaho, Wyoming, Montana, and Colorado. They furnish a large part of the domestic wool used in the United States.

Ewing Galloway
THE SANDSTONE SPIRES OF THE GARDEN OF THE GODS IN COLORADO
Amid the sagebrush and the cedars rise the fantastic shapes of wind-carved rocks.

Sheep herders often live in small cabins on wheels so that they can be easily moved when the flocks are driven to new grazing grounds. Sheep must not graze too long in one place as they crop the grass very closely and it must be given a chance to grow again. With his

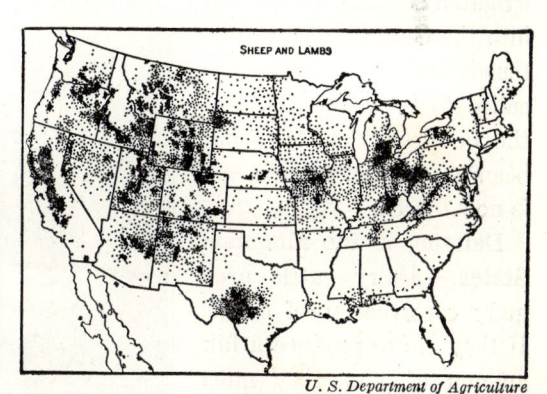

Ewing Galloway
NONNEZOSHI OR HOLE-IN-THE-ROCK
Out of the salmon-pink sandstone of Utah's rocky plateau, nature has built a perfect rainbow arch.

U. S. Department of Agriculture
SHEEP FOR WOOL AND MUTTON

Each dot on this map stands for 5000 sheep. Most of the sheep are found in the western states, where they can graze to better advantage than cattle on more arid lands. Notice the black area in Texas. What kind of land do you think the sheep graze on there? What three states in the eastern half of the United States seem to have many sheep? In these states, the sheep are kept on farms and roam over the hilly land which is not so good for growing crops.

A State Herd of Buffalo
The State of Arizona protects this herd of about two hundred wild buffalo, as they roam beneath the shadow of the Vermillion Cliffs.

faithful dog as companion and helper in rounding up the flock, and a radio to amuse him and keep him in touch with the rest of the world, the shepherd of today no longer lives the lonely life of the shepherd of olden times.

Many of the beef cattle raised on the dry areas of the Mountain States are sent into irrigated sections where food is abundant, or into the Corn Belt, to be fattened for market. These are called *feeder cattle*. Most of the better grazing land has been taken up by settlers and is now fenced.

Dairying in the Mountain States.— Dairy cattle need more care than beef cattle. If they are to produce a fair amount of milk, they must have plenty of good food and water. They have to be milked twice a day. They should also be sheltered in cold or disagreeable weather and not allowed to wander long distances in search of food. Thus dairy cattle in the Mountain States are usually found near streams or in irrigated sections.

Railroads and Roads in the Mountain States.— Another reason why fewer people live in the Mountain States is the difficulty of building roads and railroads. In the mountains most of the railroads follow the valleys, where high bridges often have to be built to span deep gorges. In climbing the mountains, both roads and railroads often wind around for long distances, slowly rising as they go. They cross the mountain ranges at their lowest places, called *passes* or *gaps*. Building roads and railroads in the mountains is hard and expensive, so few are built unless there are enough people to make them pay.

Transportation has always been a difficult problem in these Western Mountain States. In the early days the only way to carry goods was by means of long pack trains

Weber Canyon, Utah
Where once the Overland Mail and Pony Express crossed the valleys and deserts of Utah, now railroad tracks and automobile roads cling to the sides of the canyons as they follow the curving river's banks.

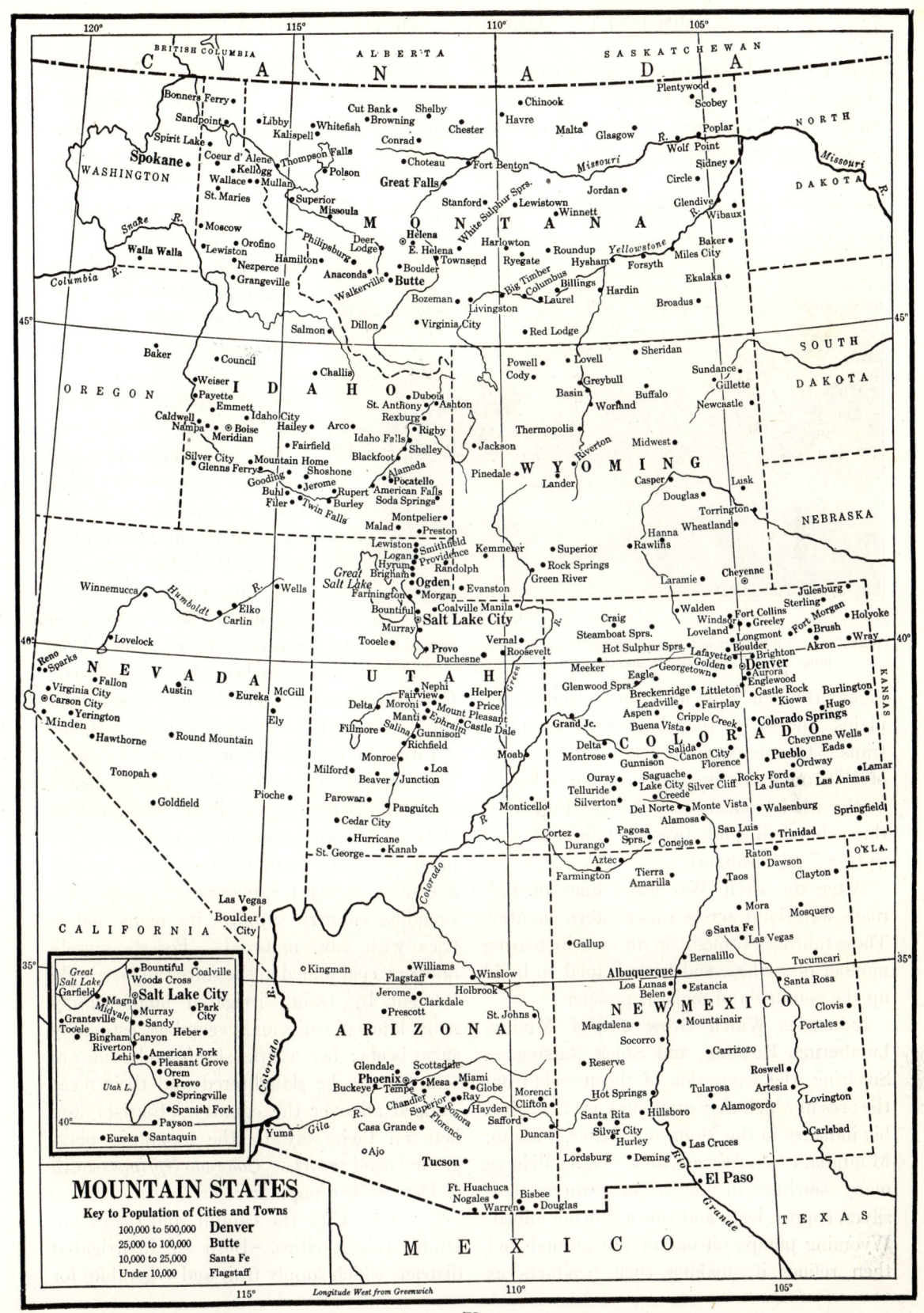

MOUNTAIN STATES

Key to Population of Cities and Towns

100,000 to 500,000	**Denver**
25,000 to 100,000	**Butte**
10,000 to 25,000	Santa Fe
Under 10,000	Flagstaff

drawn by mules or oxen. Then came the stage coach days; but the roads were rough and often dangerous. The mail traveled even faster by means of the Pony Express. "With the mail in light saddle bags riders on relays of fleet horses rode day and night, through rain and snow, across the plains and over the dangerous mountain trails. On one occasion a boy by the name of William F. Cody, who was later known to the whole country as 'Buffalo Bill,' rode three hundred and twenty miles without resting." (Burnham)

After the Civil War great lines of railroads were built across this western country. These railroads brought in an ever increasing number of settlers, and have helped to build up the country and make it prosper.

Industries Which Grow out of Mining, Lumbering, Farming, and Stock Raising. — Smelting, the separation of the metals from the ores in which they are found, is of course a big industry in the Mountain States. Idaho, Montana, Utah, Arizona, and Nevada all have many smelters in the regions where gold, silver, copper, lead, and zinc are being mined. Wyoming pumps oil out of the ground and then refines it, making such products as gasoline, kerosene, vaseline, paraffine, and heavy machine oils. Pueblo, Colorado, has a big iron and steel industry which produces many machines and tools. Iron ore and coal needed for this industry are mined in the state and also brought in from New Mexico.

From the lumber in these states are produced building materials, railroad ties, mine props, paper pulp, and telegraph poles. Lumber products are worth more than the mineral products in Idaho and Montana.

The many animals raised in these states have caused meat packing to become a big industry in Denver, Ogden, Salt Lake City, and other large cities. Flour milling uses wheat and other grains. Sugar made from sugar beets is a big industry. Canned fruits and vegetables, as well as evaporated and condensed milk are other products.

Cities in the Mountain States. — *Denver*, the "Gateway to the Rockies," and capital of Colorado, is the largest city in this group of states. At the edge of the Rockies, where the mountains and plain meet, it early became a trading center for miners. Now the surrounding country supplies its many industries with raw materials. Forests supply lumber; coal mined in the state can be readily brought by train; irrigated lands supply many kinds of fruits and vegetables, especially sugar beets; beef cattle, sheep, and swine are sent here to be slaughtered and their meat shipped all over the country; tourists stop here on their way to the mountain playgrounds and resorts. *Colorado Springs*, south of Denver, is a popular resort.

Salt Lake City, the capital, and *Ogden* are Utah's largest cities. Both are in irrigated districts which supply fruit and vegetables for

WHEATFIELDS — *John Kabel*
Wheat turned into flour is a profitable business, and a necessary food for millions of Americans, north, south and east and west of Colorado.

THE CLIFF PALACE AT MESA VERDE, COLORADO *Ewing Galloway*
Under an overhanging rock are hidden the terraced homes of the cliff dwellers — ancient relic of an early civilization.

AT THE LOOM *Josef Muench*
Two Navajo women work at the art of rug-making — one spins the yarn while the other weaves the intricate pattern on the loom.

TAOS, NEW MEXICO *John Kabel*
Straight walls with tiny, barred windows and open doorways, a few rugs of skins, a bee-hive oven out of doors — such is the primitive home of the New Mexico Indians.

canning, and sugar beets for sugar. Meat packing, flour milling, and the manufacture of tin cans and knit goods are a few of the industries. Westward from Ogden, the Southern Pacific Railway has built a bridge 30 miles long across the shallow Great Salt Lake. This is known as the Lucin or Ogden cutoff, as it shortens the route between Ogden and the cities farther west.

INTO THE SETTING SUN *Ewing Galloway*

Across many miles of trestle and solid beds of salt, the trains rush westward by the Lucin cutoff over Great Salt Lake.

Santa Fe, capital of New Mexico, is the oldest city in the Mountain States, having been founded by the Spaniards in 1609. *Albuquerque*, the largest city, founded about 100 years after Santa Fe, has two sections, the "old" town and the "new" town. It is a well-known health resort. Mining, lumbering, stock raising, and irrigated farming furnish it with products for many industries.

Phoenix, the capital and largest city of Arizona, is in a rich, irrigated, farming district, the Salt River Valley. Many people go there to improve their health in the sunshine and dry, fresh air. *Flagstaff*, farther north in Arizona, is a base of supplies for tourists on their way to view the Grand Canyon.

Cheyenne, the capital and largest city of Wyoming, is a great shipping center for cattle and sheep. It also has large railroad shops. Coal, iron ore, and petroleum near the city add to its industries.

Billings, in Montana, is a trading center from which are shipped live stock, flour, beet sugar, hay, beans, wool, and grain. Natural gas gives it excellent fuel for manufacturing as well as heating. *Helena*, the capital, *Great Falls*, and *Missoula* among the mountains are in the centers of mining districts. Falls in the Missouri River not only give Great Falls its name, but furnish power for manufacturing. These cities are also centers from which tourists and hunters go out into the mountains.

Boise, the capital and largest city of Idaho, started many years ago as a trading post for furs. *Pocatello* ships out mining and farm products from the nearby irrigated areas. Southern Idaho has a rich soil which is fine for growing crops when irrigated. Irrigated farming has helped the growth of many towns in southern Idaho. *Coeur d'Alene*, in the midst of Idaho's leading mining district, also manufactures lumber products from the surrounding forests and is a popular base for sportsmen who like to fish and hunt in the mountains.

Activities and Questions

1. Name five things for which the eight Mountain States are famous. Give reasons.
2. How does their population per square mile compare with other sections of the country?
3. Tell about the largest body of water in these states.
4. Which are the leading copper states? Which leads in the production of petroleum? Which in coal?
5. What two states have more irrigated land than the other six states together? Why?
6. Where is most of the lumbering carried on? Why?
7. Collect pictures of scenes in some of the National Parks in this section.
8. What are some of the products of irrigated lands?

THE MOUNTAIN STATES

9. Describe lode mining.

10. How are the fumes from smelters made to help plants grow instead of killing them?

11. In what five states are the capitals also the largest cities? In what three states are they different?

12. Name three important rivers rising in the Mountain States. How are the rivers used?

13. Where is the Great Basin?

14. Why has the Comstock lode been practically abandoned?

15. Where is one of the largest steel plants west of Chicago?

16. Describe the work of the forest rangers.

17. What is "dry" farming? Where and why is it carried on?

18. Name four large dams in the Mountain States. What are these dams for?

19. Why is it so hard to build railroads and roads in these states?

20. Find on the map the only place in the United States where four states come together. Which states are they?

21. Sketch a map of these states, putting in the chief rivers, leading cities, and some of the National Parks.

A STRING OF SATIN-COATED, FLEET-FOOTED ARAB HORSES ON A SOUTH DAKOTA RANCH *Publishers' Photo*

V. THE WEST NORTH CENTRAL STATES

East of the Rockies lies the Mississippi Valley, one of the most productive in the world. In the western part of the upper valley is a group of states which we call the West North Central. These are divided naturally into two groups. Next to the Mountain States are North and South Dakota, Nebraska, and Kansas, and east of these, stretching to the Mississippi, are Minnesota, Iowa, and Missouri.

The High Plains. — Most of this country is nearly level, broken only by the Black Hills in South Dakota and the Ozark Mountains in Missouri. But as we leave the Mountain States and travel east we find the western part of the Central States so much above the general level of the prairie that it is called the High Plains. Here in many places streams have cut down into the land and separated it into large sections with flattened tops called *tablelands*.

As in parts of the Mountain States the climate here is dry, so that there are fewer cultivated fields, and the native grass generally grows in bunches. This *bunch grass* has long roots, and can live through long, dry spells or *droughts*, when little or no rain falls. Cattle and sheep graze on this grass but, as it is scattered, more land must be allowed to each animal than farther east where there is more rainfall and the grass grows more thickly.

The Prairie Plains. — The lower plains nearer the Mississippi River are called *prairie plains* to distinguish them from the higher, drier plains farther west. Prairie is the name usually given to a grassland area where there are few trees. Trees are scarce on the high plains and the drier sections of the prairie plains, growing mainly along the streams and where settlers have planted a few around their homes as windbreaks. They are so scarce in the drier parts of these great plains because they need more water than is furnished by the light rainfall. Even where there is enough rainfall, long droughts occur, and hot, dry winds sweep over the land. These winds are very hard on trees, whereas grass simply dies down and comes up again after rain falls.

Before these plains were thickly settled prairie fires were common during the dry sea-

78

Statistics of the West North Central States *

State	Abbreviation	Area Sq. Miles	Population	Rank Area	Rank Pop.	Capital	Population	Largest City	Population
North Dakota	N. Dak.	70,665	641,935	16	39	Bismarck	15,496	Fargo	32,580
South Dakota	S. Dak.	77,047	642,961	15	38	Pierre	4,322	Sioux Falls	40,832
Nebraska	Nebr.	77,237	1,315,834	14	32	Lincoln	81,984	Omaha	223,844
Kansas	Kans.	82,276	1,801,028	13	29	Topeka	67,833	Kansas City	121,458
Minnesota	Minn.	84,068	2,792,300	11	18	St. Paul	287,736	Minneapolis	492,370
Iowa		56,280	2,538,268	24	20	Des Moines	159,819	Des Moines	159,819
Missouri	Mo.	69,674	3,784,664	18	10	Jefferson City	24,268	St. Louis	816,048

* 1940 Census

Important Products

North Dakota: — Grains, live stock, dairy products, flaxseed
South Dakota: — Grains, live stock, dairy products, gold, hay
Nebraska: — Grains, live stock, meats, dairy products, grain products
Kansas: — Grains, live stock, meats, grain products, petroleum
Minnesota: — Grains, grain products, iron ore, dairy products, meats
Iowa: — Grains, live stock, meats, dairy products, food products
Missouri: — Grains, live stock, meats, lead, shoes

---

son, when the long dry grass burned readily. Fanned by the winds, these fierce fires swept over the land bringing terror to the early settlers and often burning whole villages. Fires like this do not kill the roots of the grass but they destroy trees and shrubs. In fact, fires are sometimes set in cut-over areas in order to destroy the young tree growths and allow the grass to grow better.

The Tough Prairie Sod. — On the plains where there is considerable rainfall, the grass grows close together, forming a thick, tough sod. This hinders the growth of trees. The roots of the grass in the fine soil form such a tight, solid mass that rain cannot seep through to the roots of the trees. The grass gets most of the water. If a young tree starts to grow from a seed, the grass smothers it.

As lumber was scarce, the early settlers on the plains often built their homes of this sod. The walls of these houses were usually two or more feet thick, and the roof, also made of sod, was placed on top of tar paper stretched over a framework of boards or stems of young trees. A grass mat sometimes covered the floor. When the roofs were well built, these sod houses with their thick walls were warmer in winter and cooler in summer than the wooden houses which were built later. Some of these old sod houses are still to be seen on the western high plains. In fact, three distinct houses can sometimes be pointed out on the original farm.

THE HOME OF AN EARLY SETTLER
An old sod homestead on the bleak and treeless prairie plains.

First, the old sod house of the first settlers; then the simple frame house that they moved into after they got well settled, which in turn was abandoned when their children wished to live in a still larger home more like those in the nearest towns. These three homes are like the rings of growth on a tree and mark the progress one family made in getting settled in this region.

The Prairie Becomes a Land of Farms. — When people settled on the prairie plains about 100 years ago, they found this thick, tough sod very hard to cut until some one invented a sharp steel-pointed plow. The settlers were then able to make good use of these fertile plains for growing large crops of grain, hay, and other food products for themselves and their animals. Large quantities of wheat and other grains were sent to the eastern states. The former prairies are now largely fields of waving grain instead of grass.

The soil is deep, rich, and free from stones. For thousands of years, the mountain streams carried down fine rock material, and the great ice sheet which once covered the northern United States also brought much soil, and spread it over the land. Winds blew fine rock dust from the higher lands of the west into the lower valleys. All these materials mixed together helped to form a rich soil, on which year after year grass grew and died, filling the soil with *humus* (decayed vegetable matter). Some of the soil contains so much humus that it is almost black.

The land is level and much easier to farm than hilly or sloping land, where the soil washes away. Machines can be used which could not be used on hillsides. It is also easier to build roads and railroads. Roads in the West North Central States run largely along township boundary lines. In a hilly or mountainous country, they usually follow the valleys and wind about instead of going straight ahead.

Farm Life on the Central Plains. — In this area many cities and towns have grown up, connected by roads and railroads. Towns not on the railroad are connected with it by means of good automobile roads along which motor trucks carry goods back and forth.

Farmers now live in comfortable homes, many of which have electricity, running water,

THE WEST NORTH CENTRAL STATES
Map Questions and Activities

1. In what general direction do these states slope? Does the altitude increase or decrease from east to west? How does this affect the living conditions?

2. Name the most important rivers in these states.

3. Explain how the drainage of this section reaches the ocean.

4. Where is St. Louis? How has its location caused it to be a great city?

5. Name the "twin cities" in Minnesota and show how their location has contributed to their development.

6. What important river valley lies between Minnesota and North Dakota? For what is it famous?

7. Tell from the map which part is the more densely populated, east or west.

8. Why do most of the railroads in the Dakotas, Nebraska, and Kansas run east and west?

9. Why are most of the farms in this part of our country larger than the farms in the New England States?

10. What plateau is in southern Missouri? Where are the Black Hills?

11. How has Duluth's position caused it to be such an important lake port?

12. Is this section as well located commercially as the states near the Great Lakes? Explain your answer by using this map and the one of the United States, pages 28 and 29.

13. How does your map indicate the relative sizes of the cities? Name and locate the capitals and chief cities in these states.

14. What river joins the Missouri River at Kansas City, Kansas, and Kansas City, Missouri? Why have these two important cities developed here?

15. Explain how Omaha's location is an advantage to its growth.

16. What does your map suggest about the climate of the West North Central States?

17. Why are there so many lakes in the northeastern part and so few in the southwestern part of this group of states?

Physical - Political
WEST NORTH CENTRAL STATES

Scale of Statute Miles
0 50 100 150 200

⊙ State Capitals — Railroads
The type used indicates the relative sizes of towns and cities.

HEIGHTS IN FEET
- Above 5,000
- 2,000 to 5,000
- 1,000 to 2,000
- 500 to 1,000
- Sea level to 500

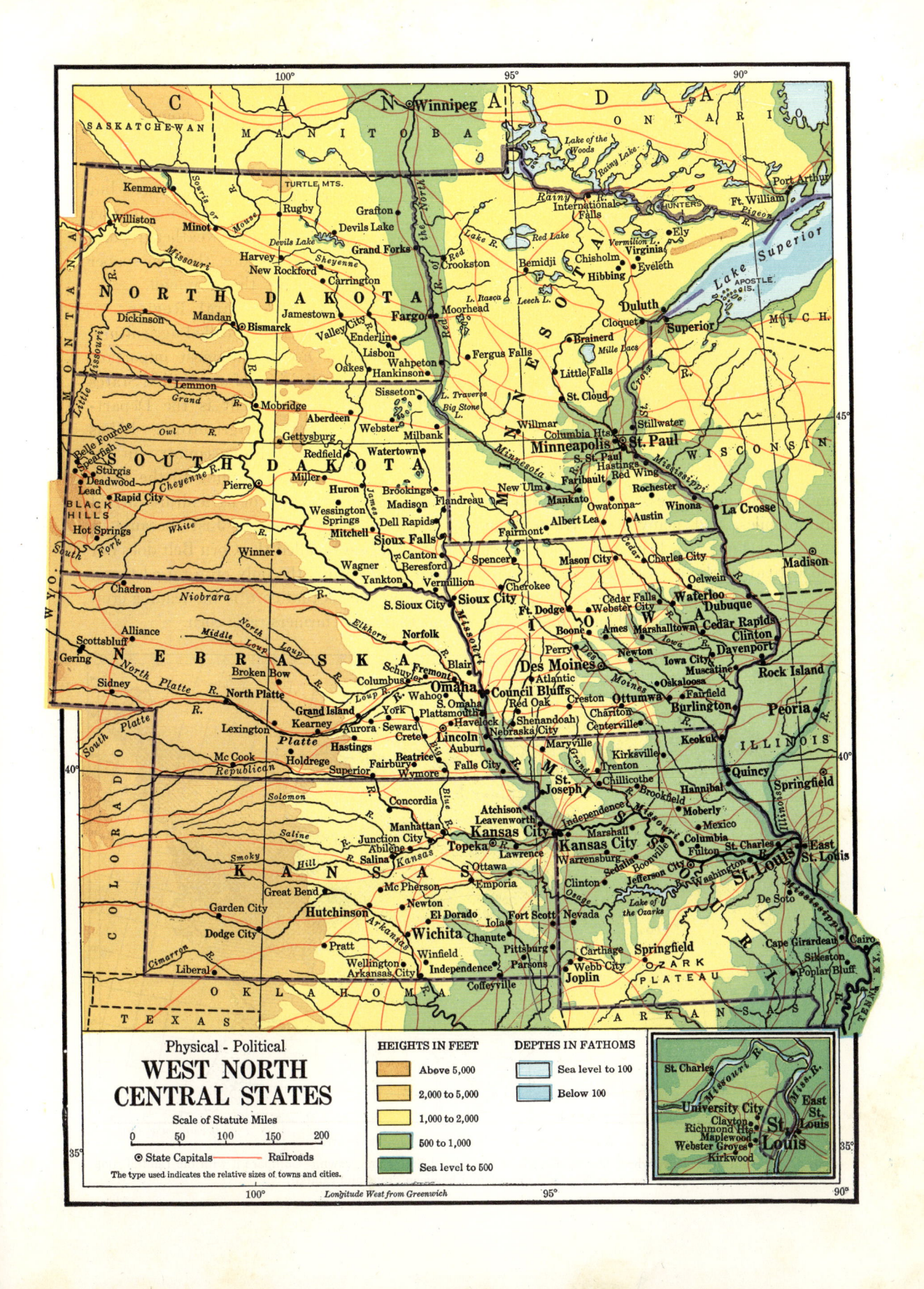

DEPTHS IN FATHOMS
- Sea level to 100
- Below 100

A MODERN FARMSTEAD
Ewing Galloway
All the conveniences of city life belong to today's settler on Minnesota's plains.

livered at their homes. The radio not only makes it possible for them to hear entertainments and lectures but also to get the news, market prices, and weather reports long before the newspaper reaches them by mail.

Agricultural Regions. — Farming is called agriculture. One of the most important divisions of our United States Government is the Department of Agriculture. It has mapped our country in regions according to the main crops grown or the kind of agriculture carried on. (See map, below.) Just because a certain region is called the Corn Belt does not mean that corn is the only crop raised there. It simply means that corn is the leading crop and that most farmers raise corn.

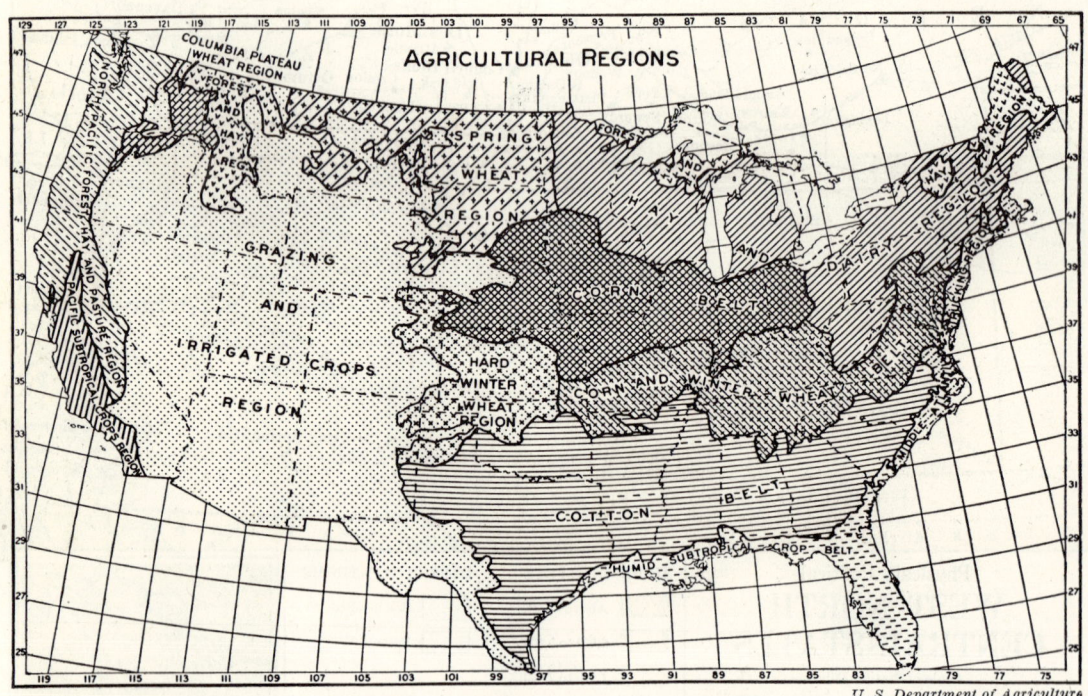

and other conveniences. Most of them own automobiles, and many have tractors and other machines to help with their work. Good roads make it easy for them to motor to the nearest city; telephones keep them in touch with their neighbors; mail is de-

AGRICULTURAL REGIONS OF THE UNITED STATES
U. S. Department of Agriculture

This government map shows where the chief crops of the United States are grown. Compare it with the rainfall map on page 56 to see the relation between crops and rainfall.

HARVESTING SPRING WHEAT
Modern machines do in a few hours what used to take days of hard hand labor.

The Spring Wheat Region. — As you will notice on the map, the spring wheat region includes most of North and South Dakota and part of western Minnesota. This land looks like one huge wheat field. The wheat farms are large, a single field sometimes containing several hundred acres. This is called the spring wheat region because nearly all of the wheat raised here is planted in the spring. In the winter wheat region farther south, the wheat is planted in the fall and is left in the ground all winter. In the spring wheat region, the winters are usually so cold and dry and the ground freezes so hard that the young wheat plants cannot live. The growing season is short, about 120 days and sometimes even less than that. But the days are long and the wheat grows so fast during the spring rainfall and the short summer that crops planted in April and May are ready to be harvested in August and September.

The great center for raising spring wheat is a very level region known as the Red River Valley of the North. After the melting of the great glacier, or ice sheet, which once covered the northern United States, a large lake covered this area for many years. Fine rock material carried into this lake by many streams settled to the bottom. After the lake was drained, its bed became the fertile level area which is now the center of one of the greatest wheat-growing districts in the world. Sometimes it is called the "Bread Basket of America."

Other Crops in the Spring Wheat Region. — Most of the farmers in this region grow spring wheat as a money crop. A *money crop* is one raised especially to sell. But they also grow other crops, mainly for their own use. These are called *supply crops*. For example, a farmer in the spring wheat region who raises wheat as a money crop will raise oats as a supply crop for his horses.

It is not a good plan to plant the same crop year after year on the same land, as this takes certain plant foods out of the soil. Wheat, for example, takes much nitrogen from the soil. If it is planted year after year in the same field, there will not be enough nitrogen left in the soil to yield a good crop. So successful farmers usually *rotate* their crops. This means that they plant one kind of crop

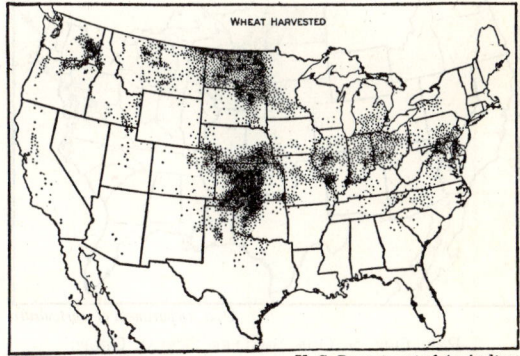

U. S. Department of Agriculture
WHEAT, OUR FAVORITE GRAIN FOR BREAD
Each dot stands for 10,000 acres of wheat. What kind of wheat is grown in North Dakota? in Kansas? Which one of the Pacific States raises much wheat?

A Combine
Acres and acres of ripened wheat fall beneath the knives on one side of the machine and pour forth in a stream of threshed grain on the other.

one year, another kind the next, and probably still another kind the third year before planting the first one again. In the spring wheat region, for example, they may plant wheat one year, clover the next, and oats, sugar beets, or some other crop the third year before planting wheat again.

Rye and barley are two other cereals grown in the spring wheat region. Rye, like wheat, grows well in a rather cool climate, and does better than wheat on poor, sandy soil. Barley makes a good feed for animals and in these northern states where corn does not grow so well, it is often used in place of corn. Flax is another important crop of these northern states.

In addition to the potatoes which they raise for their own use, farmers in this region and in eastern Minnesota raise many bushels for sale. Potatoes generally grow best in cool climates.

Winter Wheat. — Most spring wheat is hard, but there are two kinds of winter wheat, hard and soft. Hard wheat makes the best bread flour, while soft wheat is used for pastry flour. Hard winter wheat grows in the drier regions, while soft wheat does best where there is more rainfall. Much corn is also raised here, so that it is called the corn and winter wheat region.

The big wheat farms of Kansas and Nebraska are much like those in the spring wheat region. Machines do most of the work. "Gang" plows, drawn by several horses, or

Rye, One of Our Smaller Cereal Crops
Each dot stands for only 2000 acres. How does this compare with the value of the dot on the wheat map? This map shows that we raise very little rye as compared with corn or wheat. What three states grow most of the rye?

Barley, the Grain of Many Uses
A dot on this map stands for only 2000 acres, or just one-fifth as much as it stands for on the maps of corn, wheat, and oats. Barley is grown in the same areas as wheat but there are three small barley-growing areas where little wheat is grown. Name some different uses of barley.

THE WEST NORTH CENTRAL STATES

MACHINES REPLACE MAN LABOR
With one man to drive it, the harvester cuts the corn and delivers it into the wagon; the corn that does not ripen during the short growing season is used for fodder and silage.

tractors run with gasoline, turn over not just one furrow, but several furrows at a time. Other machines then smooth the surface and make the soil fine. A machine called a *seeder* plants the seeds in rows, and at harvest time, a *reaper* cuts the wheat stalks and binds them into bundles, which are placed in shocks upright in the field to dry. Then the stalks are fed in at one end of a large threshing machine, the straw and chaff are blown out at the opposite end, and the clean grains of wheat roll out through a funnel below into a hopper or bin. In the drier western parts of the winter wheat region, large machines known as *combines* are used to cut and thresh the wheat at the same time, as they do in eastern Washington.

The Corn Belt. — Corn is grown in every state in the United States, but about one-half of the corn crop is grown in the area called the Corn Belt. Though it extends east through the states of Illinois, Indiana, and Ohio, its leading state is Iowa and it includes parts of all of the other West North Central States. It lies between the spring wheat and the corn and winter wheat regions, where the soil is fertile and the weather warm. Corn grows best when it has plenty of hot sunshine and warm nights with showers enough to keep it well watered.

As with wheat, corn land is usually plowed and planted by machines. But it is generally worked with cultivators drawn by horses or mules, trained to walk between the rows. These cultivators dig up the weeds and throw the soil up around the stalks of growing corn. Unlike wheat, corn does not have to be harvested as soon as it is ripe. The close-fitting husk protects it from the weather and it can stand in the field until the farmer is ready to harvest it.

These great crops of corn and wheat in the central part of our country have been made possible only by the use of machines. One hundred years ago, a farmer using a horse averaged three hours of labor for each bushel either of corn or wheat produced. Using machines, he now averages about 40 minutes of labor for a bushel of corn and only about 10 minutes for a bushel of wheat. Horses and mules are widely used in these central states in the corn and wheat fields, but many of the large areas of wheat are cultivated entirely by machines.

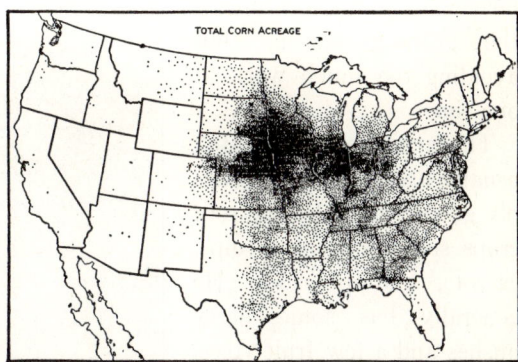

U. S. Department of Agriculture
CORN, OUR LARGEST CEREAL CROP
Each dot stands for 10,000 acres of corn. Compare this map with the map of agricultural regions on page 82, and see how the dark shaded area compares with the corn belt. Which state is nearly all black? What does that mean? What other states lie partly in the Corn Belt?

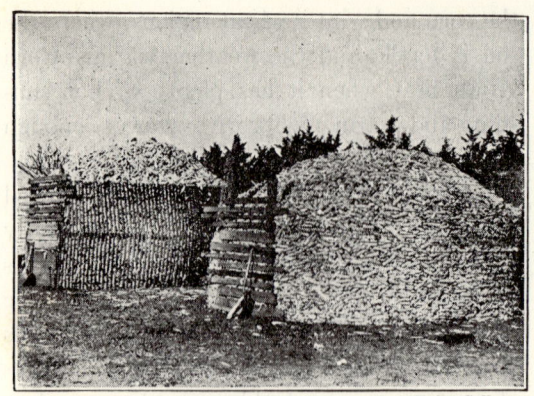

Corn Husking Time *Ewing Galloway*
The wire bins are bursting with full ears of yellow corn.

Other Crops in the Corn Belt. — Farmers in the Corn Belt raise many other crops both for sale and for their own use. Less than one-half of the farm land in the corn belt is used for corn. Oats and hay are other large crops. They can be planted in the spring before it is time to plant corn and harvested in the summer before corn-harvesting time. They are fine food for horses. Alfalfa is also raised for the farm animals. In the drier parts of Kansas where the corn crop is uncertain, grain sorghums are raised as a food for animals. Sorghum looks much like corn and can stand the long, dry spells better. By raising different crops, the farmer keeps busy all during the growing season, thus avoiding too much work at one time.

The farmer in the Corn Belt usually has a garden to supply green vegetables and root crops such as beets, turnips, carrots, and potatoes. He generally has some berry bushes and a few fruit trees. Many trees on some of the farms are planted as windbreaks.

Mixed Farming. — While the West North Central States are divided into regions according to the main crop produced in each, in many places the farmers raise a variety of products. This is called *mixed farming*. In Missouri and Iowa and eastern Nebraska and Kansas, there is more rainfall and it is easier for the farmer to grow a variety of products. In southeastern Missouri, farmers may grow cotton, which takes about 200 days to grow and ripen its bolls. Rice and sweet potatoes are also grown here. In a mixed farming region, farmers raise different kinds of grains, vegetables, and farm animals, and they also have fruit orchards. If one crop fails, or they cannot sell it, they have other crops to help them through the year.

Irrigated Farming in Western Nebraska. — Western Nebraska, like eastern Wyoming and Colorado, is usually too dry to grow crops successfully without irrigation. The Platte River, which flows across Nebraska and empties into the Missouri River along the eastern boundary of the state, is fed by two branches, the North Platte and the South Platte. Both of these have their sources back in the Rocky Mountains. The South Platte, as you will notice on the map, page 59, is almost entirely in Colorado. There,

Mixed Farming *Ewing Galloway*
The deep green of the thick trees, the pale yellow of the cut hayfields, and the rambling brown road color a landscape of scenic beauty.

THE WEST NORTH CENTRAL STATES

NOON ON A DAKOTA FARM *Ewing Galloway*
Sheep quietly graze, cattle push and crowd the troughs, and a drove of pigs roots noisily about as dinner time arrives.

the waters of this river and its tributaries are used on one of the largest irrigated areas in our country.

The North Platte flows through Wyoming for some distance before it enters Nebraska. Extending across the state boundary, partly in Wyoming, partly in Nebraska, is an irrigated area of about 400,000 acres. The river not only furnishes the water for irrigation now, but in the past it has carried down and left here the fine rock material (silt) which makes the deep fertile soil. The three main crops are wheat, alfalfa, and sugar beets. Wheat and sugar beets are the money crops. Alfalfa and the pulp of sugar beets are used to fatten cattle and sheep. Nebraska is one of our leading sugar-beet-producing states.

Animals. — Almost every farmer keeps a number of valuable animals for his own use, and many make a business of raising animals for sale. Often the farmer can sell cattle, sheep, or pigs when he cannot sell the crops on which they feed. So many swine are raised in the Corn Belt that it might just as well be called the Swine Belt. On the drier plains of western North and South Dakota and Nebraska and Kansas, cattle and sheep are grazed on the ranges. These *feeder* cattle are sent into the corn belt to be fattened for market. Many sheep are raised on farms in northern Missouri and southern Iowa, but they are not so plentiful as cattle or swine.

Horses and mules are also raised in large numbers in this land of abundant oats, corn, and hay — three good animal foods. Many of these are raised to be used as work animals on the farms. Missouri raises the most mules, which are widely used in cultivating the cotton fields of the south.

Iowa, leader in corn, also leads in swine. A large part of the corn crop is fed to swine and thus goes to market in the form of pork. Sometimes the farmer saves himself the labor of harvesting his corn crop by turning his swine into the corn field and letting them help themselves. This is called "hogging it down." Lard, rendered from the fat of hogs, is one of the most valuable products exported.

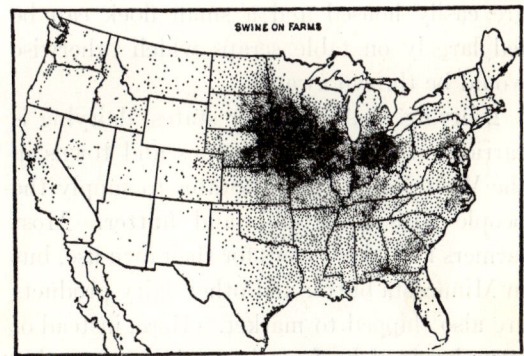

MAKERS OF PORK AND LARD *U. S. Department of Agriculture*
Each dot on this map stands for 5000 swine. Compare this map with the map of agricultural regions on page 82. In which of the agricultural regions do you find most of the swine? Can you tell why?

Nearly half the chickens in the United States are in the corn belt and bordering areas. Iowa, leader in corn and pigs, is also one of the leading states in chickens. Cheap feed is the main reason for this, as corn and other grains furnish good food. Eggs and chickens are always in demand and can be easily shipped. In addition to the chickens raised for sale, nearly every farmer keeps a few chickens for his own use. But chicken-raising is not confined to farms. People who live in villages often keep chickens, as they are easily housed and a small flock can be fed largely on table scraps which otherwise would be thrown away.

Dairying. — As in other states, dairying is carried on near all large cities and towns in the West North Central States to supply the people with fresh milk and butter. Most farmers keep dairy cows for their own use, but in Minnesota butter and other dairy products are also shipped to market. Here, instead of large herds of beef cattle roaming over wide plains, one sees small herds of dairy cattle grazing quietly in fields. Large barns shelter them and store their hay and other feed, and tall, round silos preserve the silage. There is more rainfall in eastern Minnesota than in the wheat regions farther west, so the land is better for pasturing.

Meat Packing. — Naturally meat packing is a big industry where there are so many animals. Every large city has stockyards, but Kansas City, Omaha, Topeka, St. Louis, Minneapolis, St. Paul, Des Moines, St. Joseph, and Sioux City are the largest centers. A modern meat-packing plant does much more than prepare meat. Skins are tanned for leather; fats are used for lard, tallow, and soap. Long hair is used for stuffing mattresses; shorter hair is mixed with mortar and plaster; fine, soft hair and bristles are used for making brushes. Bones and horns are made into combs, knife handles, and buttons. Gelatin, fertilizer, and glue are other much used products of a packing plant.

Flour and Other Foodstuffs. — Flour mills are usually found in cities and towns to which wheat can readily be sent, and flour shipped out. Like meat packing, it is a common industry in the West North Central States. Minneapolis is the leader, producing more flour than any other city in the United States, except Buffalo. It is near the spring wheat region, has good water and other power, and is a railroad center. Kansas City, Wichita, and Omaha, which are close to the hard winter wheat region, also make much flour. All three of these cities are on main railroad lines.

Various breakfast foods are made from wheat, corn, barley, and oats. Some of these are ground into meal, some rolled, some flaked, and some shredded. The preparation and shipping of these foods gives work to many people in the cities and towns of these states.

KANSAS CITY MEAT — *Publishers' Photo*
It takes great stockyards like this to supply meat for the markets of the country.

Courtesy Minneapolis Civic & Commerce Association
THE SKYLINE OF A FLOUR CITY

The chimneys and turrets of the "mills of usefulness" are seen twice — once, clearly against the setting sun; once, as they shiver and fade away in the ripples of the restless Mississippi River.

Ewing Galloway
MILLS THAT GRIND EXCEEDING SMALL

From a day's work of these Kansas City mills are produced barrels of wheat flour for our daily bread.

Publishers' Photo
ELEVATORS AND FLOUR MILLS AT TOPEKA

Freight cars are loaded to capacity with barrels of flour on their way north, south, east, and west.

89

Mineral Wealth. — The wealth of the West North Central States is not wholly in their farms and farm products. South Dakota ranks high in gold production and Minnesota leads in iron ore. Missouri leads all states in lead production while Kansas ranks high in zinc mining. Very often these two useful metals are found and mined together. Kansas is also rich in oil and natural gas. Beds of pumice, a kind of fine volcanic ash, are found in both Kansas and Nebraska.

THE HOMESTAKE MINE — *Publishers' Photo*
In the heart of the Great Spirit's Hunting Grounds, a mile above sea level, gold was found. Today, this mine has the record of having had one of the longest lives, so far, of any gold mine in the United States.

Iron Mining in Northern Minnesota. — The largest deposits of iron ore in the United States are found near Lakes Superior and Michigan. Minnesota shares this district with northern Wisconsin and Michigan but produces the greater part of the iron ore mined there. Most of the iron ore in Minnesota is taken out by open pit mining. Great steam shovels scoop up the ore, swing around, and load it directly into open cars which are then run to the docks of the lake ports where the ore is dumped into the holds of large vessels. These ships take it to other lake ports where it is manufactured into iron and steel or shipped on by rail to other manufacturing centers. Most of the iron ore mined in Minnesota is shipped from Duluth, but some is manufactured there. Iron ore is of little use without coal to make it into iron and steel, so some of the ore carriers, which take iron ore from Duluth, bring back coal to use in the manufacturing process.

The Black Hills. — The Black Hills are an oval-shaped group of mountains about 100 miles long and 50 miles wide. They stand all by themselves in the great plains region of southwestern South Dakota with a small portion extending into Wyoming. Like an island in the sea, they rise several thousand feet above the surrounding plains. Harney Peak, the highest point, is over 7000 feet above sea level. They get their name from the dark pine forests which cover their slopes. The richest gold mine in the United States, the famous Homestake Mine, is found here. Since 1896, this mine has produced over $200,000,000 in gold. In addition to gold, lead, silver, and other minerals are mined here.

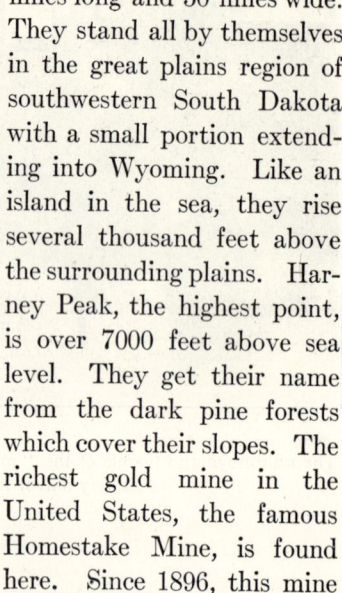

About one-third of the Black Hills is included in national forests. Here we find the famous Wind Cave National Park. The cave in this park was so named because the wind blows sometimes in and sometimes out of its mouth. It was formed by water dissolving the limestone rock, and its white walls are lined with curious forms. Sometimes they look like popcorn, sometimes like spattered snow balls; in other places they resemble the frostwork we sometimes see on the windows in winter. One of the most interesting features of Wind Cave National Park is a game preserve where there is a herd of bison. Elk, antelope, deer, and other wild life are also protected here.

Courtesy St. Paul Association

THE RAW MATERIALS OF THE MACHINE AGE

Up and down the Mississippi River at St. Paul ply the steamboats towing the flat river barges loaded with the "black diamonds" of industry.

Courtesy Duluth Chamber of Commerce

ORE BY THE CARLOAD

All day long the ore cars are being shunted on to the dock tracks at Duluth. Here the ore is unloaded into bins and the empty cars sent back for more.

Courtesy Duluth Chamber of Commerce

IRON SCOOPFULS OF COAL

Tied up at the docks in Duluth the lake freighters patiently wait while the great iron cranes swing the scoops back and forth.

WHERE SIOUX FOUGHT CROW

The road in the Black Hills runs along like quicksilver, up the steep mountain sides, winding through pine forests, up to the high divides where slim points of rock stand like spears of a guarding army.

The Ozarks. — The Ozarks are a hilly region in southern Missouri and northern Arkansas, with a small part extending into Kansas and Oklahoma. In Missouri, this area is a plateau cut by streams. The tops of the hills are rounded and the slopes gentle. There is plenty of rain and the climate is milder than farther north. In advertising the attractions of their land, the people say it is "South of the cold north and north of the hot south." State parks have been set aside where animals are protected, but hunting is allowed in the forests outside of the parks.

The farmers of the Ozarks practice mixed farming: they raise wheat, corn, and other grains, farm animals, and poultry. They also engage in dairying and truck gardening. Climate and soil are good for apples, pears, peaches, and other fruits. "The Ozarks, the Land of the Big Red Apple" is a favorite expression in this section. Canning of fruits and vegetables is an industry which developed here naturally.

Land of Ten Thousand Lakes. — Minnesota has so many lakes that it has been called the "Land of Ten Thousand Lakes." When the great ice sheet melted here, it dropped its rock material and dammed many valleys, thus forming lakes and swamps. Canoeing and fishing are favorite summer sports on these many lakes. Northern Minnesota is somewhat hilly, with patches of water, forest, and fertile land. At one time, the whole region was covered with forests, the homes of many fur-bearing animals sought by the early settlers. The lakes and streams were the highways for boats in summer, and in winter their frozen surfaces were used for trails. White pine is one of the leading timber trees of these forests. It is a soft, strong wood much prized for building purposes. Though much of the white pine has been cut, Minnesota is still a leading producer of white pine lumber. Hemlock and spruce are also cut. Some of the cleared areas are now being farmed, and the cut-over areas with stumps still standing are used as pasture lands. Much of this region, however, has the type of soil better suited for forests than for farms, so plans have been made to plant young trees and make sure of a large, steady supply of lumber. Laths, shingles, railroad ties, tele-

Courtesy Minneapolis Civic & Commerce Association
LAKE OF THE ISLES

Around the city of Minneapolis are eleven lovely lakes in settings of wooded parks and strung together by winding, tree-bordered boulevards.

graph poles, and mining props are made from the timber furnished by Minnesota forests.

Cities and Their Industries. — We have seen how one industry grows out of another. Wheat growing gives rise to flour milling; raising animals results in meat packing; lumbering furnishes wood for furniture and paper. All these result in much shipping. In the West North Central States many large cities make and ship these products.

The Twin Cities. — In Minnesota, St. Paul and Minneapolis have grown up so close together that they are called the "Twin Cities." They lie on either side of the Mississippi River with many connecting bridges. St. Paul, the capital, is at the head of navigation of the Mississippi and is a great railroad center, sometimes called the "Gateway to the Northwest." It is a meat-packing city and makes many shoes, furs, machines, refrigerators, and other articles.

THE TRAIN YARDS OF ST. PAUL
Track after track curves like a border around a bend of the Mississippi.

Minneapolis, the largest city, was first a lumber center, but later flour milling became its leading industry. Here in the Mississippi River are the Falls of St. Anthony which furnished power to run the lumber mills and later the flour mills. This water power is now used to make electricity to run the mills and for other purposes. Along the river near the falls the flour mills and large creameries are sometimes called the "bread and butter sky line."

The manufacture of linseed oil from flax seed grown in Minnesota and the Dakotas is another big industry in Minneapolis. After the oil is pressed out, the oil cake that remains is good feed for live stock.

Duluth, a Leading Lake Port. — Duluth, Minnesota's third largest city, also has a twin. But Duluth's twin, the city of Superior, is in Wisconsin. Both are lake ports, a few miles apart on the same body of water. At the western end of Lake Superior, wind and waves have worked together to form two peninsulas. One of these, called Minnesota Point, extends southward until it almost meets the other extending northward from Wisconsin. Back of these peninsulas lies an excellent harbor almost shut off from

POWER TO LIGHT A CITY
The Mississippi River, St. Anthony's Falls, and a man-made dam all combine to provide Minneapolis with electric power to run her great flour mills and to light her streets and buildings

WEST NORTH CENTRAL STATES

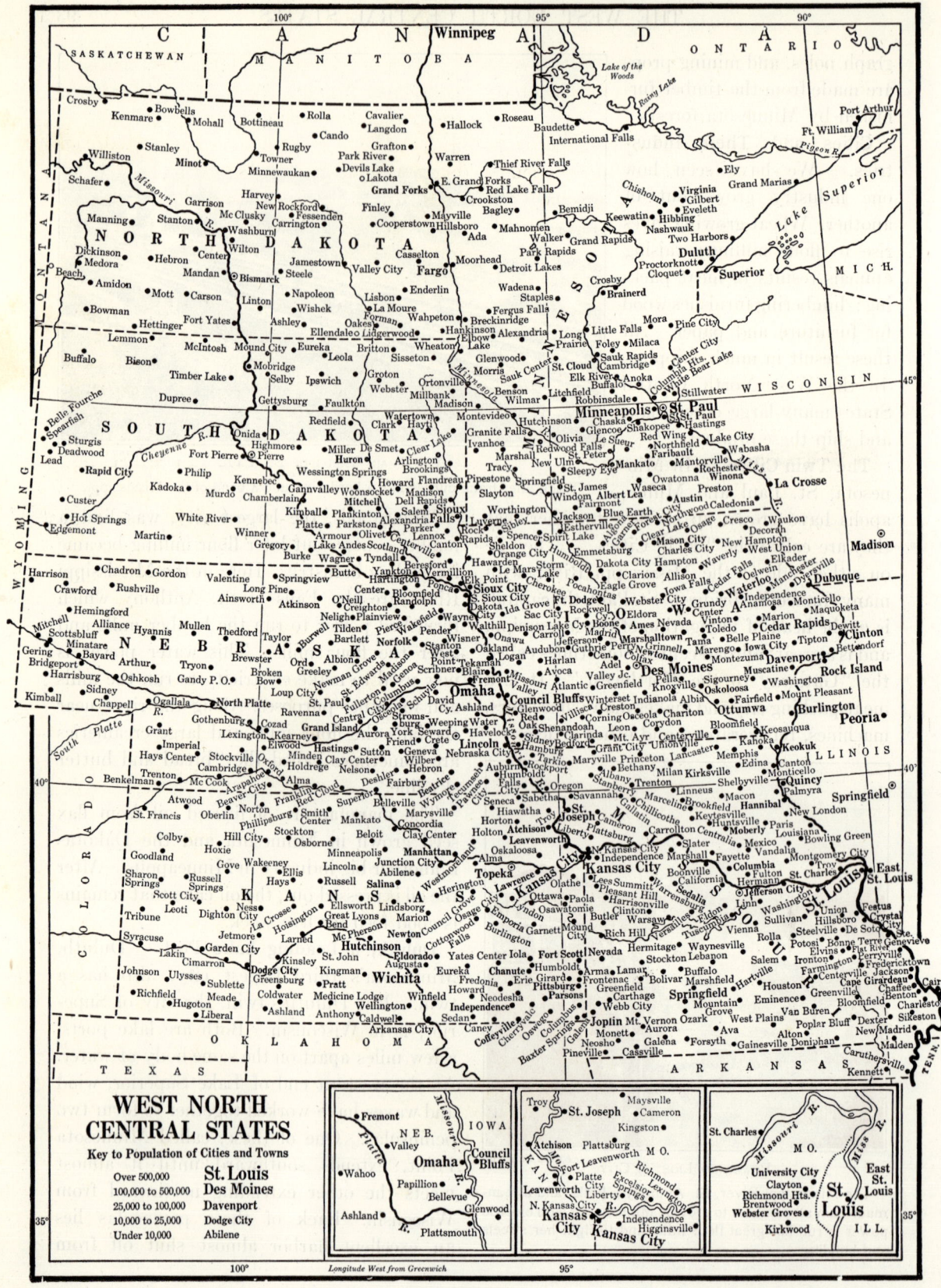

Key to Population of Cities and Towns

Over 500,000	**St. Louis**
100,000 to 500,000	**Des Moines**
25,000 to 100,000	**Davenport**
10,000 to 25,000	Dodge City
Under 10,000	Abilene

the open lake. Duluth ranks high among United States ports in the tonnage of its shipping.

It is only a short run by railroad from Duluth to the Mesabi (Mes-aw'by) iron mines in Minnesota. Cars of iron ore are run straight from the mines to the docks at Duluth where the ore is dumped into ore carriers. Duluth is not far from the spring wheat fields of Minnesota and the Dakotas, from which railroads carry millions of bushels of wheat to

Courtesy Duluth Chamber of Commerce
FROM GRAIN ELEVATOR TO GRAIN FREIGHTER
These tall, smoothly rounded grain elevators are like the columns on some ancient Greek temple.

be loaded into lake steamers and carried to Buffalo and other lake ports. This city is also near the forests of Minnesota which furnish it with lumber for shipment to other places as well as for use in its own wood-working industries. Some of the ore vessels which carry iron ore to Lake Erie ports return with coal, which Duluth uses in its iron and steel works, lumber mills, flour mills, and other industries. Some it sends to Minneapolis and St. Paul and other centers.

The St. Louis River, which flows into Lake Superior at this point, furnishes water power to make electricity. This is used to light the city and to run many different machines. The broad mouth of this river makes a good inner harbor. With the large lake in front, and the "land of lakes and forests" at its back, Duluth is popular with those who like to spend their vacations in hunting or fishing, or in boating and other water sports. All of these things have helped Duluth to grow from a small trading center into a large city.

Cities in the Dakotas. — North and South Dakota are great agricultural states and they have few manufacturing industries and few large cities. *Fargo*, the largest city in North Dakota, is a grain shipping center and distributing point for farm machinery. In addition to flour, meat, and dairy products, Fargo and *Grand Forks*, another city in North Dakota, make bricks, iron and steel articles, leather goods, and candy.

Sioux Falls, the largest city in South Dakota, is situated on the Sioux River where falls furnish water power. Like *Aberdeen* and *Watertown*, farther north, it is a railroad center, and collects and sends out farm products from the surrounding country. These cities also bring in and sell to the farmers and others the machines, automobiles, groceries, and other articles which they need. The capitals, *Bismarck* and *Pierre*, are near the center of these states on the Missouri River.

Nebraskan Cities. — *Omaha*, on the Missouri River, is Nebraska's largest city. Its stockyards and meat-packing plants rival those of Kansas City which is, like Chicago, one of the leading cities in this industry. It is also a large grain market and flour-milling center, and its bakeries help to use the flour. Creameries collect milk from the surrounding dairy farms and make large quantities of butter. *Lincoln*, the capital, is a trading center. Airplanes are manufactured in Lincoln, which, together with Omaha, is on one of the main airway routes across the United States.

Cities in Iowa. — Iowa has a number of cities which help to distribute its many farm products and manufactured articles. *Des Moines*, the capital and largest city of Iowa, is situated on the Des Moines River near the center of the state. It has many beautiful public buildings, good schools, and the great Iowa State Fair is held here each year. Nearby mines furnish coal for its meat-packing plants, flour mills, creameries, and factories which, in their turn, make farm machinery, iron and steel products, tile, brick, cement, and other much needed articles. *Sioux City*, on the Missouri River in the western part of Iowa, handles grain and live stock from South Dakota, Minnesota, and Nebraska as well as its own state, and has many manufacturing industries. *Davenport* and *Dubuque*, in eastern Iowa, have the use of the Mississippi River as well as the railroads for shipping goods. *Cedar Rapids*, on the Cedar River where rapids furnish power, and *Council Bluffs*, a short distance east of Omaha, are other large trading and manufacturing cities of Iowa.

Two Kansan Cities. — *Topeka*, the capital of Kansas, is a railway center and has large railroad shops. *Wichita* is the largest city in the winter wheat belt of the state. Wheat, cattle, swine, and oil have all helped Wichita to grow. It collects much of the wheat grown in the surrounding country, makes some of it into flour and breakfast foods, and ships the rest. Cattle and swine are brought to its packing plants where they are made into meat and other products. Here the farmers come to buy automobiles, tractors, farm machinery, and other things which they need. Several air routes which cross

LINCOLN, NEBRASKA
Chicago Aerial Survey Company

No sign of rolling prairie here; but the brick and stone of a large city. The new state capitol symbolizes "the power of the state and the purpose of its citizens."

here and aircraft factories make this city one of the foremost in aviation.

Twin Cities with the Same Name. — *Kansas City*, Kansas, and *Kansas City*, Missouri, are built across from each other along the Missouri River just where it ceases to be the boundary line between Kansas and Missouri and enters the latter state. Kansas City, Kansas, is the largest city in Kansas and Kansas City, Missouri, is the second largest city in that state. Their industries are somewhat similar and they do business almost like one big city. But, being in different states, they have their own separate city governments. They are noted for big mills, large stockyards and meat-packing

THE WEST NORTH CENTRAL STATES

KANSAS CITY, MISSOURI
Along the darkened runways, which make a great X-Y-Z monogram, planes land and take off in their scheduled flights across the country. The airport is built on the lowlands in a bend of the Missouri River.

plants. Some of the winter wheat raised in Kansas is sent here for shipment. Smelting of lead and zinc ores mined in these states is an important industry. Railroad and air routes cross here and the making of airplanes is another of the industries. Notice on the map how these cities are situated at the great bend in the Missouri where the river, flowing from the northwest, turns and flows eastward to join the Mississippi. One of the earliest trading centers grew up here as people went as far west as they could by way of the river before leaving it on their overland routes to the West or Southwest.

St. Louis. — St. Louis, the largest city of the West North Central States, is located on the Mississippi near where it is joined by the Missouri. The Mississippi connects the city with other river ports, a fleet of barges making regular trips between St. Louis and New Orleans. The Missouri River gave the early settlers a route to the Northwest from which fur traders brought their pelts to St. Louis for sale, and it is still a leading fur market. Four long bridges make it easy for railroad trains and automobiles to cross the Mississippi River at this point. Situated in the central part of our country, St. Louis has become a crossroads for railway and airplane lines. It was in "The Spirit of St. Louis" that Colonel Lindbergh, backed by men of this city, made the first solo flight across the Atlantic.

Besides its meat packing and flour milling, St. Louis makes beer, leather goods, cotton and woolen goods, chemicals, machinery, and street cars.

THE FAN-SHAPED CITY
The wide, macadamized road, the tree-lined sidewalk, and the imposing modern buildings stretching out instead of up, give St. Louis the roomy look of wide-open spaces.

Activities and Questions

1. What is one of the richest, most productive valleys in the world? Why?

2. Describe the rotation of crops. Why is it used?

3. What kinds of farming are practiced in these states? Why?

4. Name two of the main rivers. For what are they used?

5. Which state of this section leads in white pine and iron ore? in gold? in spring wheat? in corn and pigs? Give reasons in each case.

6. Where are meat packing and flour milling carried on? Why?

7. Add prairie-farming pictures to your collection.

8. Why are there few trees on the prairies?

9. What is humus? What does it do for the soil?

10. **Locate the Wheat and Corn Belts.**

11. What is meant by a money crop? a supply crop?

12. What, besides corn, is a leading product of the Corn Belt? Why?

13. What products besides meat come from a modern packing plant?

14. Name the capitals and largest cities of the West North Central States.

15. Tell the leading products of Duluth, Minneapolis, St. Paul, Omaha, Kansas City, and St. Louis. Give reasons in each case.

16. Tell what you can about the first solo flight of Colonel Lindbergh across the Atlantic Ocean.

17. Can you prove from the map of the United States that St. Louis is quite centrally located?

18. Sketch a map of these states with the rivers and largest cities. Locate roughly the Winter Wheat, Corn, and Spring Wheat Belts.

Out of the past there echoes faintly across the plains the thundering beat of horses' hoofs and the blood-curdling yells of painted savages.

VI. THE WEST SOUTH CENTRAL STATES

South of the states we have just studied lie Oklahoma, Arkansas (Ar'kan saw), Texas, and Louisian'a, which we call the West South Central Group. Texas is our largest state. It is larger than any country in Europe except Russia. The land of Texas formerly belonged to Mexico, but the people who settled it came largely from the United States. They rebelled against Mexico, declared their independence, and afterwards became a part of our own country.

Louisiana was named for the French King, Louis XIV, who encouraged the French exploration of this part of America. The French came into this region by way of the Mississippi River and laid claim to most of the territory west of it. They founded New Orleans, which they named after a city in France. After the American Revolution the French ruler, Napoleon, sold the land to the United States for $15,000,000. This Louisiana Purchase, as it was called, included not only the present state of Louisiana, but all of the land north of Texas and west of the Mississippi River as far as the Rocky Mountains.

STATISTICS OF THE WEST SOUTH CENTRAL STATES *

State	Abbreviation	Area Sq. Miles	Population	Rank Area	Rank Pop.	Capital	Population	Largest City	Population
Oklahoma	Okla.	69,919	2,336,434	17	22	Oklahoma City	204,424	Oklahoma City	204,424
Texas		267,339	6,414,824	1	6	Austin	87,930	Houston	384,514
Arkansas	Ark.	53,102	1,949,387	26	24	Little Rock	88,039	Little Rock	88,039
Louisiana	La.	48,523	2,363,880	30	21	Baton Rouge	34,719	New Orleans	494,537

* 1940 Census

IMPORTANT PRODUCTS

Oklahoma: — Cotton, grains, petroleum, petroleum products, cottonseed products
Texas: — Cotton, live stock, petroleum, petroleum products, cottonseed products
Arkansas: — Cotton, live stock, petroleum, rice, bauxite, poultry, vegetables
Louisiana: — Sugar, lumber, rice, cotton, petroleum, pelts

The Heart of Old New Orleans

Once the Place d'Armes, now called Jackson Square, this lovely park in the gracious old French city is of historic interest. In the Cabildo, the building on the left, were signed the papers that changed Louisiana from Spanish rule to French, and later from French rule to American.

Oklahoma used to be Indian territory, long held for the Indians who were forced to give up their lands in other parts of our country. Many Indians live there now although most of them have adopted modern ways of living.

Comparison and Contrasts. — Like their northern neighbors, the West South Central States are bounded on the east by the Mississippi River. They also resemble the West North Central States in being higher and drier in their western than in their eastern parts. Excepting the Ozark Highlands and Ouachita Mountains of Arkansas and Oklahoma and a few small mountain groups in western Oklahoma and Texas, these states are nearly all plains or gently rolling areas. But, being farther south and nearer the equator, these states are generally warmer and have a longer growing season. In southern Texas and along the Gulf of Mexico, this is just about twice what it is in the northern part of the West North Central States. This makes it possible to grow many products, such as sugar cane and cotton, which cannot be grown in the north.

Winds from the Gulf of Mexico bring much rainfall to Louisiana and southern Arkansas so these two states are better watered than any state in the northern group. From east to west, the rainfall decreases so that western Texas has only about one-fourth as much as most of Louisiana. All kinds of farming can be done in the eastern section where there is plenty of rainfall, but western Texas, except along the Rio Grande, is used chiefly for dry farming and grazing.

Variety of Climate and Crops. — Texas boasts that it has every kind of climate to be found in the United States. The mountainous region in the west has a climate like some more northern states, while in the

Southern Pine

A tall yellow pine is on its swift downward way to crash and then lie still, no longer part of a living forest.

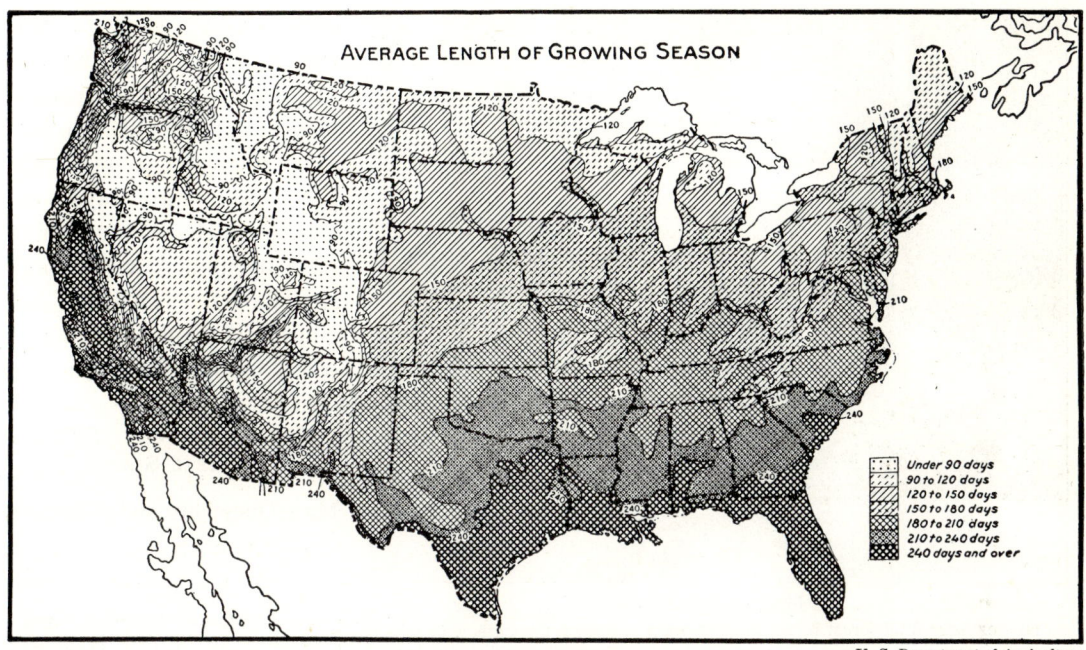

LENGTH OF THE GROWING SEASON IN THE UNITED STATES

The growing season is the time during which there are no killing frosts. Study the legend to learn the length of the growing season indicated by each shading. Beginning with Texas along the Gulf of Mexico, note how the length of the growing season shortens as you go northward through Texas, Oklahoma, Kansas, Nebraska, South Dakota, and North Dakota. What is the length of the growing season in southern Texas? In northern North Dakota?

High, dry areas have shorter growing seasons than the lower humid areas. For example, eastern Nevada with a rainfall not over 10 inches has a growing season from 90 to 120 days. In eastern Kansas in the same latitude, where the rainfall is from 30 to 40 inches, the growing season is twice as long.

Use this map often in connection with your study of farming and the different kinds of crops grown in the United States.

Lower Rio Grande Valley, semi-tropical fruits such as oranges are grown. The high plains of central and western Texas are dry and warm in summer and cold in winter, but along the Gulf, the summers are warm, the winters mild, and abundant rain falls every month in the year.

Well-watered lowlands with rich soil together with the long growing season make it possible for these states to grow a great variety of crops. Nearly everything that can be grown anywhere in the United States can be grown somewhere in these states. Forests cover large areas where rainfall is abundant, and these are remarkable for the different kinds of trees. With the exception of Florida, it is said that Louisiana produces more different kinds of trees than any other state in the Union.

Forests of the West South Central States. — When white settlers came into these states, they found Louisiana, Arkansas, eastern Texas, and Oklahoma covered with forests. When the forests of the northern states had been largely cut, lumbermen turned to these southern states which for many years furnished much of our lumber. Of the many kinds of trees grown here the chief lumber tree is the yellow pine, often called "southern" pine. This strong lumber is widely used for building houses, railroad cars, and the wooden parts of machines.

Forests of these pine trees grow on the coastal plain regions of the southern states. As the winters are mild, lumbering can be carried on throughout the year and camp shelters do not have to be so well built and heated as in the north. On these nearly level

MODERN FORESTRY

This experimental forest in southern Arkansas shows the care with which modern forestry practices are being carried out. These modern practices permit timber lands to produce a yearly harvest that may continue forever.

plains, it is easy to extend railroads into the larger forests, where machines pick up the logs and load them onto cars. Sometimes caterpillar tractors "snake" out the logs, or a long, stout cable is fastened to the log which is then pulled to the track by winding up the cable. Sometimes horses drag out the logs on carts with big wheels, which make hauling easier.

In addition to the pine forests of the West South Central States, there are many scattered forests of mixed trees such as oak, sweet gum, hickory, beech, maple, and ash.

Louisiana leads in the production of cypress, the lumber tree of the swamps. Cypress is sometimes called the "wood eternal" because it lasts so well. Like cedar, it is valuable for outdoor uses, as it is soft and easily worked. It is also fine for making food containers as it will not impart any taste or odor to the food.

Cypress usually grows in swamps where there is water most of the year. Natural waterways through the swamps are used whenever possible, but sometimes it is necessary to dig canals to float the logs out. As there is little current in the swamps, men with poles push the logs along the water courses. On the larger waterways, the logs are fastened together in rafts and pulled out by small steamboats. "Donkey" engines on flat boats are sometimes used to draw out the

MAP OF THE WEST SOUTH CENTRAL STATES

Map Questions and Activities

1. What states are included in this group?

2. Find and name the capital of each state. How can you tell them?

3. Name some of the largest cities. How are they indicated?

4. Does the map suggest one or more reasons why New Orleans has grown to be a large city? Houston? Fort Worth? Dallas? Oklahoma City? Tulsa? El Paso?

5. Where are the lowlands shown on this map? the highlands?

6. What great river flows southward through the eastern section?

7. What river helps to form the boundary line between Texas and Mexico? Do rivers make good boundary lines between states and countries? Why?

8. Does the railway network seem to be fairly thick in these states? Why?

9. Locate on the map a district where tropical fruits are grown.

10. What is the scale of miles for? Estimate the distance from Dallas to Fort Worth; to Houston; to New Orleans; to Tulsa; to Oklahoma City.

11. Does Texas seem to be a large state? How can you tell? Does it seem to be as large on the map on pages 28 and 29 as it is on this map? Why not? Remember that it is the same Texas.

Physical - Political
WEST SOUTH CENTRAL STATES

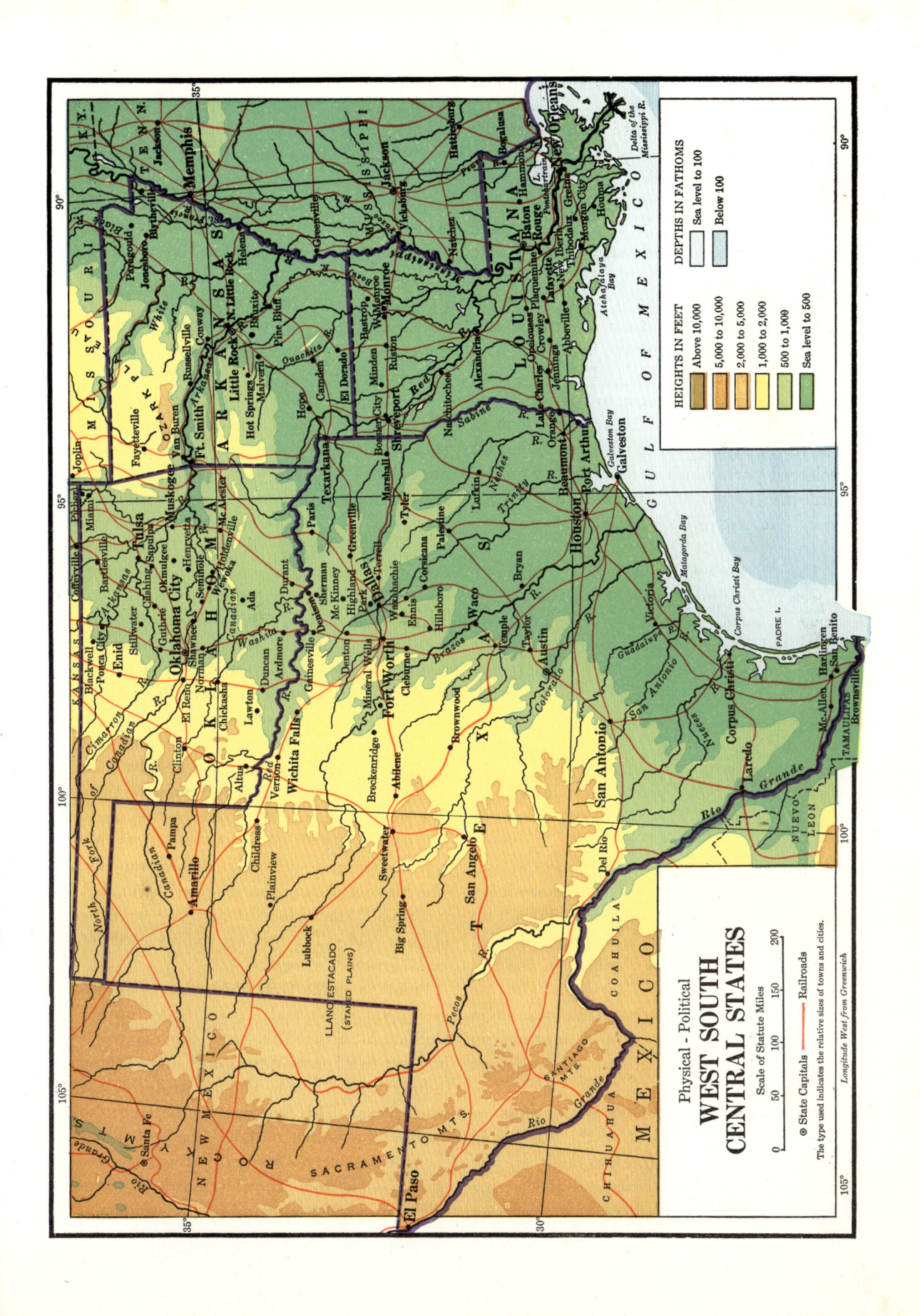

logs from where they have been cut to the main stream.

Where the swamp dries up in summer, trees are cut and hauled out as in the other forests. But cutting cypress in the water-covered swamps requires skilled men, for they have to work in boats.

Sometimes the cypress trees are "girdled" a few months before they are to be cut. Girdling or cutting away the bark all around the trunks kills the trees and they dry out, thus making them lighter so that they will float better. Cypress trees spread out at the base and they are usually cut above this enlarged part, which is often hollow and of little use to the lumberman. Most of the trees cut are very old, from 1000 to 2000 years.

The Mississippi Delta. — The Mississippi River which drains these states has carried down so much fine rock material (silt) and deposited it at its mouth that it has built land far out into the Gulf of Mexico. Land built up in this way at the mouth of a river is called a *delta*. Near its mouth, the river divides into many smaller streams which carry its waters out through the delta to the Gulf. Banks called *levees* have been built along the lower Mississippi to prevent it from overflowing the lowland during times of high water. The delta land near the Gulf is low and generally swampy, with many lakes or *bayous* (bī′ooz). One finds it difficult to use a boat as the water is shallow and filled with reeds and grasses. Neither can one find any solid land on which to walk. Because it was so hard to explore, parts of this delta region were never fully mapped until men in airplanes flew over the region and took photographs.

Numerous Animals of the Marshlands. — The marshes and lowlands of the Mississippi Delta and the nearby forested lands are the homes of many wild birds and fur-bearing animals. Wild-life shelters have been set aside where hunters are not allowed to kill or disturb the various animals. If you live in the northern United States, you have noticed how certain birds always disappear when cold weather comes. Many of these fly to the southern states to spend the winter months where it is warmer. Great numbers of wild ducks, geese, and other waterfowl which go north in the summer, return and spend the winter on the rice marshlands of Arkansas, Louisiana, and other southern states.

One usually thinks of fur-bearing animals in connection with regions which have long, cold winters and heavy snows. Yet Louisiana alone produces more pelts each year than the whole of Canada. Raccoons, opossums, minks, skunks, wildcats, foxes, and wolves are all found in the forests of Louisiana and other nearby states, and large numbers are trapped each year for their furs.

The little animals that furnish most of the fur, however, are the muskrats. These live in the salt marshes along the coast of Louisiana and feed on marsh plants. Just as we have fox farms in some of our northern states, so large areas of marsh land called "rat ranches" have been bought and held by their owners just for the muskrats. Some of these ranches contain over 100,000 acres. As many as ten and sometimes more muskrats per acre are trapped each year on these ranches. The meat of the muskrat is good to eat, but few people know about it and so very little of it is sold. The furs are mainly used for making women's coats.

Frontage on the Gulf of Mexico. — Of this group, Louisiana and Texas border on the Gulf of Mexico. This gives them a water highway to all parts of the world, and a fishing industry which can be carried on during the whole year. This frontage on the Gulf also enables the people of Louisiana and Texas to have seaside resorts and bathing beaches where people from the colder northern states like to spend the winter. Oleanders and palm

Courtesy New Orleans Association of Commerce
THE HUEY P. LONG BRIDGE AT NEW ORLEANS
This $13,000,000 bridge, located just above the city limits, is the finest of all the bridges that span the mighty Mississippi. Across its steel trestles trains, automobiles, and pedestrians travel toll free.

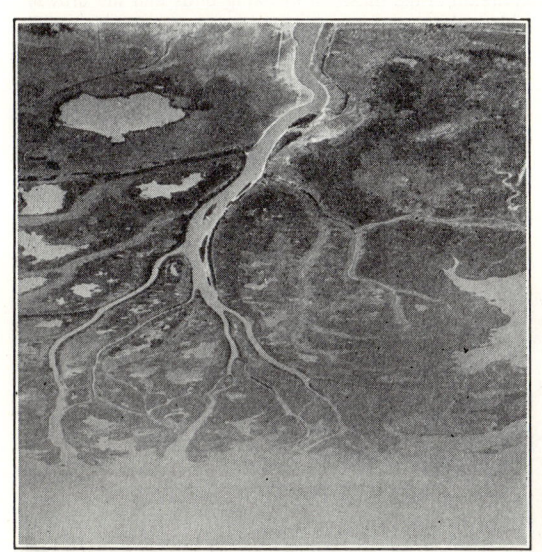

© *Airmap Corporation of America*
THE MISSISSIPPI DELTA
Over the mud flats and through countless small arteries the Mississippi River flows into the sea.

PROTECTING THE LEVEE
Instead of willow mattresses, concrete slabs are now used to keep the river from washing the levee away

ON THE OLD SPANISH TRAIL

Publishers' Photo

In the soft shadows of tropical foliage at Pass Christian one can dream of the music of mocking birds and the drowsy scent of magnolia blossoms.

LANDING A TARPON

Game fishing in the waters around New Orleans is a year-round sport.

GOOD HUNTING

Along the marshes of the Mississippi are the blinds where the wary hunter waits for a flock of unsuspecting ducks to appear.

106

trees, so different from the trees in the northern states, adorn the streets and gardens of the more southerly cities and help to make them attractive.

Fisheries.—Before people learned how to manufacture ice, fishing was not an important industry in the Gulf of Mexico and other warm sea regions. Fish spoil quickly after they are caught unless they are kept very cool. Many coastal cities of Louisiana and Texas now have ice-manufacturing plants. Fish are caught and brought to these places, packed in ice, and shipped, sometimes several hundred miles to interior cities. Texas fishermen ship part of their catch as far as New Mexico, Colorado, and Kansas. Most of the fish are caught in the broad mouths of the streams, the inland fresh-water lakes or bayous, and the inclosed bays along the shore. Only a few of the fishermen go out into the open waters of the Gulf of Mexico.

Most of the fish are caught with seines or nets. As the fishermen do not want to return to shore until they have made a fair catch, they build floating "cars" out of slats of wood. As the fish are caught, they are placed in these cars which are towed along behind the boat. In this way the fish are kept alive and fresh until they land. Many kinds of fish are caught, but a large part of the catch consists of red fish, sheepheads, pom'pano, or sea trout. Oysters, shrimp, and crabs are other sea foods caught along the coast. Packing and shipping of oysters and shrimp is a large business in Louisiana.

NEW NEW ORLEANS
Across the Mississippi River appears the skyline of a famous old Creole city gone modern.

FROM THE BAYOU LAFOURCHE *Ewing Galloway*
From the tidal bottoms of Louisiana's coastal waters come the silvery gray shrimp that turn so pink when cooked.

Farming in the Lower Rio Grande Valley.—Bordering the Gulf in the lower Rio Grande Valley is the most southerly part of the United States except the southern tip of Florida. It is a fan-shaped area, widening from a mere point about 100 miles upstream to a width of fifty miles at the coast. Sometimes it is called the American Egypt. Like the Nile in Egypt, the Rio Grande River has been busy for ages carrying down and depositing silt which makes the rich soil of this flat valley. It also furnishes water for irrigation.

As late as the beginning of this century, this valley was thought to be good for nothing except grazing cattle. It was covered with underbrush, small shrubs, and cactus. Then a railroad was built, settlers came in, and the big cattle ranches near the river were divided into irrigated farms. The climate is mild and almost free from frost. Settlers soon discovered that it was a fine place to grow citrus fruit. Many oranges are grown, but

SUGAR CANE AND SUGAR BEETS

U. S. Department of Agriculture

Each dot stands for 1000 acres. Notice how far apart the sugar beet and sugar cane areas are. What crop much like sugar cane is grown on the land between? What southern state grows most sugar cane? What western state produces most sugar beets?

grapefruit is their specialty. They can also raise almost every vegetable that can be grown anywhere in the United States. Crops grow the year round, and their cabbages, tomatoes, green beans, spinach, celery, asparagus, and other vegetables are sent to market during the late fall and winter when high prices are charged for them in other parts of the country where cold weather prevails. Not all of the land in the valley is irrigated, for the annual rainfall of from 17 to 26 inches makes it possible to grow cotton and feed-crops on non-irrigated areas.

Brownsville is the largest city and ocean port in the Lower Rio Grande Valley. On the other side of the river is the Mexican city of Matamo'ros, connected with Brownsville by two bridges. Many Mexicans come over into this part of the United States to work.

Growing Sugar Cane in Louisiana. — Next to grains, potatoes, and meat, sugar is one of our leading food products. The people in the United States use about 100 pounds of sugar per person each year. Large amounts are used in making cakes, pastry, jelly and preserves, candy, ice cream, and other sweet foods. There are two main sources of sugar: one is the beet grown in the northern states and the irrigated areas of the western states; the other is sugar cane. Sugar cane needs a long, warm growing season and fertile, well-watered soil. Most of the world's supply of cane sugar is grown in tropical regions, especially Cuba, Java, and Hawaii. We import most of our cane sugar, but a part of our supply comes from Louisiana.

Louisiana grows most of the sugar cane grown in the United States. Here on the Mississippi delta is a nearly frost-free area with a rainfall of from 55 to 60 inches each year. The soil carried down and left here by the Mississippi River is deep and fertile. Like sugar beets, sugar cane requires some hand labor. The tall stalks look somewhat like corn and have many joints or *nodes*, which are used as seed. In harvesting, the stalks are cut, stripped, "topped," and piled into carts to be hauled to the sugar mills. As the juice of the sugar cane spoils quickly after the cane is cut, each large sugar plantation commonly has its own mill. In the sugar mill, the cane is run between rollers to press out the juice, which is then boiled down or evaporated until the sugar crystals form. It is then put through machines which separate the sugar crystals from the remaining juice. Sugar at this stage is called "raw" sugar. This "raw" sugar is sent to sugar refineries, where it is made into white granulated sugar, "domino" sugar, fine powdered or pulverized sugar for candies and cakes, and light and dark brown sugar. Sugar refining is an important industry in New Orleans.

The stalks from which the juice has been pressed, called *bagasse'*, are used to make a kind of board much used in building houses. Perhaps you have seen the name "Celotex." One big factory in Louisiana turns out each

Sweet Is the Sugar Cane
The carloads of cane disappear into the refinery to appear finally in white crystals.

Cutting Cane
The sugar cane lies low on the ground, stiff as bamboo poles, but in its hollow center is hidden the sweetness for a nation.

From Cane to Celotex
Publishers' Photo
The waste product of sugar cane is salvaged and baled as celotex fiber. Six hundred pounds of fiber will produce one thousand square feet of board.

day enough of this board to make a walk four feet wide and 67 miles long. Formerly the bagasse was burned or taken somewhere and dumped.

Rice. — Unlike wheat, rice needs a great deal of water. In fact, rice plants usually grow in standing water. Near the Mississippi River in Arkansas and on the Gulf

RICE FIELDS *Ewing Galloway*
A rice field of Louisiana watered by a flooding ditch with its control gate.

Coast in Texas and Louisiana are the flat lands where grows most of the rice raised in our country. In growing rice, banks of earth or *levees* are built up around the fields to hold in the water. In the Old World, nearly all of the work of raising and harvesting rice is done by hand; but in our country, the land is prepared and the seed planted by machines, though some farmers use mules or horses instead of tractors.

After the plants are a few inches high, water is pumped into the fields. As the plants grow, the depth of the water is increased until it is about six inches. The field is kept covered with water for about three months.

When the heads of rice begin to droop from the weight of the growing grain and the fields turn yellow, the levees are opened and the fields drained. As the ground dries out, the grain ripens and in about three weeks it is ready to harvest. Now big machines are driven into the field where they cut and bind the rice stalks, which are then left in the field to dry. Later, after the grain is dried, it is threshed and hauled to the rice mill.

In some places having a good rainfall, rice will grow without irrigation, in the same manner as wheat. But the farmer is never sure of a crop because this depends so much upon the weather, especially the rainfall. Rice was raised in this way in Louisiana for many years before they started to irrigate the fields. It was called "Providence rice" because the crop was so uncertain.

Rice as it comes from the field is known as "paddy" rice. Each grain is covered by a thin husk. After the rice is husked, it is called brown rice. This contains vitamins and important food elements. In polishing to produce white rice, this has usually been removed. A new way of preparing rice drives the vitamins into the heart of the kernel where they are not worn away in the polishing process. A plant in Stuttgart, Arkansas, now uses this process.

Cotton. — Cotton, the "white gold" of the southern states, is grown in all four of the West South Central States. Cotton is always grown to sell; it is the southern farmer's money crop. It needs three things in order to grow well: (1) fertile soil; (2) 200 frost-free days; (3) at least 20 inches of rainfall. Many sections in these states meet all of these needs. (See map, page 82, showing the cotton belt, and the map on page 129 showing where the most cotton is grown.) Texas grows more cotton than any other state. The rich, dark "black-waxy" prairie soils in eastern Texas are especially good, as are also the fertile lowlands along the Mississippi.

Cotton is planted and cultivated by machines drawn by tractors, mules, or horses. Mules stand the climate of the Cotton Belt better than horses. Negroes do much of the

TEXAS COTTON

Ewing Galloway

Right up to the very doors of the cotton mills grow the cotton plants, bursting their hard brown shells into pop-corn blooms.

WHITNEY'S COTTON GIN

A series of saw-toothed steel combs fixed upon a revolving roller drew the cotton through a wire screen, leaving the seeds behind.

THE IMPROVED COTTON GIN

The principle is practically the same, but the machine grows bigger as industry demands more and more cotton. The bigger the machine, the more cotton handled.

A FORTUNE IN COTTON

Courtesy Houston Chamber of Commerce

The warehouses of Houston, Texas, are full of bales of cotton waiting to be shipped all over the world.

labor in the cotton fields, and, in Texas, large numbers of Mexicans are employed. Much cotton is picked by hand, but cotton picking machines are beginning to have widespread usage throughout the South, especially on large tracts of land. Weeding, cultivating, and fertilization are mostly done by machines and defoliation before picking is now performed largely by airplane.

When the fluffy white cotton is first picked, it contains a great many seeds which stick tightly to the fiber. To have these seeds removed it is taken to the *cotton gin*. This interesting machine was invented by a young Yale student, Eli Whitney, who in 1793 was a tutor on the plantation of Mrs. Nathanael Greene, widow of the famous Revolutionary general. One day Whitney noticed some carpenters trying to make a new window in the press where the cotton was stored. The teeth of their saw got clogged with cotton fiber and interferred with their sawing. But Whitney noticed that although the cotton fibers could be pulled through the crack that the saw had made, the cotton seeds could not. From this fact came the idea of the cotton gin, which was able to do more work in one day than a hundred Negroes before this could do by hand. After the cotton is ginned, the fiber is pressed into large bales of about 500 pounds, covered with coarse cloth called *burlap*, and bound with iron hoops. The cotton is then ready to be sent to large warehouses where it is stored until sold. Textile mills and garment factories, which were once exclusive industries of the East Coast, are now moving into the West South Central States where the raw material which feeds them is at hand and other industrial factors have been found to be favorable.

The cotton seeds are pressed to take out the oil, which is refined and used in place of olive oil, lard, and butter. The meal or cake that is left makes fine food for dairy cattle.

Other Crops in the Cotton Belt. — Farmers in the Cotton Belt in the West South Central States do not depend wholly upon cotton. They raise cattle, pigs, and chickens, and grow corn and other crops. Ripe corn is ground into cornmeal for making corn bread or cakes. Corn husks and corn stalks are fed to the animals in place of hay. They may also be chopped into small pieces and plowed under to fertilize the soil. Oats and grain sorghums are also grown for the animals. Some of the farmers have herds of beef cattle, and keep dairy cows to supply them with milk, cream, and butter. The skimmed milk is fed to the hogs. Vegetables and peanuts are raised for family use and for fodder. Pear, peach, and plum trees furnish fruit, while the pecan trees yield delicious nuts.

Sorghum and Broom Corn. — In the drier western parts of Oklahoma and northwestern Texas, sorghum takes the place of corn as fodder. Much broom corn is grown in Oklahoma. Like sorghum, it bears its seed on a long brush at the end of the stalk. For

STORAGE TANKS FOR COTTON SEED OIL
Plants like this one in Little Rock, Arkansas, store the cotton seed oils which go into shortening, oleomargarines, and other products.

making brooms, this brush is cut off before the seeds are quite ripe. The seeds are then removed, and the brush carefully dried and baled, ready for the factory. Here bunches of the brush are arranged in the form we know so well, carefully bound together, trimmed, and firmly fastened to a wooden handle.

Southern Crops for Northern Markets. — Oklahoma and Arkansas, on the border between north and south, grow the same crops as the states north and south of them. Oklahoma is a leading winter wheat state as well as a leading cotton state. Arkansas grows corn and apples like Missouri to the north, but also produces cotton and rice, two leading crops of Louisiana. One advantage that the southern farmers have is that many of their crops ripen earlier than the same crops in the north. Truck farmers in Arkansas, southern Louisiana, and Texas send their vegetables to be sold in northern markets when

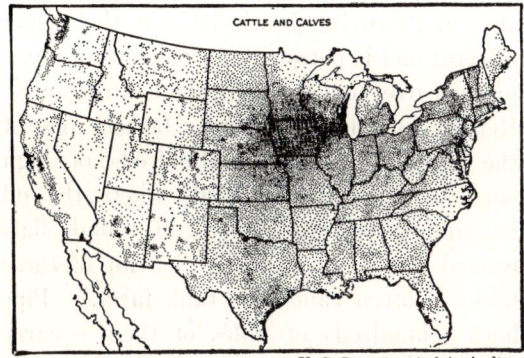

FOR NORTHERN MARKETS *Ewing Galloway*
Under Louisiana's warm sun, summer's green vegetables ripen for the northern markets buried deep in snow.

snow lies on the ground there. Arkansas and Louisiana strawberries are especially fine.

Cattle Raising. — Western Texas and Oklahoma lie in the great plains region which is sometimes called the "cow country" because the chief use made of the land was for grazing cattle. At one time, great herds of long-horned cattle called Texas longhorns roamed over these plains. Cattle owners *branded* their animals, that is, they placed marks on the animals by which they would know their own. Then they turned them loose to graze on the grassy plains. Cowboys rode about and looked after the cattle, protecting them as much as possible from wolves and other wild animals as well as from cattle thieves. Once a year, the cattle were rounded up and those to be sold were separated from the rest of the herd.

Now the fleet Texas longhorns have largely gone, and in their place are heavier types, more suitable for beef. Fences have been built, and many owners raise grain and forage crops for their cattle. The picturesque cowboy with his broad hat, flowing scarf, and leather leggings has almost dis-

U. S. Department of Agriculture
BEEF AND DAIRY CATTLE
Each dot on this map stands for 5000 head of cattle. Cattle are more evenly distributed over our country than any other animal. In what region do they appear to be thickest according to this map? Select some western states which seem to have very few cattle. What reasons can you give for this?

appeared from this land of fenced ranches and farms.

In Texas dairy cattle are scarcer than beef cattle. Most of them are found in the eastern part of the state. Of the other three states in this section, Louisiana has the fewest dairy cattle. One great difficulty in raising cattle in eastern Texas and Louisiana has been the presence of *cattle ticks*. These insects bore

THROWING A COW
The vast stretches of flat plain in Texas furnish food for thousands of cattle. Life on these cattle ranches is a life in the saddle.

into the skin of the animal and live on its blood. Sometimes they cause a fever, called tick fever, from which the cattle often die. To get rid of them, the cattle are forced to swim through a poisonous liquid, *cattle dip*, which kills the ticks, but does not harm the cattle. Great progress is being made against this pest, and the herds are steadily improving.

Sheep and Goats. — In southwestern Texas is a high, dry land called the Edwards Plateau. Here there is considerable grass, and weeds and shrubs are plentiful. This is one of the greatest sheep- and goat-grazing areas in the United States. Over half of the goats raised in the United States are in Texas and most of them are on this plateau. The cattle eat the grass, the sheep eat weeds as well as grass, and the goats feed largely on the shrubs and coarser growths. The goats raised here are Angora goats, with long, silky wool called *mohair*. This is much used for making certain kinds of fine woolen goods. Pasture lands on the plateau are sometimes fenced with wire strong enough to keep out the wolves and other wild animals. Drinking water to supply the stock during dry weather is stored in large tanks often of concrete.

Other Animal Industries. — Many horses and mules are raised in these southern states for use on the farms and ranches. Mules are commonly used in the cotton fields as they are strong and stand the climate better than horses. Swine, turkeys, and chickens are common on the farms, but they are not so plentiful as they are in the Corn Belt states.

The Land of Oil. — The West South Central States are among the leaders in the production of oil, natural gas, sulphur, salt, zinc, and bauxite (bawks'ĭt), but their chief mineral fuel is petroleum. These four states produce over half the oil in the United States. Refining of oil has naturally become one of the biggest industries. Hundreds of high derricks mark the oil fields where the oil is pumped out and stored in round, flat-topped tanks. An area with a lot of these tanks is often called a "tank farm." Pipe lines — hundreds of miles of them — carry most of the oil to the refineries in these and other states. Many products, such as naphtha, benzine, gasoline, kerosene, paraffine, vaseline, heavy oil for oiling machinery, and asphalt are made from oil. Gasoline is, of course, most in demand in our country, but

Courtesy Tulsa Chamber of Commerce
DRILLING FOR OIL

Down, down, down into the secret places of the earth! Behind the smoke and steam the power plants are driving the drills in their hungry search for oil.

Ewing Galloway
A GUSHER RUN WILD

In Oklahoma City, the famous Jones Well No. 1 "came in" in December, 1930. Millions of dollars worth of "black gold" shot into the air out of control and was wasted.

READY FOR THE CONSUMER

At this refinery in Beaumont, Texas, the oil is refined, stored in great drums, and then shipped in oil tanks here, there and everywhere.

considerable kerosene is used for lighting homes in rural districts and for cooking and heating purposes. We also export large amounts of kerosene to other parts of the world where people who do not have gas or electricity burn it in lamps.

Tulsa, Oklahoma City, Fort Worth, Dallas, and Shreveport are a few of the interior cities which owe much of their growth to the manufacture of petroleum products. Port Arthur, Galveston, Houston, and Baton Rouge are important shipping ports for both crude petroleum and the petroleum products. Port Arthur and Beaumont are near the famous Spindle Top Field in Texas where wells have been drilled very deep to tap the oil stored in the rocks below. This field was opened in 1901, and during its first year produced more than 17,000,000 barrels of oil.

Tank cars on the railroads and tank trucks carry the fuel products made out of petroleum from the refineries to the cities and towns where they are to be sold. Fuel oil, kerosene, and gasoline are usually stored in large tanks from which trucks carry supplies to consumers, but filling stations have their tanks underground so that there will be less danger from fire.

Natural Gas and Coal. — In connection with their petroleum, the West South Central States produce large amounts of natural gas. This is one of the finest of fuels, for it heats well, makes no smoke, and leaves no ash. Having so much oil and natural gas to use, the people of these states prefer to use these rather than coal, of which there are large deposits. Oklahoma, Arkansas, and Texas all have good coal, but much of that in Texas is a soft kind, called *lignite*.

Sulphur in Texas. — Sulphur deposits at a depth of several hundred feet are now being worked near the coast of Texas southwest of Galveston. Wells are drilled and the derricks remind one of those in an oil field. Natural sulphur is a solid, so it cannot be pumped out like oil, and poisonous gases make it unsafe for miners to go down in shafts to mine it like coal or ore. But if sulphur is heated, it will melt. So water heated very hot under pressure is pumped into the well. This melts the sulphur and the liquid is then forced out through a pipe by means of compressed air. It is then run into large vats where it cools and again becomes solid. Texas now produces a considerable amount of the world's sulphur. Louisiana is second to Texas in sulphur production.

Salt in Louisiana. — Louisiana is one of the leading states in the production of salt. It has three of the largest salt mines in the world. In the low swampy land west of New Orleans are five hills rising from 75 to

SPINDLE TOP OIL FIELD *Ewing Galloway*

It takes a vast forest of derricks to release the oil that has lain hidden in the earth's rocky depths for centuries. Texas is one of our leading states in the production of petroleum and petroleum products.

A WALL OF SULPHUR

Ewing Galloway

After the sulphur has been melted and pumped to the surface it is allowed to crystallize. It is then broken off in blocks. like rock from a quarry, and loaded on to freight cars for shipment.

BAUXITE MINING

Many are the aluminum pots and pans that will be made from this high quality bauxite mined in Arkansas.

PILLARS OF SALT

Under the ground, at the salt mines near New Orleans, are galleries, arched roofs. and pillars, all of solid salt.

117

100 feet above sea level. They are called "islands" because they rise above the flat marsh lands around them like islands in a sea. In the center of each of these islands is an immense core of pure salt, into which deep shafts have been sunk. Holes are bored into the salt rock and explosives break it apart. It is then loaded on small cars to be taken to the bottom of the shaft and hoisted out of

Courtesy Arkansas State Publicity Department
HOT SPRINGS NATIONAL PARK, ARKANSAS
This modern resort plays host to nearly a half million visitors each year. The above scene shows in the background, left, the Medical Arts Building, and right, the Army and Navy Hospital.

the mine. Taking out the salt leaves large open spaces called *galleries*, and pillars of the salt rock are left to support the roof of the mine. In some cases, these pillars are from 50 to 60 feet high. The mines are lighted and the little cars are run by electricity. Most of the salt is so pure that the only work necessary to prepare it for table use is to grind it fine.

Aluminum Ore in Arkansas. — Two counties in central Arkansas, Saline and Pulaski, produce 97 per cent of the ore called *bauxite* from which aluminum is made in the United States. Open-pit mining is mostly used in taking out the ore. It is loosened by blasting and picking so that steam shovels can scoop it up and load it onto cars. It is then sent to a crushing mill, where it is broken up and dried. The ore has to go through two refining processes before the metal is extracted.

Hot Springs National Park. — Arkansas contains the highest of the Ozark Mountains, the largest mountain group in the West South Central States. The Ouachita Mountains in western Arkansas have the highest mountain elevations between the Alleghanies and the Rockies. About 50 miles southwest of Little Rock is Hot Springs Mountain with a number of hot springs at its base. The 147 degree water flows from 47 hot springs in a total volume of one million gallons daily. It is owned and controlled by the Federal Government. Cold springs, containing mineral waters good for drinking, are also found, sometimes quite close to the hot springs. People suffering from various diseases go there to be healed by bathing in the hot waters and drinking the mineral waters of the cold springs. Over 100 years ago, in 1832, the United States Government set aside Hot Springs Mountain for public use and in 1921 the area was made a national park.

Large Cities and Seaports. — Away in the southwestern corner of Texas is *El Paso*, an important city. El Paso means "The Pass." Here the Rio Grande breaks through the Rocky Mountain ranges, giving an easy route east and west. Cross the river and you are in Mexico. Several railroads and roads meet here at this "Gateway to the West."

The thousands of cattle, sheep, goats, swine, horses, and mules on the ranches and ranges are another reason for El Paso's growth. The city has large stockyards and ships out meat, leather, wool, fertilizer, and other packing-house products. Mineral ores from New Mexico, Arizona, and Mexico are brought here to be smelted. Nearby forests furnish

WEST SOUTH CENTRAL STATES

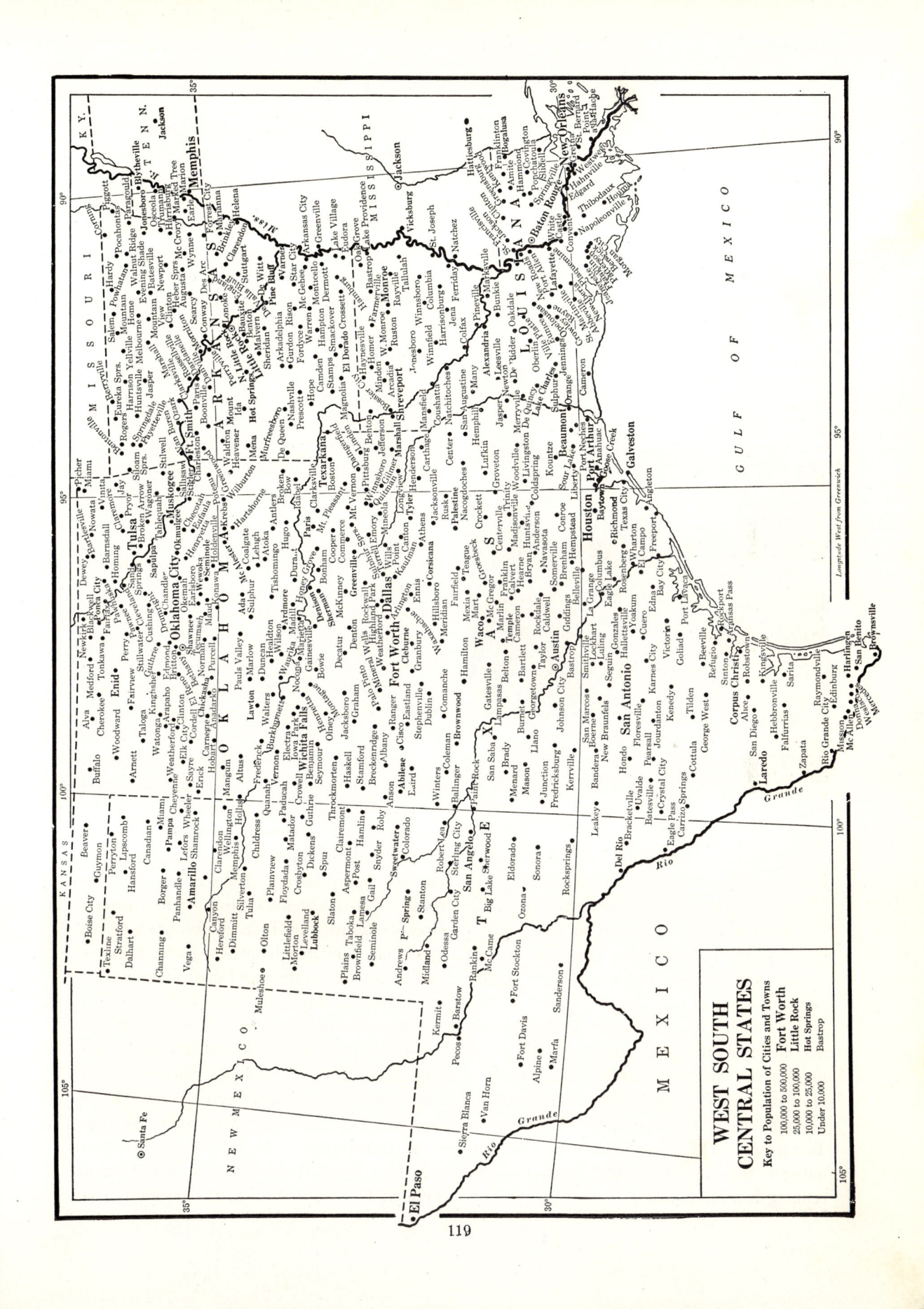

Key to Population of Cities and Towns
- 100,000 to 500,000: **Fort Worth**
- 25,000 to 100,000: **Little Rock**
- 10,000 to 25,000: Hot Springs
- Under 10,000: Bastrop

timber for the making of lumber. The Rio Grande supplies water for city uses and for growing crops under irrigation. Up the Rio Grande, the large Elephant Butte Dam holds back the waters of the river in one of the largest artificial lakes in the world. Here in this warm climate under irrigation, it is possible to grow five crops of alfalfa a year.

"REMEMBER THE ALAMO!"

At this old mission, named for the cottonwood trees that surround it, a garrison of one hundred and eighty-three men perished for the independence of Texas — among them the border heroes James Bowie and Davy Crockett. Today it stands in San Antonio as a monument of American liberty.

Still another reason for El Paso's growth is its dry, sunny climate. Less than 10 inches of rain falls each year and the sun shines over 300 days a year. People who have tuberculosis go there hoping to be cured, and caring for invalids gives work to many people.

Oil, cattle, cotton, forests, and farm products have all had a part in the growth of the four largest cities of Texas — *San Antonio*, *Houston*, *Dallas*, and *Fort Worth*. Their manufacturing industries depend largely on Texan products for raw materials. Oil and natural gas furnish handy fuels and oil refining is a big industry.

San Antonio, with its famous Alamo, missions, and old Cathedral, is a place of historical interest. It is the home of a division of the United States Army and has the largest military aviation training school in the world.

The city has many manufacturing establishments and a large trade with Southwest Texas and Mexico. As a resort San Antonio has become favorably known. The climate is mild and the hot mineral wells have curative properties.

Houston, the largest city, and Galveston are the leading seaports of Texas. Houston is 50 miles from the Gulf and a few years ago was an inland town on a small, shallow bayou. Then a 30-foot sea level canal was built, so that ocean vessels can now come right up to the city. The shallow bayou was dredged to make a turning basin for the large boats. This city now has more than twice as many people as it had in 1920.

Dallas, a cosmopolitan and well-built city, is one of the leading industrial centers of Texas. At the junction of a large number of railroads, it is an important distributing point and is a very large cotton market. It is one of the leading insurance centers of the country and an outstanding financial center with its Federal Reserve Bank of the 11th District.

Fort Worth is the center of a vast stock raising and agricultural country, has large jobbing interests, and carries on extensive trade. Its industrial establishments include large stockyards, packing houses, grain elevators, mills, and machine shops. It is noteworthy for the number and size of its recently constructed buildings.

Galveston, one of the great cotton ports of the world, is built on a low island about two miles from the mainland. A causeway wide enough for railroad and electric car tracks, a driveway, and a footway connect the city with the mainland. In 1900, a severe storm and high waves from the sea destroyed a large part of Galveston, so the people raised

HOUSTON, TEXAS
A skyline view of the largest city and important seaport of our largest state.

FORT WORTH, TEXAS
Courtesy Fort Worth Chamber of Commerce
Along a wide concrete highway one "buzzes" into Fort Worth, city of cotton and oil mills, grain marketing and meat packing.

DALLAS, TEXAS
Lloyd M. Long
Through the trees of Oak Cliff one glimpses the skyline of the east side of this "New York of the Southwest."

General Douglas MacArthur's Birthplace
In this restored old Civil War Arsenal Building, young Douglas MacArthur was born. It is located in MacArthur Park in the center of one of Little Rock's residential areas.

the level of their city several feet and built a concrete wall 17 feet high and five feet wide at the top to protect them from the ocean. Southward from Galveston for about 30 miles is a broad, level beach which is fine for surf bathing. At low tide, this beach is dry and solid enough for automobiles to use as a speedway.

Amarillo, the chief city of the Panhandle, is an important railroad center and is in the midst of a productive agricultural and stock raising region. It has growing manufacturing interests and numerous industries, including creameries, flour mills, cottonseed oil mills, meat packing plants, and petroleum refineries.

Austin, the capital, located on the Colorado River near the center of the state, is the seat of the State University.

The industries of Oklahoma's largest cities, *Oklahoma City* and *Tulsa*, are largely connected with the oil industry, though flour milling and meat packing are also important. Tulsa manufactures oil-well supplies in addition to refining oil, and nearby is one of the largest cotton mills west of the Mississippi River. Oklahoma City is the capital and largest city.

The largest city in Arkansas is its capital, *Little Rock*, situated on the Arkansas River. It is the cultural, professional, and business center of the state. Bordering on the south are some of the richest cotton producing areas in the Mississippi Valley; on the east the rice lands of the Grand Prairie; to the west the rugged Ouachitas; and to the north the Ozarks. Its stores carry on a large trade with the farmers in the surrounding country.

Fort Smith, farther up the Arkansas River in western Arkansas, sells corn and cotton and other agricultural products, and makes cottonseed oil, furniture, and other wooden articles. Nearby coal mines furnish it with fuel.

New Orleans, the largest city and shipping center of the southern states, was founded over

Tulsa, an Oil Center
This ancient meeting place of the Creek, the Cherokee, and the Osage nations is now a hustling, bustling city of commercial prosperity.

RANDOLPH FIELD, SAN ANTONIO   *Official Photographs, U. S. Army Air Corps*
The Administration Building (above) shows in the general view (middle) just beyond the front circle. Below is a detail of the planes and hangars at the right side of the field.

Courtesy New Orleans Association of Commerce
A SUPPLY BASE AT NEW ORLEANS BUILT DURING WORLD WAR I

At the juncture of the Navigation Canal and the Mississippi River were erected by the U. S. Army these three buildings. Today Unit 1 is occupied by the International Harvester Company, Twine Mill and the Chase Bag Factory; Unit 2 by the Douglass Shipside Storage Corporation (a public warehouse); and Unit 3 as an army warehouse.

BATON ROUGE, CAPITAL OF LOUISIANA

In the midst of old plantation homes rises this modern capitol building with its white tower capped by the clouds.

LACEWORK IN IRON

Delicate traceries in cast and wrought iron are embroidered on many of the buildings in old New Orleans.

200 years ago. This interesting city has a new section and an old French section. The older section contains houses with quaint overhanging balconies much as they were 150 years ago. The newer section has its skyscrapers, its streets thronged with people, and its automobiles just as in other large cities.

To protect New Orleans against floods, the Government has built the Bonnet Carre Spillway twenty-eight miles above the city. It is over 7000 feet long and consists of 350 twenty-foot bays capable of discharging more water than flows over Niagara Falls. At Lake Pontchartrain, six miles away, into which the water flows, the spillway is two and a half miles wide.

The Mississippi River gives New Orleans a good route to the sea. Many steamship lines connect it with the leading ports of the world and ocean vessels from almost all countries may be seen in its harbor. From its wharves go out grains, flour, cotton, meat, petroleum and petroleum products, canned goods, lumber, sugar, and machinery of all sorts. Into this harbor come bananas from Central America and the West Indies, sugar from Cuba, coffee from Brazil and other Latin American countries, sisal (si'zal) from Yucatan', nitrates from Chile, mahogany from tropical countries of Central and South America, and other products which are shipped to all parts of the United States. Many industries, among which are rice milling, manufacture of sugar and cane syrup, refining of petroleum, and the manufacture of summer clothing, give work to many people of this great southern city.

Other important cities in Louisiana are *Shreveport* on the Red River and the capital, *Baton Rouge*, on the Mississippi above New Orleans.

New Products. — During the last war many new industries were built up to make products which are just as useful in peace times. Among these was the smelting of tin at Texas City. Tin ore is brought to this port from the South American country of Bolivia. Another was the making of rubber from oil. Here, where oil is so plentiful, was a good place to start this industry. A big rubber making plant is found at Port Neches, near Beaumont. When one looks out over the ocean, he is not likely to think of it as a source of hard metal. But a chemical plant at Freeport, Texas, takes some of this sea water and gets from it a bright, shining metal, called magnesium. It does not tarnish, and being lighter than aluminum, it is a good metal to use in airplanes and other articles which should be light in weight.

Activities and Questions

1. By whom was Louisiana first settled?
2. Comment on the variety of crops that can be grown in these states.
3. Name three important shipping centers in these states. Why is each important?
4. In what products does Texas lead? Louisiana? Arkansas? Give reasons in each case.
5. Add to your collection pictures of some of the typical industries in the West South Central States.
6. What large rivers drain these states?
7. Where was the former Indian territory located?
8. What is the chief lumber tree of the South? For what purposes is it used?
9. Describe cypress lumbering.
10. Compare the Mississippi and the Nile in length, direction of flow, and delta land.
11. How is rice grown? Why in just that way?
12. Describe the production of sugar from cane.
13. What is sorghum? Where and why is it grown?
14. Name the capitals and largest cities of these states.
15. Make a rough sketch of these states with their principal rivers and cities. Locate some of the oil fields.

LIFE ON THE MISSISSIPPI *Courtesy Memphis Chamber of Commerce*
The "great river," boundary line of ten states, has carried upon its waters the commerce of a nation.

VII. THE EAST SOUTH CENTRAL STATES

East of the Mississippi lie the East South Central States, a group very like their western neighbors. Western Kentucky and Tennessee resemble eastern Arkansas and southeastern Missouri. Mississippi is generally low or rolling country like Louisiana and southeastern Arkansas. Northeastern Alabama, eastern Kentucky, and eastern Tennessee, however, are mountainous, as their lands extend over into the Appalachian Highlands. Alabama and Mississippi have frontage on the Gulf of Mexico, giving them seaports, seaside resorts, and a part in the Gulf fisheries.

Varied Products. — Like the neighboring states to the west, the East South Central States can raise somewhere almost every crop that can be grown anywhere in the United States. Their forests contain many kinds of trees, and they have a variety of useful minerals. Their people live and work in many different ways; some live in rude cabins among the mountains; others in big industrial cities where they work in the factories, mills, and stores. Still others live on farms where mixed farming is carried on, or on large plantations where cotton is the chief crop. A few work in the pine forests, lumbering or distilling turpentine and rosin from the gum of the pine trees. A small number make fishing their chief work.

The "Father of Waters." — The Mississippi River, sometimes called the "Father of Waters," gives these states transportation north to St. Paul and south to the Gulf of Mexico. It was the highway for early explorers and later settlers. Flatboats loaded with supplies floated down the river carrying grain, cotton, and other products to New Orleans to be shipped overseas or to eastern seaports of the United States. The flatboats could not easily be taken upstream so they were commonly sold when they reached New Orleans. Long, narrow boats about 50 feet long and 12 to 15 feet wide, called *keel boats*, were also used. They took about 40 days going downstream from St. Louis to New Orleans and about 90 days on the return trip.

Over 100 years ago, steamboats went up and down the Mississippi River as they do today. The early steamboats made the trip of about 1500 miles from St. Louis to New Orleans in around seven days, though the return journey upstream took 25 days. A fleet of barges now carries goods up and down the Mississippi River between New Orleans and St. Louis and also between St. Louis and Kansas City on the Missouri.

But travel and traffic on this river have not increased so fast as the number of people and cities along its banks. Railroads now carry most of the people and freight even along the river, because they are faster than steamboats and furnish shorter routes between places. The course of the Mississippi is so crooked that boats have to go a much longer distance than trains. (See map, page 131.) A train between St. Louis and New Orleans goes only a little over 700 miles, while a boat travels about 1500 miles. The airplane route is still shorter, being only 600 miles.

A very long time ago, an arm of the Gulf of Mexico, or *estuary*, extended north to a point just beyond where the Ohio River joins the Mississippi. For many, many years, the Mississippi and its tributaries carried down rock material which filled this estuary and also built up the great Mississippi Delta far out into the Gulf. All along its course, between the East and West South Central States, the Mississippi is bordered by a broad, flat lowland, called its *flood plain*. To prevent flooding, in times of high water, banks of earth called *levees* have been built along the river. During the flood stage, the surface of the river often is higher than that of the land on either side. If the levee gives way,

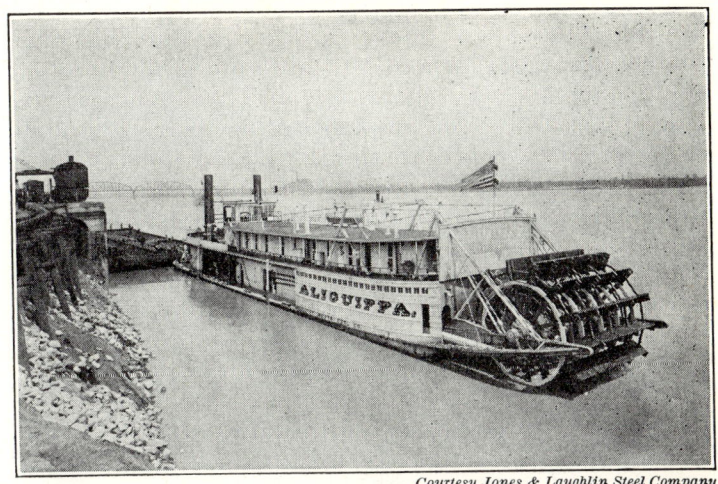

Courtesy Jones & Laughlin Steel Company

A CHAMPION

The towboat *Aliquippa* holds the record of the rivers for fast time between Pittsburgh and Memphis. It made the run of 1200 miles, with a tow of 6000 tons of steel, in 6 days and 8 hours.

Statistics of the East South Central States *

State	Abbreviation	Area Sq. Miles	Population	Rank Area	Rank Pop.	Capital	Population	Largest City	Population
Kentucky	Ky.	40,395	2,845,627	36	16	Frankfort	11,492	Louisville	319,077
Tennessee	Tenn.	42,246	2,915,841	33	15	Nashville	167,402	Memphis	292,942
Mississippi	Miss.	47,716	2,183,796	31	23	Jackson	62,107	Jackson	62,107
Alabama	Ala.	51,609	2,832,961	28	17	Montgomery	78,084	Birmingham	267,583

* 1940 Census

IMPORTANT PRODUCTS

Kentucky: — Tobacco, coal, live stock, grain, iron and steel products
Tennessee: — Tobacco, corn, cotton, timber, stone, steel products
Mississippi: — Cotton, cottonseed products, timber, vegetables, nuts
Alabama: — Cotton, iron, textiles, coal, peanuts, steel products

A BULWARK AGAINST RISING WATERS
Caterpillar tractors hasten the work of levee building along the shores of the Mississippi.

the river rushes out over the lowland, drowning people and animals and destroying millions of dollars' worth of property and crops.

In spite of the danger from floods, people live on these lowlands because the soil is so rich that it produces large crops without the use of fertilizer. For many years, the Mississippi overflowed these lowlands once a year, leaving a rich layer of fine soil or mud brought from the higher lands. Year after year this continued until the river had built up one of the most fertile areas in the world. This is one of the Mississippi's gifts to the East South Central States.

In the Land of "King Cotton." — Cotton has so long been the leading money crop of the southern states that it is often called "King Cotton." Corn, wheat, and hay are among the most valuable crops grown in our country, but cotton leads in the Southern States. Mississippi and Alabama are both leading states in the production of cotton, while some is grown in Tennessee and a little in western Kentucky.

The "Delta." — Mississippi's greatest cotton-growing section is a long, oval-shaped area known as the Yazoo Basin or the Yazoo-Mississippi Delta. The people of Mississippi usually call it simply the "Delta." It is really a part of the Mississippi flood plain, about 200 miles long and 70 miles wide in its widest part. It stretches from Memphis, Tennessee, to Vicksburg, Mississippi. Its western boundary is the Mississippi River, bordered by an unbroken levee from Memphis to Vicksburg. Its eastern boundary is a series of bluffs or a broken ridge known as Chickasaw Ridge. Near this ridge flows the Yazoo River which joins the Mississippi near Vicksburg.

The Delta is not perfectly level, but has low ridges, flat areas, and swamps. When

Courtesy Memphis Chamber of Commerce
IN KING COTTON'S TRAIN
The softest kind of a ride — on a wagon load of newly-picked cotton.

the white men came, they found it covered with forests, cypress trees in the swamps, and oak, ash, maple, tulip, and sycamore on the higher lands. Between the trees was a tangled growth of cane and shrubs intertwined with vines. Wild mammals and birds were plentiful, making it a fine hunting ground for the Indians. The settlers cleared much of the land, and started to grow cotton, the great money crop of the south. It grew so well that for many years it has been the leading crop, although a variety of other crops, such as alfalfa, clover, hay, soy beans, and peas are also raised. Swamps have been drained and steps taken to get rid of mosquitoes. Railroads and good highways make travel and shipping easy.

Cotton Plantations. — Much of the land in the Delta is in large plantations of from a few hundred to several thousand acres. On these, the land is usually divided into small units which are rented to Negro farmers. These are often called one-mule farms, because each contains just about as much land as one farmer with the aid of one mule can plant

VICKSBURG, MISSISSIPPI

Ewing Galloway

The Yazoo River is kept out of Vicksburg by a high concrete wall. At the first warning of rising water, the gates are sealed with concrete.

COTTON, OUR LARGEST MONEY CROP

Each dot on this map stands for 2000 bales of cotton. Cotton is a southern crop which needs about 200 frost-free days in which to grow and ripen its bolls. Compare this map with the map of agricultural regions on page 222 showing the cotton belt. Locate parts of states which grow the most cotton. Which state leads in cotton production? Why is Florida nearly all white on this map?

and cultivate. The Negro farmer, with his family, lives in a small cabin on the farm. The plantation owner furnishes the mule, necessary tools and other materials, and in return receives a share of the crop. In the fall, when the cotton bolls are ripe, the Negro's family helps to pick the cotton.

A few plantation owners use machines to do most of the work and hire the few workers needed. The reason more do not do this is that they need workers to pick the cotton in the fall. Since they need many helpers then, they feel that they might as well keep them on the plantation all the year.

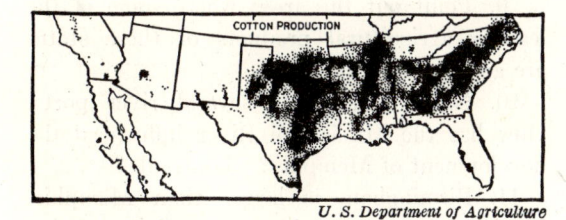

Alabama, the "Cotton State." — Alabama was once called the "Cotton State" because it raised so much cotton. Most of this was grown on plantations in a broad low area often called the Black Belt because of the rich, black soil. But this is no longer the main cotton-growing section, for most of the cotton is grown on small farms in the northern and eastern parts of the state. Though the rich soil produced large crops, the land is low and subject to floods. It was hard to keep down the cotton boll weevil which destroyed

"Away Down South in the Land of Cotton" *Courtesy Memphis Chamber of Commerce*
Up and down the rows the pickers choose the ripest bolls for today's bagful.

a large part of the crop each year. This area is now largely used to grow grasses for beef and dairy cattle.

The Cotton Boll Weevil. — The cotton boll weevils entered Texas from Mexico in 1892. Like an invading army, they spread over King Cotton's domain year by year until they reached the lands along the Atlantic Coast. The boll weevil makes a small hole in the cotton boll and lays its eggs there. When the *larvae* are hatched, they feed on the inside of the boll, which then dries up and drops off. Before they could be checked, these little insects did millions of dollars' worth of damage and ruined many crops.

Map of the East South Central States

Map Questions and Activities

1. Name the states in this group.
2. Locate the capital and some of the largest cities in each state. How are they shown?
3. Where are the lowlands? the highlands? How can you tell?
4. What great river is found on the western part of this map? on the northern part?
5. Does the map suggest one or more reasons why Memphis is an important city? Nashville? Chattanooga? Birmingham? Louisville?
6. Find Muscle Shoals. What great Government project is located there?
7. Does the railway network appear to be thick in these states? Why? How are railroads shown?
8. Where would you like best to live in one of these states? Why?
9. Point out the areas where some of the leading agricultural products of these states are grown.
10. Name and locate several river ports. How has the Mississippi River influenced the development of Memphis? Louisville?
11. Birmingham is larger than Memphis, but is not on a navigable river. Can you give causes for the growth of Birmingham?
12. Locate the following: Cumberland Mountains, Cumberland Plateau, Walden Ridge, Lookout Mountain, Great Smoky Mountains. In what general direction do the mountains run?

Physical - Political
EAST SOUTH CENTRAL STATES

Scale of Statute Miles: 0, 50, 100, 150

⊙ State Capitals — Railroads

The type used indicates the relative sizes of towns and cities.

HEIGHTS IN FEET
- Above 5,000
- 2,000 to 5,000
- 1,000 to 2,000
- 500 to 1,000
- Sea level to 500

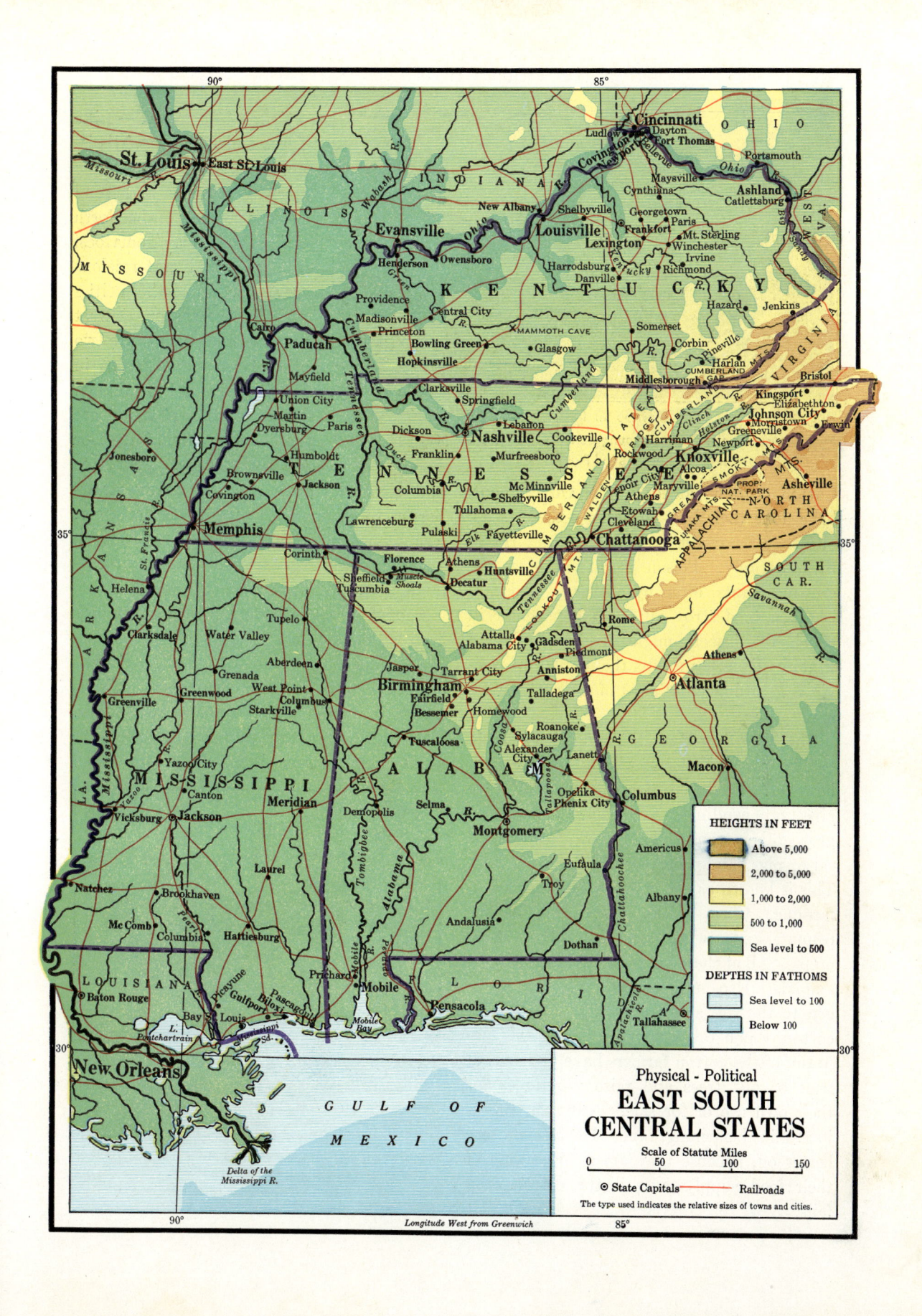

DEPTHS IN FATHOMS
- Sea level to 100
- Below 100

FIGHTING AN INSECT ARMY *Courtesy Delta Air Corporation*
Flying low over the fields of young cotton plants, the air pilot lays down a barrage of poison dust.

Cotton growers, aided by the Government, have done their best to destroy these pests, but they have not been able to get rid of them entirely. Poison is dusted over the growing plants, often by airplanes, and care is taken to destroy all vegetable matter in which the insects might live through the winter. By these means the number of weevils is kept down and most of the cotton crop saved.

The Cow-Sŏw-Hen Method of Farming. — The cotton boll weevil did some good, however. It forced the cotton farmers to give up depending so much on cotton and to grow other crops. They now keep cows, raise pigs and chickens, and grow feed. This is known as the cow-sow-hen method of farming. Corn, alfalfa, clover, soy beans, peanuts, and cowpeas are some of the leading crops. All of these are good feed for the farm animals. Excepting corn, they all add nitrogen to the soil and are good to rotate with cotton, which takes nitrogen out of the soil. Many of the cotton farmers have orchards of fruit or nut trees and raise vegetables for their own use or for sale. After all, this is just mixed farming, and the farmers are better off, because they are at least sure of their food supply even if the cotton crop fails.

Truck Farming. — Like Texas and Louisiana, Mississippi and Alabama can grow green vegetables and send them to markets in the North early in the year. Tomatoes, cabbages, and watermelons are shipped to northern cities early in the season. Sweet potatoes and peanuts are two other large money crops in Mississippi and Alabama. Most of the peanuts are made into peanut butter or fed to the swine. Tennessee and Kentucky grow and ship many strawberries to other states early in the summer. Truck farmers in these two states raise green vegetables and small fruits on the fertile lowlands to supply the people in the nearby cities.

Tobacco. — As cotton is a leading money crop of Alabama and Mississippi, so tobacco is a leading money crop of Kentucky. Tennessee also grows considerable tobacco. This is a crop that needs much care and hand labor. The seeds are so tiny that it is necessary to plant them in seed beds. Then the small

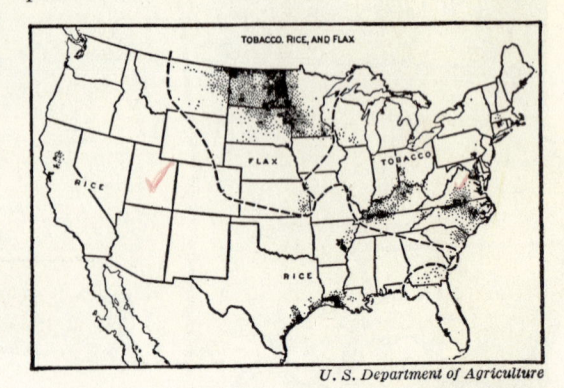

U. S. Department of Agriculture
TOBACCO, RICE, AND FLAX

Each dot stands for 2000 acres. Rice, which has to have much water while it is growing, is raised on the lowlands which are easily flooded. What group of states grow most of the rice? In what part of California is rice grown? Tobacco is grown in many states, but most of this valuable money crop is raised in five southern states. Can you find them on this map? What three northern states grow most of the flax?

plants have to be carefully transplanted to the open fields. There, they must be weeded and cultivated with great care until they are well started. Then they must be watched and protected against insects. We use tobacco to keep away some insects, but there are others that eat both the stalks and the leaves of the tobacco plants. If the farmer is to get a good price for his tobacco, the leaves must be whole and in good condition. Before the plant is fully grown, the top is cut off to prevent it from going to seed. This is done so that all its strength may go into the leaves and make them larger and thicker.

There are different ways of harvesting tobacco. Usually the whole stalk is cut, but sometimes it is split nearly to the ground, then cut off a little lower down and slung across a stick. Again, the leaves are stripped from the stalks in the field and tied together in bunches. After the tobacco is harvested, it is carried to the drying or curing shed, where the bunches are hung far enough apart so that the air may pass freely among them. The tobacco shed is a well-ventilated building, the sides of which often consist of slats with open spaces between, so arranged that the tobacco will be kept dry in case of rain. Tobacco dried in this way is called *air-cured* tobacco. Tobacco dried in closed buildings by means of hot air is known as *flue-cured*.

When the leaves are thoroughly cured, they are stripped from the stalks and tied together in bunches ready for sale. Louisville and Lexington are Kentucky's largest loose-leaf tobacco markets, and Louisville manufactures cigars, cigarettes, smoking tobacco, chewing tobacco, and snuff. Most of the tobacco raised in Kentucky and Tennessee is used for cigarettes or for chewing and smoking purposes.

Hemp in Kentucky. — Hemp is another of Kentucky's money crops. It is used for making strong cord, yarns for weaving carpet, and coarse toweling. Hemp

THE STORY OF TOBACCO

(Top) A field of tobacco, somewhere in Kentucky, with its white, lily-like blooms. (Middle) Tobacco hung on scaffolds to dry. (Bottom) The tobacco buyer inspects the baskets of tobacco laid out in the big warehouse.

fiber, which is prepared from the stalk of the plant, is much like flax fiber, but coarser. The stalks are cut by machinery and spread out on the ground to *ret*. This is a softening process, caused by exposure to the weather.

A HEMP HARVEST

A field of hemp, a crop of Kentucky, on its way to becoming string for little, and middle-sized, and great big bundles and boxes.

After this, machines separate the fiber from the woody part of the stalk and prepare it for making twine or cloth.

Farm Animals. — Many of the farmers keep dairy cattle, swine, and chickens, and some raise beef cattle, which graze on the cut-over lands in Mississippi and Alabama. One of the greatest hindrances to cattle raising in Mississippi and Alabama, as in Louisiana and Texas, has been the cattle tick. This is being overcome by "dipping" the cattle.

Many southern products, such as corn, soy beans, cowpeas, cottonseed meal, and peanuts, make good food for swine. It is not necessary to harvest many of these crops, for swine may be turned into the fields and allowed to help themselves. Pigs delight in rooting up peanuts, which are fine food for them.

A considerable amount of milk produced in these states is prepared and canned as evaporated and condensed milk. It keeps well in these forms, and can be shipped anywhere. Many people use it because it costs less than fresh milk and cream. Fresh milk takes up more room, has to be **kept** cool, and must be delivered soon after it is produced. Evaporated and condensed milk are sent to parts of the world where there are few or no dairy cattle and people cannot have fresh milk.

Sheep in Kentucky and Tennessee. — The map of the United States showing where sheep are to be found tells us that many are in north central Kentucky and central Tennessee. Both sections have rolling or hilly pasture lands which are fine for summer grazing. Both are good farming regions and it is easy for the farmers to grow grain, hay, and root crops for winter feeding. In the western states, most of the sheep are found on the big ranches, but in the eastern states, they are generally raised on farms. The flocks are small, are kept in fenced pastures, and the farmer cares for them in connection with his other farm work. Often the sheep can be grazed on hilly lands with thin soil unfit for crops.

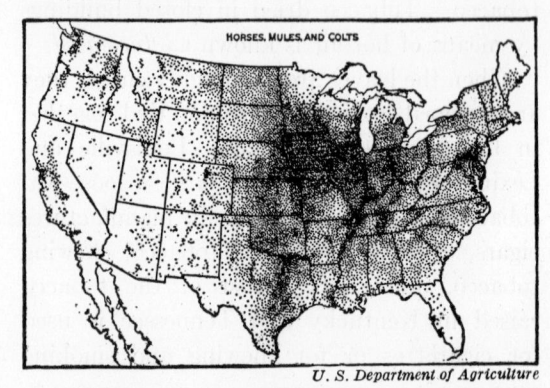

HORSES AND MULES, OUR WORK ANIMALS

Each dot on this map stands for 2000 head of horses and mules. Notice how evenly the dots are scattered over the central and southern states. What does this mean? Select three western states which seem to have very few horses or mules. Do you know any reason for this?

Mules. — Mules outnumber horses in the East South Central States. They are tougher and stronger than horses of their own size, and do not cost so much to keep. Mules are also used for hauling cars in coal mines where they are sometimes kept in underground stables. During both World Wars, our southern states sent many mules to Europe, where they were used to haul army supplies.

The Blue-Grass Region of Kentucky. — In the northern part of Kentucky, bordering on the Ohio River, is a lower region rimmed on its three other sides by higher parts of the plateau. It has a very fertile soil derived from the limestone rocks found in this section. This is the well-known Blue-Grass Region. Here have been bred many famous racing horses, as well as saddle and harness horses. But since the automobile has so largely taken the place of the horse for driving, not many light-weight harness horses are needed, and fewer are now seen in the blue-grass pastures. Mules, sheep, beef, and dairy cattle are now often pastured in this region.

Blue grass in Kentucky is mainly for pasture and little is dried for hay. It is native to Kentucky and some of the farmers make a business of growing and selling the seed. It is widely used for lawns and for mixing with other grasses for pasture. Besides raising the seed, the farmer can use the grasslands for pasture part of the year, so that he gets a double income from this rich land.

Sweet Clover and Bees. — In hilly northeastern Kentucky the soil on the hillsides is easily washed away, if planted with such crops as tobacco and corn. But sweet clover, which grows wild along the roads, does well on these hillsides, where it not only holds the soil in place but adds nitrogen to it. Clover is a good forage crop for farm animals and its blossoms provide honey for bees. Bee keeping is an industry that does not require so much

CHURCHILL DOWNS
A hush falls over the crowd as the satin-coated, fleet-footed contenders at the Kentucky Derby parade to the barrier, awaiting the signal that means, "They're off!"

work as some others because the bees gather their own food from the flowers of such crops as clover and buckwheat. Honey from clover blossoms is well liked because of its delicate flavor. Bee keeping is common on farms not only in Kentucky but wherever mixed farming is practiced. The long growing season during which the bees may gather honey helps to make the keeping of them a good industry for the southern farmers.

Gulf Fisheries of Mississippi and Alabama. — As in Louisiana and Texas, fishing along the Gulf coast is a growing industry in Mississippi and Alabama. Red snappers, mullet, sea trout or bass, catfish, Spanish mackerel, and sheepshead are some of the leading varieties caught. One kind greatly liked for its delicate flavor is the pompano, which, like many others in the Gulf of Mexico, is not found in the North Atlantic. The shallow bays along the coast make good oyster beds, from which large quantities are shipped to interior cities. Canning oysters, shrimp, and fish is a leading industry here. Fishing is a favorite pastime at resort cities

"DOWN MOBILE"
Courtesy Mobile Chamber of Commerce
On the still waters of a tree-girt lagoon, a lone fisherman quietly moves out from the deepening shadows, trolling for fish.

along the coast where landing a large tarpon furnishes lively sport.

Forests and Lumbering. — Many different kinds of lumber are produced in the East South Central States. In Alabama and Mississippi the leading lumber tree is the yellow or southern pine. So much of this comes from these two states that they rank among our leading lumbering states. Of the several kinds of yellow pine one of the best known is the longleaf. Large stands of this occur in these southern forests, where the long, straight trunks are fine for making boards and telegraph poles. Manufacturing turpentine and rosin from the gum is another important industry in Alabama and Mississippi; the pine trees may be used for this purpose for several years before they are cut for lumber.

On the lowlands along the Mississippi, red gum trees furnish a wood much used for *veneer*. By veneer is meant a thin board which is glued solid to another board. Seats and backs of chairs are often made of thin boards glued together with the grain of the wood running in opposite directions. This makes a tough board and prevents warping. Often, in making furniture, a thin layer of a more expensive wood is glued over a cheaper one so that the article looks just as if it were made entirely of the better wood.

On the slopes of the Appalachian Highlands, mixed forests of oak, birch, beech, ash, maple, hickory, walnut, chestnut, and many other kinds of *deciduous* (not evergreen) trees furnish a great variety of lumber. Spruce and hemlock, two cone-bearing trees, also grow among these highlands. The fine forests which once covered nearly all of Kentucky have been mostly cut so that this state produces only about one-tenth as much lumber as Mississippi or Alabama. Tennessee cuts several times as much as Kentucky. Original forests of native trees, which in many places cover the slopes of the mountains, are attractive features of mountainous Tennessee and eastern Kentucky. Some of these are now included in National Forests.

Coal Mining. — As the mountains of the western states have stored up metal treasures, so the highlands of Kentucky, Tennessee, and Alabama have stored up fuel treasures. First comes coal. The coal in these states is in layers which lie very nearly *horizontal* or level. Where streams cutting through the rocks have exposed the coal in the sides of the valleys, the mine is started where the **coal**

outcrops and works farther and farther back into the earth. This is called *drift* mining. The coal is hauled out in little cars, which run down the sides of the valleys, and dumped into buildings called coal *tipples*, built right over the railroads which usually run along the bottoms of the valleys. The cars are run by wire cables so arranged that the weight of the loaded car going down on one track pulls the empty car on the other track back up the hill to the mine opening. In some places, away from these valleys, shafts are sunk to the coal veins and the coal lifted out through the shafts. The coal mined in these states is soft or *bituminous* coal and much of it is used for making coke. Coal mining is a big industry in Alabama and Kentucky, which ship a large part of their output to other states. Tucked away out of sight in the beautifully forested hills of eastern Kentucky, there is said to be enough coal to supply the world for several hundred years.

Derricks scattered through the hills of Kentucky reveal another of that state's valuable fuels, oil. In addition, there is natural gas, which is nearly always found in connection with oil.

Other Useful Minerals. — Near Chattanooga, Tennessee, and Birmingham, Alabama, iron ore is mined. This gives these cities the raw material for their big iron and steel industries. The Birmingham district is second only to the Lake Superior district in the amount of iron ore mined. Tennessee also has two useful rocks, the quarrying of which is a big industry. One is phosphate rock, which is ground up to make fertilizer. The other is marble. Marble was once limestone, which has been changed into this hard and beautiful rock by heat and pressure.

Tennessee marble is used for building purposes and is well known all over the country. Alabama also quarries marble, some of which

THE COAL MINES OF KENTUCKY *Ewing Galloway*

Down in the narrow gash of valley, where the steep-sloped mountains join, the coal cars shuttle back and forth, disappearing along the winding tracks with their loaded cargoes.

is said by experts to be as good as the famous Carrara marble of Italy which has been so much used for making statues. Some of the marble in these states is beautifully colored. One kind is so plentiful near Birmingham that it is used as a flux in place of limestone in making pig iron.

Manufacturing in the East South Central States. — With their many farm products, forests, coal and other minerals, and abundant water power, these southern states have developed many manufacturing industries to supply their own needs and to produce articles for sale. Instead of sending away all their cotton, mills use part of the crop to make cotton goods both for home use and for sale. Alabama is one of our leading cotton manufacturing states. Most of the cotton mills

NORRIS DAM
This is primarily a storage dam, feeding water to the dams below on the Tennessee River.

are in the northern half of the state where coal is found and streams furnish water power. Tennessee is noted for special kinds of cotton goods and ready-to-wear articles. The silky material called *rayon* is another product, made either of wood pulp or of cotton *linters*, which are the short cotton fibers. One large mill in Tennessee makes rayon out of wood pulp; another not far away makes it out of cotton linters. Cottonseed mills making cottonseed oil and cake or meal are found in most of the cities of Alabama and Mississippi where much cotton is grown.

The manufacture of lumber into building material and furniture is another important industry. The many different kinds of woods in these states make it possible for them to produce a great variety of wood articles, and lumber mills are common.

Northern Alabama and eastern Tennessee use their coal, iron ore, and limestone to make iron and steel, from which they manufacture cotton gins, and oil well, saw mill, mining, and quarrying machinery. They also export many iron and steel manufactures.

Birmingham, the "Pittsburgh of the South." — As Pittsburgh has long been the center for the iron and steel industry in the North, so Birmingham has become the great iron and steel center for the South. Good coking coal, iron ore, and limestone, the three things necessary for making iron, are all found within a few miles of the city. This has helped to make Birmingham one of the greatest manufacturing cities in the southern states. Cast iron pipe, sugar mill machinery, cotton gins, mining machinery, stoves, grates, and radiators, and other heavy iron and steel articles are manufactured here, and shipped by the many railroads that enter the city. A short railroad connects Birmingham with Birmingport on the Black Warrior River 26 miles to the west, where barges run to Mobile, carrying

Courtesy Birmingham Chamber of Commerce
FURNACES AT NIGHT
The black shadows of the night roll back before the intense white light of the steel furnaces at Birmingham, Alabama.

EAST SOUTH CENTRAL STATES

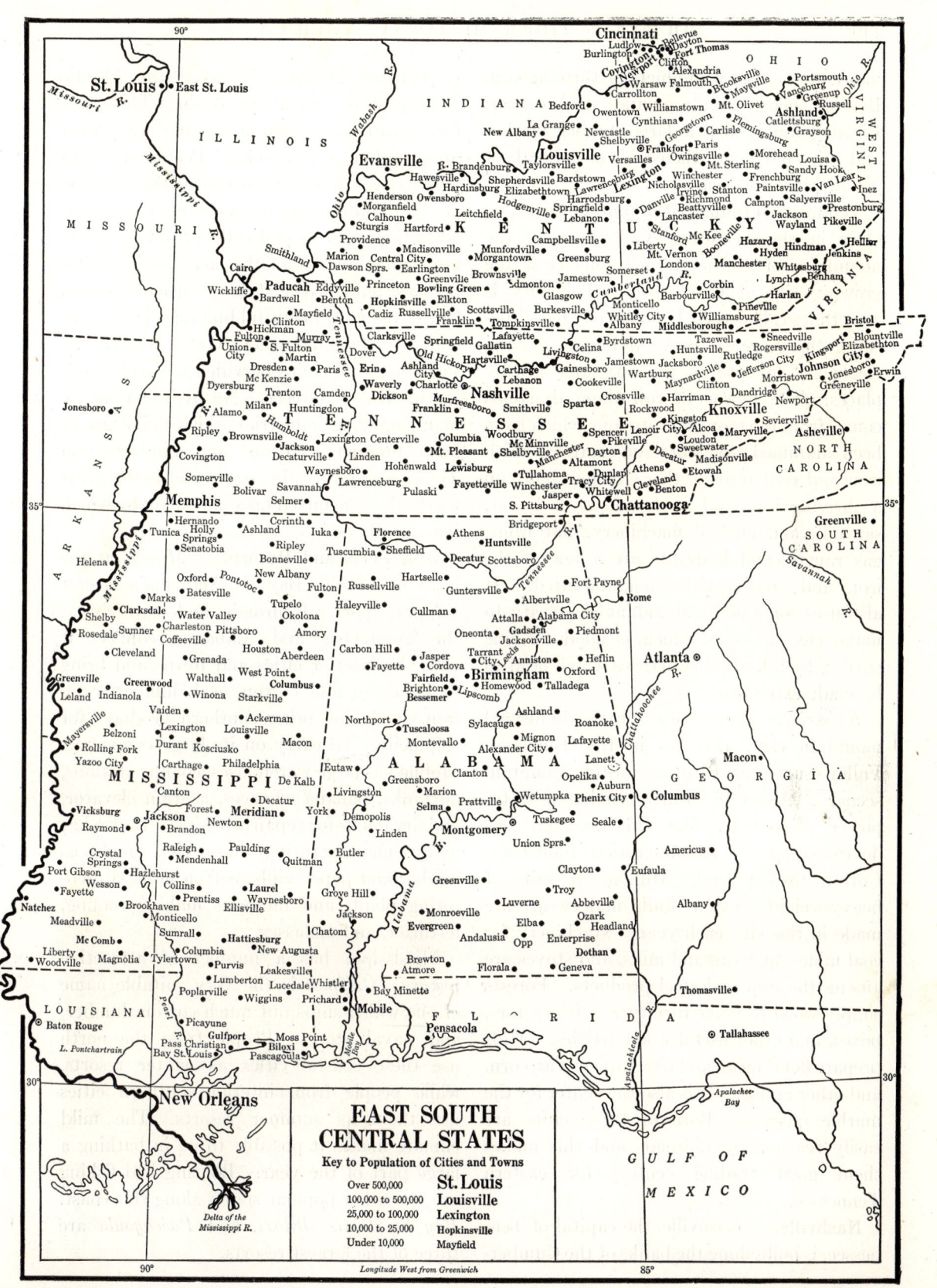

Key to Population of Cities and Towns

Over 500,000	**St. Louis**
100,000 to 500,000	**Louisville**
25,000 to 100,000	**Lexington**
10,000 to 25,000	Hopkinsville
Under 10,000	Mayfield

many of the heavy products of Birmingham. Besides being an iron and steel center, Birmingham is also a large lumber market and ships out many thousands of carloads of yellow pine each year.

Tennessee's Industrial Mountain Cities. — Over in the Tennessee Valley among the mountains of southeastern Tennessee is the growing city of *Chattanooga*. This city is sometimes called the "Dynamo of Dixie" because there are so many dynamos making electricity for use in the city and nearby places. The power to run these dynamos comes from the mountain streams which have been dammed to store up water. With iron and coal nearby, this city has built up a thriving iron and steel industry. Boiler, sawmill, and oil-well machinery, flat irons, gas ranges, and hydrants are a few of the iron and steel articles manufactured. It also uses some of its abundant electricity to make electric steel, which is good for fine cutting tools and other articles which need to be made extra hard.

Knoxville, Tennessee's other industrial mountain city, also lies in the Tennessee Valley surrounded by beautiful mountain scenery. Aided by nearby coal and water power, Knoxville, like Chattanooga, has developed many manufacturing industries. Cotton textiles lead. Millions of suits of heavy-weight cotton knit underwear are made in this city each year. Machinery for coal mines, quarries and mills, and stoves are among the iron and steel products. Forests supply wood to make furniture, refrigerators, boxes, and other useful wood articles. Mills prepare flour, meal, and feed from wheat, corn, and other grains. It is also the center for the marble quarries. Both of these cities are easily reached by railroads and this makes them good trading centers for eastern Tennessee.

Nashville. — Nashville, the capital of Tennessee, is built along the banks of the Cumberland River in what is called the Middle Tennessee or Nashville Basin. This is a fertile farming region much like the Bluegrass region of Kentucky. People of Nashville like to think of their city as the "Athens of the South." It is a great center for education, with several colleges and one large university. Many of the large public buildings are built in the style of ancient Athens. One of the most beautiful buildings is an exact copy of a famous ancient Greek temple, the Parthenon, the ruins of which are still standing in Athens, Greece. Nashville has many manufacturing industries which make use of farm products, cotton, and lumber from Tennessee and nearby states and is the great market for the mixed farming region by which it is surrounded.

Gulf Ports and Resorts. — *Mobile*, at the head of Mobile Bay, is Alabama's largest shipping port. Railroads and two rivers, the Tombigbee and Alabama, connect it with the interior cities and towns and bring to it cotton and cotton seed, lumber, coal, iron, steel, and other southern products for shipment. To carry on its large commerce, Mobile has large warehouses, coaling stations, oil tanks, banana wharves, a grain elevator, and dry docks for repairing ships. It also has many manufacturing industries, such as lumber and paper mills, cotton mills, a creosoting plant, and factories making roofing, fertilizer, and molasses.

Mississippi has a number of attractive resorts. *Gulfport* is the very suitable name of one which ships out much cotton, lumber, and naval stores. People from the north use these coastal cities as winter resorts, while people from interior southern cities use them as summer resorts. The mild climate makes it possible to go in bathing a large part of the year. Boating and fishing are two other popular sports along this coast. *Bay St. Louis*, *Biloxi*, and *Pascagoula* are three of the largest resorts.

FROM THE GOLDEN AGE OF GREECE
The Art Museum of Nashville is a copy of the hauntingly beautiful Parthenon of ancient Greece.

CHATTANOOGA

On the Cumberland Plateau is the famous Lookout Mountain from which, so it is said, seven states may be seen.

TEXTILE MILLS IN KNOXVILLE, TENNESSEE

The vast new hydroelectric resources of the state have increased the size of Tennessee's industries immeasurably.

HERE TODAY, GONE TOMORROW

With her smoke stack flaunting a thick, black banner of smoke, a river boat pushes and shoves two cotton-laden barges into the port of Mobile.

River Ports. — As you have already learned, the Mississippi River has played a part in the settlement and development of the East South Central States. Its tributary, the Ohio, has been most important to Kentucky, which has a number of cities using the river for transportation. Largest of all is *Louisville*, situated at a point where a low fall occurs in the Ohio and a dam helps to furnish water power for a large hydro-electric plant. Louisville is not only a large grain, livestock, and tobacco market, but it exports agricultural implements and has extensive manufactures. It is noted for its fine horse shows and, together with *Lexington* in the Blue-grass Region, is a trade center for that rich farming area. *Ashland, Covington,* and *Paducah* are other industrial cities on the Ohio. Locate all of these places on the map on page 131.

Memphis, the largest city in Tennessee, at the northern end of the Delta or Mississippi-Yazoo Basin, is a great shipping center for cotton, timber, and other products of this area and the fertile lowlands west of the Mississippi. Like *Vicksburg* at the southern end of the Delta, it is built on the high bluffs close to the river. *Greenville*, in the center of this region, and *Natchez*, farther south on the Mississippi, are both market centers and shipping ports for farm and forest products.

Two Industrial Capital Cities. — *Jackson*, Mississippi, and *Montgomery*, Alabama, are not only state capitals, but important railroad and trading centers. Both have many manufacturing industries. Cottonseed mills, fertilizer plants, lumber mills, and foundries are among Jackson's industries. Montgomery on the Alabama River, may be reached by river steamers most of the year. Located near cotton fields, coal and iron mines, and forests, and with cheap electricity furnished by water power from river dams, this city manufactures cotton goods, fertilizers, cars, paper boxes, furniture, and other lumber products.

THE EAST SOUTH CENTRAL STATES

Muscle Shoals, a Giant of Power. — The Tennessee River, a source of power back in the mountains of Tennessee, again becomes a source of power in northwestern Alabama, where in a series of rapids it falls about 134 feet within 37 miles. Here the United States Government has built the long Wilson Dam to store up the waters of the river and provide power for hydro-electric plants. When completed, this development will furnish over 600,000 horsepower, enough to do the work of 3,000,000 men. During World War II, the Government built a plant here and manufactured nitrates for use in making explosives by taking nitrogen from the air. Now it is planned to use this same plant to manufacture electricity and nitrates for use as fertilizer by the farmers.

Courtesy Memphis Chamber of Commerce
THE TWIN BRIDGES OF MEMPHIS
Two great iron bridges span the river carrying railroads and national highways across from Tennessee to Arkansas.

Mountaineers of Eastern Kentucky and Tennessee. — Among the mountains people once lived very differently from those in the cities or on the fertile farms of the lower lands. These hill farmers lived in rude log cabins built with their own hands, often containing only one room. They sometimes slept on cornhusk mattresses laid on the floor, going to bed when it became dark and getting up at

Ewing Galloway
WATER POWER AT MUSCLE SHOALS
Engineers have flung a great concrete dam across 4,500 feet of raging waters, a dam which holds the strength of the rapids in check, converting it into power for man's machines.

dawn. The farmer was fortunate if he had one mule or horse to help him with his work. For food, farmers depended mostly on what they could raise on the poor soil of the steep slopes. Corn and pork were their chief foods. With only poor roads, or none at all, leading to and from their mountain homes, many of these people had lived apart, knowing little of what was going on in the big world around

CABIN HOMES — *Ewing Galloway*

Astride his best possession, this dweller among the mountains of Kentucky rides along the bleak hillside that he calls home.

them. Many of them were unable to read or write. Children could not walk miles through such a country to attend school. But now a new world has come to their doors. Good roads are being built through these mountain lands; some of the people have obtained phonographs and radios; others are coming down to work in the factories, where they make good, self-reliant workmen. A new life is opening up for them — a life of books and newspapers and education, of music, electric lights, of automobiles, and, perhaps best of all, of mingling with people from other parts of the country.

National Parks. — Two National Parks are found in the East South Central States. One contains the Mammoth Cave, the underground wonderland of Kentucky, where water has dissolved the pure limestone and hollowed out a cave whose rock columns, pinnacles, and beautiful forms are the wonder of all who see them.

The boundary line between Tennessee and its eastern neighbor, North Carolina, runs along the crest of the most rugged mountains of the Appalachian Highlands. These are the Great Smoky Mountains, so named because of the smoke-like haze which often surrounds their summits. Their slopes are covered with forests which have never been cut and a great variety of shrubs and other native plants. To preserve the natural beauty of this region, the United States Government has set aside a large area to be known as the Great Smoky Mountain National Park, and roads are being built to open up this beautiful district.

Activities and Questions

1. Tell what varieties of crops the East South Central States can raise.

2. Name the chief rivers by which these states are drained. What are the rivers used for?

3. What is the leading money crop? Name others that are important and tell where they are grown. What is a money crop? a supply crop?

4. Name three states which yield much lumber and three which have vast coal deposits.

5. Which cities have important iron manufactures? Why?

6. What river in these states furnishes the most water power?

7. Add to your collection pictures of scenes and industries in these states.

8. In what ways has the Mississippi contributed to this section? What is meant by its flood plain?

9. Describe the raising and picking of cotton.

10. What is the boll weevil and how is it kept under control?

11. Name some products that are shipped north in winter and early spring.

MOUNT LE CONTE IN TENNESSEE

Among the ridges of the Great Smoky Mountain Range this peak stands out in all its wild beauty as one of the highest mountain peaks east of the Rockies. The highest is Mount Mitchell in North Carolina.

AN OVERHANGING CLIFF

Looking up at this mass of rock it seems as if the topsy-turvy cliff in the Great Smokies were striving to tip over and right itself.

STAR CHAMBER

Ewing Galloway

In the vast underground cavern known as Mammoth Cave is this chamber with its ceiling of black manganese studded with crystals of snowy gypsum.

12. Describe the raising and harvesting of tobacco.

13. What is hemp used for?

14. Tell about drift mining. How does it differ from shaft mining?

15. What useful minerals besides iron and coal are found in these states?

16. Where is the Blue-Grass country? For what is it best known?

17. From what is rayon made?

18. What different kinds of mills are found in these states? Why?

19. Name three important river ports in this section. Why is each important?

20. What are the capitals and largest cities in these states?

21. Tell about the power plants on the Tennessee River. For what purposes will they be used?

22. Describe the life of the mountaineers.

23. Name two National Parks found in these states.

24. Sketch a map of these states showing the main rivers and largest cities.

Tufted fields for agriculture and the mills of industry proclaim the New South. — *Ewing Galloway*

VIII. THE SOUTH ATLANTIC STATES

Different sections of our country are commonly spoken of as "The North," "The East," "The South," "The West," and "The Middle West." The South Atlantic States, which extend along the Atlantic coast from Florida to Maryland, together with the East and West South Central States, are called "The South." With their large areas of fertile land, abundant rainfall, and warm, sunny climate, the people of the South have always made a large part of their living by farming. They raised so many crops that this section became known as "The Agricultural South."

Statistics of the South Atlantic States*

State	Abbreviation	Area Sq. Miles	Population	Rank Area	Rank Pop.	Capital	Population	Largest City	Population
Florida	Fla.	58,560	1,897,414	21	27	Tallahassee	16,240	Jacksonville	173,065
Georgia	Ga.	58,876	3,123,723	20	14	Atlanta	302,288	Atlanta	302,288
North Carolina	N. C.	52,712	3,571,623	27	11	Raleigh	46,897	Charlotte	100,899
South Carolina	S. C.	31,055	1,899,804	39	26	Columbia	62,396	Charleston	71,275
Virginia	Va.	40,815	2,677,773	35	19	Richmond	193,042	Richmond	193,042
West Virginia	W. Va.	24,181	1,901,974	40	25	Charleston	67,914	Huntington	78,836
Maryland	Md.	10,577	1,821,244	41	28	Annapolis	13,069	Baltimore	859,100
Delaware	Del.	2,057	266,505	47	47	Dover	5,517	Wilmington	112,504

*1940 Census

Important Products

Florida: — Citrus fruits, vegetables, phosphate rock, naval stores, timber
Georgia: — Cotton, textiles, peanuts, naval stores, fruits
North Carolina: — Tobacco, cotton, textiles, tobacco products, furniture
South Carolina: — Cotton, textiles, tobacco, peanuts, live stock
Virginia: — Tobacco, tobacco products, textiles, peanuts, corn
West Virginia: — Coal, natural gas, iron and steel, lumber, glass
Maryland: — Vegetables, clothing, food products, fruits, oysters
Delaware: — Vegetables, canned foods, fruits, grains, chemicals

CHARLESTON, WEST VIRGINIA

This prosperous industrial and residential city, state capital and county seat of Kanawha County, is located at the junction of the Elk and Great Kanawha rivers. Its beautiful capitol building was completed in 1932. The city nestles snugly in the western foothills of the Appalachians

Park. In North Carolina, the Blue Ridge broadens out into a mass of high, forested mountains. The most rugged section of these is so beautiful that our Government has included it in the Great Smoky Mountain National Park which North Carolina shares with Tennessee.

West Virginia, the only state in this group not on

The New Industrial South. — But today the people of the South are also doing many other kinds of work. They spin and weave their cotton, make furniture from their lumber, rayon from their cotton and wood pulp, and iron and steel from their ores. Out of the iron and steel, they manufacture cotton gins and textile machinery to weave their cotton and rayon goods. They use water power from their streams to run their mills and factories, and farm machinery helps them grow bigger and better crops. Because of these great changes, this section is now often called "The New South" or "The New Industrial South."

Highlands and Lowlands. — Much of the area of the South Atlantic States lies in the broad, low Atlantic Coastal Plain. Next is a broad belt of rolling land known as the Piedmont. Piedmont means "the foot of the mountain." Rising sharply from the Piedmont is the long range known as the Blue Ridge. A large section of this range in Virginia is now included in the Shenandoah National

MAP OF THE SOUTH ATLANTIC STATES

Map Questions and Activities

1. What states are included in this group?
2. Locate the capital and some of the largest cities in each state.
3. What do the various colors of the map stand for? How do they show you where the lowlands are? the highlands?
4. Does the map suggest one or more reasons why some of the cities became large? Select several and give the reasons.
5. Is Washington centrally located in the United States? See map on pages 28 and 29. Why, then, is it the capital of our country?
6. Which one of these states has no seacoast? How does that affect it?
7. Does the map suggest any reasons why Florida is one of our greatest winter resort states? Locate some Florida resorts.
8. Are there any natural boundary lines in these states? What and where are they?
9. Where would you like to live in one of these states? Why?
10. What cities are near the fall line? Give reasons for so many cities being located here.
11. Why are most of the swamps along the coastal plain?
12. What two capes are at the entrance to Chesapeake Bay? In what state are they?
13. Name the leading rivers in these states. In what general direction do they flow?

Physical - Political
SOUTH ATLANTIC STATES
Scale of Statute Miles
0 50 100 150 200
State Capitals
Railroads
The type used indicates the relative sizes of towns and cities.
HEIGHTS IN FEET
Above 5,000
2,000 to 5,000
1,000 to 2,000
500 to 1,000
Sea level to 500
DEPTHS IN FATHOMS
Sea level to 100
Below 100
Longitude West from Greenwich
85°
80°
75°
40°
35°
30°
25°
ATLANTIC OCEAN
GULF OF MEXICO
BAHAMA ISLANDS
WEST VIRGINIA
VIRGINIA
NORTH CAROLINA
SOUTH CAROLINA
GEORGIA
FLORIDA
ALABAMA
TENNESSEE
KENTUCKY
OHIO
INDIANA
ILL.
PENNSYLVANIA
MARYLAND
DEL.
N.J.
DIST. OF COLUMBIA
Pittsburgh
Philadelphia
Baltimore
Washington
Richmond
Norfolk
Charleston
Raleigh
Columbia
Atlanta
Tallahassee
Jacksonville
Miami
Tampa
St. Petersburg
Savannah
Chattanooga
Knoxville
Nashville
Birmingham
Montgomery
Louisville
Cincinnati
Columbus
Indianapolis
Key West
Nassau
Mt. Mitchell ×6,684
GREAT SMOKY MTS.
CUMBERLAND PLATEAU
BLUE RIDGE
ALLEGHENY MTS.
Okefenokee Swamp
The Everglades
Lake Okeechobee
Florida Strait
FLORIDA KEYS
C. Hatteras
C. Lookout
C. Fear
C. Canaveral
C. Sable

the coast, is mountain and plateau land which has been cut by streams into steep-sided valleys so that there is not much level land in the state.

Rivers and Bays. — Notice on the map, page 149, the many rivers which flow down from the Appalachian Mountains. Their lower courses are often lined with swamps, of which little use is made, for the farms and homes are on the higher lands back from the rivers. Most of the rivers have wide mouths called *estuaries* (ĕs'tū-ăr-ĭz), which furnish good harbors for many of the seaports in the South Atlantic States. Rivers were the only highways for the first settlers, as there were no roads or railroads. While boats still run on the rivers, railroads and highways are now chiefly used both for traveling and carrying goods. Railroads and highways are easily built on the coastal plain and the Piedmont where most of the people live and work.

Many of the rivers empty into shallow bays or sounds. Along the coast of North Carolina and Florida, long islands off shore almost form an inland waterway. One of these islands in North Carolina forms a point called Cape Hatteras, and one of these long, narrow inland waterways in Florida is called Indian River.

The Fall Line. — The belt between the Piedmont region and the coastal plain is called the *fall line*, because there are low falls or rapids in the rivers where they descend from one region to the other. Many cities have grown up along the rivers at or near the fall line. There are two reasons for this: the falls furnish water power for manufacturing; and boats can run only as far as the falls. In Virginia and Maryland, the fall line is at the head of the estuaries where the rivers come down to sea level. Here the tide rises and falls as in the open sea, so the coastal plain sections of Virginia and Maryland are known as "tidewater" Virginia and Maryland. Many of the old plantations bordered on the tidewater streams so that the owners could have their own private wharves for shipping and receiving goods.

A NORTH CAROLINA RIVAL OF NEW ENGLAND *Ewing Galloway*
Dams like this one at Blewitt Falls mean water power, and water power means mills, and mills mean rapid growth of industry.

Florida. — Florida is the southernmost of the South Atlantic States. It was to this peninsula that the gallant explorer, Ponce de Leon, came in search of the "Fountain of Youth." He had been told by an Indian chief that in a beautiful island north of the West Indies was a magic fountain that would make any man who bathed in it forever young. In his search, he reached this "island" on Easter Sunday, 1518, and since the Spanish for Easter Sunday is "Pascua Florida" he named the "island" Florida.

Florida's Climate and Soils. — Florida differs from the other South Atlantic States. It is a peninsula about 400 miles long, with

The Seminoles

Life is very simple in this Indian village — a thatched hut under the shade of the tall palms, today like yesterday and tomorrow.

An Alligator Farm

These ugly reptiles look much better as pocketbooks and bags than slithering around in the mud and water.

The Dismal Swamplands

In the marshy swamp grass gleam hidden pools of sluggish water, and branches of dead trees protrude at grotesque angles like bleached skeletons. The Spanish Moss hanging in long festoons from the trees will be gathered, dried, and used in upholstering furniture.

the longest coast line of any state in the Union. The trip by rail and road from Pensacola to Key West is about as long as from New York to Chicago. The mild climate of the southern part enables people to farm the year around, even raising tropical fruits, and makes its seaside cities and beaches popular winter resorts. Some of the soil is fertile and the ground nearly level and often swampy.

G. W. Romer
AN EVERGLADES CANAL BARGE
Produce is towed out to where swifter transportation can carry it to waiting markets.

There are a great many lakes in Florida. The underlying rock in Florida is limestone, which when dissolved by underground water makes "sink holes," which form the beds of many of these lakes.

The Everglades. — South of Lake Okeechobee in southern Florida is a large swampy area called the Everglades, famous for tropical growths, giant ferns, and beautiful flowers. The wild animals that made the Everglades the hunting grounds of the Seminole Indians are growing scarce. The alligators for which this region has always been noted are now protected by law lest they be used up too quickly in providing skins for pocketbooks and handbags. Refuges have been established to protect the birds, many of which go north in summer and return to Florida for the winter.

Not many years ago, little was known about the interior of the Everglades, but now they are crossed by good automobile roads along one of which runs a canal. The material dug out to make the canal was used to build the road. With roads and canals running through them and airplanes flying overhead, the Everglades are no longer an unknown wilderness.

Farming in the Everglades. — Thousands of acres of the Everglades have been drained and turned into farm land. Canals and ditches have been dug and dikes built around the areas to be farmed. Huge pumps lift the water out of the ditches into the main canals which carry it off to the sea. If there is a spell of very dry weather, the pumps can be turned about to lift water out of the canals on to the land. The fertile soil of the Everglades is made up largely of *humus*, decayed vegetable matter. Large quantities of vegetables are raised on these drained areas and shipped to northern cities. Sugar cane, different kinds of grass for cattle, and some citrus fruits are also grown on these rich muck soils.

Florida Fruits. — With plenty of sunshine and nearly every day in the year a growing day in a large part of Florida, farmers raise many kinds of vegetables and fruits which they send to northern markets in the middle of the winter. If you live in the North, you may have seen Florida strawberries on sale in January. With their long growing season, thrifty Florida farmers can grow three or four different crops each year on their land.

All kinds of citrus fruits, from the big grapefruit to the little kumquat, are grown in Florida. It grows vast quantities of delicious oranges and leads all the states in the production of grapefruit. Tangerines and lemons are also leading products. Most of these fruits are raised in the central part of Florida known as the Lake District, where there is very little danger from frost. Picking and packing the citrus fruits ready for shipment give work to many people. The fruit is picked, sorted, and carefully packed, each piece being usually wrapped in soft paper.

With its mild, sunny climate southern Florida grows tropical fruits which can be raised in few other parts of the south. Three of the most important are the avocado (ăv-ō-cä′dō), the papaya (pä-pä′yä), and the mango. The avocado is often called the "alligator pear." Like the olive, it is rich in oil and tastes more like a vegetable or a nut than a fruit. The papaya is a delicious melon-like fruit which grows along the stem of the tree, and is sometimes called the "tree cantaloupe." The mango may be cooked and preserved in a number of ways, its bright color and rich flavor making it fine for dessert. Tons of avocados are shipped from Florida to northern markets, but the papaya and the mango are often too delicate to ship.

Other Products of Florida. — One of the newer industries in Florida and other Gulf States is growing tung nuts for producing tung oil. This is used in making paints and varnishes. Mixed with rosin, it makes a waterproof varnish which even boiling water will not destroy. The tung oil tree is a native of China and bears clusters of nuts shaped somewhat like small apples. Each nut contains five or more seeds which are pressed by machines to take out the oil. Mississippi, Louisiana, and Florida produce most of the tung nuts grown in our country.

Florida's bulkiest product is a most useful mineral called phosphate rock. This state produces much of the phosphate rock now mined in the United States. Most of it is used in making fertilizer, but in the magic hands of the chemist, it also helps to refine sugar, puts the "phiz" into soda fountain drinks, and in baking powder makes our biscuits and cakes light and fluffy. The port of Tampa ships millions of tons of phosphate rock each year to European countries where farmers make much use of fertilizers.

Florida Fisheries. — Florida, with her long coast line on both the Gulf of Mexico and the Atlantic Ocean, is one of the leading southern states in fish. About 500 kinds of fish are found in the waters around Florida, but only a few of these are good food fish.

John Kabel
COCONUTS FROM FLORIDA
The odd-shaped, cumbersome seeds of the coconut tree are planted just as any seeds. From the three dark spots at one end of the nut, its "eyes," seedlings will sprout.

Fishing boats go out from Pensacola sometimes as far as Mexico in search of red snappers, Spanish mackerel, and mullet. Three shellfish, oysters, clams, and shrimps, are also caught. Oyster beds are most plentiful in the shallow Apalachico′la Bay region, and one of the largest hard-clam beds in the United States lies near the coast of southwestern Florida. St. Augustine, the oldest city in Florida, is noted for its shrimp industry.

Florida has one fishery that is not found in any other state. That is the sponge

SEA AND SUN AND SAND *Ewing Galloway*

Forgotten are the cold and ice and snow of northern climes as one lies on the warm white sands of Miami Beach — a cloudless sky above and blue water lazily lapping away at the shore's edge.

fishery. Sponges grow in shallow, rather warm water, fastened to some object on the bottom of the sea and have to be cut or torn loose. If the water is not too deep, the sponge fisherman may use a long pole with a hook on the end, but in deeper water, they put on diving suits and go down to the bottom. Florida sponge fishing is carried on largely by a colony of Greeks living at Tarpon Springs, the center for this industry. Greek sponge divers who first settled here learned their trade in the Mediterranean Sea. The older men train their sons and other young men to carry on the work.

Winter Resorts in Florida. — With the Gulf of Mexico to the west and the warm Gulf Stream near the eastern coast, southern Florida never has cold winters like those in the North. This climate draws many people to Florida to spend the winter. Some have bought homes here; others stay at the magnificent hotels in the resort cities. Two of the most popular winter resorts are *Miami* on the southeastern coast and *St. Petersburg* on the western coast. When the people in the North are wearing fur coats, people at Miami may stroll along the beach clad only in bathing suits.

Old Ponce de Leon never found his "fountain of youth," but today thousands of tourists go to Florida every year to rest, enjoy the bathing, and grow young again. There seems to be magic in the wonderful sunny climate of Florida. With this tourist trade Miami has grown to be the second largest city in Florida. It also serves southeastern Florida as a seaport, and is an airmail center with passenger planes making

DAYTONA BEACH AT EVENTIDE
A perfect automobile road, fifteen miles long, of hard, white sand.

A Winter Pastime

Astride the rails of the million dollar pier, the tourist fisher folk of St. Petersburg try their luck in the rippling waters of the bay.

Publishers' Photo

One Who Walks on the Ocean's Floor

In his clumsy suit and heavy helmet this Greek diver searches the ocean's depths at Tarpon Springs for sponges of all sizes.

A Day's Catch

Scorning fishing from the pier these residents of St. Petersburg sailed out into the bay and cast their lines in deeper waters, to be rewarded with a catch like this.

regular trips to Havana, Cuba. Its airport is also a base for South and Central American flying routes. The people of St. Petersburg advertise their city as the "Sunshine City" because it has so few days when the sun does not shine. *Daytona Beach* and *Palm Beach* are other popular seaside resorts on the eastern coast of Florida. The beach at

COTTONSEED TANKS — *Publishers' Photo*
Cottonseed is stored in these tanks in North Carolina until ready to be sent to the oil plant. After the oil is extracted the remainder is used as cattle fodder.

Daytona is so level and hard that record-breaking automobile runs have been held here.

Florida Seaports. — *Jacksonville*, the largest city in Florida, is the leading seaport as well as a railroad and manufacturing center. It is not directly on the coast, but the broad, deep mouth of the St. Johns River gives it an excellent harbor. Jacksonville ships out much lumber, rosin, turpentine, and other products from northern Florida.

Tampa, on the west coast near St. Petersburg, is near the citrus fruit area and the phosphate deposits, and ships large quantities of these products. It has many cigar factories, which make it the leading Florida city in this industry. *Pensacola*, besides being a base for the Gulf fishing industry, ships lumber, rosin, and turpentine from the pine forests.

Key West is the southernmost city in the United States. It is built at the end of a long string of islands called the Florida Keys. One of the most remarkable railways in the world connected Key West with the mainland of Florida until 1935 when the tracks were so damaged by a hurricane that the line had to be abandoned. Long bridges built to carry this railroad have now been altered to form part of an automobile highway between Key West and the mainland. Key West is noted for its manufacture of cigars from tobacco which comes from Cuba.

Mixed Farming in the South. — The South Atlantic States can raise every crop that can be grown anywhere in the United States. Certain sections have become known for the production of special money crops such as watermelons, peaches, apples, and peanuts. But most of the southern farmers do not depend on one crop. They practice mixed farming, and try to have more than one product for sale. It is easy for them to do this because they have a long growing season and plenty of rain. The United States Government and the State Governments conduct Agricultural Experiment Stations, bringing in plants and seeds from other parts of the world. Whenever they find a useful plant that grows well, they distribute seeds or plants to the farmers, and in this way the new crop gets started.

Cotton Growing and Manufacturing. — Cotton, the wonder crop of the South, has been the leading money crop of Georgia and South Carolina ever since the invention of the cotton gin over 150 years ago. North Carolina also grows much cotton, but tobacco is the most valuable crop in that state. Virginia and Florida raise only a small quantity of cotton. Most of Virginia is too far north and in Florida there is often too much rainfall during the picking season. This discolors the fluffy, white cotton and also interferes with the picking.

Cotton growing was much easier in these states before the cotton boll weevil came.

TAMPA OF THE WEST COAST
Courtesy Tampa Chamber of Commerce

Freighters from the ocean lanes crowd their way into this busy port on Tampa Bay where they unload the old and load on the new cargoes.

Courtesy Tampa Chamber of Commerce
THE FLAVOR OF AN HAVANA

Rows of bins where day after day the hand-rolled cigars are made for which Tampa is famous. Notice the light, airy room and the comfortable dress of the workers.

Ewing Galloway
PHOSPHATE MINING

A slow-moving dredge scoops up the rock, the dirt and sand are washed away, and the rock is loaded on to cars and carried to the *tipple*, high in the background.

Now the plants must be dusted with poison, either by hand or by airplane, to destroy the boll weevils. Cotton is usually planted and cultivated with machines, but it has to be picked by hand. Georgia and the Carolinas not only grow cotton but together with Massachusetts they are now the leading states in its manufacture. Most of the mills are run by hydro-electric power developed in

Courtesy Norfolk Advertising Board
"BAREFOOT BOY WITH CHEEK OF TAN"
This young tobacco farmer is holding a bunch of tobacco leaves, corded ready for curing.

the Piedmont region, but many are run by steam, using coal as a fuel. North Carolina, with over 400 mills, leads the other states of the South.

Southern mills make chiefly knit underwear and the coarser woven goods such as sheeting, pillow tubing, denim, and gingham, though they make some fine voiles, lawns, and dainty handkerchiefs. Many of the workers are native-born Piedmont and mountain farmers who are glad to work in the mills because life in the cities and towns is more comfortable than in their mountain homes.

Tobacco. — Tobacco, like cotton, is nearly always grown to be sold. It has been a money crop in Virginia for over 300 years, ever since the day when Sir Walter Raleigh introduced into England the smoking of tobacco. Smoking was so strange to the Englishman of the 16th century that when Raleigh's servant first saw his master smoking, he threw a bucket of water over him, because he thought he was on fire. When, in 1649, the Virginia settlers advertised their colony in England, they told of all the wonders of this new land, ending with " tobacco is our great crop."

Virginia's neighbor, North Carolina, now produces more tobacco than any other state. Much is also grown in South Carolina and smaller amounts in Georgia, Florida, and Maryland. Some of the tobacco in Florida and Georgia is raised under cheesecloth held up by poles and wires. This shades the plants from the hot sun and produces fine leaves for cigar wrappers, while other tobacco is used as cigar filler. Tobacco raised under the cheesecloth is known as "shade" tobacco. Viewed from an airplane, these cheesecloth-covered fields look like patches of snow.

Compared with cotton fields, tobacco fields are small. But the value of an acre of tobacco is usually several times that of an acre of cotton. Tobacco growing requires much hand labor, and the farmer's family sometimes help take care of the plants and harvest the leaves. Tobacco takes so much potash and other plant food out of the soil that it soon makes it poor unless it is rotated with other crops or fertilized. The kind of soil affects the quality of the tobacco, so different kinds are grown in different places in the South Atlantic States. Some of it is air cured and some is flue cured or fire cured. Naturally, where tobacco is such a large crop, its manufacture into cigars, cigarettes, smoking and chewing tobacco, and snuff is an important industry in many of the cities. Richmond, in Virginia, and Durham and Winston-Salem in North Carolina are noted for their large tobacco factories.

Peanuts. — Fresh-roasted peanuts at the stand on the street corner, salted peanuts

IN GEORGIA *Publishers' Photo*
A tractor like a street sprinkler sprays the young cotton plants with protecting poison.

IN SOUTH CAROLINA *Ewing Galloway*
When the cotton is ripe the whole plantation turns out and helps to pick it.

EIGHT BALES AN HOUR *Ewing Galloway*
Mule-drawn loads of cotton feed this "ginnery" at Hawkinsville, Georgia.

IN NORTH CAROLINA *Ewing Galloway*
A beautiful site for this up-to-date cotton mill which gets its power from the winding river.

AT NORFOLK, VIRGINIA *Norfolk-Portsmouth Chamber of Commerce*
Bulging bales of cotton are piled on the docks, waiting to be loaded into the gaping holds of freighters tied alongside.

PEANUTS!
Publishers' Photo
It won't be long before the drying peanuts will appear on the whistling stands of the cities' peanut vendors.

and peanut brittle at the candy store, peanut butter in the grocery — you find them everywhere. Tons and tons are needed to supply the demand, and the South Atlantic States grow most of them. Southwestern Georgia extending over into Alabama is one large peanut region. Northeastern North Carolina and southeastern Virginia is another. Peanuts grow on the underground stems of the plants just below the surface. They are planted in rows and cultivated with mule- or horse-drawn cultivators. In the fall, the plants are pulled and stacked in the field to dry. Then they are threshed or picked off by hand, and the vines often used for feed. Peanuts are fine food for swine, which may be turned into the field and allowed to harvest the crop for themselves.

Georgia's Leading Food Crops. — Pecans, one of our most delicious nuts, are grown in several of the southern states and southern Georgia is an important center. Pecan growers find ready markets in all parts of our country for this favorite nut.

Another crop in which Georgia leads is watermelons. These may be grown in other states farther north, but Georgia watermelons, large and juicy, are early on the market and sell readily during the hot summer days.

In sweet potatoes, also, Georgia is very important with about 7,000,000 bushels each year. They do not require a very rich soil, are relatively inexpensive to raise, and when carefully dried may be kept for months and shipped long distances.

Peaches are another of Georgia's well-known crops. These are shipped north in early summer long before northern peaches are ripe.

Truck Farming on the Coastal Plain. — Raising of vegetables and small fruits is one

U. S. Department of Agriculture
FIELD BEANS AND PEANUTS
Each dot on this map stands for 1000 acres. Peanuts are a southern crop, but most of the field beans are grown in the northern states. Select two large peanut-growing areas and tell what states they are in. What northern state grows most field beans?

U. S. Department of Agriculture
VEGETABLES FOR SALE
Each dot on this map stands for 500 acres of vegetables, including cabbage, cantaloupe and muskmelons, lettuce, onions, sweet corn, tomatoes, and watermelons. Growing vegetables for sale is called truck farming. Many of the truck-farming areas shown on this map are clustered around large cities. Where is the largest vegetable-growing area in the eastern states? What southern states grow vegetables and send them to northern city markets during the winter?

GEORGIA PEACHES

What fun to pick the luscious, warm-skinned fruit from the low peach trees!

Baskets of ripening fruit are packed for shipping to northern cities.

Ewing Galloway *Ewing Galloway*

GEORGIA PECANS AND SORGHUM CANE

Poison must be thoroughly sprayed over the nut trees to insure a bumper crop.

Out of these leafless stalks will flow gallons and gallons of sweet, sticky molasses.

GEORGIA WATERMELONS

Among the watermelon vines is a grand place to be! One good tap on that green shell and all the sweet, juicy, pink pulp would lie revealed.

161

AN APPLE A DAY —
This motionless sea of apples awaits shipment from Winchester, Virginia, the apple center of the state.

of the biggest industries on the coastal plain. Level land, and sandy, easily worked soil with plenty of rain all favor this industry. Fast trains or motor trucks rush the products to city markets before they have a chance to spoil. Beginning with Florida, which sends green vegetables and strawberries to the North in January, each state takes its turn at supplying the northern markets.

One of the largest centers for this industry is on the peninsula east of Chesapeake Bay, where almost every kind of fruit and vegetable is grown. The grower has a choice of railroad, boat, or motor truck to get his products to market, or he may have them canned. Canneries which put up fruits and vegetables during the summer and fall may can oysters and fish during the winter season.

The Valley of Virginia. — West of the Blue Ridge in Virginia is part of a long lowland extending through the Appalachian Highlands from New York to Alabama. This Great Appalachian Valley is known in southwestern Virginia as the Valley of Virginia. In the northern area of the state, the well-known Shenandoah Valley is a part of it. It is not level, but consists of low ridges with long, fertile valleys between. The Great Valley was a highway for early travelers and today it is a route for roads and railroads. It is a good farming region, with underlying limestone rock which makes a fertile soil. The famous blue grass grows here and furnishes pasture for cattle, horses, and sheep. This ridge and valley region extends over into West Virginia and is a great apple-growing center. The apples are carefully sorted and the best ones selected for shipment, the poorer ones being used for making cider or vinegar.

Luray Caverns. — Among the interesting attractions of the Shenandoah Valley are the Luray Caverns, caused by underground water dissolving the limestone. Long, pointed rock forms (stalac′tites) hang from the ceilings in many of the rooms while others (stalag′mites) stand up from the floors. In other places, masses of colored rock resembling seaweed,

LURAY CAVERNS, VIRGINIA
An underground gallery where the stalactites glimmer and sparkle — pink, blue, amber, and snow white — and the tall limestone columns ring with a hollow, bell-like tone.

A MINER'S COTTAGE *Courtesy Bituminous Coal Institute*
Who could ask for a nicer little cottage than this one in a West Virginia valley?

coral, and other curious shapes cover the surface, and sparkle as the light shines upon them. The Caverns are lighted by electricity and cement walks and steps make it easy for the visitor to walk through and view the wonders of this fairy underground palace.

Farming in West Virginia. — Mountainous West Virginia is usually thought of as a land of forests and coal mines, but even in this mountain state, many of the people depend on farming for a living. The best farming regions are the northeastern part in the Great Appalachian Valley and the lands along the Ohio River. It is a land of mixed farming, because a single farm may have several kinds of soil suitable for different uses. The rolling lands may be used for grains, the lower slopes of hills for apple and peach orchards, and the higher places for pasture or hay lands, or they may be left to grow up into woodland. Farmers in many of these southern states have their wood lots to supply them with wood for fences and fuel.

Corn, the leading grain in all of the South Atlantic States, also leads in West Virginia, but wheat, oats, rye, and buckwheat are also grown. Farmers near cities grow vegetables and small fruits for the local markets. Hay is a big crop here as it grows well on the slopes and helps to hold the soil in place. Of farm animals, cattle are the most plentiful, as they can graze on the hillsides which are too steep or have too poor a soil to grow crops; moreover, it is easy to raise the other foods they need, and there is always a demand for dairy products. Many sheep also roam over the hills of West Virginia.

Fisheries of the South Atlantic States. — Fisheries of the South Atlantic States differ from those farther north; instead of the cod, flounder, haddock, herring, and mackerel, southern fishermen catch red snapper, mullet, sheepshead, pompano, and blackfish. In the many shallow bays along the coast the fish feed

BOATLOADS OF FISH *Ewing Galloway*
Often a fisherman's seine will haul up from out of Chesapeake Bay ten thousand wriggling, flapping, twisting, frightened fish.

upon the tiny vegetables and other fish food brought down by the rivers. Many are caught in these waters, where they come to feed and to lay their eggs. Some are taken by seines; others by gill nets. In the gill net, the opening is just large enough to admit the head but not the body of the fish. When the fish tries to back out, it is caught by the gills, and held fast.

Canning of shrimp is one of the most important industries along the coasts of Georgia and the Carolinas. Oysters are found all along the coast, but the great center for this industry is Chesapeake Bay. Annapolis and Baltimore are two centers for the oyster industry, where many are shipped out fresh and the rest canned. Some are shipped in the shell, while others are "shucked," that is, the shells are removed. Familiar sights around the oyster canneries and packing houses are the huge piles of oyster shells, some of which are thrown back into the water while others are ground up to make fertilizers.

Publishers' Photo
TAPPING FOR TURPENTINE
When the pine trees of the southern forests are tapped, cone-shaped basins catch the gum as it oozes slowly down the rough bark.

Forests and Forest Industries.—Forest trees in the South Atlantic States are of three main kinds. In the swamp lands of Florida and the Dismal Swamp of southeastern Virginia and northeastern North Carolina, the leading lumber tree is the cypress. It usually grows in water, so the lumbermen have to stand in boats to saw through the trunk. The cypress logs are generally floated or towed out on canals or natural water lanes in the swamps. Cypress trees form a large and valuable part of the lumber cut in Florida, which has some of the world's largest cypress mills.

The greatest lumber-producing forests of these southern states are the pine forests which grow on the coastal plain. Yellow or southern pine is one of the most used woods in our country. The northeastern states which use so much lumber depend on these southern pine forests for a large part of their supply. Knowing that these pine forests will soon be gone unless new ones are allowed to grow, southern lumbermen are now *reforesting* (planting young trees) cut-over areas and protecting them from fire.

Lumbering is easy on the coastal plain where the land is quite level and the mild winters make it possible to work comfortably all the year. Tractors, horses, and mules are all used in "snaking" the logs to the railroads or main roads, by which they are taken to the sawmills. Tall, straight, slender young pine trees are much used for telegraph and telephone poles. Others to be used for railroad ties are dipped in creosote to make them last longer.

Pine trees in these southern forests furnish two other very useful products, turpentine and rosin. The trees are cut and cups adjusted to catch the resin or *gum* as it runs from the trees. The gum is then collected in barrels and hauled to the turpentine still where it is made into turpentine and rosin. Turpentine and rosin are called *naval stores* because when pine tree products — pitch, tar, turpentine, and rosin — were first produced, they were used mostly for *calking* (closing tightly and making waterproof) the seams of the wooden ships then in use, and for preserving the rigging and painting the ships. Hence every ship kept these supplies in store. Trees may be used for "turpentining" for a number of years before they are cut for lumber. Today a great amount of these naval

A Scene near White Sulphur Springs

Ewing Galloway

Rank after rank of oak and southern pine make these Allegheny Mountain slopes a living forest from base to peak, broken only where a golf course lies unrolled like a bolt of soft green velvet.

John Kabel

MIDDLETON GARDENS, CHARLESTON

Wide sloping lawns, a lazy, curving river, camellias and spice bushes, sunken gardens and rose gardens, azalea walks and reflective pools make these oldest of gardens one of the loveliest garden spots in America.

CYPRESS GARDENS, NEAR CHARLESTON

A great water forest of giant cypress trees has been turned into a mysteriously beautiful garden, where rare and gay flowers bloom to reflect their flaming colors in the dark waters.

stores are secured by cutting the trees into fine chips and then distilling out the materials. Georgia now produces more of these products than any other state and the port of Savannah leads in their export.

Piedmont and mountain forests contain many different kinds of trees which shed their leaves, such as the oak, maple, birch, beech, red gum, hickory, chestnut, and poplar.

THE SILVER GRAY QUARRY *Ewing Galloway*
Out of the hillside at Tate, Georgia, are cut great square slabs of marble cake — chocolate and vanilla mixed.

These are commonly called hardwoods to distinguish them from the cone-bearing trees whose wood is called soft wood. Animals are largely used both for "skidding" the logs and hauling them to the mills. On the steeper slopes, chutes or slides often carry the timber down.

Southern forests furnish wood for making such articles as furniture, parts for automobiles, handles for tools, *veneer* (thin boards) for use in fruit and vegetable containers, and barrels.

Minerals. — From the older Appalachian Mountains which run through most of these states, millions of tons of granite are quarried each year. Granite is a hard rock which takes a high polish, and is much used for monuments and buildings. Marble, a favorite stone for statuary and ornamental building purposes, is quarried in northern Georgia and sent to many other states. Its color ranges from white to almost black.

Stored up in the forested hills of West Virginia are two of our most useful minerals, coal and petroleum. West Virginia is a leading state in the production of *bitu'minous* or soft coal. Southwestern Virginia produces a small quantity. Sometimes the coal outcrops in the side of a valley and the miners dig back into the hill; in other places shafts must be sunk down to the beds and the coal is lifted out through these openings. Bituminous coal is generally smoky, but some of West Virginia's coal is of a fine, hard quality which burns with so little smoke that it is called "smokeless coal." Railroads do a big business carrying the coal from West Virginia to other states.

In the western and northern parts of West Virginia the production of petroleum and natural gas is a big industry. The presence of these fuels helps to build up other industries. Oil is pumped through pipes to refineries which make gasoline, kerosene, naphtha, and vaseline. Natural gas is one of the finest of fuels for heating homes, cooking, and making glass and china. A great deal of gas from West Virginia is piped into other states.

South Atlantic Seaports. — Each of the South Atlantic States has one or more seaports which play a large part in the trade of the state. *Jacksonville* and *Miami* are

THE SOUTH ATLANTIC STATES

Florida's main gateways. In Georgia, the old city of *Savannah* shares the state's trade with *Brunswick*, farther south along the coast. Savannah is about 18 miles from the ocean, but the river furnishes a good harbor. It leads in the export of cotton and naval stores, and sends out lumber, tobacco, and fertilizer. The winters are so mild that Savannah is a popular all-year resort.

Charleston, South Carolina's interesting port with its fine old homes and attractive gardens, is built on a peninsula lying between the mouths of two rivers. It exports much cotton, cotton goods, fertilizer, and other South Carolina products. Nitrogen from coke ovens, fish from the ocean, waste products from meat-packing plants, cottonseed meal, phosphate and potash from southern and western states all are collected here and made into fertilizer, for which the city is noted.

Wilmington, on the broad estuary of the Cape Fear River, serves North Carolina as a port and is also a resort. It sends out cotton goods, lumber, and furniture.

Virginia has one of the largest harbors of any of these states. It is called *Hampton Roads*. *Norfolk*, *Portsmouth*, and *Newport News* all face this harbor. Several trunk railways come to these cities, linking them with all parts of the country. Railroads leading to the coal fields of West Virginia and southwestern Virginia bring large quantities of coal here for shipment to other places along the Atlantic seaboard and to other countries. Immense piers have been built especially to take care of the coal.

Wheat, tobacco, and petroleum products are other leading exports for which these ports have provided special storage buildings and handling facilities. Newport News is a great shipbuilding center.

Baltimore. — Maryland's main port is Baltimore, on an arm of Chesapeake Bay.

NORFOLK, VIRGINIA *Fairchild Aerial Surveys*

Many are the boats which put into this busy harbor at the mouth of Chesapeake Bay — sailing ships and freighters, warships and steamers. For it is not only an important coaling station and oil-bunkering port, but a naval station as well. And the sightseers and pleasure seekers eagerly go ashore to visit the famous Virginia Beach and Old Point Comfort, Fortress Monroe and the Navy Yard, St. Paul's Church (1737), and Hampton Institute.

Baltimore has a fine deep harbor into which very large ocean vessels may come. With the sea in front and a rich country back of it to furnish coal, oil, and raw materials of many kinds, Baltimore has become one of the greatest manufacturing cities and seaports of the eastern United States. It is noted for its big iron and steel industries, its copper refining, its large canning industry, its production of spices, porcelain, and fertilizer, and its clothing and printing industries. It has over 2000 manufacturing plants. So many tomatoes and other vegetables and fruits are raised near Baltimore and brought there that it has become one of the greatest canning centers in the country. In addition, it makes the tin cans. When through with the vegetables and fruits in the late fall, the plant may then keep busy by canning oysters.

Where other large cities have built apartment houses for their people, Baltimore has

WILMINGTON, DELAWARE

Dallin Aerial Surveys

From the Indian village Minquas, Wilmington has grown to be the first city of Delaware — a city proud of its municipal buildings, its parks, its schools, and its Du Ponts.

continued to build single homes. Rows of brick houses with marble steps and trimmings are an attractive feature of the city.

On account of its central location between North and South, Baltimore has always played an important part in the history of our country and is now very active in the coastal as well as foreign trade. Ships are built as well as repaired here. Products from the interior, such as coal and wheat, are brought here for shipment.

Wilmington, Delaware. — Nearly half of the people of Delaware live in Wilmington, the chief port and manufacturing city. The Delaware River gives Wilmington a splendid harbor. The farming country back of it supplies its many canneries with vegetables and fruits and in turn makes use of fertilizer manufactured there. Coal, easily brought from Pennsylvania, supplies it with fuel.

The leading industry in Wilmington is the manufacture of explosives, chemicals, dyestuffs, and paints and varnishes. Rayon and motion picture films are also made here. Some of these articles are made from the same kinds of raw materials, and, up to a certain stage, they are prepared in very similar ways. Here is where the chemist, working almost like a magician, takes the bunch of cotton fiber and makes out of it a deadly explosive, or a beautiful piece of rayon, or a film for a motion picture, just as he wishes.

Industrial Cities. — The capitals of some of the South Atlantic States are also busy manufacturing cities. *Atlanta*, at the foot of the Appalachian Mountains in northern Georgia, is a great railway center and carries on a big business in selling and distributing goods as well as collecting and shipping out state products. Cotton goods, cotton gins, fertilizers, machinery, and lumber are a few of the many manufactures. Water power helps to run its industries.

Columbia, the capital of South Carolina, is a railroad center with hydro-electric power and some manufacturing industries. *Greenville* is noted for its large cotton and rayon mills.

North Carolina's capital, *Raleigh*, is named after Sir Walter Raleigh, who made several attempts to colonize in this region. North Carolina leads in tobacco, cotton, and rayon goods, but also makes furniture, machinery, building materials, and many other things. Two large manufacturing cities are *Greensboro* and *Charlotte*. *Asheville*, located among the mountains in western North Carolina, is a famous resort. The abundant water power

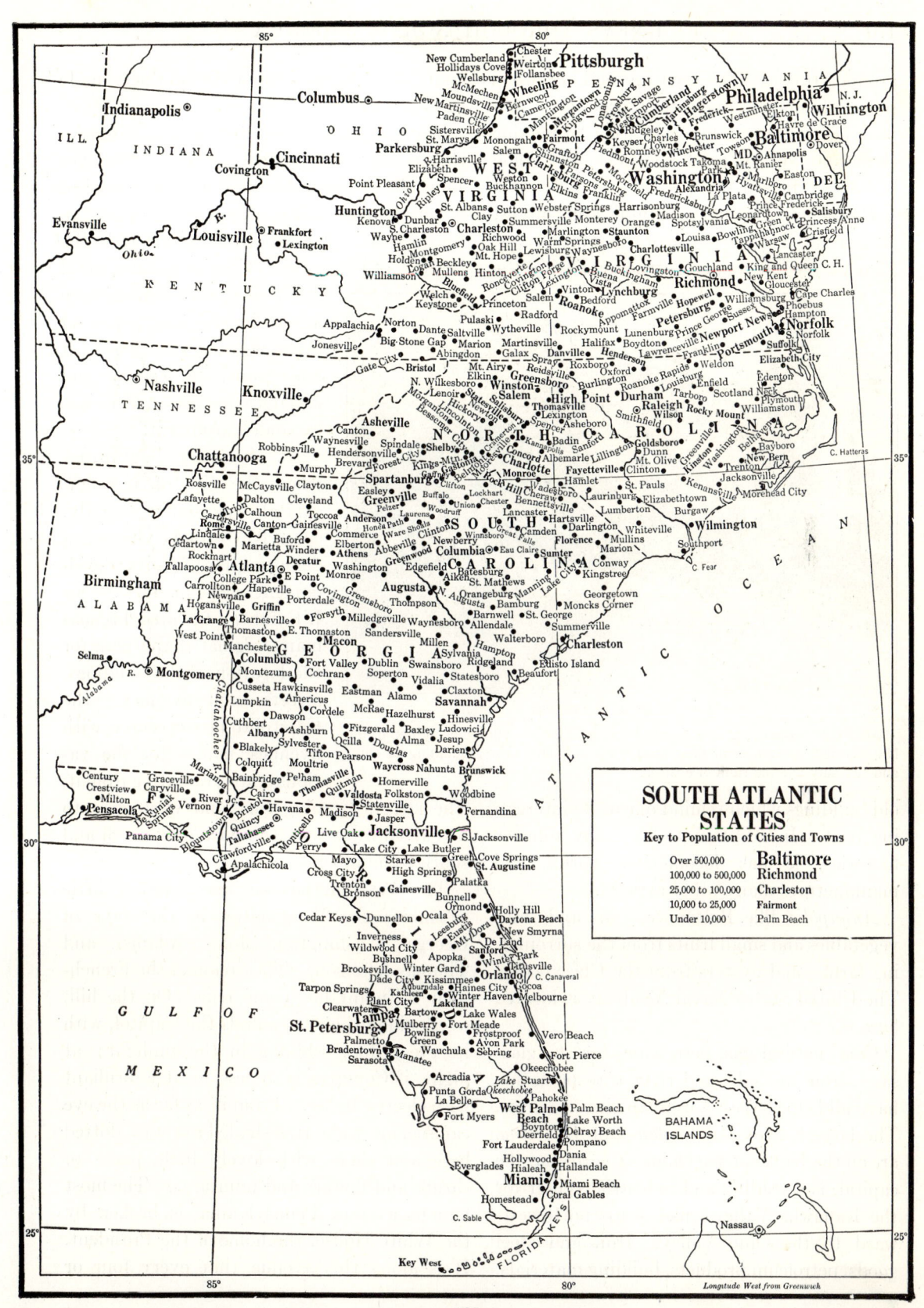

SOUTH ATLANTIC STATES
Key to Population of Cities and Towns

Over 500,000	**Baltimore**
100,000 to 500,000	**Richmond**
25,000 to 100,000	**Charleston**
10,000 to 25,000	Fairmont
Under 10,000	Palm Beach

around this city is used in making wood pulp, aluminum, and other products. Deposits of *kā'olin*, a fine clay used in making china and pottery, are found near by. Some kaolin is exported.

Richmond, Virginia's capital and largest city, situated on the banks of the James River, mingles its tall modern structures with the old buildings which remind one of its interesting past. In addition to its many tobacco factories, it has locomotive works, and manufactures many other articles.

Annapolis, like Baltimore, cans and ships vegetables and small fruits from the surrounding farms, and oysters from the Chesapeake. The United States Naval Academy is located here.

Coal, natural gas, petroleum, forests, glass sand, iron ore, salt, and river transportation have all helped West Virginian cities to grow. The largest two, *Huntington* and *Wheeling*, are on the banks of the Ohio. *Charleston*, the capital, is a trading and industrial center for the Kanawha Valley which leads northwestward to the Ohio Valley. Iron and steel goods, petroleum products, building materials, and chemicals are some of the products made in these cities.

Washington. — This seat of the American Government belongs to no state, but lies along the Potomac River in a strip of land of seventy square miles, originally belonging to Virginia and Maryland, and now called the District of Columbia. Chosen as the capital of the new nation of thirteen states in the early days of Washington's presidency, it has grown in beauty and loveliness as the nation has expanded around it.

At the very beginning, when the site of the new capital was but a muddy, sparsely settled village, a definite plan for its development was made. Major L'Enfant, a talented Frenchman, originated the plan for the location of the buildings, streets, and avenues — the Capitol to be the center, with avenues, named for the various states, radiating from it. The streets running east and west were to be named by letter; those running north and south by number.

The Washington we know today little resembles the Washington in the days of George Washington, John Adams, and Thomas Jefferson. The dream of the Frenchman L'Enfant has come true. On the hill, overlooking the city, stands the Capitol, with its great dome shining in the sunlight; at night, if Congress is in session, it is brilliant with electric lights. From it, as far as the eye can see, are wide, tree-shaded avenues, dotted here and there with lovely little parks of shrubs and flowers and fountains. The most famous avenue, Pennsylvania, is broken by the White House, the home of the President. It is along this avenue that every four or

JUNE WEEK AT ANNAPOLIS

After four years of hard study and iron-clad discipline the midshipmen of the Naval Academy march in their final dress parade before graduating to ships and sea duty and the rank of ensign.

HISTORIC HARPER'S FERRY

Courtesy Baltimore & Ohio Railroad

The village, made famous by John Brown's raid, lies just where the waters of the Shenandoah and Potomac rivers meet at the foot of the Blue Ridge Mountains.

IN THE "LAND OF THE SKY"

Above the Piedmont Plateau rise the Blue Ridge Mountains, and beyond, the Black Mountains and the Great Smoky Mountains with their steep cliffs and lofty peaks. Up in these densely wooded mountains of western North Carolina, where the scenery is beautiful beyond words and the climate most healthful, is Asheville, a noted year-round resort.

THE CAPITOL AT RICHMOND

Jefferson, while minister to France, obtained a model of an old building in southern France erected by the Romans, in Greek temple style, and from that model was completed, in 1792, this public building. It was here that Aaron Burr was tried for treason; and it was here that Jefferson Davis had his offices as President of the Confederate States of America.

eight years, as the case may be, the new and the old president ride side by side; one to take his oath of office, the other to say farewell.

Near the White House are many interesting buildings: the Treasury building — gray and grim; the Pan-American building, with its lovely courtyard of tropical flowers and birds; the Corcoran Art Gallery; and the Smithsonian Institution, where many famous things are preserved, including Colonel Lindbergh's airplane "Spirit of St. Louis."

There are many other interesting buildings — the Department of Commerce occupying an entire block, where several thousand employees work; the Union Station, where many visitors arrive and depart daily; the Folger Shakespeare Memorial Library; the office buildings of the Senate and the House; the Supreme Court building; the Congressional Library, on whose shelves can be found any book published in the country. In the northwestern part of the city, around circles whose names are famous, are the beautiful homes of Washington's élite and the imposing embassies of the foreign nations. Near by, also, is Rock Creek Park with its sixteen hundred acres of wild and lovely country.

Washington cannot be described in words. It is too beautiful, and too full of associations with the great things in American history. But no one could mention Washington without trying to describe the majestic beauty of the Lincoln Memorial, that shrine where an impressive figure of the martyred President sits and gazes out at the city where he spent the last momentous days of his life. In front of him rises the tall, narrow shaft of Washington Monument mirrored in the pool at his feet; behind him stretches the long white bridge to Arlington Cemetery and the home of Lee — as if a silver chord went from the heart of the man, who loved all parts of his country so well, to those who fell "that this nation might live."

Courtesy U. S. Army Signal Corps

ABRAHAM LINCOLN

"In this temple, as in the hearts of the people for whom he saved the Union, the memory of Abraham Lincoln is enshrined forever."

Activities and Questions

1. What are the leading money crops of the South Atlantic States? Why?

2. Where are most of the cotton mills located? Why?

3. Describe the Everglades.

4. What fruits does Florida export most? Why?

5. Why does Florida grow tropical fruits?

6. In what product does West Virginia lead all other states? Why?

7. Describe the Luray Caverns.

8. Which state has one of the longest coast lines in the United States?

9. Where in these states are oysters found? sponges? What use is made of them?

10. Why are most of the manufacturing cities at the edge of the Piedmont region?

11. Collect and bring to class pictures of cotton and tobacco fields, orange groves, and other scenes in these states.

THE CAPITOL
In one wing is the House of Representatives, in the other the Senate.

THE WHITE HOUSE

The most interesting house in the whole United States, where Presidents have lived and labored. Every day visitors eagerly crowd into the basement rooms and up to the famous East Room on the first floor, with its glittering crystal chandeliers, its gold piano, and its romantic memories.

ARLINGTON BRIDGE

The long, white road that leads from the city where heroes have marched — Grant, Dewey, Pershing — to the place where heroes sleep their long, last sleep; from a city of well-known and famous men to the tomb of the Unknown Soldier, before whose shrine a soldier paces, keeping eternal watch.

174 JOURNEYS THROUGH NORTH AMERICA

12. Make a list of the chief rivers in these states. How are they used?

13. Name some of the leading exports. Give reasons in each case.

14. What are the chief products of Georgia? of North Carolina? Give reasons in each case.

15. Sketch a map of these states, putting in the rivers and chief cities.

WHAT THE LAND IS LIKE *Courtesy Wilkes-Barre Chamber of Commerce*
A view of Wilkes-Barre, where the Susquehanna flows through Wyoming Valley.

IX. THE MIDDLE ATLANTIC STATES

The colonies which formed the original states of our Union stretched along the Atlantic coast from New Hampshire to Georgia. They formed a long row, facing the Atlantic Ocean, the great highway for all. With Maine and Florida, which were afterwards added, these states are usually divided into three groups: (1) the North Atlantic States, generally called New England; (2) the Middle Atlantic States; and (3) the South Atlantic States.

The Middle Atlantic States. — The Middle Atlantic States are New York, New Jersey, and Pennsylvania. Because of its central position, Pennsylvania is likened to the center stone in an arch and is called the "Keystone State." It does not border directly on the Atlantic Ocean, but the Delaware River and Bay make a good waterway for its large port of Philadelphia.

Many people live in these Middle Atlantic States. New York has more people than any other state in the Union; Pennsylvania is second; New Jersey ranks second in numbers of people per square mile. Most of the people are crowded together in the cities and towns which cluster around the great centers like New York, Buffalo, Philadelphia, and Pittsburgh, or are scattered along the Mohawk Valley and south of Lake Ontario.

What the Land Is Like. — If we were to travel by airplane from Philadelphia to Pittsburgh along the route of the Pennsylvania Railroad, we should first pass over the rolling land of the Piedmont region, which extends along the Appalachian Highlands from New York to Alabama. Streams wind about among the low hills, and patches of woods mingle with the fields. Cities and towns dot the countryside, never more than a few miles

STATISTICS OF THE MIDDLE ATLANTIC STATES*

State	Abbreviation	Area Sq. Miles	Population	Rank Area	Rank Pop.	Capital	Population	Largest City	Population
New York	N. Y.	49,576	13,479,142	29	1	Albany	130,577	New York	7,454,995
New Jersey	N. J.	7,836	4,160,165	45	9	Trenton	124,697	Newark	429,760
Pennsylvania	Pa.	45,333	9,900,180	32	2	Harrisburg	83,893	Philadelphia	1,931,334

*1940 Census

IMPORTANT PRODUCTS

New York: — Clothing, dairy products, vegetables, printing, meats, fruits
New Jersey: — Refined petroleum, textiles (silk), vegetables, fruits, smelted copper
Pennsylvania: — Coal, iron and steel, silk, iron and steel goods, dairy products

apart, and all are woven together in a network of roads and railways.

Less than an hour's ride brings us to Harrisburg, the capital of Pennsylvania, on the banks of the Susquehanna near where it comes out from the mountains. The Susquehanna River is nearly a mile wide at Harrisburg. With its tributaries it drains central Pennsylvania and a part of south central New York. Its valley was the hunting ground of the Susquehannocks, the Indian tribe after which the river was named.

Just north of Harrisburg, the railroad crosses the river and runs along its western bank. The valley of its tributary, the Juniata, has some of the most beautiful mountain scenery in Pennsylvania. Long, forested mountain ridges, with narrow valleys between, stretch out for miles from both sides of the river. These ridges continue until we reach Altoona, west of which is a valley from which rise the Allegheny Mountains. The railroad climbs this steep front by a wide bend known as the "Horseshoe Curve." Within this curve lies a picturesque man-made lake, the reservoir from which Altoona gets its water supply.

The Middle Atlantic States

Map Questions and Activities

1. Name the states in this group.
2. Find and name the capital and the largest city of each state.
3. Does the map suggest one or more reasons why New York City has grown to be the largest city in the United States?
4. Does it also suggest one or more reasons why the following cities have become large: Philadelphia? Pittsburgh? Buffalo?
5. Trace with your finger the course of the New York State Barge Canal.
6. What two of the Great Lakes border on these states?
7. What do the various colors of the map mean?
8. What mountains do you find in these states?
9. What great river forms a part of the boundary line between New York State and Canada? What other important river is in New York State?
10. Where would you like to live in one of these states? Why?
11. Look at the map and give several good reasons why New York is so much larger than Philadelphia.
12. How do ocean steamers get to Philadelphia?
13. What river runs between New Jersey and Pennsylvania? Name several cities on this river.
14. What part of this section lies in the Atlantic Coastal Plain? Which state is almost wholly within this plain? How does the map show this?
15. How has the location of Pittsburgh caused it to become a great city and a leading steel center? What rivers come together here to form the Ohio River?

NEW YORK CITY And LONG ISLAND

Physical - Political
MIDDLE ATLANTIC STATES

Scale of Statute Miles
0 10 20 30 40 50   100

⊙ State Capitals — Railroads

HEIGHTS IN FEET
- Above 5,000
- 2,000 to 5,000
- 1,000 to 2,000
- 500 to 1,000
- Sea level to 500

DEPTHS IN FATHOMS
- Sea level to 100
- Below 100

The type used indicates the relative sizes of towns and cities.

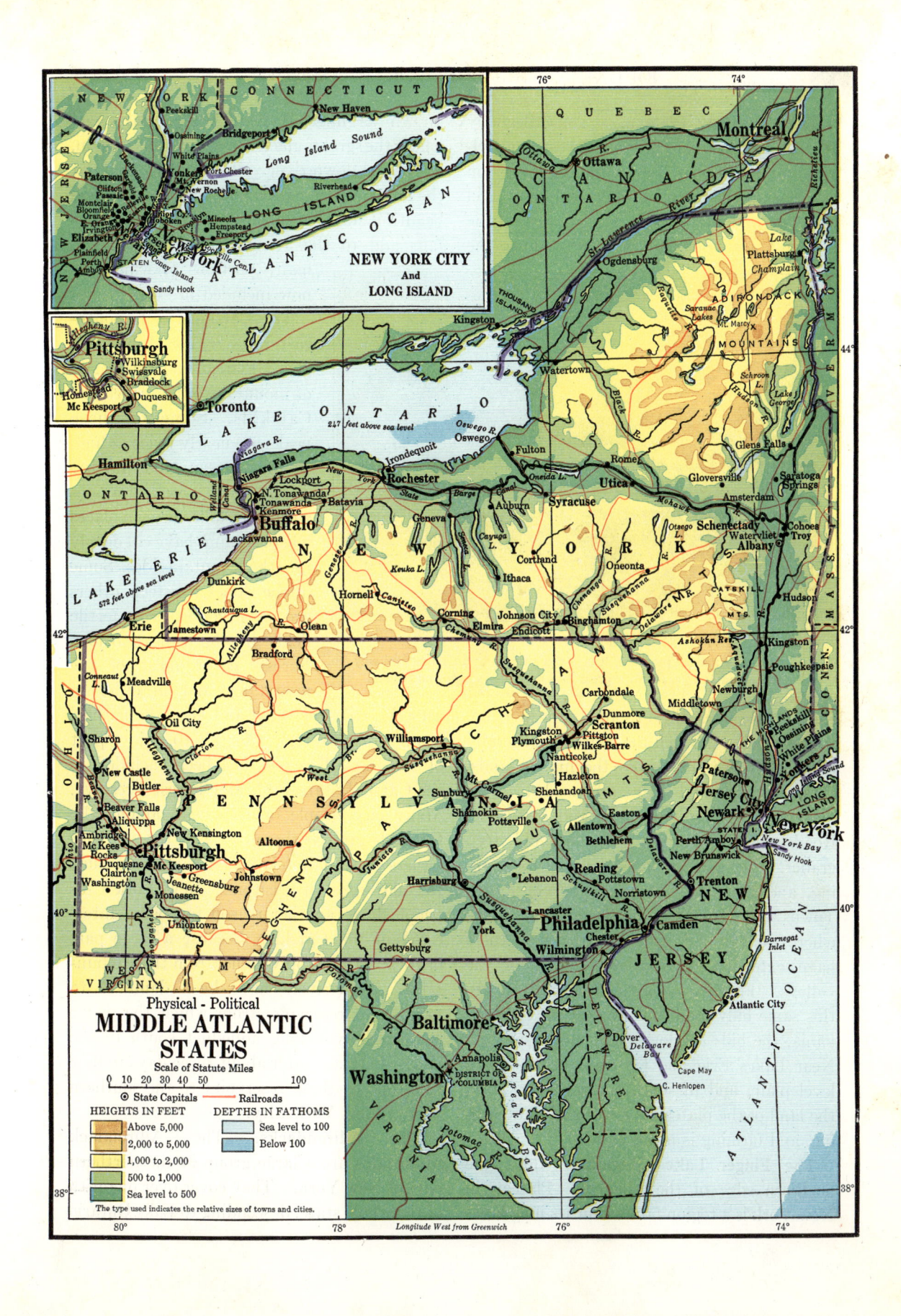

Longitude West from Greenwich

The Allegheny Plateau. — The Allegheny Plateau makes up much of northwest Pennsylvania and southern New York. This region is so cut up by streams that scarcely any level land can be found except small places on the higher lands and narrow plains along the rivers. Most of the streams run in deep, winding valleys, which the railroads generally follow. Where they cross the higher lands, cuts, fillings, and bridges are needed. This makes railway building hard and expensive. Roads wind and turn in order to avoid steep grades. The gentler slopes are used for farming, and there are many patches of forest. Towns are generally found in the valleys where the railroads run and many of them have extended up the steep sides of the valleys. From Altoona to Pittsburgh we see this same hilly land but in western Pennsylvania, the hills are lower and more rounded. Near Lakes Erie and Ontario the land is a level plain, and in south central New York, the land of the plateau is lower and more rolling, and farming is much easier.

The Finger Lakes Region. — Along the northern edge of the Allegheny Plateau in New York is a region famous for its long lakes known as finger lakes. Many years ago, when the great glacier covered this region, ice moved down river valleys and scoured out the long, narrow basins now occupied by these beautiful lakes. Numerous gorges and waterfalls add to the attractions of this region, many portions of which are now included in state parks.

The Catskills. — In southeastern New York, the Allegheny Plateau ends in a mass of mountain peaks called the Catskills. Some of these peaks are nearly twice as high as the plateau lands farther west. Deep, rocky ravines with waterfalls occur in places where streams have cut deeply into the mountain sides. Some of the slopes are steep, others are more gentle, with fertile fields in the valleys below. Forests cover most of the mountains, and in order to preserve some of these and keep the natural beauty of this region for all to enjoy, part of the Catskill region has been included in the Catskill State Park and Forest Preserve. Many city people own cottages among the Catskills and go there to spend the summer. Others stay at hotels which have been built to take care of visitors. New York City people have another reason for being interested in the Catskills, because a large part of their water supply comes from these mountains. Two rivers have been dammed to form large reservoirs from which the water is carried by a long aqueduct south to the city. It takes water about three days to flow from one of these reservoirs to the southern part of New York City.

The Adirondacks. — The Adirondack Mountains are a large group in the northern part of New York. They cover over one-fifth of the whole state, descending to Lake Ontario

WEST OF ALTOONA — *Fairchild Aerial Surveys*
The railroad, in a playful moment, leaves the straight and narrow pathway up the mountain and curves in a great loop to girdle a man-made lake.

STORM KING MOUNTAIN

Where the sound of Rip Van Winkle's little men at bowling still reverberates when the storm clouds gather, the Storm King Highway winds along the river.

WATKINS GLEN

Publishers' Photo

This great natural wonder is located near the head of Seneca Lake, known far and wide as one of the gems of the Finger Lakes of New York State.

KENSICO DAM AND RESERVOIR

Publishers' Photo

From its storage place in the Catskills, through miles of pipes, flows the water that is used by New York City's millions.

WHERE "WINTER SPORT" IS KING
Ewing Galloway

The Lake Placid Club is a favorite winter resort for those who love the feel of clear, cold mountain air, the thrill of skiing, and the rhythmic movement of ice skating.

and the St. Lawrence Valley on the west and north, to Lake Champlain on the east, and on the south to the Mohawk Valley which separates them from the Catskills. Many of the peaks are over 4000 feet high. Highest of all is Mount Marcy, with an altitude of 5334 feet. The Indians called it "Tahawus," meaning "Cloud Piercer." Many beautiful lakes lie scattered among the mountain peaks. Some of these are favorite resort centers, such as Lake Placid and Saranac Lake, which are popular alike in winter and in summer. People go there to enjoy winter sports such as skiing, tobogganing, hockey, and skating. Like the Catskills, the Adirondacks are heavily wooded and contain the finest forests in the state. Much of the best timber has been cut, but lumbering is still an important industry. The central part of the Adirondacks is now a state park, a playground for all who wish to go there and enjoy the cool air in the summer, hike over the mountain trails, or fish in the many lakes and streams. Good automobile roads lead through the mountains, and railroads also reach some of the resorts.

Highlands and Lowlands of New Jersey. — Like most of the Atlantic States, New Jersey has both mountains and coastal plain. Long mountain ranges extend from southern New York across northern New Jersey into Pennsylvania. The Delaware River, which forms the boundary between New Jersey and Pennsylvania, cuts across one of these ranges in a deep, picturesque gorge known as the Delaware Water Gap. Southeastern New Jersey is largely a sandy plain, covered in places by pine forests. The coastal region is low and often swampy, with long sand bar islands along the coast. These provide the

THE DELAWARE WATER GAP
Ewing Galloway

High in the Pocono Hills, where the Delaware River cuts through forested mountains, is the beautiful Kittatinny Hotel, a famous summer resort.

SPLIT ROCK FALLS

All through the Adirondacks little streams tumble merrily along over the rocky feet of steep cliffs — dropping now and then in a sheet of rainbow-spangled mist.

LAKE PLACID
Ewing Galloway

Breathless stillness — the snowfields shot with black shadows — rows of evergreens — houses crouching close to the ground — and over all the magic of silvery moonlight.

A BECKONING ROAD IN THE ADIRONDACKS
Ewing Galloway
As the road winds on its way toward Loon Lake it has that "Come hither" look that lures us on.

many bathing beaches and seaside resorts which make New Jersey the largest coastal resort region in the world. Millions of people come here each year to swim, sail, fish, or just simply rest from the noise and heat of crowded cities. Atlantic City, the largest and best known of all, is built on an island separated from the mainland by a narrow strait and tidal meadows. Motor busses, trains, automobiles, and boats all carry the thousands of people who visit this city every day in the year. Large hotels take care of the many visitors. One of the interesting features here is a wide boardwalk, several miles long, fronting the ocean where visitors may walk, or ride in a wheel-chair pushed by a porter.

Cape May, at the southern end of New Jersey's Atlantic shore, is one of the oldest resorts in the United States. Its most important industry now is fishing. Bass, mackerel, tuna, and other fish bring the fishermen a large sum of money each year. Not many miles away, on Delaware Bay, is Bivalve, whose name suggests the oyster industry for which it is noted.

Long Island. — Long Island furnishes most of New York's coast line. This long, narrow island extends about 125 miles eastward from the southern point of New York with Long Island Sound separating it from Connecticut on the north. The north shore of the island is a long row of peninsulas with bays between. Boating is a popular sport here and in summer the blue water of these bays is flecked with the white sails of pleasure boats.

The northern half of Long Island is hilly. These hills are masses of sand, gravel, and clay, left by the great glacier which reached just this far and then melted back. The natural beauty of the landscape is marred in many places by immense gravel pits where thousands of tons of sand and gravel have been taken out for building purposes.

Southern Long Island is a low, nearly level plain, bordered with swamps and shallow bays. Long sand bars next to the ocean are used as bathing beaches and seaside resorts. Thousands of people visit these resorts on warm summer days to escape the heat of the city and enjoy the many amusements provided for them along the shore. The best known is Coney Island, a name familiar to all New York boys and girls.

The western third of Long Island is all part of the great city of New York, but the rest of the island has many towns and villages, and much of it is in large estates and small farms. Many people who work in New York live in towns on Long Island and *commute*, that is, they travel back and forth daily to their work. Railroads sell monthly tickets at reduced rates and run extra trains during the morning and evening when the commuters are going to and coming from work.

Farming in the Middle Atlantic States. — Hay is a leading crop almost everywhere in these states, where there is plenty of rainfall. Grass and clover grow well on the steeper slopes where it is hard to use farm machinery. In the plateau regions the waste land with thin soil is often used for pasture. Much milk and butter are needed to supply the many cities, so dairying is one of the big industries. New York City alone uses over 3,000,000 quarts of milk each day. Part of this huge supply is brought by train from the northern part of New York and Vermont, part from northern New Jersey, Pennsylvania, and nearer places.

Dairy cows are scattered on farms all over these states. The St. Lawrence and Champlain valleys, the central and western parts of New York, eastern Pennsylvania, and northern New Jersey all have many dairy cattle. New York is second among the states in numbers of dairy cattle. It was once the leading cheese-producing state, but now most of the milk in all of these states is shipped to the cities to supply the demand for fresh milk. There are many large dairy farms, but most

ATLANTIC CITY

The shallow water and the long beach, with its striped tents and colored umbrellas, offer pleasure and enjoyment to throngs of people during all the hot days of summer.

SURF-CASTING OFF MONTAUK POINT

It takes a lot of practice to become perfect with this heavy pole — for casting against the ocean breezes is exacting and tiring.

LONG ISLAND SOUND

A sunny day, a steady wind, a white-winged boat, and a skipper's heart beats high.

The "Cow-Go-Round"

At this dairy plant at Plainsboro, fifty cows enter the platform, one by one, are showered with warm water, and their udders wiped with individual towels. The rubber-lined cups of the milking machine are then attached and the milk forced into glass jars above the cows. In 12½ minutes the job is done and the cows are released and returned to the barns, while others take their places.

of the milk is produced where mixed farming is practiced.

Mixed Farming. — Most of the farmers in the Middle Atlantic States practice mixed farming. In the plateau regions of New York and Pennsylvania, many of the farms include different kinds of land. Hilly and stony land is used for pasture or for growing trees. In the higher plateau regions, the fields are generally too narrow and steep to cultivate, but in the fertile valleys wheat, corn, oats, hay, and potatoes are common field crops.

Elizabethtown, Pennsylvania

A motor-driven tractor crawls along the potato hills and harvests the many-eyed vegetable instead of the old-fashioned hand-digging methods.

Each farmer usually has an orchard of apple trees, and perhaps a few peach, pear, and cherry trees, and grapevines. A garden supplies green vegetables for the family. Root vegetables such as turnips, carrots, and parsnips are raised and stored away for winter use. A few horses, cows, swine, and occasionally sheep, and a flock of chickens complete the plateau farm, which furnishes most of the foodstuffs needed by any one family, with a surplus of some crops for sale.

In southeastern Pennsylvania is a part of the corn and winter wheat region. Though corn and wheat are leading crops, this, too, is a mixed farming region. Fertile soil makes this one of the finest in our country. Farmers rotate their crops and add fertilizers to the soil so that it keeps on producing good crops year after year. One of the crops for which this region is noted is tobacco, which is rotated with other crops so that it does not destroy the fertility of the soil. They also keep dairy cattle and other farm animals. Sometimes beef cattle from the West are shipped to this region to be fattened before being sent to market.

Fruit Raising in the Great Lakes Region. — In passing over the lake plains of New York on our air trip across the United States, we saw many orchards and vineyards. The water of the lakes does not heat so fast nor cool so rapidly as the land. In the spring, the cooler air from the lakes keeps the trees from blossoming until danger from frost is past. In the fall, the winds from the lakes are warmer than those blowing over the land and prevent frost until after the fruit is fully ripened. Apples, peaches, and pears are most plentiful along Lake Ontario while grapes lead along Lake Erie. Many grapes are also raised on the shores of the Finger Lakes in central New York. The grapes raised in the eastern United States are mostly eaten fresh or used for making grape juice and wine. They are too soft and juicy and do not contain enough sugar to make raisins.

Truck Farming in New Jersey and on Long Island. — The level plain of southern and eastern New Jersey is mainly used for grow-

TRUCK FARMING IN SOUTHERN NEW JERSEY *Ewing Galloway*
One of the gardens in this "garden state" has yielded basket after basket of big yellow sweet potatoes.

HAY FOR FARM ANIMALS *U. S. Department of Agriculture*
Each dot on this map stands for 10,000 acres of hay. Much hay is needed to feed the many animals in the United States, and hay of some kind is generally one of the leading crops in every farming district. A cool, moist climate is good for hay. What kind of hay is usually grown in the irrigated districts of Nevada, Utah, Arizona, and other dry states of the west?

ing various vegetables, such as okra, beans, peas, tomatoes, sweet potatoes, and cabbages. Many of these products find a ready market in New York, Philadelphia, and the cities of northern New Jersey, but large quantities are canned. Camden, on the Delaware River opposite Philadelphia, is a great center for the canning of soups and vegetables.

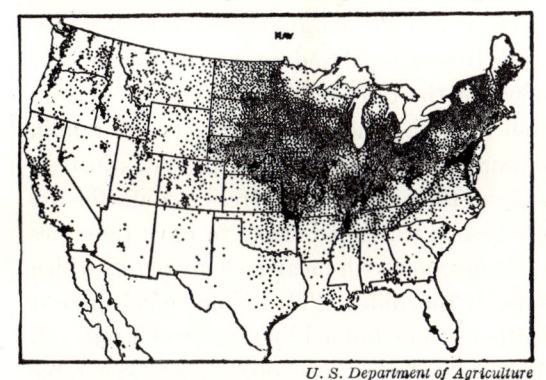

Near the coast, among the pines west of Barnegat Bay, is a clearing where cranberries are grown. A cranberry bog, like a rice field, has to be located where it can be flooded. Dikes and ditches are necessary to inclose and drain it. Most of the year this cranberry area is relatively dry but during the winter it is flooded to protect the plants from cold. A cranberry bog then looks like a lot of little, man-made lakes. Flooding also protects the plants from certain kinds of insects. The berries are picked by means of a scoop which has prongs close enough to catch the berries as the scoop is run through among the plants. New Jersey is next to Massachusetts in the production of cranberries, many of which are prepared as sauce and canned so that we may enjoy this delicacy all through the year.

The soil of the pine barrens is poor for most crops, but seems just right for producing large, sweet blueberries. Quantities of these are carefully raised in the pine region of New Jersey which produces most of the cultivated crop of these sweet berries. They are care-

MAN-HIGH BLUEBERRY PLANTS *Ewing Galloway*

Southern New Jersey farmers are cultivating the lowly blueberry and turning into the markets of eastern cities large and juicy and richly flavored berries.

fully packed in boxes and covered with transparent paper. On account of their unusually large size, they bring high prices in the market.

Southern Long Island, like southern New Jersey, is a nearly level plain with sandy soil which is fine for growing vegetables. The great demand for all kinds of vegetables in New York City has caused this industry to lead all other farming industries on Long Island. Produce can be readily packed, loaded in large motor trucks, and taken straight to market.

In addition to truck farming, many chickens and ducks are raised in New Jersey and on Long Island. Long Island has some of the largest duck farms in the world.

Forests and Lumbering. — The fine forests which once covered most of the Middle Atlantic States have been nearly all cut. Naturally, the lower lands were cleared first as the settlers wanted to use the land for farming. But even the forests which now cover the highland areas of the Allegheny Plateau and the mountainous regions are mostly second growth, many of the older trees having been cut or destroyed by forest fires.

Lumbering was once a big industry in the Allegheny Plateau region, but it is no longer of great importance. The logs were hauled or skidded over the snow to the streams. In the spring, when the creeks and rivers were high, the timbers were fastened together in large rafts and floated to market. Lumbermen built small shanties on these rafts and lived in them while guiding the rafts downstream. These rafts were a familiar sight on the Allegheny River when lumbering was more important than it is now.

In the Adirondacks, the rivers are still used for floating the logs to the sawmills which are usually near the edge of the forests, but much of the lumber is now hauled by railroads and trucks. The making of wood pulp, for which smaller trees can be used, is one of the leading industries in the Adirondack region.

Tanning of Leather. — The bark of certain trees, such as the oak, hemlock, and chestnut, contains a large amount of *tannin*, which is used in tanning leather. Many tanneries were once scattered among the forests where these trees were abundant, but there are fewer now, for the trees have been largely cut, and the tanneries now use extracts of tannin obtained from many different woods instead of from the bark of these trees. With the use of these extracts it is easy to have tanneries in connection with meat-packing plants which furnish the hides. Then, too, much of our leather is now tanned by the use of a mineral. This takes but a few hours, where vegetable tanning requires weeks. Philadelphia is an important center for the mineral tanning industry.

Mineral Wealth of the Middle Atlantic States. — As Pennsylvania was the keystone state of the thirteen original states on account of its location, it might be termed the keystone state of the Middle Atlantic States in industry, for it furnishes the keystone fuel, coal, on which most of these industries depend.

Two kinds of coal are produced in Pennsylvania, hard or *an'thracite* coal, and soft or *bitu'minous* coal. Scranton and Wilkes-Barre in eastern Pennsylvania are centers for the anthracite industry. Anthracite coal burns with little soot or smoke and is much in demand for heating purposes, especially in cities. Bituminous coal is very plentiful in the plateau of western Pennsylvania, where the largest mines are centered around Pittsburgh. Bituminous coal burns readily and gives out much heat but it makes a great deal of smoke and soot. Pittsburgh was formerly known as the "Smoky City," because of the clouds of black smoke which rolled from the chimneys of its many iron works and factories. Smoke consumers now make it possible to burn this coal without allowing all this black smoke to darken the air.

Coal occurs in layers or *veins* between other rock layers. In the Allegheny Plateau, these rock layers are nearly horizontal or level. Rivers cutting deep into the valleys in this region often expose the coal on the sides. In such places, mining begins where the coal outcrops, and as the coal is taken out, the mine goes deeper and deeper into the hillside following the coal deposits. This is called *drift* mining. Coal is taken out of the mine in cars which are then run down tracks on the slope to a building below known as the coal tipple. This is built right over the railroad track so that the coal can be dumped directly into the railroad cars underneath. In other places, shafts have to be dug to reach the coal below, and the cars of coal are brought to this opening and hoisted to the surface above. This is known as *shaft* mining.

In the anthracite coal region, the rock layers do not lie horizontal and mining is much more difficult. Anthracite has to be sorted

HOUSEBOATS ON THE ALLEGHENY RIVER
Shades of Tom Sawyer and Huckleberry Finn! Lumbermen live on rafts as they float the logs down the river.

and cleaned of refuse rock material after it is mined. Huge piles of this *culm*, as it is called, are a feature of the anthracite mining region. After it is cleaned, the coal is broken and sorted into different sizes commonly known as egg, stove, nut, pea, and buckwheat, intended for different kinds of furnaces and stoves. Pennsylvania furnishes nearly all of the anthracite coal mined in the United States.

The bituminous coal found near Pittsburgh is especially good for making coke, the fuel used in the manufacture of iron and steel. Coke is also a good fuel for heating purposes. Formerly all coke was made in what are called beehive ovens. Long rows of beehive coke ovens are a common sight south of Pittsburgh. These beehive ovens allow the valuable gases from the coal to escape while coke is being

THE COKE INDUSTRY AT KEARNY, NEW JERSEY
Besides turning out 3000 tons of coke a day, this great plant supplies much of northern New Jersey with gas, a by-product.

made. Little use was formerly made of the coal tar left from the coke, but now coke is made in a way which saves the gases, ammonia, and other useful products, while from the coal tar the chemist makes such varied articles as perfumes, dyes, drugs, carbolic acid, and a host of other products.

The Allegheny Plateau, a treasure house of coal, also holds two other valuable fuel treasures, petroleum and natural gas. The first oil well in the United States was drilled near Oil Creek, a small stream which empties into the Allegheny River at Oil City, the first center for the oil industry. At first oil was carried down the Allegheny in barrels loaded on flatboats. Now railroads and pipe lines convey the oil to the refineries. For many years Pennsylvania was the leader in the production of petroleum and it still produces a considerable amount of this much-used liquid fuel. The petroleum produced in Pennsylvania is of an unusually good quality and brings higher prices than the thicker, darker oil of the mid-continent and western fields. Natural gas nearly always occurs in connection with petroleum, and great quantities of it have been allowed to go to waste, because there was no market for it. Now that more people live here and there are more factories, much use is being made of it, for it is one of the finest of fuels, being clean, of high heating quality, and easy to regulate.

Iron ore in small quantities is mined in all of the Middle Atlantic States but most of the ore used in these states is imported. Northern New Jersey has zinc mines which make that state a leader in the production of that useful metal. Building stone, clay for bricks, sand and gravel for making the concrete now so much used for buildings, bridges, and roadways are all abundant in these states, where immense quantities of building materials are necessary.

One of the most valuable resources, especially in New York, is water power. Hydro-electric plants at Niagara Falls produce electric power which is used not only in

ON THE SACANDAGA RIVER, NEW YORK
From the power generated at plants like this, thousands of homes and mills and public buildings throughout northern New York are lighted at the touch of a button.

MINERS AT WORK
Publishers' Photo

Turning the crank produces no music, but conveys great hunks of black coal to loading cars.

THE INSIDE OF A TIPPLE
Courtesy Bituminous Coal Institute

The coal is passed through screens or sieves to sort it according to size, then dropped down chutes, as shown below.

A MODERN TIPPLE OR BREAKER
Courtesy Bituminous Coal Institute

Here the coal is cleared of rock and slate, washed, cleansed and sorted into various sizes.

METROPOLITAN NEW YORK *Aerial Explorations*

The heart of a great city, where man-made palisades of concrete and stone, rising to spectacular heights, are ringed by the waters of two rivers.

Niagara Falls and Buffalo, but in places very much farther away. Northern New York has a number of hydro-electric developments near the St. Lawrence, where power is supplied by streams flowing down from the Adirondacks. One of the largest aluminum plants in the country is located here. The manufacture of aluminum requires large amounts of electricity, so it is manufactured mainly in places where cheap electricity can be produced from water power.

New York, Our Great Eastern Gateway. — Over 300 years ago, in 1609, a famous explorer, Henry Hudson, sailed into what is now New York Bay, and up the large river which bears his name. He did not discover the northern water passage to Asia which he was seeking, but he did discover what afterwards became the great eastern gateway to our country. More passengers and more goods enter and leave the United States by way of New York City than any other port.

If we try to discover some of the reasons for its growth, we note first of all its splendid harbor. Thousands of years ago, when the land was higher than it is now, the Hudson River cut a deep valley leading out to the Atlantic. Then the land sank and the waters of the ocean flowed into the valley. Now the Hudson River is at sea level for a long distance northward and makes a fine, deep waterway far into the state.

A few miles south of the Hudson, two islands, Long Island and Staten Island, come close to each other, forming a wide entering strait known as "The Narrows." The bay thus inclosed is known as Upper New York Bay and the open bay beyond the Narrows is called the Lower Bay. All around this Upper Bay and up the Hudson for some

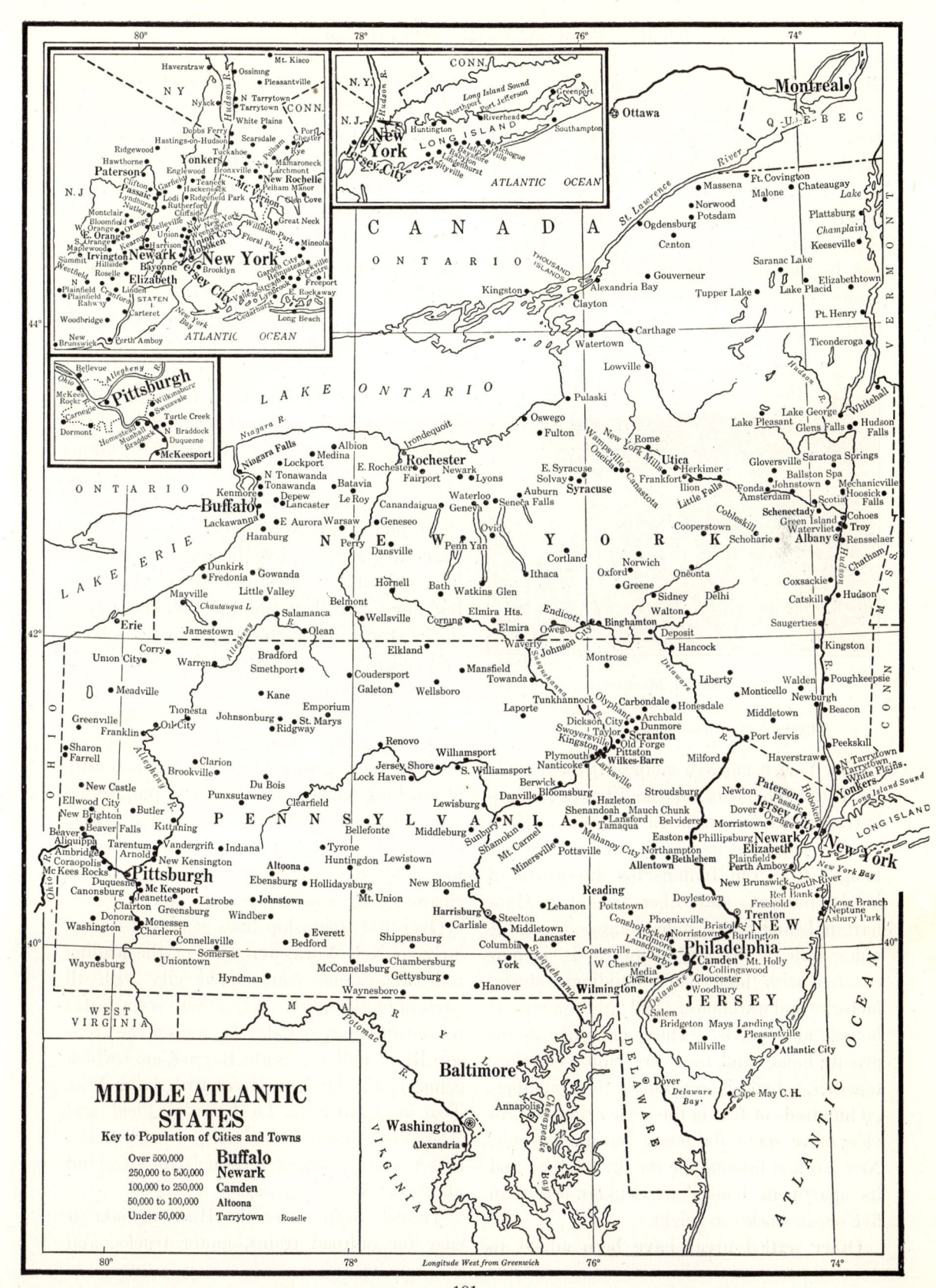

MIDDLE ATLANTIC STATES
Key to Population of Cities and Towns

Over 500,000	**Buffalo**
250,000 to 500,000	**Newark**
100,000 to 250,000	Camden
50,000 to 100,000	Altoona
Under 50,000	Tarrytown Roselle

distance, long piers project into the water and between these are docks for ships. The largest ocean liners sail through the Narrows up the bay and river to their docks along the water-front of New York City. The river is nearly a mile wide so that even the largest boats, which are about a thousand feet long, can be backed out from their piers, turned around in the river, and headed for the ocean.

Courtesy American Airlines

THE TOWERS OF MANHATTAN

Today, planes of several airlines soar in restless flight over the neck of land known as Manhattan.

New York began as a small settlement made by Dutch colonists on the island of Manhattan, which lies on the east side of the Hudson River right at its mouth. The island was bought from the Indians for $24 worth of beads, buttons, and other trinkets. Manhattan Island is $13\frac{1}{2}$ miles long and only $2\frac{1}{4}$ miles wide in its widest part. It is now covered with high office buildings, stores, factories and warehouses, and large apartment houses and hotels. There are only a few private homes and these are built very close together. Land is so valuable that buildings go hundreds of feet in the air in order to provide office room for many business people. New York is famous for its skyscrapers, and its apartment houses are seldom less than five or six stories in height.

Other settled areas have been added to New York until now it is 35 miles from the most northerly point to the most southerly point of the city, and about 17 miles from east to west in its widest part. All of Staten Island on the west side of New York Bay and a large part of western Long Island, including Brooklyn, are part of this great city in which live about 7,000,000 people. Brooklyn, on Long Island, is separated from Manhattan Island by the East River which connects Long Island Sound with New York Bay. Five large suspension bridges and two other high bridges span the East River while tunnels for railways and subways run under the river and link these two sections of the city.

Many immigrants from Europe have made their homes in New York. People from over fifty nations live in this city. They have helped not only to construct the many buildings, but they and their children work in the stores and factories, go to the schools and colleges, and help to carry on the business of this metropolitan city.

In addition to its work of receiving and shipping goods, many manufacturing industries have grown up. The manufacture of clothing leads. Printing and publishing, the manufacture of hats, boots, and shoes, slaughtering and meat packing, sugar refining, and the manufacture of cigars and cigarettes are among the many industries.

Over 100 steamship lines send ships regularly to New York, and nine of the leading railroad systems connect the city with all parts of our country. Then there is the water route to the Great Lakes by way of the Hudson River and the State Barge Canal which connects the Hudson River with Lake Erie. Two large airports, La Guardia Field and New York International Airport (Idlewild), are America's largest terminals for overland and trans-Atlantic planes.

Tunnels deep under the Hudson make it easy for railroad trains, motor trucks, and automobiles to pass between New York and New Jersey. Farther up the river, a long suspension bridge, the George Washington Bridge, spans the Hudson River and makes it easy for automobilists and people on foot to pass from one state to the other.

Cities of New Jersey. — Nowhere in the United States would one find such a cluster of cities as in northern New Jersey west of New York. Along the Hudson, facing New York, are *Hoboken, Jersey City*, and *Bayonne*. Hoboken is a railway terminal into which trains from nearby places in New Jersey empty each morning of every working day thousands of commuters bound for their work in New York. Here the daily travelers change to ferry boats, or tube trains which run under the Hudson River, to complete their journey. In Jersey City, also a railroad terminal, similar scenes can be witnessed each day. Jersey City, in addition to its shipping business, has many manufacturing industries, including printing and type making, refining of petroleum, meat packing, and the manufacture of soap and candles. Next is Bayonne, noted especially for its oil refineries. The petroleum reaches this city in oil tankers, tank cars and pipe lines, some of which lead from oil fields in Texas and Oklahoma. All of these three cities have large docks and piers and share in the trade of the port of New York.

Across a low, swampy region called the Newark Meadows west of these three cities is New Jersey's largest city, *Newark*. Thousands of articles are made in this city, including electrical goods, paints and varnishes, chemicals, jewelry, and leather. Newark has a waterway leading to New York Bay by which barges and even larger vessels can reach the city. Near Newark is its once famous airport. Airplanes make regular stops at Newark for passengers and mail, but New York City's two large airports are now the main terminals, and transfer points for the air lines.

North of Newark is *Paterson*, noted especially for its silk mills. Here the Passaic River, tumbling over a ledge of hard rock, furnished one good reason for starting textile industries. The waters of this river are fine for dyeing silks. Paterson also makes motors

Ewing Galloway

ONE HOME OF THE STANDARD OIL

Oil tanks, like mammoth pill boxes, cover an immense area beside the railroad yards at Bayonne, New Jersey.

for airplanes. Close by is *Passaic*, turning out woolens and worsteds, cotton, silk and rubber goods, artificial leather, and oil cloth. South of Newark is *Elizabeth*, busily making sewing machines, brass and copper goods, asbestos and petroleum products, electric fans, and vacuum cleaners. Southwestward from this group of cities is *New Brunswick*, which makes cigars and boxes to put them in, Red Cross supplies, music wire, wall paper, and many other articles.

Trenton, the capital city on the east bank of the Delaware River, makes steel cables, cigars, tires and other rubber goods, but it is especially noted for its pottery. Clay found near by is used for the coarser grades but *kā′olin* for the finer china is imported from

A CITY HOME

In the city of Philadelphia the grass is still green and the trees flaunt their leafy crowns as if the country had crept to the city's very heart, banishing canyons of sunless streets, crowded pavements, and overreaching apartment houses.

England. *Camden*, opposite Philadelphia on the Delaware, in addition to canning soups and vegetables, makes phonographs and radios, steel pens, and dozens of other articles. Its shipyards have built many of our naval vessels, as well as ships for other purposes.

Philadelphia, the City of Brotherly Love. — Philadelphia, founded by William Penn, who started the first colonies in Pennsylvania, is of much interest to Americans because of the part it has played in our history. Here in Independence Hall was signed the Declaration of Independence and here in Carpenters' Hall met the first Continental Congress which ruled our land during the Revolutionary War. Philadelphia, with nearly 2,000,000 people, is the third largest city in our country. It is sometimes called the "City of Homes" because so many of its people live in their own homes, instead of large apartment houses as they do in New York and some other large cities.

Philadelphia makes so many different articles that it brings raw material for them from every country in the world. Carpets and rugs are one of its specialties, hosiery and knit goods another. Large locomotive works, which were recently moved to a place near by, send their product to far-away China, South America, and central Africa. Ships made in Philadelphia travel all over the world. The United States Navy Yards are located here. Petroleum and sugar refining are big industries, and iron and steel articles of many kinds are manufactured. Though not on the sea, the Delaware River gives it a good waterway to the ocean and railroads and fine automobile highways link it to other cities in our country.

Pittsburgh, the Iron and Steel City. — Pittsburgh is sometimes called the "Gateway to the West." It is built where the Allegheny River, flowing from the north, joins the Monongahē′la River from the south to form the Ohio, a waterway to the west now as it was in the early history of our country. From a little settlement on the point of land between the two rivers, the city has grown until it now

© *Aerial Surveys of Pittsburgh, Inc.*

THE "GOLDEN TRIANGLE"

Pittsburgh's administrative center, backed by its manufacturing and industrial sections, is laced to opposite shores by a series of bridges.

THE PASSAIC RIVER, NEW JERSEY *Ewing Galloway*
The main arch of the Pulaski Bridge frames the Public Service Power station of Newark, visible through the smoke of the little, fat, puffing tug.

INDEPENDENCE SQUARE *H. Armstrong Roberts*
Philadelphia is one of the most interesting cities, historically, in the whole United States, and Independence Hall is one of its most famous buildings.

TRENTON, NEW JERSEY *Ewing Galloway*
A glimpse of the capital city's capitol dome through the Ionic columns of the new Soldiers and Sailors Memorial Auditorium.

has over 600,000 people, bordered by smaller cities and towns. The triangular piece of land between the Allegheny and the Monongahela Rivers where the heart of the city lies, is called the "Golden Triangle" because the land is so valuable.

In the midst of coal, iron ore, and limestone, Pittsburgh early became the great center for the iron and steel industry. When the better ores of the Lake Superior district were discovered, the local ore mines were abandoned in favor of ore brought from the Lake Superior mines. Many other cities now have large iron and steel industries, but Pittsburgh still leads with its huge production of steel rails and plates, and other iron and steel goods.

Pittsburgh is also a center for glass making. Natural gas, the best and cleanest fuel for this industry, is much used in making glass, and its presence is one of the main reasons for the many glass factories in western Pennsylvania.

Other Industrial Cities of Pennsylvania. — *Scranton* and *Wilkes-Barre*, anthracite coal-mining centers in eastern Pennsylvania, have a variety of other industries based on cheap power from coal. Scranton cards and spools a considerable amount of the raw silk imported into this country. Another product is buttons. Both these cities are in the midst of beautiful mountain scenery, and nearby resorts attract many people. *Reading*, farther south, is a prominent city in the production of hosiery and hardware; *Bethlehem* is an iron and steel center; and *Allentown* makes over one-third of our cement and in addition manufactures silk goods. *Lancaster*, in the midst of Pennsylvania's finest farming region, not only acts as a market center, but makes linoleum, umbrellas, cotton and silk goods, and cigars. It is also a meatpacking center.

Harrisburg, the capital at the eastern foot of the mountains, is a railroad and distributing center, and manufactures a number of articles, including silks, hosiery, tobacco, boilers, and machinery. Thousands of railroad workers live here. The city has many fine public buildings, especially its high schools " for all the children of all the people."

Altoona, the mountain city, is a half-way point for the railroad. It owes its growth largely to the railroad shops located here. Farther west, deep in a valley, is *Johnstown* with its big iron and steel plant. Near Pittsburgh, *New Castle* and *McKeesport* excel in tin and tin plate. *Williamsport*, on the west branch of the Susquehanna River in north central Pennsylvania, was once called the "Sawdust City" because of its large lumber industries. It still manufactures lumber products, but foundries and machine shops and other industries now lead.

Erie, which has one of the finest harbors on the Great Lakes, not only distributes iron ore brought to it from the Lake Superior mines, but ships out tons and tons of coal carried to it by the railroads. It makes iron and steel goods from the iron ore and coal brought to it. The city also manufactures pipe organs, baby carriages, clothes wringers, and hundreds of other articles. Erie is an important center for lake fisheries.

Cities of the Hudson-Mohawk Valley. — Adjoining New York City on the north is *Yonkers*, with its large sugar refineries, carpet factories, and elevator plants. North of Yonkers, on the west side of the Hudson River in the midst of a beautiful highland region, lies *West Point*, seat of the United States Military Academy where United States Army officers are trained.

The next large city is *Poughkeepsie*, where a high railroad bridge crosses the Hudson. Then comes *Albany*, the capital and an important river port. North of Albany is *Troy*, famous for its collars and shirts. On the Mohawk River lies *Schenectady*, well known for all kinds of electrical appliances. *Amsterdam*, rug and carpet maker, is next. Not far

WILKES-BARRE, PENNSYLVANIA
Courtesy Wilkes-Barre Chamber of Commerce

Located in a valley of the Appalachian Mountains, this city, founded in 1769 and twice burned during colonial wars, has become of great importance because of its location in the anthracite coal region.

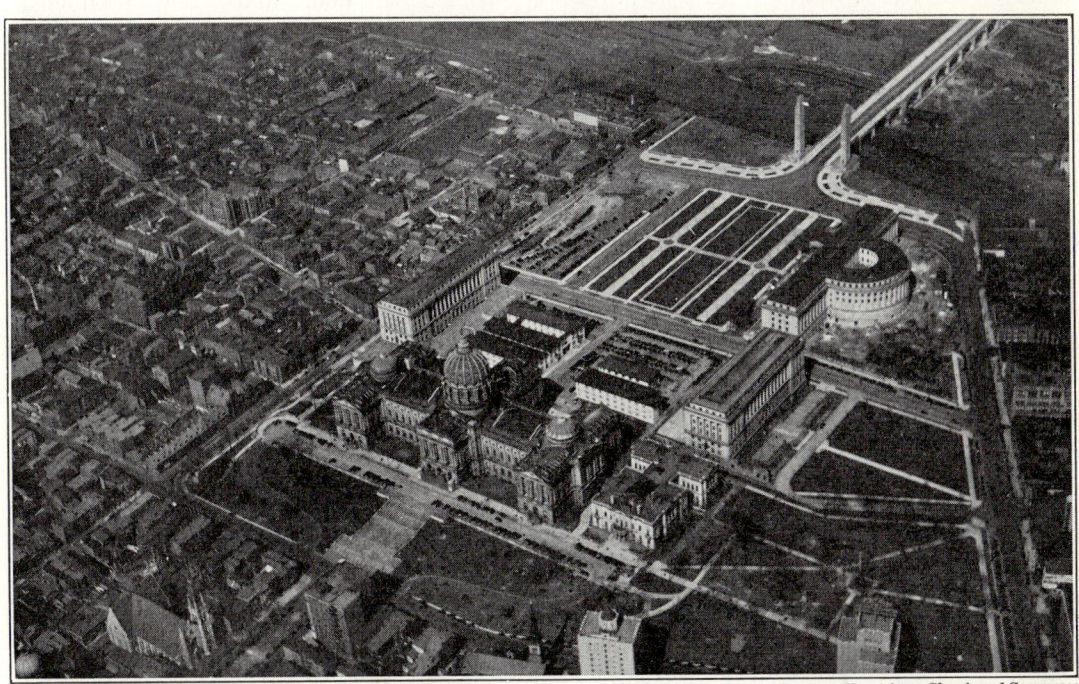

HARRISBURG, PENNSYLVANIA
Courtesy Harrisburg Chamber of Commerce

The capitol building is surrounded by a park of fifteen acres, a beautiful setting for its austere beauty.

away are *Johnstown* and *Gloversville*, makers of gloves, while farther west comes *Utica* with its knit goods, and its cotton sheets and pillow cases. *Rome*, farther west, makes so many copper articles that it is sometimes called the "Copper City."

Cities of the Plateau and Finger Lakes Region. — *Binghamton*, on the Susquehanna River in the plateau of southern New York, is a meeting place for highways and railroad routes. Shoes and cigars are among its many manufactured goods. *Syracuse*, which grew up near salt springs, no longer produces salt because other places which have better deposits can make it more cheaply. The city now makes typewriters, tool steel, automobiles, chemicals, and other products. It is also a railroad center where north and south, and east and west routes cross. About twenty miles south of Syracuse, soda and bleaching fluids are made from salt brine.

Rochester used to be called the "Flour City" because of its flour mills. Later it became known as the "Flower City" because of its many large nurseries and its production of flowers and seeds. Now it is known as the "Kodak City" because it makes more cameras than any other place. It also makes thermometers, optical goods, camera supplies, telephone apparatus, radios, typewriter ribbons, carbon paper, and many other useful articles. Falls in the Genesee River are an attractive feature of Rochester and also provide water power.

Buffalo, New York's leading Lake Port. — Buffalo, at the eastern end of Lake Erie and the western end of the State Barge Canal, has become the second largest city in New York. Ore carriers and lake vessels loaded with wheat both discharge their cargoes here. Buffalo uses a large part of the wheat in her flour mills, now producing more flour than any other city in the world. In Buffalo and nearby *Lackawanna*, iron ore is converted into iron and steel with coal brought by rail from coal fields of the plateau farther south. Niagara Falls, that great source of power only a few miles away, has been harnessed to make electricity which lights the city and runs some of the manufacturing plants. Buffalo does not stop with flour and iron and steel. It makes airplanes, packs meat, and manufactures hundreds of other articles. Lake steamers make regular trips between Buffalo and other lake ports to the west.

Niagara Falls. — No natural attraction of New York is better known than Niagara Falls. Flowing from Lake Erie into Lake Ontario, the Niagara River falls over a cliff 160 feet high, and then runs for miles through a steep-

Courtesy Buffalo Chamber of Commerce
BUFFALO, NEW YORK
Into Buffalo's port come shipments from the Great Lakes or across from the Atlantic coast; into its hotels come the many tourists attracted by its nearness to Niagara Falls; into its business houses come the orders for manufactured goods from its around-the-corner neighbor, Canada.

STATE CAPITOL OF NEW YORK

From this many-windowed stone building in Albany, New York, two Roosevelts have stepped from the governor's chair to the office of President of the United States.

SPANNING THE HUDSON AT POUGHKEEPSIE

This toll bridge for cross-country motor traffic collects a fare for every car which crosses it.

Ewing Galloway

FUTURE GENERALS

These five West Point cadets hold the most distinguished scholastic records in the graduating class.

SYRACUSE, NEW YORK
Courtesy Syracuse Chamber of Commerce

Syracuse is a city of wide, straight streets. Around Clinton Square are grouped the new post office, the Soldiers and Sailors Monument, and the Board of Education building.

Courtesy Niagara Falls Chamber of Commerce
NIAGARA FALLS

Most famous of all falls, the force of these rushing waters is utilized by power companies on both sides of the river. A restriction is placed on the amount of water which may be diverted for making electricity.

Courtesy Rochester Chamber of Commerce
GENESEE FALLS

The Genesee River (meaning *shining valley*) rises in Pennsylvania, flows north through New York, and enters Lake Ontario near Rochester. Here it falls in three cataracts, a source of water power for the city.

sided gorge. Visitors from all over our country and other countries come to see these wonderful sights. An island in the center divides the falls into two parts. Those next to the United States are called the American Falls and those next to Canada are called the Canadian Falls. The twin cities of Niagara Falls, Ontario, and Niagara Falls, New York, have grown up nearby. Formerly, taking care of the many visitors was the leading industry, but now hydro-electric plants furnish power for making aluminum, breakfast foods, chemicals, and many other manufactured products.

Activities and Questions

1. What river drains central Pennsylvania and south central New York?

2. Describe the Allegheny Plateau.

3. Where are the finger lakes?

4. What and where are the chief mountains of New York? How are they used by the people?

5. Where are the most famous bathing resorts in the Middle Atlantic States?

6. What is the commonest type of farming practiced in these states? Why?

7. In what section are the most cranberries and blueberries grown? Why?

8. What are the two kinds of coal which Pennsylvania produces?

9. Compare coal mining in Pennsylvania and Kentucky. Why the difference?

10. Name some articles made from coal tar.

11. Describe New York harbor.

12. The people of how many different nations live in New York City?

13. Give some of the reasons for the greatness of New York City.

14. Where do many of the people live who work on Manhattan Island in New York City?

15. Name some of the chief cities of New York; of Pennsylvania; of New Jersey.

16. What are the leading products of New York City? of Philadelphia? of Pittsburgh?

17. Sketch a map of the Middle Atlantic States, putting in the chief cities, rivers, and mountains.

EARLY SETTLERS
Marietta, Ohio, — founded by a company of Revolutionary officers from New England under General Rufus Putnam, and named in honor of the lovely Marie Antoinette of France.

X. THE EAST NORTH CENTRAL STATES

Our airplane trip across the East North Central States showed us a land of fine farms with many large cities and towns. These five states are a great food-producing and manufacturing region. A little over one hundred years ago it was mostly prairies and forests, but wonderful changes have taken place since the first settlers started to cut down trees, build homes, and farm the land.

Difficulties of the First Settlers. — The first white settlers were chiefly explorers, trappers, and farmers. Much of the land was covered with timber, which took time and labor to clear away before the fertile soil could be put into cultivation. Most of Illinois and parts of the other states were originally prairie lands, covered with tough sod which was hard to cultivate without steel plows.

These early settlers had few comforts, for they came before there were railroads or modern steamboats. Some came by small boats on the Great Lakes from New York and New England. Others came overland from the Middle and South Atlantic States. After the eastern highlands were crossed, the Ohio River and its tributaries furnished water highways to different parts of Ohio, Indiana, and Illinois. It was a long, hard journey, but this beautiful, rich territory was well worth the effort.

Transportation in the early days was one of their chief difficulties. The rich, level lands grew much feed for animals, but these had to be driven hundreds of miles overland to eastern markets. There were no railroads or paved roads, and steamboats had not yet come into general use. After the Erie Canal was opened in 1825, wheat grown by these farmers was sent by way of the Great Lakes and this canal to the eastern cities.

How the Railroads Helped. — For many years their chief markets were in the Atlantic states, though some products were shipped down the Ohio and Mississippi to New

THE EAST NORTH CENTRAL STATES

Statistics of the East North Central States*

State	Abbreviation	Area Sq. Miles	Population	Rank Area	Rank Pop.	Capital	Population	Largest City	Population
Wisconsin	Wis.	56,154	3,137,587	25	13	Madison	67,447	Milwaukee	587,472
Michigan	Mich.	58,216	5,256,106	22	7	Lansing	78,753	Detroit	1,623,452
Illinois	Ill.	56,400	7,897,241	23	3	Springfield	75,503	Chicago	3,396,808
Indiana	Ind.	36,291	3,427,796	37	12	Indianapolis	386,972	Indianapolis	386,972
Ohio		41,222	6,907,612	34	4	Columbus	306,087	Cleveland	878,336

*1940 Census

Important Products

Wisconsin: — Dairy products, vegetables, grains, machinery, paper
Michigan: — Automobiles, iron ore, vegetables, fruits, furniture
Illinois: — Grains, live stock, meats, coal, iron and steel goods
Indiana: — Grains, live stock, meats, farm machinery, iron and steel
Ohio: — Iron and steel, grains, dairy products, automobiles, rubber goods

---

Orleans. But with the coming of the railroads about 1850, these states began to develop rapidly. Grain, live stock, lumber, minerals, and other products were now quickly and cheaply shipped to the eastern markets there to be exchanged for manufactured goods.

Not only did the coming of the railroads aid the settlers, but it brought many new families from the eastern states and from Europe. During the past seventy-five years, millions of people have come into Wisconsin, Illinois, Indiana, Michigan, and Ohio, to help develop these important states. The level land has made it easy to build railroads and roads, so now it takes only a few hours for fast trains to run from any part of this area into Chicago, Detroit, Cleveland, or the other large cities near the Great Lakes. Raw materials and other products are easily and quickly sent to every part of the United States, for no other section of the world is better supplied with such a fine network of railroads, which carry fast freight, express, passenger, and refrigerator trains in every direction both day and night. Farm machinery, automobiles, clothing, furniture, live stock, food, coal, and other raw and manufactured goods are sent by rail from this section to population centers throughout America. Chicago, our greatest commercial and industrial lake port, is the

CHICAGO
Ewing Galloway

Along the banks of the river which bears the city's name, rise the great uptown skyscrapers that mark Chicago's business district. A steamship glides slowly along — a toy boat beside the enormous buildings — while along the double-deck thoroughfare beside it automobiles scurry like rows of black beetles.

chief railroad center in the world. Splendid systems of modern highways which reach every important town and community act as feeders to the railways and help in the transportation of people and goods.

The Great Lakes. — While fast trains are running in all directions throughout this prosperous section, hundreds of large steamboats are busily transporting iron ore, coal, grain,

A BUSY WATERWAY *Ewing Galloway*
A long line of freighters, defying even cold weather, steams its slow but sure way through the St. Marys River, a short waterway connecting Lake Superior with the other Great Lakes.

stone, lumber, and people on the Great Lakes, the most used inland waterways in the world. It is much cheaper to ship heavy and bulky products by special boats than by rail, and the lakes are deep enough for large vessels. Some of these carry more than 12,000 tons of iron ore, enough to fill 400 railroad cars, or half a dozen long freight trains. Many of these boats also carry thousands of tons of coal on their return trips for the industrial cities and towns in Michigan, Wisconsin, and northern Illinois and Indiana. Look at the map on the next page and tell on what lakes, rivers, and canals one of these boats would return from Cleveland, Ohio, to Duluth, Minnesota.

All of these East North Central States border on the Great Lakes and have excellent lake ports, where railroads from all parts of the United States connect with boat lines. This fact is one of the main reasons why this section is one of the leading commercial and industrial regions in America.

Many Resorts. — Many places on the Great Lakes have excellent bathing beaches and resorts, where people may swim, play games, go boating or fishing, dance, or just rest and enjoy the cool lake breezes. The city of Chicago has built a four-million-dollar recreation pier which is often visited by

THE EAST NORTH CENTRAL STATES

Map Questions and Activities

1. These states might well be called the Great Lakes States. Why?
2. Name the states included in this group.
3. Find and name the capital and largest cities of each state.
4. What do the various colors of the map stand for?
5. Why is the railway network so thick in these states? How are the railroads shown?
6. Does most of the land seem to be low or high? How can you tell?
7. Does the map suggest one or more reasons why the following cities have become large: Chicago? Detroit? Cleveland? Milwaukee? Cincinnati? Columbus? Indianapolis?
8. What two important rivers form much of the boundaries of these states? How does this help trade?
9. Study your map closely and make a list of several reasons why there are many cities and railroads near the Great Lakes.
10. Name the four Great Lakes that touch this group of states. Which of these lakes lies wholly within the United States?
11. How do the Great Lakes benefit agriculture in this region?
12. Locate ten rivers on this map and tell where and how the waters of each reach the ocean.
13. Can small boats go from Chicago to the ocean? How?

Physical - Political
EAST NORTH CENTRAL STATES
Scale of Statute Miles
0 50 100 150
State Capitals
Railroads
The type used indicates the relative sizes of towns and cities.
HEIGHTS IN FEET
Above 2,000
1,000 to 2,000
500 to 1,000
Sea level to 500
DEPTHS IN FATHOMS
Sea level to 100
Below 100
Longitude West from Greenwich
LAKE SUPERIOR
602 feet above sea level
LAKE MICHIGAN
581 feet above sea level
LAKE HURON
580 feet above sea level
LAKE ERIE
572 feet above sea level
Chicago
Milwaukee
Detroit
Cleveland
Indianapolis
Cincinnati
St. Louis
Louisville

thousands of people during a warm day in summer. Cool breezes from the lake sweep across this pier, which offers many means of making these vast crowds comfortable and happy.

Farming in the East North Central States. — The East North Central States lie in the hay and pasture region, the Corn Belt, and the Corn and Winter Wheat Belt. Some of the finest farming areas in the United States are found in the corn region of Ohio, Indiana, and Illinois. Here millions of acres of rich,

A CORNFIELD IN THE CORN BELT *Ewing Galloway*
Two girl farmers of Wabash Township, Indiana, are running cultivators through a fine field of corn for the last time before harvest. The field is a forest of droopy green leaves, as far as the eye can see.

dark soils produce abundant crops of grain, hay, and vegetables. The gently rolling, nearly level land makes it easy to use machinery to plant, cultivate, and harvest the crops. Corn is the most important grain but wheat, oats, and other grains are grown. Most of the corn is fed to swine, cattle, horses, chickens, and other live stock on the farms. In the southern part of Illinois, Indiana, and Ohio, winter wheat is also important.

Much of the wheat grown in these East North Central States is shipped to large flour mills in Chicago, Indianapolis, Toledo, Milwaukee, and other cities near by, or to markets in the East, and some is exported to foreign countries. Little wheat is grown in northern Wisconsin and northern Michigan because of the rough land and the fact that other crops do better.

Barley, grown largely for malting and feed, thrives better than other grains just north of the corn belt. Rye also grows best in a cool, moist climate. It is raised quite extensively in Wisconsin and Michigan on soil too poor for wheat. As rye bread is not so tasty as wheat bread, relatively few people in the United States use it, but millions of people in Europe eat it daily. Oats are cultivated with corn in the Corn Belt. They can be planted before corn and harvested long before the corn is ripe. Oats are an excellent feed for animals, especially horses, which are plentiful in the Corn Belt. Only two states, Minnesota and Iowa, produce more oats than Illinois. Wisconsin and Illinois grow much hemp, which is made into burlap, twine, ropes, and fishing nets. These two states, together with Iowa, are our largest growers of hemp. Hay is one of the leading crops in all these states, where it is a general feed for live stock.

Sugar beets are an important crop in southern Michigan. It requires much labor to cultivate and harvest these plants, so many people from the cities go to the fields in summer and help with the crops. The most important vegetable crop is the potato, which is grown in all of these states, especially in northern Ohio, southern Michigan, and central Wisconsin. Millions of bushels are raised, and most of the crop is used in the cities near the Great Lakes. Large cities like Detroit, Chicago, Cleveland, and Milwaukee

GOING AND COMING

Courtesy J. I. Case Company

The latest and most modern piece of machinery for handling a valuable hay crop — the pick up hay baler — being used on an alfalfa field at Racine, Wisconsin. The loose hay is picked up over rollers, fed into a compression box in the rear and expelled, firmly wired, into a square bale.

also need many carloads of the fresh cabbages, celery, beans, and other vegetables grown in the rich, black muck soils of southern Michigan and northern Indiana. Onions, celery, and peppermint for flavoring do especially well in these soils. Central Michigan produces large crops of white field beans, which are prepared as baked beans. Wisconsin is one of our leading states in the production of canned beans. These states around the Great Lakes also can corn, peas, beans, and other vegetables.

Fruits. — Fruits grow in each of these five states, and one of the best fruit sections in the United States lies along the east shore of Lake Michigan. Apples, peaches, plums, pears, and grapes grow here abundantly. The many orchards present a beautiful scene during blossom time, as well as later in summer when the fruit is ripe. Westerly winds crossing Lake Michigan modify the climate; the cold, spring winds delay the blossoming until the danger from frost is past; and the warm fall winds keep back frosts till the fruit is ripe. Michigan ranks fourth in the production of apples in the United States, and is a leading state in the production of small fruits. Northern Ohio, south of Lake Erie, also has a fruit belt similar to that found in Michigan.

Animal Industries. — Good climate, abundant food, and large markets near by make this section one of the chief dairy regions in America. No other group of states produces more milk, butter, and cheese. Wisconsin manufactures about one-half of all the cheese made in the entire United States. Much of the milk produced is sold to nearby markets for local use as fresh milk, but millions of cans of condensed milk are manufactured and sold throughout our country.

Plenty of corn and other grains, hay, and good pastures help these states to produce much of our beef. Many fine breeds of cattle are raised here and other cattle are shipped into this territory to be fattened for the great packing plants in Chicago, Indianapolis, Cincinnati, Milwaukee, and other large meat-packing centers. Chicago is the greatest meat-packing city in the world. Millions of live stock are slaughtered here and shipped all over our country and to foreign ports.

Swine also are plentiful where it is so easy to grow corn and other grains to feed them. Every state in our country raises swine, but the Corn Belt has more hogs than any other section. Most of the swine in these five states are in the three south of the Great Lakes. Swine grow quickly when they

Ewing Galloway
A MODEL POULTRY FARM AT HUNTINGTON, INDIANA

Flocks of snow-white chickens cackle and crow as they flutter around their pens, pecking here and there at seeds or stones or bits of shell.

are well fed. By the time they are six or eight months old they are large enough to be sent to market for pork, while steers must be from two to three years old before they are ready for the packing house. But the hog weighs only two or three hundred pounds, while the steer weighs a thousand or more by the time it is ready to be slaughtered. Most farmers raise a few swine for themselves, but in the corn belt many have hundreds or even thousands of swine, which are shipped by rail to the meat-packing centers near the Great Lakes.

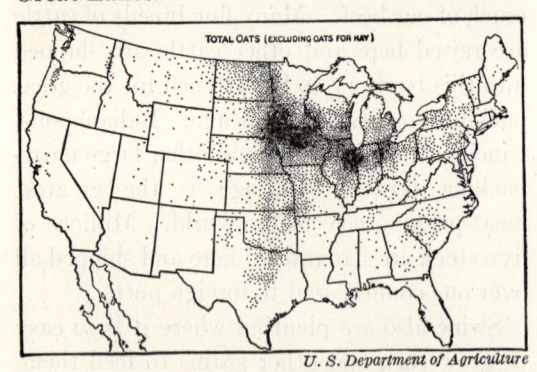

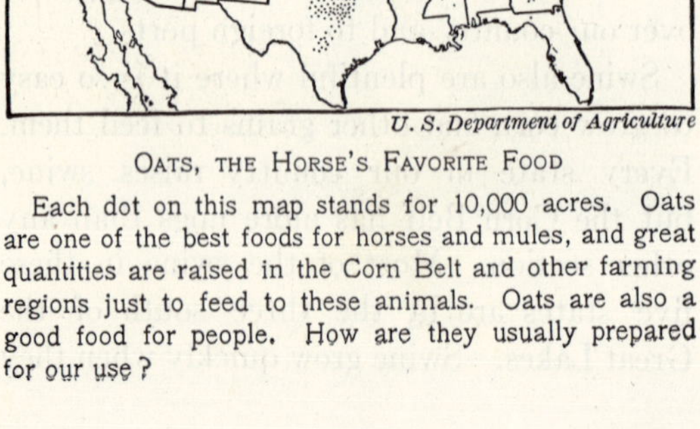

All these states raise some sheep for mutton and wool. Eastern Ohio and southern Michigan are important sheep-raising areas, shipping some to the large woolen mills near Boston, Massachusetts. Trainloads of sheep and lambs are shipped to great packing centers in this section and slaughtered for markets in New York City, Philadelphia, and other eastern cities. The Corn Belt also raises horses for draft, driving, racing, and for the saddle. Feed is relatively cheap for them here, since much corn, hay, and oats are grown right on farms where the horses are raised.

There are millions of chickens in the United States, and almost every farm has a flock. In the central states they feed chiefly on the abundant grain. Chickens give us two excellent foods, eggs and meat, to eat with our bread, vegetables, and fruits. Most of the eggs and poultry meat in this section are eaten locally in cities and towns near the Great Lakes, but millions of dozens of eggs are put in cold storage and shipped to other parts of the United States. These states also raise ducks, geese, and turkeys, but more chickens are grown than any other fowl.

Fishing in the Great Lakes. — The waters of the Great Lakes furnish some excellent

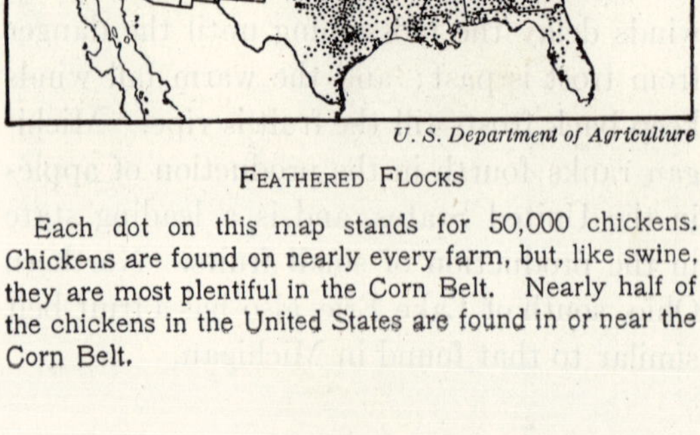

U. S. Department of Agriculture
OATS, THE HORSE'S FAVORITE FOOD

Each dot on this map stands for 10,000 acres. Oats are one of the best foods for horses and mules, and great quantities are raised in the Corn Belt and other farming regions just to feed to these animals. Oats are also a good food for people. How are they usually prepared for our use?

U. S. Department of Agriculture
FEATHERED FLOCKS

Each dot on this map stands for 50,000 chickens. Chickens are found on nearly every farm, but, like swine, they are most plentiful in the Corn Belt. Nearly half of the chickens in the United States are found in or near the Corn Belt.

HONEY IN THE MAKING

Ewing Galloway

The flavor of honey varies according to the source of the nectar. White clover, alfalfa, sage, orange blossom, and even buckwheat are all used by the bees. This modern apiary is on a farm in Mt. Vernon, Indiana.

PICKING PEACHES AT DECKER, INDIANA

Ewing Galloway

The United States produces the most and the best peaches in the world. The trees grow about fifteen feet high, have long slender leaves and sweetly scented pink blossoms.

CHERRIES AND PEARS

Forty acres of cherry and pear trees in Old Mission, Michigan, are undergoing a bath of poison spray to protect them from insect attack.

fish, especially the delicious lake trout and whitefish. Fishing is pursued for both pleasure and business. The United States government maintains hatcheries in and near the Great Lakes in order to increase the supply of fish. Brook trout, the small-mouth black bass, and other game fish lure the angler to the many glacial streams and lakes, especially

A GOLDFISH FARM

So popular has the goldfish bowl become that this farm in Martinsville, Indiana, keeps three tractors busy digging new ponds in which to raise enough fish to supply the demand in England, Canada, and all over the United States.

in northern Michigan and northern Wisconsin. These game fish are also raised in state-supported hatcheries.

Forests and Lumbering. — When the first settlers came, much of the land was covered with trees such as ash, oak, maple, hickory, birch, tulip, poplar, pine, and hemlock. Most of this timber has been cut by farmers and lumber companies. Fifty years ago Michigan and Wisconsin were leading states in the production of lumber, but now Washington, Oregon, and California lead. The need for farms in these fertile lands and the demand for lumber to supply the growing cities caused most of these forests to be cut. However, they still furnish lumber for building purposes and for the manufacture of furniture, farm implements, wood pulp, packing, and crating. Wisconsin ranks high in the production of wood pulp for paper.

Mining Industries. — Coal is mined in all the East North Central States except Wisconsin. Illinois, Ohio, and Indiana rank third, fifth, and sixth respectively in the United States in coal production. Our country produces three chief kinds of coal, *anthracite* or hard coal, *bituminous* or soft coal, and *lignite*, a still softer brown coal. This central section has soft or bituminous coal. Much of this is used to run the great locomotives which carry thousands of people, coal, grain, live stock, food, and other products over the network of railroads. Coal is the chief fuel and source of power in these states, and thousands of men work underground in mines to supply homes, factories, and railroads with this useful mineral.

Illinois, Ohio, and Indiana also produce petroleum. Michigan's production of petroleum has increased until it now ranks among the ten leading states. Millions of barrels of petroleum from this section as well as the Southwest run through large pipe lines across these states to Chicago, and to large cities on the Atlantic coast. Crude petroleum is refined into many valuable products such as gasoline, kerosene, benzine, lubricating oil, vaseline, and paraffin.

For many years, the northern peninsula of Michigan near Houghton and Calumet on the Keweenaw Peninsula was the leading copper region in the United States. This metal is mined here in almost a pure state. Some of the western states now lead Michigan in copper production. Zinc, which is used for galvanizing iron and steel and for mixing

Ewing Galloway
COAL MINING BY STRIPPING IN CLAY COUNTY, INDIANA

The steam shovel eats its way into the hillside, taking big scoopfuls of coal and fire clay. Because the coal vein is so near the surface it can be worked like an open quarry.

Ewing Galloway
ZINC AND LEAD MINE

In the southwestern part of Wisconsin there are valuable deposits of zinc and lead. These are very useful metals whose ores occur in veins or large masses.

Ewing Galloway
INDUSTRY ON PARADE

This battery of cracking stills belongs to the Whiting Refinery of Standard Oil Company of Indiana, and it is one of the largest gasoline-producing plants in the world.

211

with copper to make brass, is found in southwestern Wisconsin.

These states have a variety of stone and other valuable products taken from the earth. The famous Indiana limestone, found in the Bedford-Bloomington district, is used in monuments, state capitols, and other public buildings. Central Wisconsin produces good granite. Illinois and Ohio have good sand for making glass. Natural gas furnishes the best of fuels for extensive glass and pottery industries in Ohio.

Iron and Steel. — Iron ore, cheap transportation on the Great Lakes, and growing cities which need large quantities of building materials are some of the reasons why these states rank high in the iron and steel industry. While gold is one of the most valuable metals in the world, iron is the most useful.

The United States produces nearly half of the world's iron ore, and the mines around Lake Superior in Minnesota, Wisconsin, and Michigan furnish nearly all of it. The richest and greatest iron ore mines in the world lie in the Mesabi Range near Duluth, in Minnesota. Michigan is our second leading state in iron ore production. Trainloads of dirt-like ore are scooped up by enormous steam shovels and sent to Duluth, Minnesota, or other shipping ports on Lake Superior where the ore is dumped into large lake vessels, which carry it to steel mills in Cleveland, Chicago, Detroit, Gary, and other steel centers. The ore carriers, which hold as much as 12,000 tons of ore, are unloaded quickly by machinery, and are soon ready to return with coal or other cargo for cities on the upper lakes.

If you were to visit one of these large steel mills near Chicago, you would see tons of this ore pouring into great blast furnaces, where it is mixed with limestone and melted. This crude iron is called *pig iron*, which is refined into various grades of iron and steel, which in turn is made into rails for railroads, sewer and water pipes, bridge material, tools, and thousands of other articles. Some is refined into steel for razor blades, watch springs, needles, and other articles which need an extra fine quality of steel.

Automobiles. — No other industry has had a more rapid growth than that of the American automobile. Some one has truly said that "America rides on rubber." There are enough automobiles in our country to carry every person in the United States, if each car were filled with passengers. This group of states on the Great Lakes manufactures three-fourths of all our cars, Michigan alone making over one-half. Detroit leads, but Flint, Lansing, Jackson, and Pontiac also manufacture automobiles and automobile parts. Cleveland and Toledo in Ohio, and other cities in this group of states have important automobile factories. There are several reasons why this section of the

A Steel Mill at Indiana Harbor
Ewing Galloway
The heavy sheets of cut steel are easily moved on upright rollers that stand up like the stiff bristles on a giant hairbrush.

FORD ASSEMBLY LINE

An endless belt carries all the necessary parts past the long line of workmen. There is no lost time nor waste motion because every man has a particular part to put in place. No wonder these machines can be turned out "while you wait."

Ewing Galloway

POTTER'S CLAY

At the Weller plant in Zanesville, Ohio, a workman takes a lump of moist, formless clay and with the turn of a wheel molds it into a flower pot.

Courtesy J. I. Case Company

FARM MACHINERY EN ROUTE

Carloads of boxed machinery leaving the Tractor Works at Racine, Wisconsin, via ferry, on the first lap of their journey to various parts of the country.

United States produces so many automobiles. Excellent transportation by land and water, plenty of iron and steel and other raw materials, a large number of skilled mechanics, an early start, and a good market for automobiles are some of the main reasons.

Other Industries. — *Furniture.* Furniture making is also a very important industry in these states where there is plenty of hardwood, leather, and other materials which go into furniture. The chief woods used are oak, maple, and birch, all of which grow extensively in these states. Many other woods, such as mahogany, must be shipped in from other parts of the world. Grand Rapids, Michigan, has long been famous for its furniture manufacturing. Evansville, in southern Indiana, and Rockford, Illinois, are also noted for this industry, and many other cities and towns make various kinds of furniture.

Agricultural Machinery. These states produce about three-fourths of all farm machinery made in the United States. Chicago's location and fine transportation facilities make it the chief center, but several other cities, such as South Bend in Indiana, Columbus, Cincinnati, and Springfield in Ohio, Moline in Illinois, and Milwaukee in Wisconsin, manufacture various kinds of agricultural machinery.

Tanning of Leather. Milwaukee is the center of the leather industry in these states, and is one of the leading cities in the United States in the production of leather and leather goods. Hides from the great meat-packing plants in Chicago are sent to Milwaukee to be tanned with hemlock bark from the forests of Michigan and made into shoes, boots, gloves, and other leather goods.

Pottery. Ohio is one of our leading states in manufacturing fine pottery. The center of this industry is at East Liverpool on the Ohio River in eastern Ohio. Excellent grades of clay and coal are near at hand, and highly skilled labor is available. Much of the clay for this pottery is now shipped to East Liverpool from Florida and Georgia, and some is even imported from foreign countries.

Chief Cities of this Group of States. — *Chicago.* Chicago's excellent location on the southwest border of Lake Michigan has made this city the second largest in America. Its population of three and a half millions is exceeded only by New York, London, and Berlin. Few cities in the world have grown as rapidly as Chicago.

One hundred years ago Chicago consisted of less than 100 huts on the mud flats of lower Lake Michigan near the Chicago River. Its amazing growth has taken place in the space of

NORTH SHORE, CHICAGO — *Chicago Aerial Survey Company*

The mass of imposing buildings, tall and short, lean and squat, in this thickly crowded city give way, at the lake shore, to a long strip of boulevard and parkway and sandy beach.

EAST NORTH CENTRAL STATES

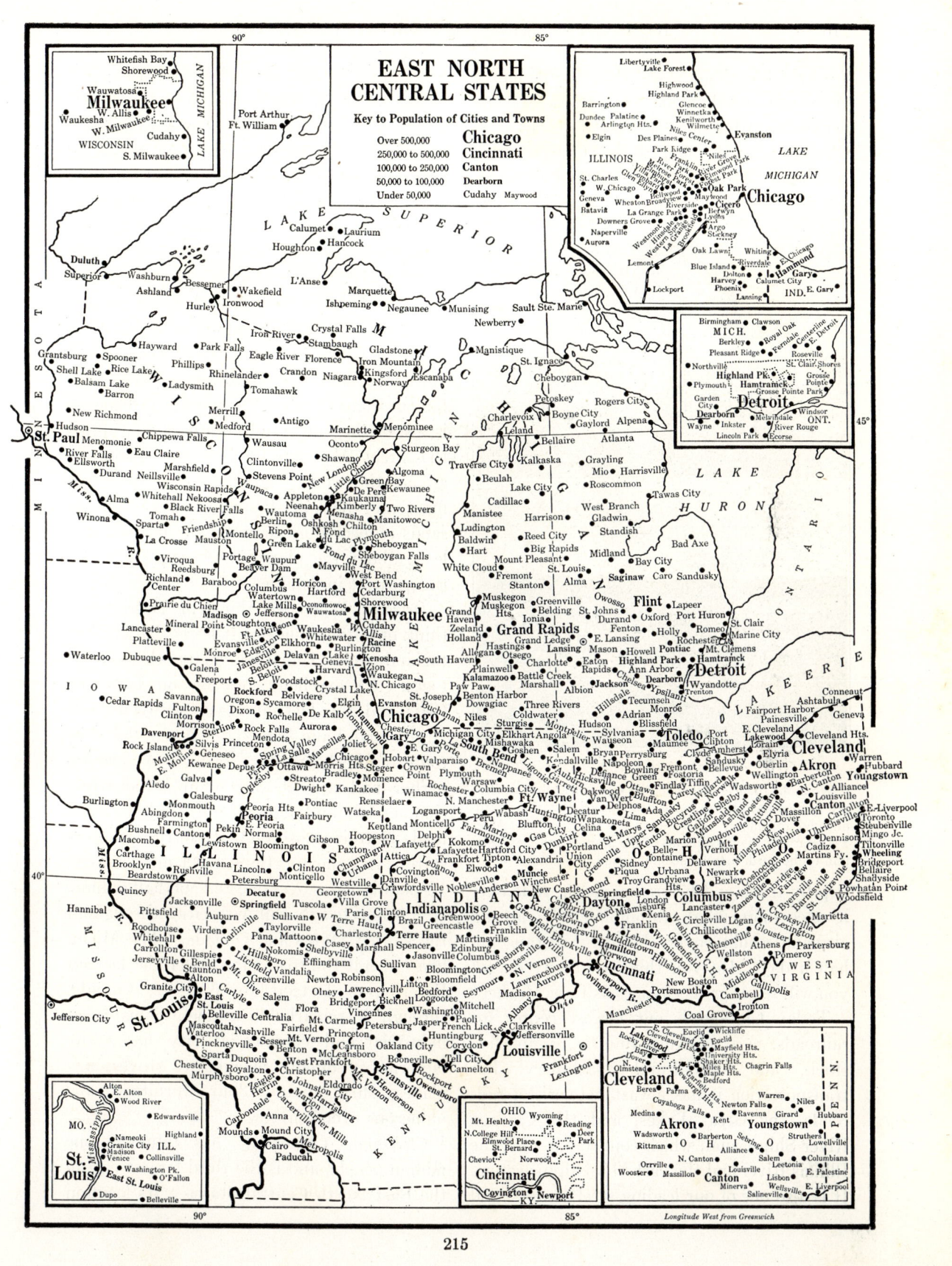

Key to Population of Cities and Towns

Over 500,000	**Chicago**
250,000 to 500,000	**Cincinnati**
100,000 to 250,000	**Canton**
50,000 to 100,000	**Dearborn**
Under 50,000	Cudahy Maywood

a single life time. Less than one hundred years ago, a lad in his teens, Ezra Meeker, helped his father drive a covered ox-cart from Chicago over the long, dusty Oregon Trail. In middle life he was able to take the same

LET'S STAR-GAZE!

When the room is darkened, the wonders of the universe are flashed upon the rounded dome by means of the complicated machinery in the center. Here, at the Adler Planetarium, the movements of the planets and their relation to the earth may be seen and studied.

trip by train, and before his death, rode over it once more in an automobile. Today an airplane would cover the same distance in half a day. Do you think that any one of you will see as great changes as Ezra Meeker?

Today Chicago is our largest center for railroads, meat packing, lumber, grain, live stock, and agricultural machinery. For transportation it has a vast network of railroads, the Great Lakes, and the Chicago River Ship Canal, which connects it with the Illinois River and the vast Mississippi system. It is also one of our leading steel centers, and at South Chicago blast furnaces use much iron ore from Michigan and Minnesota, and coal and limestone from Indiana and other states. Chicago is a great industrial city with more than ten thousand factories using much raw material. Almost any article you can think of is made here, and the city trades with all the world. Freight is sent under the city in subways. The water supply comes from miles out in Lake Michigan.

Chicago is noted for its skyscrapers, extensive parks, beautiful drives, fairgrounds, museums, schools, and universities. The famous John G. Shedd Aquarium in Chicago is one of the finest and largest in the world; the Field Museum of Natural History is among the world's greatest scientific museums; and the Adler Planetarium, where thousands of people go to study the heavens and learn about the planets and stars, is among the greatest in America.

Detroit. When we think of Detroit, we think of automobiles for it leads the world in this industry. But it has many other advantages. Its excellent location on Lake St. Clair and the Detroit River between Lake Huron and Lake Erie puts it on the chief route of the heavy lake traffic. A splendid harbor and a vast surrounding, industrial, commercial, and agricultural territory have made Detroit the second city in this group of states, and the fourth in the United States. Its population is over one and one-half million. It is connected by rail with cities throughout the United States and Canada. The Michigan Central Railroad runs under the Detroit River from Detroit to Windsor, Canada, through a remarkable tunnel. This great industrial and commercial city has many factories producing machinery, stoves, airplanes, ships, paint, flour, furniture, and numerous other things.

Cleveland. Cleveland has almost one million people, and is the third largest city in the East North Central States. Its location

DETROIT, MICHIGAN

Along the short river that connects Lake Erie and Lake Saint Clair is Detroit, famous for the making of automobiles. This "City of the Straits" leads the world in the production of "horseless carriages." It is famous, also, for its beautiful parks, loveliest of which is Belle Isle, an island in the river shown clearly in this picture.

MILWAUKEE, WISCONSIN

In Washington Park, where chains of lagoons are linked together like a string of crystal beads, is a lovely lily pond, over whose clear, still waters a Narcissus might once have knelt to see his image.

CLEVELAND, OHIO

The windings of the Cuyahoga River divide the city into two parts, East side and West side. The Flats along the river are used for factories, docks, and railroad yards. Around the Mall, in the foreground, are grouped the city's public buildings.

on Lake Erie helps to make it the chief iron ore port in the world. Millions of tons of ore are brought to Cleveland to be used in steel mills here or shipped by rail to important steel centers at Youngstown and other places in eastern Ohio, and to Pittsburgh in western Pennsylvania. It also handles coal from Pennsylvania, Ohio, and West Virginia to be used in the great manufacturing industries of the Great Lakes region. The many trains that carry so much iron ore from Cleveland to the steel centers, south and east of Cleveland, would return empty if there were no coal to be shipped back to cities on the lakes. Some of Cleveland's leading industrial products are iron and steel goods, automobiles, clothing, heavy machinery, ships, hardware, and women's clothing. The people take a great pride in their public buildings, schools, parks, and drives, which show excellent planning.

Milwaukee. About 85 miles north of Chicago on the west shore of Lake Michigan lies the busy city of Milwaukee, Wisconsin. This is the fourth city in size of the East North Central States, and has almost three-fourths of a million people. Milwaukee's lake commerce rivals Chicago's. Lake boats bring it coal and iron ore and carry away grain and lumber. Freight cars loaded with grain are ferried across Lake Michigan, and shipped to eastern points. It is not only a beautiful city, with parks, boulevards, and fine buildings, but it is a leading industrial and commercial center. Some of the chief manufacturing plants or products are tanneries and shoe factories, automobile body paints, foundries and machine shops, steel mills, knitting and hosiery mills, breweries, and meat-packing plants. Milwaukee is noted for heavy machinery such as steam shovels and crushers. The great excavators which dug the Panama Canal were made in Milwaukee, and there are crushers in Chile, South America, weighing five hundred tons which were also built here.

Cincinnati. The fifth largest city in these states is Cincinnati, Ohio, in the southwest corner of the state on the Ohio River. This city is the metropolis of the great Ohio Valley, and through it run leading lines of railroads connecting the South and North. Much of the traffic from the East North Central States goes to the South by way of Cincinnati. It owes its growth largely to its nearness to coal, rich farms, and hardwoods, as well as to its river traffic. This has made it an important manufacturing and commercial city, producing boots, shoes, men's clothing, soap, leather, metal products, and motor vehicles. Cincinnati is also noted for slaughtering and meat packing, printing, and publishing.

Indianapolis. Indianapolis is the capital and chief city of Indiana. It is sixth in popu-

INDIANAPOLIS, INDIANA
Fairchild Aerial Surveys
In the heart of the downtown section of this capital city (the second largest state capital in the country) is the World War Memorial Plaza, covering five blocks of parks and beautiful buildings. The city is famous as the home of James Whitcomb Riley, the poet.

CINCINNATI, OHIO

Courtesy Cincinnati Chamber of Commerce

Above the shores of the Ohio River rise the business blocks that give Cincinnati the ragged, jagged skyline of a modern American city. Its name was given to it in 1790, while still a fort, in honor of the Society of the Cincinnati, an organization of officers of the Revolution.

PUT-IN-BAY, LAKE ERIE, OHIO *Ewing Galloway*

This granite shaft, 352 feet from the ground to its beacon light, overlooks the battleground on Lake Erie, and commemorates the Perry victory and the treaty which provided for disarmament along the Canadian border.

COLUMBUS, OHIO *Ewing Galloway*

At the head of the bridge crossing the Scioto stands the American Insurance Union Citadel Building, slim guardian of the newly developed Civic Center of Columbus, capital of the state.

lation in this group of states and is one of the largest cities in the United States not on a navigable waterway. It is located near the center of the state and in the heart of the corn belt, a fact which makes it a very important commercial and industrial city. It has meat-packing plants, automobile factories, and flour mills. Indianapolis is also noted for its foundries, and its machine-shop products.

GRAND RAPIDS, MICHIGAN
© Abrams Aerial Survey Corp.
Another city on a river, this time the Grand, and its descent of eighteen feet in the course of a mile gave the city its name. Some of the power required by the city's many industries is furnished by means of a dam.

Columbus. Columbus is the capital of Ohio, and is about the size of Toledo which has a population of nearly 300,000. It was incorporated about 100 years ago, when it had only a very few people. It has meat-packing plants, railroad shops, foundries, and machine shops. Columbus is the center for Ohio's several hundred clay-products plants, whose annual production is more than one hundred million dollars. It has excellent transportation facilities by land and air. It is served by several important railroads such as the New York Central and the Pennsylvania, and the first coast to coast air-mail line, the Transcontinental Air Transport, Inc., has its eastern terminal here.

Other Cities. — *Toledo,* Ohio's second lake port, has a location similar to that of Chicago, each being on the southwest border of a large lake. This has helped to make these two cities great railroad centers. Toledo is a leading grain and milling center. Among its important industrial products are automobiles, one plant being one of the largest in the world, cut and plate glass, steel goods, oil-well supplies, and refined petroleum.

Akron leads the world in manufacturing rubber tires and tubes. More than half the automobile tires and tubes made in our country are produced here, where tens of thousands of people are employed by more than a dozen companies. About four-fifths of all the tires made in the world are manufactured in the United States, and about half of these are made in Akron.

Dayton is the home of the "National Cash Register," which has one of the largest plants of its kind in the world. It also has one of the largest "frigidaire" factories in the United States. The United States government maintains its testing and experimental laboratories here at Wright Field, one of the largest in the world. Dayton has other important industries such as the making of airplanes, railroad cars, and Delco lighting systems.

Youngstown. The making of iron and steel and their products is the chief industry in Youngstown, Ohio. Look at your map of northeast Ohio and see if you can tell why this city is near the center of one of the greatest iron and steel districts in the United States. Youngstown makes steam shovels, threshing machinery, rubber tires, silk, and other goods.

Grand Rapids. The leading industry of Grand Rapids, Michigan, is furniture making, and it is called "the furniture capital of America," though *Rockford*, Illinois, and *Evansville*, Indiana, are also important furniture centers. Like other large cities in the East North Central States, its industries are numerous and varied.

Flint. When we think of Flint, Michigan, we think of automobiles; for, like Detroit, Flint is a leading center for this industry. The General Motors Corporation makes several leading cars here, and employs thousands of persons in its various factories.

South Bend and *Fort Wayne* are important cities in Indiana. South Bend, in the northwestern part of the state, manufactures automobiles, wagons, farm machinery, sewing machines, clothing, and various other articles. Fort Wayne is in the northeastern part of the state, and produces flour, food products, and clothing; it is also noted for machine shops, knitting mills, and packing plants.

Springfield, the capital of Illinois, is a manufacturing center. It is historically interesting as the home of Abraham Lincoln, for here is located the tomb of the "Great Emancipator," and the only home he ever owned. Tens of thousands of people visit Lincoln's tomb every year.

Peoria, Illinois, is an important city located near the center of the state on the Illinois River. It has vast coal fields near by, and is a good corn market and manufacturing center. Farm implements, washing machines, drugs, chemicals, cigars, liquors, and many other things are made in this city.

East St. Louis and *Quincy* are important cities in western Illinois on the Mississippi River. East St. Louis is just across the river from St. Louis, Missouri, and is a leading meat-packing and commercial center.

Canton, Ohio, situated near the heart of the great industrial center of Youngstown, Akron, East Liverpool, and Cleveland, is a busy manufacturing city of much importance. It produces a great variety of goods, among them being steel products, metal furniture, farm implements, enamelware, brick and tile, cutlery, and rubber gloves. Like Springfield, Illinois, it has historical significance, for it

SPRINGFIELD, ILLINOIS *Ewing Galloway*
From the steps of the Superior Court Building is seen the state capitol, built in the form of a Greek cross, with a dome 361 feet high.

was the home of William McKinley. The McKinley National Memorial, the last resting place of our martyred and beloved president, is one of the beauty spots of Canton.

Kalamazoo, Michigan, is known for its paper mills and factories producing windmills, gas lamps and heaters, stoves, musical instruments, and clothing. Kalamazoo is near the southwestern part of the state where much celery and peppermint are grown.

Terre Haute, Indiana, is a thriving city in the bituminous coal fields of the state, and produces much coke. Other important industries are railroad shops, paper and box factories, glass factories, and flour mills.

ACTIVITIES AND QUESTIONS

1. What difficulties did the early settlers of this region encounter? Why?

2. Tell how railroads helped these states to develop.

3. Describe the commerce of the Great Lakes.

4. Make a list of the leading grain crops in the East North Central States.

5. Where are most of the vegetables consumed?

6. Name the chief animal products of these states.

7. What are the chief mineral products of these states?

8. Make a list of five of the leading cities and their products.

9. Which city specializes in rubber? in meat packing? in leather goods? in steel production? Can you give the reasons in each case?

10. Name the capitals and largest cities in these states.

11. Sketch a map of these states, locating the chief cities, the copper country, the dairy district, the fruit belt, and the corn region.

A NEW ENGLAND HARBOR

All summer long the fast-sailing, trim yachts flit about the harbor of Marblehead like enormous white butterflies.

XI. THE NEW ENGLAND STATES

Many, many years ago all of the northeastern part of the United States, which we now call New England, was covered with ice. This ice sheet, or glacier, was very thick and heavy. It ground off the tops of the mountains, scoured out deep valleys, dug large pits, and left behind much glacial drift. On the hillsides and in the valleys today are many boulders, or large stones, dropped by the glacier. Through the valleys now flow rapid rivers. The deep pits formed many of New England's beautiful ponds and lakes; and old Cape Cod, shaking its fist in the face of the stormy Atlantic, is made up partly of glacial drift. Many years ago, also, some great force caused the land to sink, and as it sank the water of the ocean came in. The area along the New England coast is often referred to as "drowned land," and such a coast line is nearly always irregular in shape with many good harbors. This is in direct contrast to the coast line of the South Atlantic states with its coastal plains extending far out into the ocean. The Cape Cod peninsula marks the northernmost limit of this Atlantic Coastal Plain. The sandy shores of the Cape are quite different from the rugged, bold coast line of the state of Maine.

Mountains and Rivers. — Many years after the ice had gone, large forests came to cover the surface of the land. As you will see from the map (page 225) most of New England is hilly, and there are two distinct mountain groups, the White Mountains in New Hampshire and the Green Mountains in Vermont. Western Massachusetts has its beautiful Berkshire Hills, with Mt. Greylock its tallest peak. Cape Cod, on the other hand, and the land around Buzzards Bay and all along Long Island Sound are mostly low and sandy.

Statistics of the New England States*

State	Abbreviation	Area Sq. Miles	Population	Rank Area	Rank Pop.	Capital	Population	Largest City	Population
Maine . . .	Me.	33,215	847,226	38	35	Augusta	19,360	Portland	73,643
New Hampshire	N. H.	9,304	491,524	43	45	Concord	27,171	Manchester	77,685
Vermont . .	Vt.	9,609	359,231	42	46	Montpelier	8,006	Burlington	27,686
Massachusetts	Mass.	8,257	4,316,721	44	8	Boston	770,816	Boston	770,816
Rhode Island .	R. I.	1,214	713,346	48	36	Providence	253,504	Providence	253,504
Connecticut .	Conn.	5,009	1,709,242	46	31	Hartford	166,267	Hartford	166,267

*1940 Census

Important Products

Maine: — Potatoes, wood pulp, timber, paper, stone
New Hampshire: — Hay, dairy products, textiles, corn, shoes
Vermont: — Stone, dairy products, maple syrup, hay, fruits
Massachusetts: — Textiles, shoes, fish, hay, leather
Rhode Island: — Textiles, jewelry, dairy products, stone, machine tools
Connecticut: — Tobacco, hardware goods, textiles, brass goods, silk

Many rivers like the Connecticut, the Housatonic, the Kennebec, the Penobscot, the Merrimack, and the Charles flowed

MOUNT WASHINGTON
The backbone of the White Mountains in New Hampshire is the Presidential Range, the giants of which are Mounts Washington, Adams, Jefferson, and Madison.

through primeval forests to the sea. Some of the smaller streams like the Merrimack were swift and rapid, and were to be harnessed in later years for water power. Others of these rivers, like the Connecticut, reached far back into the land through wide, deep valleys. These valleys were to make the best of the farming land in New England.

The New England States
Map Questions and Activities

1. Which one of the New England States has no sea coast? How does this influence its commerce? Which state has the shortest coast line?

2. Look at the map and compare the size of Maine with Rhode Island. Their populations are about the same. Can you give some reasons for this situation?

3. Name and locate six of the largest rivers in this group of states and tell what general direction each runs. What advantage is this for New England?

4. From the looks of your map would you expect much water power here? Why?

5. Mention the different kinds of resorts and playgrounds which the map indicates this part of our country has. Name and locate a famous summer resort in Rhode Island.

6. Locate the following: (*a*) capital and largest city of each state; (*b*) five important mountain peaks; (*c*) Lake Champlain and three other large lakes.

7. Trace on a map how an ocean steamer might go from Boston to New York City. Compare this distance with an air-line distance between the two cities.

8. Name and point out the most important bays and harbors on the Atlantic.

9. How does the coast line help the fishing industry in this section?

Physical - Political
NEW ENGLAND STATES

Scale of Statute Miles
0 10 20 30 40 50 100

● State Capitals   — Railroads
The type used indicates the relative sizes of towns and cities.

HEIGHTS IN FEET
- Above 5,000
- 2,000 to 5,000
- 1,000 to 2,000
- 500 to 1,000
- Sea level to 500

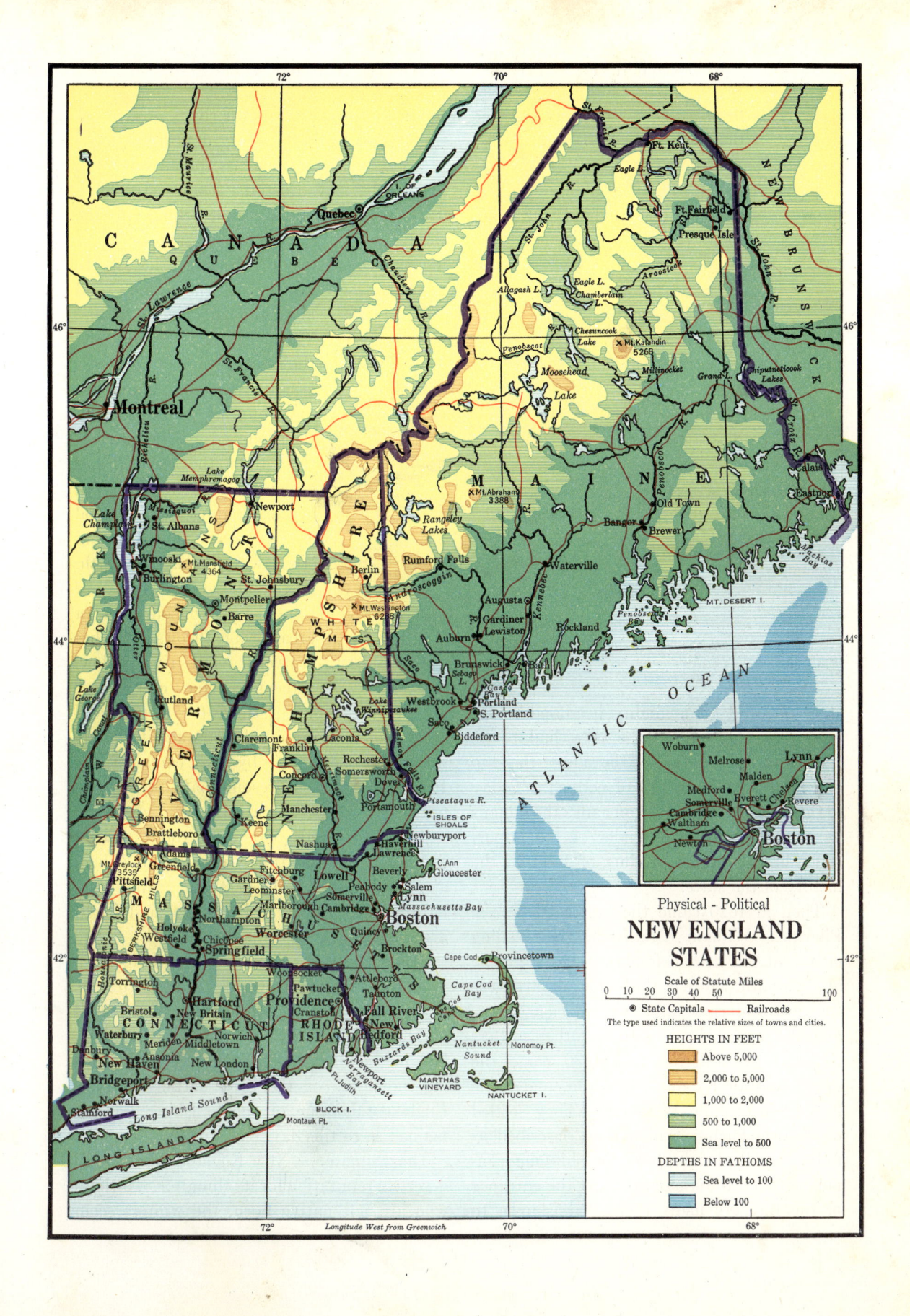

DEPTHS IN FATHOMS
- Sea level to 100
- Below 100

Early Settlers. — The years went by, and the first of the bold explorers began to map out our northeastern coast line. It was old Captain John Smith of Virginia fame who gave it its name "New England," in 1614. In the year 1602, Captain Gosnold sailed into "Cape Codd" harbor and took "a great store of codd off a mighty headland." He even reported that all the crew had to do was to lower baskets over the side of the ship and haul them back full of codfish. Today in the State House in Boston hangs the famous "sacred codfish," a reminder of the importance of this staple product of food in the history of the state.

Then in 1620 came the first settlers, the Pilgrims. William Bradford, the leading citizen of this little community of 102 people at Plymouth, wrote of the country that it was "a vast wilderness filled with savage beasts and still more savage men." Other settlers followed the Pilgrims. In 1630 came the great Puritan Exodus to Boston, under the leadership of John Winthrop. They settled on Boston harbor, which they described as follows: "Better harbors for shipping cannot be found than here are. At the entrance of the Bay are many rocks and islands, to shoulder out the sea, with rivers of fare entrance and peninsulas easy of fortification." Many daughter settlements spread out from Plymouth and Boston. These struggling little communities at first clung to the shore at convenient harbor-side or river mouth. Then rude clearings began to appear in the woods and along the banks of the rivers. The years go by. Where stood the rude clearing in the forest is a thriving community to-day counting its citizens by the thousands. The frail settlement on the seacoast has grown into a mighty city with ever-expanding commercial activity. That thronging street was once a river path. Right above the route of the old-time toilsome ferry a great bridge throws its arches skyward. The river below, a teeming artery of trade, is alive with traffic destined for a thousand ports, yet three hundred years ago its waters were disturbed only by the canoe of the Indian, or the venturesome bark of the pioneer ever moving westward.

Three hundred years ago these earliest settlers had to take things as they found them and make the best of them. And they naturally turned for help to the land itself. There were the fields to be farmed. Along the coast were some of the best fishing grounds in the whole world. And the forests would supply them with logs for their homes and lumber for their ships. These three then, farming, fishing, and forestry, were the leading industries of the early settlers in New England, and one of them, fishing, has remained so to this day.

The Climate. — New England has a well-deserved reputation for its climate. To those who are not native born, the winters seem

PLYMOUTH COLONY IN 1622
© A. S. Burbank

On the harsh, bleak shores of Plymouth Bay the dauntless Pilgrim Fathers had firmly anchored their new colony. Their days were busy ones, spent in farming, fishing, and forest clearing.

long and cold and the summers short and warm. But spring and autumn are beautiful, and there is something in the vigor and freshness of the air which gets into the blood. The prevailing winds are westerly, but a cold current from the ice-floes of the Arctic sweeps down all too near the coast and brings the "icy East winds" for which New England is famous. A great many of the storms which sweep across the United States from west to east cross the New England states, helping to give them very changeable weather.

WOODSVILLE, NEW HAMPSHIRE
Shoving, crowding, eddying with the river's flow, the big logs jam the lower Ammonoosuc on their way to the sawmills.

As one of New England's great spokesmen once said: "Although she has a harsh climate, a barren soil, a rough and stormy coast yet we love the Puritan land for mountain and river, for hillside and valley, for rugged cliff and high sand-dunes with the measureless sea ever murmuring beneath."

Lumbering and Shipping. — Three hundred years ago, much of New England was covered with a splendid growth of forests. These for the large part were native white pine, hemlock, and spruce, although there were many hardwood trees like the oak, maple, chestnut, and elm. For the early settlers there was wood in abundance, and this fact was both a help and a hindrance. Clearings had to be made in the woods so they could get fields to plow and plant. To be sure many of the logs were used for their cabins, and for firewood for the large kitchen fireplaces.

But often it was necessary to chop down trees and burn the logs in order to open up fields for farming. Two of the hardest jobs of a New England farmer were stump-pulling and stone-wall building, and the first New Englanders had a great deal of this back-breaking work to do. Some one has said that "boulders are one of the chief crops of New England," and as one drives or walks over the countryside today the many stone walls that run on and on, bordering the fields and pushing on into the wood lots, seem to bear evidence of the truth of this remark.

As time went on the people of New England learned how to use their forest wealth to advantage. Gangs of hardy axmen would go into the thick of the woods in winter, build

"THE STERN AND ROCKBOUND COAST"
At few places in the world is the pine-scented air so sweet or the sound of the waves as they break on the rocky shores so soothing as in the vacation land of Maine.

a large log shack, and camp out for several weeks. Then the great trees would come crashing to the ground, be cut into logs, and then sledded by means of oxen to the banks of some near-by river. The logs would then be rolled out on the ice to wait for the spring "break-up," when they would come booming

"BLACK AND WHITE AND READ ALL OVER"

Paper, that was once the tall tree trunks in a forest, is fed into the printing presses from big rollers and comes out a part of a book, a magazine, or a newspaper.

down to the sawmills at the falls of the river. Here they would be cut into lumber for building materials.

At the time of the Revolution and for many years after, the largest single manufacturing industry in New England was shipbuilding. There were many famous shipbuilding centers, such as Portland on the Maine coast, Portsmouth in New Hampshire, Medford, Salem, and New Bedford in Massachusetts, Newport in Rhode Island, and Bridgeport and New London in Connecticut. These Yankee ships became famous the world over. The poet Longfellow gives us a fine picture of all this in his poem "The Building of the Ship":

"Till, after many a week at length,
Wonderful for form and strength,
Sublime in its enormous bulk,
Loomed aloft the shadowy hulk."

Many of the "Yankee Clippers," as these ships were called, sailed to our western coast, carrying with them manufactured articles from England and Europe and some home products. After trading with the Indians and the Spanish, they would strike boldly across the Pacific for the "China trade." Here they would make another change of cargoes, this time taking on tea, silk, and spices, and then off once more for a run to some port in Europe. Another exchange for articles desired in the United States and then "home-ward bound" on the last leg of their voyage around the world. During the War of 1812 Yankee ships built and manned by New Englanders were of great service on the high seas in our war with England. The famous brig "Old Ironsides" was built at this time and is a good example of the ships of this period.

But as time went on, the best of the forests were cut down. Iron and steel ships took the place of the Yankee Clippers and whalers. Before long the great forests of the states farther west began to send timber to New England. Even the great standing pines of the state of Maine are nearly all gone, and the annual growth is far less each year than the amount cut. This has raised a new problem in New England, and today all the states are trying to safeguard their best timber by setting aside certain tracts of land and saving forests by what is known as the State Forest Service. In the northern part of Maine, for instance, the state has set aside an area of several million acres known as the Maine Forestry District. Here there are some seventy-five look-out towers and a

"OLD IRONSIDES"

The U. S. Frigate "Constitution" was launched in Boston in 1797. Her first flag was made by Betsy Ross and the copper in her hull was wrought at the foundry of Paul Revere. She won everlasting fame in her victory over the "Guerrière" in 1812.

WHALING

Harpooning a whale became an exciting struggle as the small whale boat maneuvered around the blowing, lashing, wounded monster. When his struggles finally ceased, he was towed to the mother ship, which may be seen waiting some distance off.

"GREAT REPUBLIC"

© *New Haven Railroad*

Built by Donald McKay, at East Boston, Massachusetts, in 1853, this was the largest clipper ship ever constructed. Fully rigged, her square sails wind-full, she proudly cut her way through the white-capped waters.

force of fire wardens, whose business it is to locate and put out forest fires before they burn over large stretches of land and cause great loss.

In addition to this protective policy all the New England states have forces of men engaged in setting out new trees. Thousands of acres of young trees are planted each year on areas which have been cut over.

THE FISHING CAPITAL OF THE UNITED STATES *Ewing Galloway*
The air about the docks in the little seaside town of Gloucester is saturated with the odor of fish, for day after day loads of fish like these are brought to shore, dried, boxed or canned, and sold.

Those early sawmill workers who made lumber out of great logs that came down the river would hardly have thought that the day would come when instead of sawing logs they would grind them into pulp. Such, however, is the case, for today nearly all of our paper is made from pulp wood. Some of the soft woods like poplar and spruce are cut into small logs, put through machines which tear them into shreds, and then this ground-up product is made into pulp in huge vats. It is then thinned out, rolled over cloth carriers, and finally wound onto great drums. It is then shipped to our cities where tons upon tons of this paper are used each week so that we may read our daily newspapers.

No account of New England trees would be complete if we did not mention the maple and the elm. One of the great joys of early spring in New England is "sugaring off" time. When the sap begins to flow in early spring, the maples are "tapped." A sap-bucket catches the clear, sweet juice, which is then boiled down slowly until it thickens. Thus is formed a thick syrup which when it cools makes the very sweet and delicious sugar that is known everywhere as Vermont Maple Sugar. No one could write of New England without speaking of her stately elm trees. The little towns in New England owe much of their beauty to the graceful elms that line the main streets, encircle the Town Common, and stand guard over the roof of many a modest New England home.

Fisheries. — The early settlers found an abundance of fish, lobsters, oysters, and clams all along the New England coast. Says one old writer: "The Mackerals have shott themselves ashore with the surfe of the sea so that whole hoggsheads have been taken up on the sands. They measure 18 and 19 inches in length." The shad and the alewives (herring) were very abundant in the spring. "In two tides they have gotten 100,000 of these Fishes," says another writer, "in a Wayne (net) just below the falls of the Charles River." These fish were often used by the colonists as fertilizer, placing one in each hill of corn. Lobsters were "infinite in store" and of great size. Oysters were also found in "greate store in the entrance of all Rivers,"

Maple Sugar Time in Vermont

"Sap's running!" That is the cry that heralds two weeks of busy activity in the Vermont woods. Horse-drawn sleds make the rounds from tree to tree, collecting the sap which has dripped into the buckets fastened to the trees. It then goes to the sugar house and becomes syrup and maple sugar candy.

Wethersfield, Connecticut

For 264 years this great elm — said to be the largest elm in the United States — has spread its dark arms to the sky.

The Church of Our Forefathers

The little white church on the common is a landmark in nearly every New England village.

and of clams "there is no want; every shore is full." Mackerel, cod, and haddock were caught just off the coast. Thriving fishing hamlets grew up along the shore from Eastport in Maine to Long Island Sound. Because of the good harbors at Marblehead and Gloucester these towns became centers of the fish trade. The Newfoundland banks were finally to prove the best fishing grounds, and year after year fishing fleets have left these harbors for a quick run to "the Banks,"

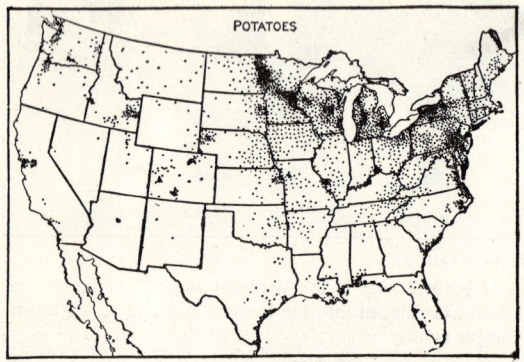

U. S. Department of Agriculture
POTATOES IN ALL STATES

Each dot on this map stands for 1000 acres. Potatoes are grown in every state, but they grow best in a rather cool climate. The map tells us that most of them are grown in the northeastern and north central parts of the United States north of the corn belt. This map refers to white potatoes only. What other kind of potatoes are grown in the southern states?

then back to dry, salt, pack, and ship the fish into the interior. To this day the New England states rank high in the value of their fish products, with Boston and Gloucester the chief centers of this trade.

The fish are split in half, salted, and then spread out to dry. Artificial drying apparatus is used indoors when the weather is unfavorable for outdoor drying. When dry, they are boned, shredded, and packed neatly in boxes. The canning of fish, particularly herring, cod, and haddock, is a thriving industry. Rhode Island is famous for its oysters, Maine for its lobsters, and Massachusetts for its clams. All these are frozen, also, and because this preserves them, they can now be shipped all over the United States.

No account of the fisheries of New England would be complete if mention were not made of the fact that many sections are noted as sportmen's paradises for fishing with the rod and reel. Maine, in particular, has many streams and lakes, where one may catch the beautiful speckled trout, land-locked salmon, bass, pickerel, and perch. All the states stock their best streams with small fish each year.

Farming. — Generally speaking, New England does not have good farming land. The hillsides have steep slopes, often covered with large stones. The soil is thin, and except in the larger river valleys, ledges of granite and other hard rocks often crop out at the surface. Long winters make it difficult for the farmer to get in his seed or harvest his crops because of the frost and snow. The farms are usually rather small, and a great variety of crops is raised on each one. Every farmer tries to raise at least enough hay and grain for his own stock. He intends to put in enough vegetables, such as potatoes, beans, squash, carrots, and turnips, to see his family through the winter; and has a small fresh vegetable garden of peas, beans, beets, lettuce, squash, corn, and tomatoes for his summer "green goods."

New England apples have a flavor all their own and are the chief fruit crop. The apple industry is developing rapidly and apples should become one of the best market crops. Other fruits, such as peaches, strawberries, and raspberries, are being grown in greater quantities, particularly along the shore of Long Island Sound. There are other special crops in New England that are famous all over the United States; such as Cape Cod cranberries, Aroostook County potatoes, long-leaf tobacco in the Connecticut Valley, and the big blueberries that grow over the cut-over, burned-over uplands.

AT DYER BROOK, MAINE *Ewing Galloway*
Long rows of the famous Aroostook potatoes are being harvested for market.

AVON, CONNECTICUT *Publishers' Photo*
Under great canopies of white cheesecloth the tender young tobacco plants are carefully cultivated.

GILFORD, NEW HAMPSHIRE
On the wooded hillsides of New Hampshire are the typical New England farms; a group of buildings, a plowed field or two, irregular stone walls. and two narrow, brown dirt tracks worn through the meadow grass.

CHINOOK KENNELS, WONALANCET, NEW HAMPSHIRE
Many of these huskies have been with Admiral Byrd on his Antarctic expeditions. The wire-net houses were used on the ship going out and coming back.

John G. Whittier has drawn for us, in his poem "Snowbound," a fine picture of New England farm life and character. The typical farm house is a story and a half structure, joined by a shed or two to a large rambling barn with a silo. Then come sheds for the wagons and farm implements. These buildings are nearly always connected, which is a convenience during the winter when the heavy snow falls. On the other hand, farm property is often a bad fire risk, for if a fire gets started, the whole place frequently burns to the ground.

A number of years ago many of the farmers in New England raised sheep. Then came the great influx of wool and mutton from our Western states and from Australia and New Zealand, and sheep disappeared almost wholly from the hillsides and rocky valleys of New England. In recent years, however, farmers have again taken up sheep-farming, for it has been found that the rough pasturage is well suited to sheep and they can be raised with profit if the flocks do not grow too large.

It is interesting to note that it has become profitable in New Hampshire and Maine to raise dogs for polar expeditions. Many of the "huskies" used by Admiral Byrd and others were selected from New England stock.

Manufacturing Industries. For many years before the American Revolution it was part of the policy of Old England to discourage manufacturing in the colonies. There were laws against importing any manufacturing tools or machinery. In the words of an English statesman, "If I had my way the Colonies should not make a hob-nail." Yet in spite of all this a young mechanic by the name of Samuel Slater arrived in the colonies and brought a cotton-spinning machine with him. To be sure he brought it in his head and it was only after much labor on his part with the aid of Yankee skill that he was able to set up and operate the first spinning-machine factory in this country. This was at Pawtucket in Rhode Island in 1790. The old mill is still standing.

THE SLATER MILL
The first in New England's long line of industrial mills, and the beginning of her industrial wealth.

This was the beginning of a great industrial era in New England. Massachusetts was a leader in this work, and today great factories and mills perform the work formerly done by the spinning-wheel, the hand-loom, and the village cobbler.

People have been moving away from the farms and crowding into the great industrial centers. This accounts for the many large cities we find in New England, and today in the three states of Massachusetts, Connecticut, and Rhode Island most of the people live in cities. How do all these people make a living? Let us go into some of the great manufacturing centers and watch the people at work.

The Textile Industries. — In 1813 a large cotton mill was erected at Waltham on the Charles, and for the first time in America all the processes of clothmaking were carried on under one roof. The mill operated 1700 spindles. The power-loom was put into operation in 1814 by F. C. Lowell, and after this the textile industry grew by leaps and bounds. Crude mills were erected at Lawrence and Lowell on the Merrimack, and many other streams in New England were harnessed and their water power used to run the mills.

In 1791 the woolen industry was almost wholly confined to families producing homespun goods. Three years later the first woolen factory was built in Haverhill, Massachusetts, and shortly afterward Amos Whittemore invented a new carding machine which transformed the business. Woolen mills sprang up at Uxbridge and Pittsfield, and from this beginning the industry spread throughout New England. Worsted manufacturing did not begin until 1858. Ten years later cloth for suits was made, and this industry grew rapidly. Many large cities have sprung up around the sites of the first textile mills, and thousands of people have made their living tending the machines in the big factories which cover acres of ground. Though many cotton mills have moved to the southern states, New England is still the leader in the production of woolens and worsted, and the manufacture of rayon goods is a growing industry.

Courtesy Boston and Maine Railroad
MANCHESTER, NEW HAMPSHIRE
The Merrimack River has helped to furnish power for more cotton spindles than are found along any other river. The smoking chimneys and whirring wheels of mills are found all the way from Franklin, New Hampshire, to Newburyport, Massachusetts.

Rhode Island has developed into one of the strongest textile manufacturing states in the Union. The population of the state has grown rapidly and has centered in its cities. Providence, the largest city, is one of the most important seaports in New England, and because of both water and rail facilities Rhode Island is able to transport its manufactured products easily.

Leather Manufactures. — It is a long cry from the days of the traveling cobbler to the immense shoe factories one finds today in such cities as Brockton and Lynn in Massachusetts, and Manchester in New Hampshire. The first real shoe factory in New England was established at Danvers in 1786. For many years there was a strange prejudice against machine-made shoes. Most shoes were made in little shops employing five to ten men. In 1861 a sole sewing machine was invented and other labor-saving machines followed. Massachusetts and New Hampshire are leaders in this industry today. Massachusetts is easily the leading state of the Union in the production of boots and shoes. In fact quite a large number of

Courtesy Vermont Marble Company
WEST RUTLAND, VERMONT
Up a steep inclined plane, blocks of white marble ride to sunlight from the dark heart of the quarry.

the people of the United States walk in shoes made in Massachusetts.

Foundry Products. — The products of the foundry play a large part in all industrial activity. Joseph Jenks of Lynn was the first founder who worked in brass and iron on our western continent. Hugh Orr in 1746 made the first musket ever turned out in America. Now the foundry business centers around the city of Worcester, Massachusetts. It has been said that should one draw a cricle with a ten-mile radius around Worcester, a larger range of metal manufacturing would be found there than in any circle of the same diameter elsewhere in the world. Connecticut, also, has been outstanding for its foundry and machine shops. It is a leader in the manufacture of brass, bronze, and copper articles, as well as in the manufacture of firearms. Meriden is famous for its silverware; and Waterbury for its watches.

Quarrying. — Every one has heard of New England granite and Vermont marble. Granite makes a good building stone and there are fine quarries in Massachusetts, Rhode Island, Vermont, and New Hampshire. New Hampshire is known as the "Granite State," but the quarries at Quincy in Massachusetts are famous, and Barre, Vermont, is called "the granite center of the world."

Vermont possesses a practically unlimited supply of a very fine marble. For years this Green Mountain State has ranked first of all the states in the Union in the output of marble. Many public and private buildings throughout the United States have used Vermont marble for much of their interior finish. Proctor and Rutland are the leading marble centers.

Slate and other stones are also used for building purposes. The thin leaves of slate are used chiefly for shingles for some of our finest homes and public buildings. The coarser slabs are often used for sidewalks, but the finer ones make good blackboards for schools.

Scenery and Resorts. — New England during the summer months is one of the loveliest recreation grounds in the United States. It can offer both mountain and shore, lake and forest. Many hotels have been erected on the slopes of the White Mountains in New Hampshire and the Green Mountains in Vermont. Thousands of people leave the cities in the summer to go to their cottages on the shores of the lakes in Maine, or along the sandy beaches of Massachusetts and Long Island Sound.

Moosehead Lake in Maine has an area of

MT. CHOCORUA, NEW HAMPSHIRE

Courtesy New England Council

A favorite hike for outdoor enthusiasts, and a place of beauty for all who enjoy the gifts of Nature.

SKI-JUMPING

A swift rush, a leap into space, and a sure landing — that is sport!

THE SNOW TRAIN

When the north wind howls and the fields lie blanketed in white, powdery snow, an army of winter sport-lovers entrain for mountain playgrounds — shouldering skis like muskets.

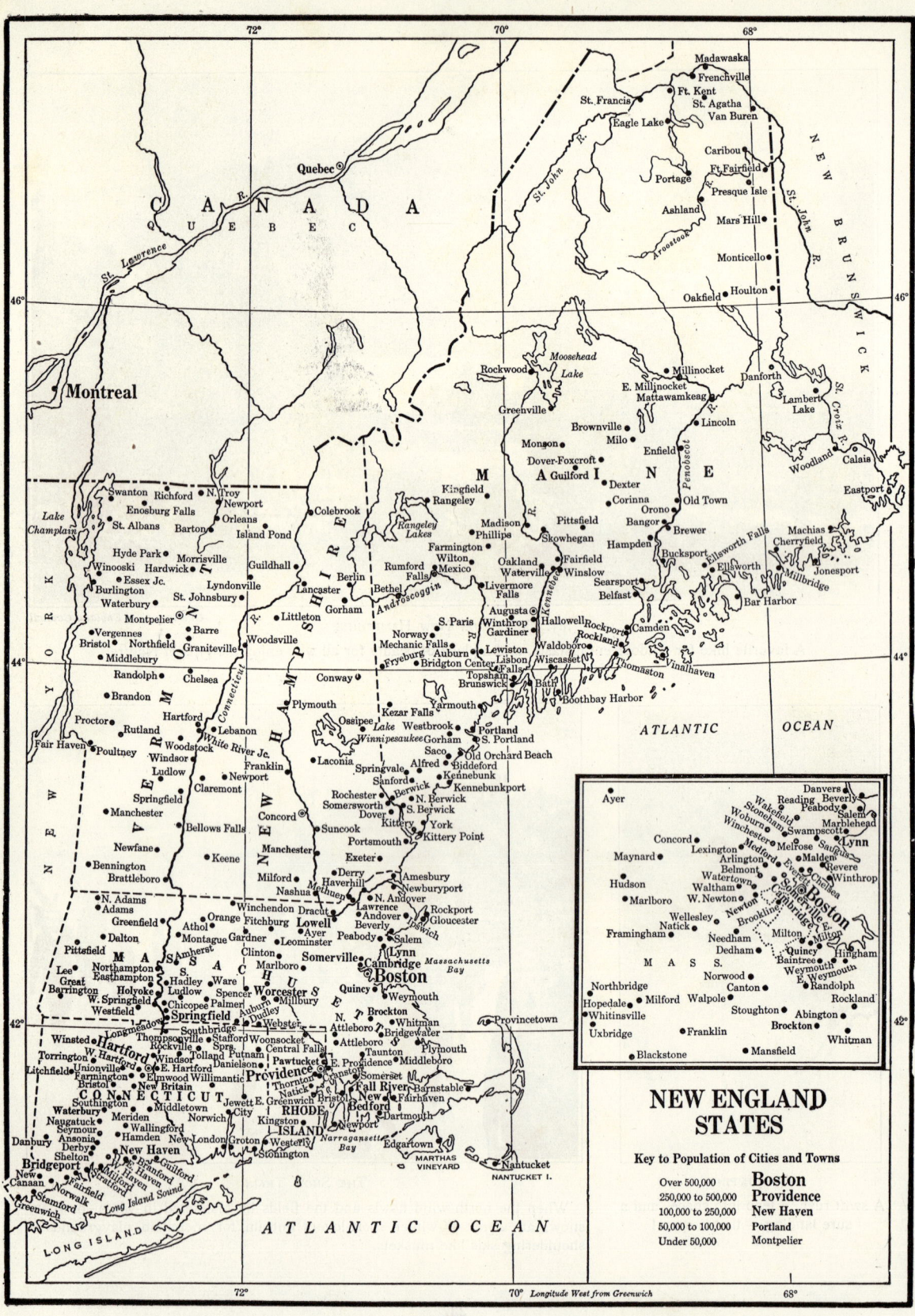

NEW ENGLAND STATES

Key to Population of Cities and Towns

Over 500,000	**Boston**
250,000 to 500,000	**Providence**
100,000 to 250,000	New Haven
50,000 to 100,000	Portland
Under 50,000	Montpelier

120 square miles and the Rangeley lakes are almost as large. Mt. Desert Island has been for years the crowning glory of the beautiful Maine coast, and a few years ago was made into a National Park. As soon as schools close in June, many boys and girls from the cities rush off to summer camps in New England. Here they can take part in all the wholesome outdoor sports. If the campsite is along the shore, they can enjoy ocean bathing and deep-sea fishing and sailing. Moreover, New England is beginning to advertise her winter sports, and there are many places in Maine, New Hampshire, Vermont, and Massachusetts which make their appeal to those who love the vigorous winter sports of skiing, snowshoeing, tobogganing, and skating.

Cities. — New England has many famous cities. We have already spoken of several of these in connection with some fact in their history or their leading industrial products. In every case there is a reason why each city is located where it is. For instance, *Boston*, the capital of Massachusetts, has the best harbor along the entire New England coast. The map shows you clearly how centrally located it is, right back of Cape Cod Bay. As Emerson said: "It was destined to grow great." *Worcester*, about fifty miles inland, has often been called the "Heart of the Commonwealth"; and the city of *Springfield* with its beautiful civic center and fine public schools is also important for its manufactures of metal goods of all sorts. *Lowell, Lawrence, Haverhill, Fall River, New Bedford,* and others are leading textile centers. *Holyoke* in western Massachusetts is famous for its fine paper mills. These mills make some of the paper money for the United States Treasury notes. *Pittsfield* on the Housatonic River is located in the beautiful Berkshire Hills. It is a favorite summer resort, and is noted, also, for its manufacture of electrical and automobile supplies. *Cambridge* is the

ON THE PENOBSCOT RIVER *Ewing Galloway*
The swift-flowing river coils about the frayed edges of the wooded shores or hurries by a group of village homes, huddled close for company.

home of Harvard University, founded while still the howl of the wolf could be heard along the Charles River, "in order that learning should not perish in the graves of the fathers."

Most of the large cities in the state of Maine are located either on the coast, near the mouths of rivers, or a few miles up these rivers at some convenient and natural site where usually there is water power. *Eastport* on the Passamaquoddy Bay is our most eastern town. It is at the mouth of the St. Croix River, which is the boundary between Maine and New Brunswick in Canada. Just opposite Eastport is Campobello Island, where President Franklin D. Roosevelt had his summer home. *Bar Harbor* is on Mt. Desert Island, famous as a summer resort. *Bangor*

PROVIDENCE, RHODE ISLAND

Fairchild Aerial Surveys

The capital of Rhode Island spreads out over seven hills, along the Seekonk and Providence rivers. Many of its streets still bear the names that reflect Quaker influence — Power, Benevolent, Benefit, Friendship, and Peace.

is situated at the head of navigation on the Penobscot River, sixty miles from its mouth, and is the center of transportation in this section of the state. *Bath* was one of the old shipbuilding centers, and is famous today for its manufacture of marine engines and cordage mills. *Lewiston* is on the Androscoggin River at the great falls. *Augusta*, on the Kennebec, is the capital of the state, and *Portland*, on beautiful Casco Bay, is the largest city. Portland has a fine harbor, and is the center of the fishing and lumber interests of this section of the state. It was the birthplace of the poet Henry W. Longfellow.

Portsmouth is the only seaport in the state of New Hampshire. It has a fine deep harbor. A United States Navy Yard is located here, where many fine ships have been built and launched. *Concord* on the Merrimack is the capital of the state. *Nashua*, also on the Merrimack, is noted for the manufacture of boots, shoes, and machine-shop supplies. *Manchester*, its largest city, also located on the Merrimack, is known for its large cotton and woolen mills and its boot and shoe factories. *Hanover*, on the upper reaches of the beautiful Connecticut River, is the home of Dartmouth College.

Montpelier is the capital of Vermont. We have already mentioned *Rutland, Barre*, and *Proctor* as centers of the granite and marble quarries in Vermont. *Burlington* is the largest city and is situated on the eastern shore of Lake Champlain. It is a beautiful city with a fine tower erected to the fame of Ethan Allen and his Green Mountain Revolutionary soldiers. It has a large trade in lumber, building stones, woolen goods, and

BOSTON

City of famous people — Paul Revere, John Adams, John Hancock, Longfellow, Lowell, Louisa M. Alcott; of historic buildings — Faneuil Hall, Old North Church, King's Chapel, Old South Meeting House; of famous institutions — Boston Latin School (oldest high school in America), Boston University, Simmons College, New England Conservatory of Music.

DUNSTER HOUSE, HARVARD UNIVERSITY

Tower and chimneys and dark red walls lie reflected in the quiet, star-studded waters of the Charles River.

THE CAMPANILE AT SPRINGFIELD

More and more, American cities are remodeling their civic buildings on the classic lines of Greek art.

BENNINGTON BATTLE MONUMENT
The tower that commemorates the Battle of Bennington, fought August 16, 1777

HARTFORD, CONNECTICUT
The state capitol building rises from a setting of shady green parks and flowering rose gardens.

furniture. *St. Johnsbury* is the home of the famous works of the Fairbanks Scales Company.

The capital city of Connecticut is *Hartford*, and this city, with *Bridgeport* and *New Haven*, is especially important for the manufacture of metal goods. New Haven is the seat of Yale University; and Bridgeport is a large shipbuilding center. *Waterbury* is famous for its watches, and *Meriden* for its cutlery and silverware. *New Britain* is noted for its large output of hardware, and it is often called "the Hardware City." It also has large plants which manufacture cigars and cigarettes.

Rhode Island is a leading textile state, and its chief cities, *Providence*, *Pawtucket*, and *Woonsocket*, are the chief centers of this industry. Woonsocket is known also for its rubber goods. *Newport* is not only widely famed as a summer resort, but is a place of great historic interest. It is situated at the entrance of Narragansett Bay. Providence, the capital of Rhode Island, is the second city of New England. Providence is a beautiful city with fine parks and public buildings. The most famous of its parks is named in honor of its founder Roger Williams. The State House is an imposing building of white marble. Brown University is located in Providence. It is the leading city in the United States in the manufacture of jewelry and silverware and has one of the largest mechanical tool factories in the world.

Activities and Questions

1. Describe the surface of New England.
2. On what did the early settlers depend for a living? Why?
3. What are now the leading manufactures of New England? Why?
4. How have the forests been used?
5. Describe the New England climate.
6. Collect pictures of New England coast and mountain scenes, and of various industries.

THE NEW ENGLAND STATES

7. What states produce granite and marble?

8. Where does the fishing industry center? Why there?

9. Which is the largest New England state? the smallest?

10. Where is the most tobacco grown? Why there?

11. Name the chief New England rivers.

12. What are the chief highlands of New England?

13. Compare New England lumbering with that in the South. Why the difference?

14. Name three famous New England universities.

15. Sketch a map of New England, putting in the chief mountains, rivers, and cities.

HALIFAX *Courtesy Canadian National Railways*
From Citadel Hill — a fortress since 1749 and the capital of the land that was once Acadia.

XII. CANADA, OUR NORTHERN NEIGHBOR

A Steamer Trip to Halifax. — On a Saturday morning in early June, we leave New York City on a good-sized cruising steamer for a trip to Halifax, Nova Scotia. Once more we pass the Statue of Liberty, steam through the Narrows, and out upon the broad Atlantic. As we travel northeastward, at first we see the shore of Long Island on the left, but we soon pass out of sight of land. After a while we turn north and then we learn that we are off the New England coast. Here are the famous fishing grounds through which sailed the *Mayflower* and other historic ships of long ago. We spend Saturday night and Sunday on the water, finally arriving at Halifax Monday morning. (See map on page 2.)

Halifax, the Capital of Nova Scotia. — Halifax is the capital and largest city of Nova Scotia, one of Canada's eastern provinces. The divisions of Canada are named provinces instead of states, as they are called in our country. We are surprised at the beauty and size of the harbor of Halifax. It is about sixteen miles long, one to two miles wide, and has an area of about twenty square miles. It is one of the finest and deepest harbors in all Canada and compares well with other great harbors of the world. Lying on the slopes of hills which face the roomy harbor, surrounded by a dozen forts, Halifax is a famous naval station of the British Empire. Seldom a day passes without a visit from one of Great Britain's warships. It is also a center of trade and industry for eastern Canada and a terminus and shipping point for great railroad lines.

The Maritime Provinces. — We spend several days making railway and automobile trips to various parts of the Provinces of Nova Scotia, New Brunswick, and Prince Edward Island. These are called the Maritime Provinces of Canada because they are near the sea or ocean. We find the railway service excellent and the automobile roads in fairly good condition. The coasts of the Maritime Provinces remind us of our own New England States. They are bold and rocky with many inlets, some of which are very large. The Bay

THE BORE OF THE PETITCODIAC
As the tide turns, a thick layer of foaming, rushing water covers the quiet river in the twinkling of an eye.

drying sheds, and canneries. Nearly two-fifths of Canada's total catch of fish comes from these provinces, Nova Scotia being the most important. Most of the cured fish go to the West Indies, South America, and the Mediterranean countries of Europe, but a large part of the catch is shipped fresh each day to the provinces of Quebec and Ontario, and to our own New England States.

All through the Maritime Provinces there is also much fishing for pleasure and sport in the many rushing trout streams and inviting lakes.

of Fundy extends far into the interior of Nova Scotia and New Brunswick and has many large harbors. Its tides are among the highest in the world, rising many feet and rushing into some of the rivers as a solid wall of water. This is called the tidal *bore*. The roar of the water can be heard a long way off and vessels are tossed about like corks. Much of the lowland around the Bay of Fundy is diked and used as meadow land, for the soil is rich and produces large crops of grass and hay.

Fishing. — Everywhere we travel along the shores of the Maritime Provinces we see signs of the fishing industry, where cod, lobster, halibut, herring, mackerel, and haddock are caught, some in nets and some by hook and line. The inshore fisheries, that is, those within ten or twelve miles of the coast, are more important than the offshore or deep-sea fisheries. They are safer, easier, and cheaper, for the deep-sea fishermen may be gone for several weeks or even months, and so must clean, salt, and pack the fish on board ship.

Halifax is an important center of the industry, but nearly every coastal village has its fishing vessels — some large, some small —

Agriculture. — Like our own New England, most of the land is rugged, with many hills and valleys. Many of the slopes are covered with forests, but the lowlands are used for agriculture. Prince Edward Island is wholly lowland, most of which is cultivated. Hay, clover, and oats make up about four-fifths of all crops, but fruits and vegetables are also grown. Lesser crops are spring wheat, buck-

AN OX TEAM, GREENFIELD
A slow-moving yoke of oxen makes rapid enough transportation in a land where even the thrifty and industrious farmer need never hurry.

Courtesy Canadian National Railways
FISH DOCKS AT LOCKPORT

Handling the fish, as the hauls are brought to the dock in small fishing dories, is a job that keeps many workers busy.

A SHIPPING SCENE, CAMPBELLTON

The white-winged fishing boats rest a little before going out once more to buffet the pounding waves with the wind shrieking through the halyards.

FISH DRYING AT LUNENBERG
Courtesy Canadian National Railways

The peaceful little harbor is protected by low, wooded hills, and at every home, with its long wharf, white mounds of skinned and cut-in-half fish are laid out in the sun and air to dry.

CANADA, OUR NORTHERN NEIGHBOR

Statistics of the Dominion of Canada

Provinces of Canada	Abbreviation	Area Sq. Miles	Population 1941	Rank Area	Rank Pop.	Capital	Population 1941	Largest City	Population 1941
Quebec	Que.	594,860	3,331,882	1	2	Quebec	150,757	Montreal	903,007
Ontario	Ont.	412,582	3,787,655	2	1	Toronto	667,457	Toronto	667,457
British Columbia	B. C.	366,255	817,861	3	4	Victoria	44,068	Vancouver	275,353
Alberta	Alta.	255,285	796,169	4	5	Edmonton	93,817	Edmonton	93,817
Saskatchewan	Sask.	251,700	895,992	5	3	Regina	58,245	Regina	58,245
Manitoba	Man.	246,512	729,744	6	6	Winnipeg	221,960	Winnipeg	221,960
Yukon	Yukon	207,076	4,914	7	11	Dawson	1,043	Dawson	1,043
New Brunswick	N. B.	27,985	457,401	8	8	Fredericton	10,062	Saint John	51,741
Nova Scotia	N. S.	21,068	577,962	9	7	Halifax	70,488	Halifax	70,488
Prince Edward Island	P. E. I.	2,184	95,047	10	9	Charlottetown	14,821	Charlottetown	14,821
Northwest Territory	N. W. T.	1,304,903	12,028		10				

Important Products

Quebec: — Dairy products, potatoes, wood pulp, textiles, asbestos.
Ontario: — Dairy products, wheat, flour, automobiles, pulp and paper.
British Columbia: — Lumber, fruits, lead, copper, fish.
Alberta: — Live stock, grains, flour, coal, petroleum.
Saskatchewan: — Wheat, dairy products, flour, live stock, coal.
Manitoba: — Grains, flour, vegetables, live stock, dairy products.
Yukon: — Furs, silver, gold, copper, fish.
New Brunswick: — Dairy products, paper and pulp, coal, vegetables.
Nova Scotia: — Fruits, dairy products, fish, paper and pulp, coal.
Prince Edward Island: — Potatoes, dairy products, vegetables, furs, fish.
Northwest Territory: — Furs, reindeer, silver.

---

wheat, barley, and beans. The Maritime Provinces are famous for their hardy fruits. The Annapolis Valley in northwestern Nova Scotia is very well known for its fine apples and cherries.

CANADA AND NEWFOUNDLAND

Map Questions and Activities

1. What are the names of the provinces shown on this map?
2. Point to and name the capital of each province.
3. From the map, which province would you estimate to be the largest?
4. Does Labrador belong to Canada or to Newfoundland?
5. What is the name of the very large bay which touches the provinces of Quebec, Ontario, and Manitoba?
6. Are there any high mountains in Canada? Where? How does the map tell you?
7. What part of Canada seems to be fairly well supplied with railroads? In what general direction do they run?
8. Why are there no railroads in the Northwest Territories?
9. Do the Great Lakes belong to Canada as well as to the United States?
10. With the help of the scale of miles estimate the airline distance from Halifax to Victoria.
11. Which one of the Canadian provinces would you like most to visit? Why? If you have ever been to Canada tell some of the things you saw there.
12. Does the map suggest one or more reasons why Montreal has become the greatest city of Canada?
13. Why has Canada so few large seaports, when its coast line is so very long?
14. What and where is Newfoundland?
15. What bearing has the coast line of Nova Scotia and Newfoundland on the fishing industry in these two sections?

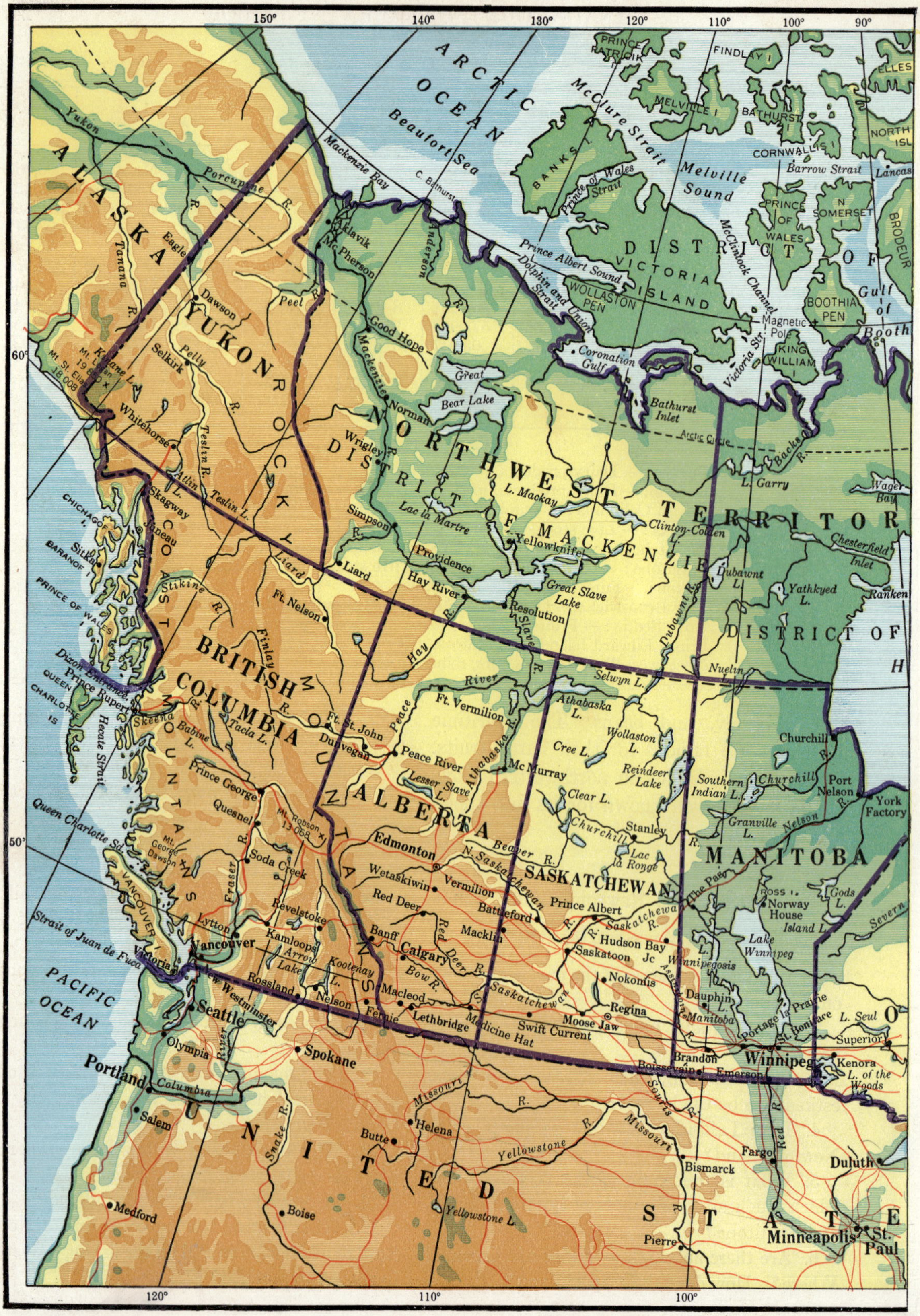
ARCTIC OCEAN
Beaufort Sea
Mackenzie Bay
ALASKA
YUKON
ROCKY MOUNTAINS
NORTHWEST TERRITORIES
DISTRICT OF MACKENZIE
DISTRICT OF
BRITISH COLUMBIA
COAST MOUNTAINS
ALBERTA
SASKATCHEWAN
MANITOBA
UNITED STATES
PACIFIC OCEAN
Melville Sound
McClure Strait
DISTRICT OF VICTORIA ISLAND
Great Bear Lake
Great Slave Lake
Lake Winnipeg
Whitehorse
Dawson
Juneau
Prince Rupert
Prince George
Edmonton
Calgary
Vancouver
Victoria
Seattle
Portland
Spokane
Regina
Saskatoon
Winnipeg
Churchill
Yellowknife
Aklavik
Minneapolis
St. Paul
Duluth
Bismarck
Helena
Butte
Boise
Medford
Salem
Olympia
Lethbridge
Medicine Hat
Moose Jaw
Swift Current
Prince Albert
Brandon
Fargo
Pierre
Kenora
Mt. Logan 19,850
Mt. St. Elias 18,008
Mt. Robson 13,068
Strait of Juan de Fuca
Queen Charlotte Sd.
Hecate Strait
150°
140°
130°
120°
110°
100°
90°
60°
50°

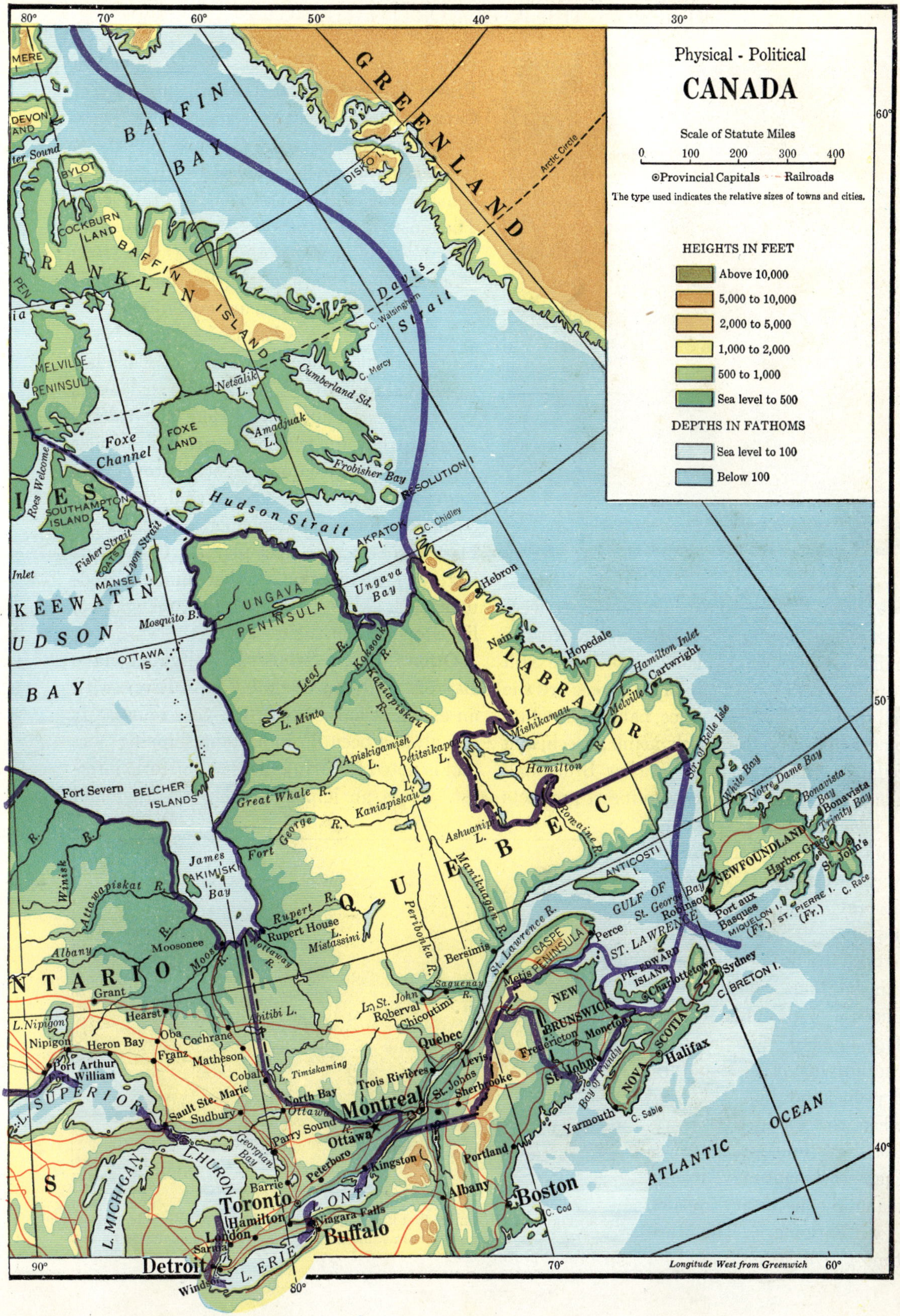
Physical - Political
CANADA
Scale of Statute Miles
0 100 200 300 400
⊙Provincial Capitals
Railroads
The type used indicates the relative sizes of towns and cities.
HEIGHTS IN FEET
Above 10,000
5,000 to 10,000
2,000 to 5,000
1,000 to 2,000
500 to 1,000
Sea level to 500
DEPTHS IN FATHOMS
Sea level to 100
Below 100
GREENLAND
BAFFIN BAY
DISKO I.
Arctic Circle
Davis Strait
C. Walsingham
C. Mercy
Cumberland Sd.
BAFFIN ISLAND
FRANKLIN
COCKBURN LAND
BYLOT I.
DEVON
MELVILLE PENINSULA
Netsalik L.
Amadjuak L.
FOXE LAND
Foxe Channel
Frobisher Bay
RESOLUTION I.
Hudson Strait
C. Chidley
AKPATOK I.
SOUTHAMPTON ISLAND
Roes Welcome
Fisher Strait
Lyon Strait
MANSEL I.
KEEWATIN
HUDSON BAY
Mosquito B.
OTTAWA IS
UNGAVA PENINSULA
Ungava Bay
Hebron
Nain
Hopedale
Hamilton Inlet
Cartwright
LABRADOR
Melville L.
Mishikamau L.
Hamilton R.
Str. of Belle Isle
White Bay
Notre Dame Bay
Bonavista Bay
Bonavista
Trinity Bay
NEWFOUNDLAND
Harbor Grace
St. John's
C. Race
Port aux Basques
MIQUELON I. (Fr.)
ST. PIERRE I. (Fr.)
Robinson
St. George Bay
GULF OF ST. LAWRENCE
ANTICOSTI I.
Leaf R.
Koksoak R.
Kaniapiskau R.
L. Minto
Apiskigamish L.
Petitsikapau L.
Kaniapiskau L.
Great Whale R.
BELCHER ISLANDS
Fort Severn
Fort George R.
Ashuanipi L.
Romaine R.
QUEBEC
Manikuagan R.
Peribonka R.
James Bay
AKIMISKI I.
Rupert R.
Rupert House
Mistassini L.
Bersimis
St. Lawrence R.
GASPE PENINSULA
Perce
Matis
Winisk R.
Attawapiskat R.
Albany
Moose R.
Moosonee
ONTARIO
Nottaway R.
Abitibi L.
L. St. John
Roberval
Chicoutimi
Saguenay R.
Grant
Hearst
L. Nipigon
Nipigon
Heron Bay
Oba
Cochrane
Franz
Matheson
Cobalt
L. Timiskaming
Port Arthur
Fort William
L. SUPERIOR
Sault Ste. Marie
Sudbury
North Bay
Ottawa R.
Parry Sound
Georgian Bay
L. HURON
L. MICHIGAN
Montreal
Ottawa
Quebec
Levis
Trois Rivières
St. Johns
Sherbrooke
Kingston
Peterboro
Barrie
Toronto
Hamilton
L. ONT.
Niagara Falls
Buffalo
London
Sarnia
Detroit
Windsor
L. ERIE
NEW BRUNSWICK
Fredericton
Moncton
St. John
Bay of Fundy
PR. EDWARD ISLAND
Charlottetown
NOVA SCOTIA
Halifax
Yarmouth
C. Sable
Sydney
C. BRETON I.
Portland
Albany
Boston
C. Cod
ATLANTIC OCEAN
Longitude West from Greenwich
80° 70° 60° 50° 40° 30° 60° 50° 40° 90° 80° 70° 60°

A FOX FARM AT CHARLOTTETOWN
Ewing Galloway
These sharp-nosed black beauties are high-bred fox pups, raised for breeding purposes.

Forests. — The Maritime Provinces were once heavily covered with forests, and many billion board feet of good timber are still standing. The most important trees are the red spruce, but white spruce, balsam fir, white pine, hemlock, yellow birch, maple, beech, and cedar are also common. In New Brunswick alone, the yearly income from forest products is about two-thirds of that from agriculture. The forests were once the basis of an important local shipbuilding industry. There are many natural dry docks where ships can be built and repaired. Because of the great tides a ship in need of repairs can run into one of these natural dry docks at high tide, and when the water goes down, the ship's hull is exposed so that workmen may readily make the necessary repairs.

Fur Farming. — The Maritime Provinces are noted for their fur farms. The industry was started on Prince Edward Island, the only province of Canada which is entirely an island. These eastern provinces are still the most important, but the industry has spread to all parts of Canada, where there are over 1000 fur farms. The most valuable furs are those of the silver fox, the pelts of which are often worth $1000 or more, but almost all fur-bearing animals of the northern countries are now raised.

Minerals. — New Brunswick and Nova Scotia produce about two-fifths of Canada's total coal output. The *Sydney* coal fields are the most important. Here the thicker seams are now followed for several miles under the sea. With iron ore imported from Newfoundland and good coking coal at home, Sydney has become an important center for blast furnaces and steel plants. Gypsum is next to coal in value. Other mineral products, such as oil shale, gold, salt, manganese, limestone, are of slight value.

Other Cities. — *Saint John* is situated on the Bay of Fundy on the Saint John River, with an excellent harbor open the year round. It has always been an important shipping port and is noted for many places of historic interest. It is an important ship-repairing and

Courtesy Canadian National Railways
SAINT JOHN RIVER VALLEY
Flowing through country that is beautiful to behold, with rolling hills, flower-sprinkled fields, and graceful elms, the Saint John River is sometimes named the "Rhine of America."

shipbuilding center, having one of the world's largest dry docks. The Saint John River is about 450 miles long and is navigable for large river steamers as far as *Fredericton*, the capital of New Brunswick. Fredericton is a picturesque old city with well-shaded streets, fine homes, and quaint old churches.

Moncton is the second city in size in the province of New Brunswick and is sometimes called the "Hub of the Maritimes" because from here railway trains run to Halifax, Sydney, Cape Breton Island, Saint John, and other parts of the Maritime Provinces. *Charlottetown* is the capital and leading city of Prince Edward Island. It is a very beautiful city and has had a long history, going back to the days of the early French settlers. Its site was chosen because of its fine harbor and central location.

The Gaspé Peninsula. — After our long, roundabout journey through the Maritime Provinces, we finally return to Halifax and board a steamer for a trip up the St. Lawrence to Quebec and Montreal. Once out on the Atlantic we turn northward and pass through the Strait of Canso which separates Nova Scotia and Cape Breton Island. We then continue on through the Strait of Northumberland, which separates Prince Edward Island from Nova Scotia and New Brunswick, into the Gulf of St. Lawrence and finally arrive at the little village of Gaspé. Be sure to follow your Canadian journey on the map to be found on page 2.

Courtesy Canadian National Railways
SHIP HEAD CAPE, GASPÉ
Here, where the Appalachian Range straggles over the boundary into Canada, lies the peninsula of Gaspé, hemmed around by the Shickshock hills.

FARM EQUIPMENT, GASPÉ
This queer, awkward-looking windmill of bygone days provides the power for farm tasks in the twentieth century.

We learn that the Gaspé Peninsula is a part of the Province of Quebec and is about 150 miles in length and 40 miles wide in places. Its backbone is made up of old rugged mountains which are a part of the Appalachian system. We stop at the quaint little fishing village of Gaspé long enough to explore the surrounding country, partly by auto and partly by horseback. The forest-covered interior has been very little developed, but picturesque fishing villages line the shore. The hunting and fishing are very good: salmon and trout abound in the streams, while moose, caribou, elk, deer, bear, and fur-bearing animals are to be found in the forests. The people in the villages have many quaint customs which have been handed down from long ago, for this was one of the first parts of Canada to be settled by white men.

In addition to hunting and fishing for pleasure, the Gaspé cod fisheries are very important. They are nearly 400 years old and are said to be the finest in the world. The fish are caught so close to the shore that they can be quickly dressed and prepared for market. Millions of cod are taken annually, cured, and exported, mainly to Italy and Brazil.

The Saguenay River. — Leaving Gaspé, we steer past Anticosti Island, enter the Bay of St. Lawrence, and proceed westward along the north shore. This shore is very rugged, but it has a number of lumbering, fishing, and fur-trading centers. Life is hard for these sturdy people who still get a living by hunting and fishing, just as their ancestors did many, many years ago.

Journeying west, we reach the mouth of the Saguenay River, which we follow northward through beautiful scenery, much like Norway. In fact, some one has called it "a Norwegian fiord transplanted to American soil." We travel up this stream, past capes Trinity and Eternity, towering 2000 feet above the water level, as far as the city of Chicoutimi. The Saguenay River, which goes back to Lake St. John, is not only beautiful, but is becoming very well known for its water-power resources and development. The river has a drop of 300 feet between Lake St. John and tidewater at Chicoutimi. Thousands of horse power have already been developed and many thousands more are planned. Large pulp and paper mills, aluminum plants, and other factories have been attracted to this region by the cheap water power.

The City of Quebec. — Leaving the Saguenay River, we continue up the St. Lawrence to the famous old city of Quebec. This is one of the oldest cities in North America. The site was visited by Jacques Cartier in 1535; the city was founded and named by Champlain in 1608. It was the center of French rule in America for 150 years. The St. Lawrence was the main highway into central North America for the early French explorers and settlers.

Quebec is situated at the point where the river first becomes narrow enough for a fort to command it and defend the land against enemy warships. Here we see the first bridge across the St. Lawrence. It has been said that whoever controls Quebec controls Canada. The fall of Quebec in the French and Indian War decided that this region was to pass from French into British hands.

Part of the city is built on a high cliff overlooking the lower section. These two sections differ so much that they seem like two Quebecs. The lower part along the river reminds one of Old World France; the upper part is modern in its streets, residences, and public buildings. On the highest part of the cliff stands the Citadel, a large stone-walled fort built over a hundred years ago.

UP THE SAGUENAY *Courtesy Canada Steamship Lines*
Out of the unfathomable depths of the dark river rise the rocky walls of Cape Eternity — austere and lonely in the unbroken solitudes.

Courtesy Canadian National Railways
MONTREAL

From the wooded crest of Mount Royal we can see over the modern skyscrapers to the bridge-spanned river and the flat lands beyond.

Courtesy Canadian Pacific Railway
QUEBEC

In the upper town is the Chateau Frontenac; below the hills is the old town, a narrow strip of rocky ground steeped in historic memories.

Fairchild Aviation Limited
QUEBEC BRIDGE

This bridge across the St. Lawrence binds the two shores together in a graceful figure of silvery steel girders.

Courtesy Canadian National Railways
WINTER IN MONTREAL

Along the drives in Mount Royal Park the crisp snow crunches under the feet of pedestrians, and through the clear, cold air echoes the high, thin jingle of sleigh bells.

Montreal. — Our steamer trip ends at Montreal, the largest city in Canada and its most important port. We spend several days here viewing its many points of interest. We go to the top of Mount Royal, a low mountain after which the city takes its name and from which we secure a magnificent view of the city. We hear the hum of its many activities, for it has a population of nearly a million engaged in manufacturing, shipping, buying and selling, and other kinds of business. There are many fine homes and apartment houses.

Situated at the head of deep-sea navigation on the St. Lawrence River where it is joined by the Ottawa River, Montreal has a fine harbor and a busy water front with many massive elevators and shipping docks. We visit McGill University, the magnificent Church of Notre Dame, and many other points of interest.

The Province of Quebec. —While at Montreal we learn more about this Province of Quebec. It is the largest of the provinces of Canada and more than twice as large as our largest state, Texas. (See map of Canada, page 249.) Quebec has a population of over 3,000,000, being second only to the Province of Ontario. It leads all the other provinces in lumbering, paper and wood pulp production, and in water power development. In the northern part are the rugged, wild, forest-covered Laurentian Mountains with almost numberless glacial lakes, falls, and rivers. Seen from above, the area has a patchy appearance — patches of forest, patches of bare rock, and patches of water mixed between. These waterways are so closely connected that it is possible, with frequent short trips overland between streams or lakes, to travel in almost any direction by canoe. Many fur-bearing animals roam through the forests. South of the St. Lawrence, we learn that there is an older settled district, and this we decide to visit.

The Farming Section of Quebec. — We hire an automobile at Montreal to take us into the prosperous farming section. We find again that the roads are surprisingly good and well marked. We pass through village after village and, occasionally, cities of fairly

Courtesy Canadian National Railways
ST. FRANCIS VALLEY, QUEBEC

On the long level plains, south of the St. Lawrence, are fertile fields where farm crops are grown and live stock raised.

TORONTO

In a landlocked harbor on the north shore of Lake Ontario is Toronto, chief commercial city of Ontario and famous for its aquatic sports.

good size. *Sherbrooke*, for instance, has a population of about 30,000 and is sometimes called the hub of the Eastern Townships. Everywhere we see fertile farmlands, famous for their pure-bred live stock and their dairy products. One thing that impresses us throughout Quebec is that most of the people speak two languages, French and English. We learn that two-thirds of the people of Quebec are French and that the Roman Catholic church is the most important.

The Province of Ontario. — We next explore the Province of Ontario by automobile. Ontario is the second largest province in size with an area of about 400,000 square miles. It has more people than any other province, — about 3,787,000, — and is also the richest. We travel at a good rate of speed over the well-paved and well-marked automobile roads. We first visit *Ottawa*, the capital of Canada, and find it a very modern city. The government building, with its high tower and chiming bells, is the main point of interest. From Ottawa we travel south to *Kingston*, a lake port located at the northeastern end of Lake Ontario. Then we travel westward along the north shore of Lake Ontario until we reach Toronto. As we motor along, we observe rich farming lands on every hand and notice that the land is quite thickly settled. This is not quite so true in the area north of Quebec and Montreal.

Toronto, the Queen City of the Lakes. — We spend several days in Toronto, because it is the second city in size in Canada and more like one of our own cities than any we have yet visited. It has a population of over 600,000 and is a thriving manufacturing center. We visit the busy waterfront on Lake Ontario, explore Queens Park with its well-known University of Toronto, walk through the

GOVERNMENT BUILDING, OTTAWA

The Memorial Tower, in Italian Gothic style, rises like a sentinel above the summit of the highest hill overlooking the Ottawa River

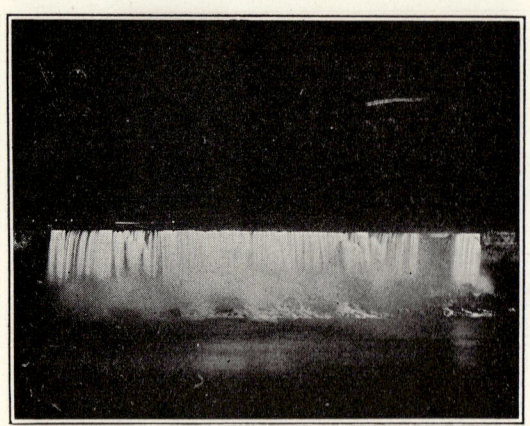

Courtesy Niagara Falls Chamber of Commerce
ILLUMINATED BY THEIR OWN POWER
Niagara Falls furnishes the power for Toronto's light, heat, and industrial plants.

Parliament Building, for Toronto is the capital of the Province of Ontario, and are delighted with the buildings of the Canadian National Exhibition where a large national fair is held annually.

Through Ontario. — Continuing westward from Toronto we reach *Hamilton*, a prosperous city at the western end of Lake Ontario, in the heart of the fruit belt. Although much of Canada has long, cold winters, the summers are warm in the southern sections, and there are several important fruit-growing areas. As we travel along the south shore of Lake Ontario eastward from Hamilton to Niagara Falls, we pass through miles and miles of apple, peach, plum, and cherry orchards. Acres of vineyards with their long, straight rows of grapevines appear on both sides of the highway.

At last we reach Niagara Falls and remember that the Great Lakes belong to Canada as well as the United States. The Canadian Horseshoe Falls are larger than those on our side of the Niagara River, and increasing use of the water power for the production of electricity is being made in large hydro-electric plants here.

After viewing the mighty Niagara Falls for some time, we again travel westward, this time along the north shore of Lake Erie until we finally reach *Windsor*, opposite Detroit. We pass through prosperous villages and cities, and farms which are well cared for. We see fields of potatoes, tobacco, wheat, hay, oats, barley, and many other crops which are related to mixed farming. From Windsor we travel through a mixed farming and dairying area north to Sarnia, across the St. Clair River from Port Huron, Michigan.

Our next trip takes us along the eastern shore of Lake Huron, through Orilia to the city of North Bay. This is a very long trip and we notice that the country is wild and not so well settled. From North Bay we visit the mines at Sudbury, Ontario, famous for their nickel and copper ores. We learn that Ontario produces more valuable minerals than any other Canadian Province, and Canada produces from 70 to 75 per cent of the world's nickel, 65 per cent of its asbestos, and about 25 per cent of its platinum. Gold, lead, silver, zinc, cobalt, and copper are also mined in considerable amounts.

Across the Canadian Bridge. — Our next journey, after we return to North Bay, is by rail westward across what is sometimes called the "Canadian Bridge." This area is north of Lake Superior and connects the well-populated Eastern Provinces with the fairly well-

Courtesy Canadian National Railways
FISHING THROUGH THE ICE
In this setting of natural beauty at Lake of Bays, Ontario, a fisherman catches his dinner.

settled Prairie Provinces. We find the railway trains and services equal to any in the United States. In fact, Canada has two of the finest railway systems in the world. They are called the Canadian Pacific and Canadian National Railways. Not only do they serve all parts of the settled areas of Canada but they also own and operate steamship lines to all parts of the world. We find the "Bridge" wild, unsettled, and forested, with rushing streams and tempting lakes on every hand. This is a great country for trout fishing and wild animal hunting.

Courtesy Canadian Pacific Railway
THE WHEAT FIELDS OF ALBERTA
Wheat fields so vast that six harvesters can easily work side by side.

The Prairie Provinces. — After a long but pleasant journey, we reach *Winnipeg*, the capital of Manito'ba, one of the three so-called "Prairie Provinces." The other two are called Saskatch'ewan and Alberta. We find that Winnipeg is a modern city something like our western prairie cities. It has a population of over 200,000 and is the fourth in size among Canadian cities, only Montreal, Toronto, and Vancouver being larger.

We travel through the Prairie Provinces by rail and are much impressed by the miles and miles of grain-producing lands which we see on every hand. The soil is fertile and the land is nearly level, permitting the use of labor-saving machinery. The summers are short but the summer days are long enough to mature abundant crops of spring wheat, oats, and other grains. Canada is one of the greatest wheat-producing countries in the world, with an annual yield of about 400,000,000 bushels. We see grain elevators in nearly every city and the railroads do a thriving business when shipping time arrives.

Some of the wheat is sent to ports on the Great Lakes, some to Vancouver, and some even to Churchill on Hudson Bay to be shipped to Europe and other ports of the world. Churchill has an elevator which holds 2,500,000 bushels of wheat and can load three or four ships at a time. Other cities which we visit on our trip west from Winnipeg are Regina, Saskatoon, Edmonton, and Calgary. They are all prosperous cities whose business

Courtesy Canadian National Railways
EMPEROR FALLS
Over the edge of a steep cliff in the Canadian Rockies, a stream cascades in a river of mist.

LAKE LOUISE
Josef Muench

In the depths of the lake are reflected the snowy ridges of the Victoria Glacier, and iceland poppies bloom in magic splendor.

depends mainly on the grain farming and stock raising which surround them.

Scenic Wonders. — From Calgary we travel westward, again by rail, on one of the most delightful parts of our Canadian journey. For we are to cross the Canadian Rockies, through the Province of British Columbia, to the port of Vancouver on the Pacific Ocean. As the train pulls out of Calgary, the full glory of the Canadian Rockies bursts into view. We pass from grasslands, through evergreen forests, until we finally come to snow-clad peaks, with glaciers in their valleys and rushing streams coming from the ends of the glaciers. The country is wild, with here and there cool, blue lakes nestling in the midst of evergreen forests. After a beautiful ride we arrive at *Banff* in the Rocky Mountain National Park, and stay at the Banff Springs Hotel, from which we secure a grand view of the Bow River Valley. We take horseback rides to view the scenery and enjoy the bracing mountain air, play golf and tennis, and climb mountains. In fact we enjoy Banff so much that we vote this one of the pleasantest parts of our Canadian trip.

We continue on the railway about 40 miles west to *Lake Louise*, where we stop for another grand view of mountain scenery. Lake Louise lies in a deep, steep-walled basin caused by glacial erosion. Surrounding it there is a glorious circle of snow-clad peaks.

VANCOUVER
Courtesy Canadian National Railways

Into the fine, natural harbor of this metropolis steam the vessels from the shipping lanes of the Pacific.

Josef Muench

THE VALLEY OF THE TEN PEAKS

In the cracks of these jagged peaks are the remnants of glaciers. At their base lies lovely Morrain Lake.

Courtesy Canadian National Railways

VANCOUVER ISLAND'S BIG TREES

This island is the southern end of a partially submerged mountain chain whose slopes are covered with forests of fir, cedar, and spruce.

PARLIAMENT BUILDING, VICTORIA
This building overlooks James Bay and contains not only the government offices, but the provincial library and natural history museum.

Beautiful mountain flowers are to be found right up to the water's edge. From Lake Louise we continue westward for miles through similar gorgeous scenery which has been aptly called "Fifty Switzerlands rolled into one." At length, we reach Vancouver, and the end of our railroad journey.

British Columbia. — *Vancouver* is the largest city on the Pacific Coast of Canada and the third in size among Canadian cities. It has a population of about 275,000. With its fine harbor, it is a busy shipping port, and carries on much manufacturing. The University of British Columbia is located here.

Of course, British Columbia has many other things besides scenery. It has forests like those of our own Pacific coast and the lumbering industry is well developed. There are productive irrigated valleys where vegetables and fruits are raised. The mines in the mountains furnish much gold and silver. Salmon fishing is also important on Canada's Pacific Coast, as it is in our own states of Washington and Oregon.

A TRAPPER AND HIS FURS
In the cold, cold north was the starting point of the Hudson Bay Company's fur-trading activities, and today the fur trappers and traders are still at work.

A few hours' sail across the Strait of Georgia brings us to the beautiful city of *Victoria*, which is the capital of British Columbia. It is located on the island of Vancouver, and has a very good harbor. It is a city of beautiful homes and has a fine Parliament Building.

The Northwest Territories. — In order to visit the northern part of Canada, we decide upon a novel venture. We hire a large passenger hydroplane for our trip. Early one morning we take off from the waters of Vancouver Harbor and fly over the Rockies into the interior of the country. We fly quite low when we reach the interior so that we can see what the country looks like. We see few signs of human life. There are no cities or farms such as we saw farther south, but almost endless stretches of forests and grasslands, cut through here and there by rivers and lakes. Now and again we catch glimpses of vast herds of caribou feeding on the rich grasses. We pass over huge lakes which seem as large as our own Great Lakes. Whenever we land, it is usually on the waters of these lakes. We wonder what use is being made of this vast wilderness, and our pilot tells us that the forests furnish shelter to fur-bearing animals and that trapping is one of the principal industries. Then, too, gold and silver and radium and other valuable minerals have been discovered and are being worked. The main mode of travel to these mining areas is by airplane. Our journey takes us even to the mouth of the Mackenzie River. From there we travel to Churchill on Hudson Bay, to which a railway has been built for shipping purposes. The final flight in our air journey takes us across the wilder parts of northern Ontario and Quebec and lands us in the harbor of Montreal, from which city we return to New York by train.

Our trip around Canada has been well worth while. We have traveled by boat, automobile, train, horseback, and airplane. We have seen mighty cities and forests and farm lands and much magnificent scenery. Well can we realize that Canada is a great country, larger in area than the United States, though it does not have so many people, because as yet only the southern part is settled. However, Canada probably will never be so densely settled as the United States because a considerable amount of it lies so far north.

Activities and Questions

1. Name the provinces of Canada and their capitals.

2. What are the chief products of the Maritime Provinces? of the Prairie Provinces?

3. Which provinces produce furs? wheat? minerals?

4. At what places in the east and the west did we see the finest scenery?

5. Which province has the greatest area? the largest population?

6. Name the four largest cities in the order of their size.

7. What is the capital of Canada? of Ontario?

Courtesy Newfoundland Information Bureau

The moon shines softly on the fishing fleet as it rides at anchor on the molten silver waters of St. John's harbor.

XIII. NEWFOUNDLAND AND LABRADOR

Newfoundland is a large island lying across the mouth of the St. Lawrence River. In the northwest, it is only nine miles across the narrowest part of the Strait of Belle Isle to the mainland of Labrador. In the southwest, it is only sixty miles across Cabot Strait to northern Nova Scotia. In this air age, its location makes it important as an air base for trans-Atlantic planes. The inhabitants are proud of the fact that theirs was the first British colony to be established in America. Newfoundland was a member of the British Commonwealth of Nations until 1933 when Great Britain took over the rule of the country. In 1948, the people of Newfoundland voted in favor of a union with Canada.

Nearness to Europe. — Newfoundland lies farther east than any other part of North America. It is only a little over 1600 miles from the west coast of Ireland, about half the distance between New York and Ireland. This is one of the reasons why the explorer, John Cabot, came first to Newfoundland when he left England on his voyage of exploration in 1497. Cabot did not stay to explore the island but soon returned to England where the King gave him ten pounds for "discovering the New Isle." He reported the sea about Newfoundland to be full of fish. This news aroused great interest in Europe and attracted fishermen, not only from England, but from France, Spain, and Portugal. Many of the bays and smaller islands of this section have French and Spanish names.

Courtesy Newfoundland Information Bureau
MODERN EXPLORERS

The frail, box-like machine of Alcock and Brown rolled down the runway at St John's in 1919 on the first successful transatlantic flight.

ST. PAUL'S INLET
Ramparts of rocks and rugged cliffs make Newfoundland renowned as the "Norway of the New World."

Courtesy Newfoundland Information Bureau
MARBLE HEAD ON THE HUMBER
Streams like this, in the deep silence of hovering mountains, offer the sublime to the sportsman.

Ewing Galloway
THE GRENFELL MISSION
At Cape St. Anthony are the hospitals, welfare centers, and orphan homes established by W. T. Grenfell in 1902, to care for the needy among the fisherfolk who live and labor on the coasts of Labrador and Newfoundland.

A FISHING VILLAGE

Below the houses, squatted on the hillside, the long fish wharves reach out for the day's catch. On the skeleton platforms the fish are left to dry in the sunshine and clean, salt air.

The Land of Newfoundland. — There are two things which we see at once as we look at a map of Newfoundland. First, it is shaped very much like a triangle. If lines were to be drawn connecting the most northerly point of Newfoundland and the most westerly and easterly points, they would form a triangle each of whose sides would be about 300 miles long. We should notice also the many peninsulas and bays which give it a very irregular coast line over 6000 miles long. The peninsulas, bays, rivers, and lakes all run in the same direction, northeast and southwest. There are many islands along the coast; in fact one bay along the western coast is called the Bay of Islands.

The coast of Newfoundland is generally rugged with many cliffs and rocky headlands. Long, fiord-like bays extend far back between rocky peninsulas. These furnish not only attractive scenery, but good harbors for the little fishing villages usually found at their heads. In the southeast, the heads of two long bays come within a few miles of each other in one place and almost make an island of the large peninsula called Avalon. Nearly half the people live on this peninsula, which is nearest to Europe, to the ocean steamer routes, and to the best fishing grounds, the Grand Bank.

Newfoundland is mostly rolling land, but there are ranges of hills, the highest of which runs along the western side and ends in a long peninsula to the north. This is known as the Long Range, and some of its peaks are over 2000 feet high. Many smaller ranges and peaks dot the interior and between these lie the river valleys and the lake basins. There are hundreds of lakes in Newfoundland, some deep, with rocky borders, others shallow and more like bogs or marshes.

Plants and Animals. — The interior of Newfoundland is not so bare as the coast might indicate. Part of the land is covered with forests, which sometimes reach to the tops of the highlands. Grasses grow on the lowlands. Even the less known rocky regions known as the "barrens" are covered with mosses and ferns, and, like our own highlands, are gay with flowers in the summer time.

CARIBOU CROSSING ROUND POND

Safe against the hunter, families of caribou roam the forests and swim the streams as they have for generations.

Berries of different kinds are also plentiful, especially blueberries, some of which are shipped to the United States. Herds of caribou, and other wild animals, such as the moose, wolf, bear, fox, beaver, and rabbit, roam through the forests and meadows and over the "barrens." Birds, which spend their winters in the south, return in summer to liven the woods and lakes with their presence.

Where the People Live. — Very few people live in the interior of Newfoundland. This is largely the land of the hunter and fisherman, and few people have settled here and built up farms. A railroad now runs from St. John's, the capital in the southeastern part of the island, to Port Aux Basques in the southwest. Nearly all the settlements in the interior are along this railroad. But most of the people live along or very near the coast, in little villages at the heads of bays which furnish safe harbors, especially on the peninsula of Avalon, near the best fishing grounds.

The Land of Codfish. — Newfoundland's best known industry began soon after Cabot returned to England and told how the waters were full of fish. Other kinds of fish such as haddock and halibut are caught, but cod have always led to such an extent that when one speaks of fish in Newfoundland one nearly always means cod. Newfoundland is the greatest country in the world for salt-dried codfish. Many are caught in the bays and shallow waters near the shore, but the famous fishing ground is a shallow area lying south and southeast of Newfoundland. Here the bottom of the sea is a plateau within 150 to 300 feet of the surface. Several parts of this plateau are called banks, the largest and most famous of which is the Grand Bank. It has an area of about 48,000 square miles and is larger than the island of Newfoundland. The fishermen go out to the banks in sailing vessels carrying small boats called dories. In these the men row out from the main vessel with tubs of long baited

Courtesy Newfoundland Information Bureau
A BEAUTIFUL DANGER
Past the fort that guards the narrow entrance to St. John's harbor there floats a fairy palace — white as alabaster and beautiful to behold. It is a wandering iceberg.

lines. The long line, perhaps 2000 feet or more in length, has fastened to it many short lines with hooks on their ends. Buoys along the main line show its location in the water. After the lines are set, the men row out to them at different times, draw them up, remove the fish, and put fresh bait on the hooks. Then they return to the larger vessel and unload their catch. At the end of each day's fishing, the fish are cleaned and salted, or placed on ice in the hold of the vessel.

Fogs and Other Dangers on the Grand Bank. — Fishing on the Grand Bank is dangerous because of storms and fogs. The fishing banks are on the most traveled route across the North Atlantic and the fishermen's vessels are often in danger of being run down in heavy fogs. Fogs and storms often come

SEAL BABIES

Four little soft balls of fur — with black noses and shoe-button eyes.

up suddenly before the men out in the dories can get back to the main vessel and they may be lost for days at a time. The skippers of the fishing vessels become very skillful in locating the dories in times of fog or storm.

The cold Labrador current from the north and the warm Gulf Stream from the south which flow past eastern Newfoundland carry with them much food for the smaller fish upon which the cod and larger fish feed, and help to make this a great fishing ground. But when the chilled air over the Labrador current meets the moist air warmed by the Gulf Stream from the south, fog results. Here, too, is the melting place of icebergs carried south by the cold current from the north. It is claimed that the banks are partly built up from rock material dropped by the icebergs when they melted in the warmer waters of the Gulf Stream.

Seal Fisheries. — Floating ice cakes are usually a source of danger, but they carry close to the shores of Newfoundland another source of fishery wealth, seals. These are not fur seals like those caught in the Pacific Ocean. Their skins are used in making leather articles such as handbags, and their blubber or fat in making soap. They feed on fish. A famous sea captain who has done much seal hunting has estimated that when the seal herds are feeding on the Grand Bank, they eat as much as 3,000,000 pounds of codfish each day. The young seals live on the ice floes for some time before they take to the water; thus they are readily caught by the seal hunters. The sealing ships go out in March and work their way among the ice floes until they spot a herd of seals. Then the men take their weapons and a small amount of food and go out on the ice after the seals. Airplanes now aid in spotting the seal herds and tell the ships where to go.

Other Industries of Newfoundland. — Fish have always been so abundant and so easily caught that they have actually held back the settlement of Newfoundland and the development of its other resources. Fishermen from Europe used to come over to do their fishing and then return with their catch. Few people stayed all the year. Laws were actually passed forbidding people to build houses and to fence and cultivate the land. These laws were not repealed until after 1800. Until about 1900, Newfoundland's one industry was fishing. People settled along the coast and every harbor became a fishing center. Most of the people were either engaged in fishing or dependent upon this industry in some way for a living. Now they are beginning to make use of the forests, the water power, and the minerals, so that other industries have grown up.

Forests and Water Power. — Forests of pine, spruce, fir, birch, maple, and other

Courtesy Newfoundland Information Bureau
THE SEALING SHIP

With its airplane aboard, through dangerous waters, thick with ice floes, the ship picks its way, hunting out the herds of seals.

A Strike!
Ponds, lakes, brooks, and many salmon rivers make Newfoundland a paradise for the angler.

Fisherman's Stages, Logy Bay

The chief industry is the fisheries — cod, salmon, herring, halibut, haddock, turbot, and trout — and the drying sheds spill over the rocks like disarranged jackstraws.

Salmon Jumping the Falls

Fighting their way upstream from the sea in the spring, the salmon seek out the foaming pools of the swift-running rivers and defy the angler to pull them out.

A Catch of Cod

These fish are so valuable to Newfoundlanders that they are often called "Newfoundland Currency."

Photos Courtesy Newfoundland Information Bureau
Hauling a Cod Trap

While much Newfoundland fishing follows the Grand Bank, hauls like this are also made nearer shore.

Courtesy Newfoundland Information Bureau
AT GRAND FALLS

In this large mill, power from rushing water helps to change wood from Newfoundland forests into paper which later will carry the news to millions of English readers.

trees cover large parts of Newfoundland. The lumber, wood pulp, and paper produced from these trees and exported are now worth more than the fishery products which are sent to other countries. Large pulp and paper mills are found at Grand Falls and Bishop's Falls near the central part of the island. Paper for London daily newspapers comes from these mills, which are situated where falls in the Exploits River furnish water power. Other large pulp and paper mills are found at Corner Brook, a little town near the mouth of the Humber River in western Newfoundland. These mills, too, are run by water power furnished by a near-by lake which is over 200 feet higher than the river along which the mills are built. Many of the towns as well as mills and factories in Newfoundland are now supplied with electricity produced from water power.

Mineral Wealth. — Minerals as another source of wealth have been little used in Newfoundland. Some of the old rocks which make up the surface of this island are rich in metals, and considerable copper has been mined in the northern part of the island. Nickel, lead, silver, and gold have also been discovered. A mine in the central part of the island produces an ore containing zinc, lead, copper, and small quantities of silver and gold. Belle Isle, in a bay west of St. John's, the capital city, contains one of the world's largest deposits of iron ore. Most of the iron ore mined here is sent to Sydney in northern Nova Scotia, and to the United

Courtesy Newfoundland Information Bureau
BAY D'EAST RIVER

Beautiful lakes fill the deep gulches between the mountains, where canoeists may spend happy hours.

THE NARROWS, ST. JOHN'S
Ewing Galloway
From Signal Hill, 500 feet above the sea, Marconi made his first successful trans-oceanic test in 1901.

Kingdom. Lead and zinc are also mined and exported. Petroleum and oil shale have been found also but are very little used.

Farming in Newfoundland. — Thin soil and a rather cool climate hinder farming in Newfoundland. But there are areas of fertile soil upon which good crops can be grown. The best land for farming is in the southwestern part of the country. The growing season is short and the winters are long, but the thermometer rarely goes below zero. There is scarcely any spring, summer coming suddenly in May or June. Planting is begun late in May or in June and the growing season ends by October, when frosts occur. Plants grow rapidly during the long hours of sunlight of the summer days. Oats, barley, hay, and root crops such as potatoes and turnips grow well, and cabbage is also easily raised. The numbers of farm animals, such as cattle, horses, sheep, and swine, are increasing, as these can easily be fed on the crops which grow here. Much of the food now imported could be raised in the country, but the people have found it more convenient to make a living by fishing.

Newfoundland's Attraction for Tourists. — Newfoundland offers many attractions for tourists and people on vacations. The lakes and rivers abound with many kinds of game fish. The forests contain wild animals sought by the hunter: the moose, bear, fox, wolf, and rabbit. Many of the picturesque little fishing villages along the coast are becoming favorite summer resorts. With the ocean on all sides, Newfoundland is neither as cold in winter nor as warm in summer as the interior of our own country or Canada. The fogs for which the fishing regions are noted do not extend far into the interior of Newfoundland, where clear skies and bright sunny days occur just as they do in other lands.

St. John's, the Capital City. — About 60,000 people live in St. John's, the capital of Newfoundland. It is located at the southeastern end of the island where it is much nearer than New York to the British Isles. An inlet from the ocean furnishes a fine harbor. The entrance to this harbor appears from the ocean just like an opening in the rocky wall along the shore. Its steep sides rise sharply 300 to 400 feet above the water.

This entrance, which is about one-half mile long, is about 1400 feet wide near the ocean and narrows to 600 feet in one place. On the right is Signal Hill, 500 feet above the ocean, on top of which stands the Block House with which vessels seeking to enter the harbor communicate by signals. On the left is a rocky projection which makes a good base for a lighthouse. The city itself, built on the slopes of the hills rising from the harbor,

Publishers' Photo
THREE ESKIMOS OF HOPEDALE

These fur-clad people inhabit the barren north, living in rude huts of stone or wood, often banked with snow and shaped like beehives.

cannot be seen until the boat is over half way through the narrow entrance. St. John's, in addition to being the capital, is the chief trading center for the island. Machine shops and a large dry dock for the repair of ocean vessels are located here.

The Land of Labrador. — Across the narrow Strait of Belle Isle from the northern tip of Newfoundland lies the southern tip of Labrador which belongs to Newfoundland. For about 1000 miles the coast of Labrador extends along the Atlantic Ocean in a northwesterly direction, ending at Hudson Strait. Like Newfoundland, the land of Labrador is shaped like an irregular triangle. The southern part reaches back into the interior over 400 miles from the coast. For many years, Canada and Newfoundland had a dispute over the inner boundary of Labrador. This was finally settled by giving to Labrador all the land as far back from the sea as the Labrador River valleys extend. Labrador has an area of 110,000 square miles and is about two and a half times as large as Newfoundland.

The Coast of Labrador. — The coast of Labrador, like that of Newfoundland, is deeply cut by inlets of the sea and fringed with islands. It is a bare and rocky region where the sea with its fisheries gives people the only chance of making a living. Toward the north the land is higher, and the scenery is wild and rugged. Deep, picturesque fiords run far back into the land, and little glaciers lie in the hollows of the highlands. A cold ocean current from the north sweeps along the coast and chills the region in both summer and winter. Ice closes the harbors and shuts off the people from the rest of the world for six months of the year.

The People of Labrador. — A few Indians live in the interior of Labrador and make a living by trapping the fur-bearing animals in the forests. Native Eskimos live near the coast, generally in the northerly sections. These depend largely on the sea for a living. About 5000 people, mainly of Scotch and English descent, inhabit the more southerly coastal regions. These are called "livyers" to distinguish them from Newfoundlanders and others who come to these coasts during the summer to fish, and then leave. Some of the people fish during the summer and then move inland in winter to the more sheltered wooded areas, where they live by trapping and hunting. Fuel is obtained from the forests.

Life is hard for the people of Labrador. The winters are long and cold. Frosts even in the summer time make it hard to raise vegetables to vary their food supply. Attempts have been made to establish reindeer herds, but hungry wolves from the interior kill them. Farm animals and chickens are curiosities to many of these people who lack

LABRADOR

Battle Harbor is one of the principal fishing villages in this sparsely populated region of the Dominion of Newfoundland.

A WET DRYDOCK

A bleak and barren harbor at Hopedale, where the rocks lie smooth and polished by the constant wash of icy waves.

A MISSION STATION

The homelike buildings of the white man's mission have become a part of the Eskimos' village.

THE LAND NOBODY KNOWS *Ewing Galloway*

These unknown falls, located at the junction of the headwaters of the Unknown and Hamilton rivers, near the Grand Falls, had never been seen by white man until aerial photographers flew over the spot and "shot" them.

Labrador has forests of spruce and poplar trees and when she uses her water power of the interior may some day develop a large wood pulp and paper industry. One of the wonders of this little known land occurs where her largest river, the Hamilton, tumbles over a cliff at Grand Falls. These falls are over 300 feet high, nearly twice as high as the Niagara Falls.

Activities and Questions

1. What is the general shape of Newfoundland?
2. How far is it from Ireland?
3. Where do most of the people live? Why there?
4. What is its best known industry? its most valuable export? Why?
5. Describe the coast line.
6. How do the people in the interior live? Why?
7. See if you can find pictures of Newfoundland.
8. What hinders farming there?
9. Tell about the people and life in Labrador.
10. List four natural resources of Labrador and explain how each may aid in the development of Labrador and make life more pleasant for people who live there.
11. Where was Labrador's inner boundary set?
12. Sketch a map of Newfoundland and Labrador.

the fresh milk, butter, and eggs so common in our country. Dog teams furnish the only means of winter transportation.

Resources and Industries. — As in Newfoundland, fishing has always been the main industry of Labrador. Cod are abundant along the coast in the summer time and form the main part of the catch, but salmon are also caught. Vessels come to the shores in the summer with supplies of various kinds and take away the fishery products.

Rich deposits of iron ore have been found in Labrador, and plans are now being carried out to develop these. The many rapids and waterfalls furnish much water power which may be used in manufacturing industries.

BRIDGE AND LAKE, ALASKA

XIV. ALASKA, OUR NORTHERN WONDERLAND

Alaska occupies the northwest corner of the American continent between the Arctic and Pacific oceans. It is about one-fifth as large as the United States. Its northern tip, Point Barrow, is about 1200 miles from the North Pole, while its southern part is in the latitude of Denmark or Southern Scotland. Its most easterly point lies some 600 miles west of Seattle, while the Aleutian Islands extend like stepping stones far out toward Asia.

Physical Characteristics. — Alaska has some of the wildest, most rugged mountains of North America. Among them is Mount McKinley, the highest peak on our continent, and Mount St. Elias, almost as high and rising close to the ocean. Deep, rocky fiords, with waterfalls and rapids rippling over their steep sides, dent the mountainous coast and reach far back into the interior. Glaciers, hundreds of feet thick and miles long, slide down the mountain valleys to the shore where huge icebergs break off from them and crash into the ocean. Magnificent scenery, active volcanoes, and steaming hot springs are some of the wonders which lure tourists, as well as explorers, to Alaska. Central Alaska, in the valley of the Yukon, is a low plateau. Indians and Eskimos inhabiting this region mountain large herds of reindeer. One of the most thrilling sights in Alaska is the breaking up of the ice in the Yukon in the spring.

Climate. — Alaska has a wide range of climate, due to its great extent and to the warm ocean currents and west winds which give many of the coast towns milder winters than cities in our North Central States. There is a heavy rainfall along the coast, but very little north of the high mountains. Although the summer season is short, the days are long and the sun is warm, so that flowers, fruit, and vegetables grow in abun-

273

dance during this short growing season. Polar Alaska north of the Brooks Mountains is so cold and barren that its Eskimo inhabitants live by hunting and fishing, as there is hardly enough vegetation for their reindeer.

Population. — The population of about 72,000 (of which only a little more than one half is white) is found largely in the various cities. The natives of Alaska can be divided into four groups — the Aleuts, Eskimos, Tlingits or Tlinkits, and Athapascan, the last being one of the North American Indian families. The Aleuts live on the Alaska Peninsula and the Aleutian Islands. The Tlingits live in Southeast Alaska, and the Eskimos live chiefly along the shores of Bering Sea and the Arctic Ocean. Most of the natives live in small settlements, some of which are near the cities and towns built by the whites.

Cities of Alaska. — Nome and Fairbanks, situated near the Arctic Circle, are mining centers, and the latter is connected with Seward on the coast by a government railroad. Most of the other places of importance are situated in the Panhandle, as the narrow strip between Canada and the Pacific is called. This district has many fine harbors and is nearest to supplies and markets. Here are Sitka, the former capital; Juneau, the present capital; Wrangell and Petersburg, lumbering and fishing centers; Anchorage, a rapidly growing town; and Ketchikan, near the extreme southern end of Alaska. These cities, on what is called the Inland Passage, have a mixed population of whites and native Indians.

Methods of Travel. — There are few railways in Alaska, most travel being by boat with several thousand miles of sled and wagon roads in the mining country. There are about 5,000 miles of navigable waterways but the rivers are free of ice only for five months of the year. In the north, the Eskimos use sledges drawn by dogs and reindeer. The Government has built some roads, but the rough nature of the country makes this work expensive in view of the scanty population. For inland travel airplanes are coming into use, making in a few hours trips which formerly took several weeks.

Indian Totems. — One of the interesting things to be seen in Wrangell and other nearby towns are the totem poles carved by the ancestors of the Indians who live here. The carvings on the totems are in the form of men, birds, and mammals, and record the family history of the Indians. They are commonly made of cedar and painted in red, brown, blue, and green with dyes made from plants and minerals. The Indians who live here now make totem poles for sale to tourists and others who may want to buy them.

Products of Alaska. — Alaska is famous for gold, but its coal, lead, platinum, mercury, and other minerals are also valuable. Over 200,000 tons of coal are now being mined each year and the production of petroleum is

POINT BARROW, ALASKA *Ewing Galloway*
The Eskimos hunt the long-tusked walrus for the meat, which is stored away for the long winter.

AN ALASKAN HIGHWAY
John Kabel
The road from Juneau to Mendental Glacier rolls by rugged and awe-inspiring scenery, where the mountain tops are often hidden in the clouds.

Courtesy Alaska Steamship Company
CHILDS GLACIER
"A wonderful blue-white torrent, suddenly frozen as it was about to plunge into the sea."

Publishers' Photo
ALASKA
Camped beneath the blizzard-worn cliffs on the south side of Mt. McKinley, where the snow never melts.

275

Courtesy Alaska Steamship Company
THE LOOP DISTRICT

The government-owned railroad winds through the narrow valleys, crossing and recrossing the streams on trestles.

Ewing Galloway
SEAL ROOKERIES

The Pribilof Islands are the home of the fur seals, the safety of whose herds is protected by law

JUNEAU, ALASKA
Courtesy Alaska Steamship Company

Dwarfed by the towering cliffs, crowding it into the icy waters, Juneau goes fearlessly about its business of mining and fishing and everyday living.

Courtesy Hewitt's Photo Shop, Anchorage, Alaska
A MATANUSKA VALLEY HAY CROP

Publishers' Photo
PACK DOGS OF ALASKA

The Alaskan dog is one of the economic factors of this northern land, for winter and summer he helps to carry the white man's burdens.

increasing. Lumber and fishing are other important industries, and the seal fisheries of the Aleutian and Pribilof Islands are famous. We paid Russia $7,200,000 for Alaska in 1867, and its products have already yielded over 100 times that amount.

A New Home in Alaska. — In 1935, the United States Government made it possible for 200 families from this country to go to Alaska and found a settlement in the Matanuska Valley in southern Alaska. Each family was given 40 acres of land, and allowed 30 years to pay for it. The Government sent workers and supplies to help the settlers clear the land, build homes, and start farming.

Fertile black soil, often several feet thick, enables these settlers to produce good crops of wheat, barley, oats, potatoes, hay, vegetables, and berries. Farm animals, such as cows, sheep, goats, horses, swine, and chickens, thrive here. Grazing animals can be pastured five months of the year, and butter, cheese, and meat are leading products. Fishing and hunting provide sport as well as food.

Some of the families returned to the United States but most of them remained and by hard work and co-operation are making a success of farming in Alaska.

Activities and Questions

1. Compare the size and population of Alaska with those of your state. How many times as large as your state is Alaska? Your state has how many times as many people as Alaska? What does this tell you about the number of people in Alaska in comparison with its size?

2. Plan a trip to Alaska, naming in order the places you would visit, how you would travel between places, and the interesting things you would expect to see along the way. Collect pictures to illustrate your trip.

3. Trace the route of a steamer going from Seattle to Point Barrow.

4. Name at least one article which you think might come from each of the following Alaskan seaports: Wrangell; Cordova; Seward; Nome.

5. Do you think you would like to live in Alaska? Where and why?

6. What things can you tell about Alaska that prove it was worth more than the United States paid for it?

7. Make a list of things that you might see in Alaska that you would not see in the United States, unless, as in the case of animals, they had been carried here from Alaska or some other far northern country.

Orizaba, or Star Mountain, with a halo of fleecy clouds about her snowy peak. *Publishers' Photo*

XV. MEXICO, OUR SOUTHERN NEIGHBOR

The Mexican Cornucopia. — Mexico is shaped like a huge cornucopia, or horn of plenty, and many valuable gifts pour forth from this horn. In area it is nearly three times the size of our largest state, Texas, or about one-fourth of the size of the United States. All of western Europe, including Germany, France, England, Spain, Portugal, with Holland and Belgium thrown in for good measure, could be placed in Mexico.

Mexico is, indeed, a rich country. Four authorities who know Mexico have used the following expressions in order to give us an idea of Mexico's great natural wealth.

1. "Mexico is the treasure house of the world."

2. "Mexico has the most enormous and diversified wealth ever bestowed upon a single people in a single area."

3. "Mexico is the most highly mineralized region in the world."

4. "Mexico has a greater variety of soil, surface, and vegetation than any equal extent of territory in the world."

Physical Characteristics. — This horn of plenty is about as broad as it is long. It is about 1800 miles in width where it borders on United States territory, 1900 miles in length and tapers to about 150 miles in width at the Isthmus of Tehuantepec. There are two large peninsulas jutting out from the main area, one in the northwest, the Peninsula of California, and the other in the southeast, the Peninsula of Yucatan.

On closer view of the land itself one sees that it is mostly a vast mountainous plateau with a plain along either coast. These plains are called hot lands for they are hot and steamy, and have rain forests and unhealthy jungles. The Peninsula of Yucatan, however, gets fresh winds from two sides, which clear away the unhealthful conditions of the jungle swamps. Mexico lies in three altitude zones: the hot lands at sea level; the temperate lands on the plateaus; and on the slopes of the highest mountains, the cold or frigid lands. Nearly all Mexicans live on the temperate lands.

There are many tall mountains and volcanoes in Mexico. The highest, Mt. Orizaba, is over 18,000 feet. One gets a good view of its white cone on sailing into the harbor of Vera Cruz. Popocatepetl, "the mountain which smokes," is next, 17,800 feet in height. The Mexicans speak of it rather affectionately as "Popo."

Climate. — During the dry season from November to May, Mexico is a land of almost continuous sunshine. Then comes the rain, often pouring down in torrents, yet with great regularity. Often the forenoons are sunny, and the rain comes in the afternoon. In the hot belt near the coasts, as one would expect, the vegetation is tropical, the land fairly fertile, and the principal products are coffee, bananas, rubber, pineapples, cocoa, sugar cane, and cabinet woods.

The temperate region is the chief agricultural section in Mexico. It resembles the climatic conditions in parts of our own country. Here are fertile valleys, smooth slopes, and high plains where a variety of crops like corn, cotton, and fruits are grown.

Rivers and Harbors. — Most Mexican rivers are short and run from the interior plateau down the steep slopes near the ocean. This gives the country much water power, but only a small part of this has been developed. Boats cannot go far up the rivers, so they are little used for navigation. On the central plateau many rivers end in salt

CONTRASTS — *Ewing Galloway*
While the cows and donkeys and smaller sheep walk along the dusty road in the blazing summer heat, Ixtaccihautl and Popocatepetl wear their snow caps, like a painted backdrop on a stage.

TAMPICO — *Publishers' Photo*
Where once an ancient Aztec city stood, a busy seaport now stands — the center of oil production in Mexico.

MAP OF MEXICO

Map Questions and Activities

1. On what bodies of water does Mexico border?
2. How are the highlands shown on this map? the lowlands? the sea depths?
3. Estimate the flying distance from Mexico City to New Orleans.
4. What kind of country does the map show most of Mexico to be?
5. Why has Mexico no large rivers?
6. How does Yucatan seem to differ from the rest of Mexico?
7. Locate Mexico City, Vera Cruz, Tampico, and Mt. Popocatepetl.

CALIFORNIA
Salton Sea
San Diego
Yuma
Colorado R.
Prescott
ARIZONA
Phoenix
Gila R.
Tucson
Nogales
Santa Catalina
LOWER CALIFORNIA
GULF OF CALIFORNIA
Sebastian Vizcaino Bay
SONORA
Hermosillo
Guaymas
Yaqui R.
Topolobampo
Magdalena Bay
Culiacan
La Paz
Tropic of Cancer
C. San Lucas
Mazatlan
SINALOA
WESTERN SIERRA MADRE
CHIHUAHUA
Chihuahua
Conchos R.
Jimenez
Torreon
DURANGO
Durango
ZACATECAS
Zacatecas
NAYARIT
San Blas
Tepic
AGU.
Aguascalientes
Leon
Guadalajara
C. Corrientes
JALISCO
Manzanillo
Colima
COLIMA
Morelia
MICHOACAN
Mexico
Toluca
Nev. de Toluca
Cuernavaca
Popocatepetl
Guanajuato
GUANAJ.
Celaya
QUER.
Queretaro
HIDALGO
Pachuca
MEXICO
TLA.
Puebla
PUEBLA
Jalapa
Orizaba Vol.
Orizaba
Vera Cruz
Chilpancingo
Southern Sierra Madre
GUERRERO
Acapulco
OAXACA
Oaxaca
S. Felipe del Agua
Salina Cruz
Gulf of Tehuantepec
SAN LUIS POTOSI
San Luis Potosi
COAHUILA
Saltillo
Eastern Sierra Madre
NUEVO LEON
Monterey
Victoria
TAMAULIPAS
Tampico
Tuxpam
VERA CRUZ
Piedras Negras
Eagle Pass
Laredo
Brownsville
Matamoros
Ciudad Juarez
El Paso
Rio Grande
Pecos R.
Santa Fe
Albuquerque
NEW MEXICO
Canadian
Cimarron R.
KANSAS
OKLAHOMA
Oklahoma City
Tulsa
Arkansas R.
Red R.
Fort Worth
Dallas
Brazos R.
Colorado R.
Austin
San Antonio
Houston
Beaumont
Sabine R.
Galveston
TEXAS
UNITED STATES
MISSOURI
ILL.
IND.
KENT
Ohio R.
Nashville
TENNESS
Tennessee R.
Memphis
ARKANSAS
Little Rock
Mississippi R.
Shreveport
MISSISSIPPI
Jackson
Vicksburg
Birmingham
ALABAMA
Montgomery
Mobile
Tombigbee R.
Alabama R.
LOUISIANA
Baton Rouge
New Orleans
F L
GULF OF MEXICO
Yucatan Channel
C. Catoche
Progreso
Merida
YUCATAN
Yucatan Pen.
Campeche
CAMPECHE
QUINTANA ROO
Payo Obispo
GULF OF CAMPECHE
Puerto Mexico
TABASCO
Villa Hermosa
CHIAPAS
Tuxtla
BRITISH HONDURAS
Belize
Gulf of Honduras
Puerto Cortez
Coban
Pto. Barrios
GUATEMALA
Tacana Vol.
Quezaltenango
Champerico
Guatemala
Zacapa
HONDURAS
Tegucigalpa
San Jose
Santa Ana
San Salvador
EL SALVADOR
San Vicente
San Miguel
Amalpa
Gulf of Fonseca
NICAR
Matagalpa
Leon
Managua
Granada
L. Nicaragua
CENTRAL
PACIFIC OCEAN
Longitude
West
115°
110°
105°
100°
95°
90°
85°
35°
30
25
20
15
10
5

MEXICO AND THE CARIBBEAN LANDS

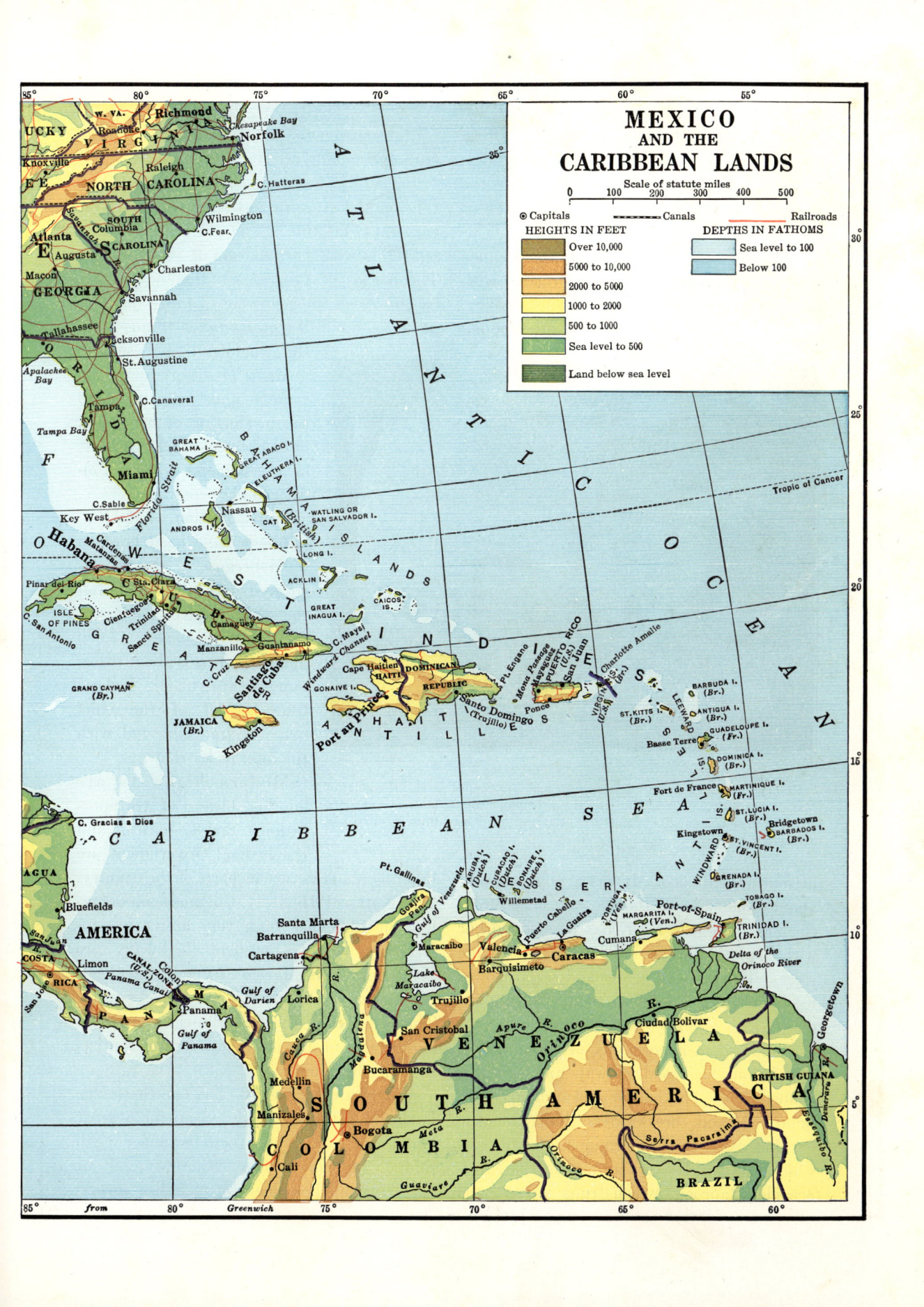

Scale of statute miles
0   100   200   300   400   500

⊙ Capitals   ┄┄┄ Canals   ─── Railroads

HEIGHTS IN FEET
- Over 10,000
- 5000 to 10,000
- 2000 to 5000
- 1000 to 2000
- 500 to 1000
- Sea level to 500
- Land below sea level

DEPTHS IN FATHOMS
- Sea level to 100
- Below 100

lakes as in the Great Basin of our western states. Mexico has few good harbors; Tampico and Vera Cruz are the best on the eastern coast, and Manzanillo and Acapulco on the western coast.

Tampico, near the mouth of the Panuco River, is connected by railroads with Monterey, with the fertile Panuco Valley, and with Mexico City, as well as other points in southern Mexico. It has a population of about 68,000, and though six miles from the mouth of the river, has a good harbor with loading wharves on both sides of the river. This railroad center and seaport owes its importance chiefly to the petroleum industry.

Vera Cruz, a historic city of about 68,000 population, has good railway and shipping connections. The harbor has been recently improved and breakwaters built at the entrance. It is the terminus of railroads which lead to Mexico City and to the Interoceanic Railroad which runs across the continent from the Gulf of Campeche to the Gulf of Tehuantepec.

Progreso is the third center of transportation on the Atlantic side, in the northwest corner of Yucatan. The chief city nearby is Merida with a population of about 95,000. The harbor of Progreso is shallow so that ocean vessels anchor some distance out and passengers and freight are taken to and from the mainland by smaller boats. The port owes its growth and importance to the production of henequen, or sisal fiber, nearby. Most of its commerce is carried on with foreign countries.

Transportation. — Mexican railroads have been hard to build because of the jungle-covered coastal plains and the steep slopes of the mountains. Of the nearly 17,000 miles of railroads about three-fourths are under Federal control. All of the chief seaports are connected with the interior by railways.

Modern highways are another means of transportation. States, cities, and the Federal Government are building roads in various parts of the country. The National Highway Commission, organized in 1925, has been very active in constructing roads. Excellent highways are being built from Mexico City and other leading centers to different parts of the country. This is a part of the Government's means of aiding agriculture and encouraging tourists to visit the country.

Agriculture. — Mexico has much fertile land and a long growing season for a great variety of crops, but there is not enough rainfall in some parts. Where rainfall or irrigation supplies plenty of moisture, several

MEXICO CITY

Publishers' Photo

From an Indian village of mud and rush huts, six centuries old, the capital of Mexico has become a beautiful city of flat-roofed dwelling houses, a modern office building scattered here and there, and boulevards beautified by trees and shrubs and flowers.

crops may be grown in one year. But Mexico is using only a small part of her land for agriculture; most of the present farms are used for grazing live stock. In some sections where the rainfall is abundant, valuable forests of pine, cedar, mahogany, and rosewood are found.

Corn, beans, and wheat occupy one-half of the cultivated land in Mexico, and are the main crops for human food. Corn will grow almost anywhere in Mexico and it is the chief food of the Mexican people. Beans are second to corn in their diet. An increasing amount of wheat is being produced on the broad stretches of the Mexican plateau.

Mexico is also adapted to growing fruits of many varieties. The banana ranks first. This requires a well-drained, fertile soil, tropical climate, and protection from high winds. Southern Mexico grows and sends to the United States a large share of the many millions of bananas we eat each year.

Lower California and the north central part of Mexico produce some cotton, but henequen, or sisal hemp, is probably the chief fiber plant in Mexico. It has long, heavy leaves which grow up from a central stalk. It takes five or six years for the plant to reach maturity. Then the leaves are cut, the fiber extracted, bleached, and pressed into heavy bales. From this product is made binder twine, cord, and rope. Henequen is raised chiefly for export, and is grown mostly in the Yucatan peninsula. This small section supplies about half the world's sisal hemp, and most of the world's binder twine comes from henequen grown in this part of Mexico.

Live Stock. — The grazing of live stock has long been important in Mexico. High plains in the northern part form one of the best grazing sections in the world. The winters there are milder than they are in most parts of the United States, so cattle do not have to be sheltered.

Minerals and Mining. — While most of the people of Mexico are engaged in agri-

MAGUEY, OR SISAL HEMP, FIELDS *Ewing Galloway*
This spiny-looking plant is of two varieties; one produces a fiber and the other produces a sap from which a national drink is made.

culture, mining is the best organized industry. The mining of metals was carried on long before Columbus discovered this land. The early Spanish explorers carried vast sums of these precious metals back to Spain, taken largely from the temples. Until recently, foreigners controlled most of the Mexican mines and the minerals were largely exported. Much of the import trade consists of mining machinery, supplies, and tools. During the long history of this industry silver and gold have been the chief metals; and with the exception of oil, these two metals still form about one-half of the production. The total value of silver mined in Mexico during the past four hundred years has been more than three billion dollars, a considerable part of the world's output. Mexico now yields about one-third of the world's silver. Lead has now become second to silver in importance, and the best known deposits are usually found in connection with the latter.

Petroleum. — When oil was discovered in Mexico, they did not have the equipment or the money to develop the oil fields. So about thirty-five years ago the Mexican Government invited United States capitalists to go into

A GUSHER UNDER CONTROL *Ewing Galloway*
A well in the Panuco River region is controlled by a big valve, held down by a steel arch. Some of the most violent gushers have been brought under control in seven minutes during recent years.

Mexico and develop the oil industry. As a result, Americans invested large sums of money in the business and much of the oil came to our country. People from other countries also invested money in this profitable industry. In 1938, the Mexican Government took over all of the oil properties. A large part of the production has always been shipped to different European countries. As transportation is difficult, it is fortunate that most of the oil wells are near the coast. Some of the greatest gushers in the world have been found near Tuxpam, and Tampico owes its growth and importance to the rich oil fields nearby.

Manufacturing. — Mexico is not a leading manufacturing country. Revolutions, lack of money, old customs, and the nature of the people have hindered the growth of this industry. Good coal is lacking, but much water power can be had near the steep slopes. Among some of the most important manufactured goods are shoes, clothing, tobacco products, pottery, refined petroleum, hats, and baskets. A good many of these articles are still made by hand.

The commerce of Mexico is chiefly with the United States, Great Britain, and Germany. Most of her exports are to the United States, in fact this amounts to almost 90 per cent of the total. A few years ago our trade with Mexico averaged more than one million dollars a day.

The People. — Mexico has a population of about 25,000,000, most of whom are native Indians, direct descendants of the ancient Mayas and Aztecs. About one million, however, boast pure Spanish blood, and the rest are a mixture of these two races. These are the *mestizos*, and together with the Indians they form the laboring class or *peons*.

Long before Columbus the Mayas and Aztecs built up a remarkable civilization, of which numerous ruins remain, especially in Yucatan. The Mayas invented a wonderful calendar from which we know that the first great Maya empire was founded about the time Christ was born. Their greatest period was around 500 A.D., the beginning of the so-called Dark Ages in Europe. At that time the Mayas were among the most civilized people in the world. Then, for some reason that scholars do not know, they abandoned their wonderful cities and moved away, leaving only the ruins of their remarkable temples.

The Mayas were followed by the Aztecs, a warlike tribe, who built their capital at Mexico City on an island in a lake. Narrow causeways with drawbridges led to the main-

SAN PEDRO, SAN LUIS POTOSI

Behind a fence of organ cactus appear the low stone buildings of a mining village — gold mines have been worked here since 1590.

Ore cars are quickly loaded under the chutes, and then carry the ore-bearing earth, partly by gravity, down to the smelters.

PACHUCA, MEXICO

Pachuca is a thriving mining city situated in a valley among the Sierra Madre Mountains, over 8000 feet above sea level. Silver has been mined here for centuries and the surrounding hills are honeycombed with mines. Waterfalls in the vicinity furnish electric power.

THE "PYRAMID OF THE SUN"

This man-made mound of earth and stone is the most imposing existing monument to Aztec civilization — a temple for sun-worshipers and their religion of cruel sacrifices.

Ewing Galloway

...OUR DAILY BREAD

An Indian woman in her backyard kitchen at Mitla is making tortillas, the main staff of life to Mexicans.

AZTEC CALENDAR STONE

This lunar calendar of complicated picture writing is a record of unusual accuracy.

land. The Aztecs grew rich and powerful, and ruled harshly over all central Mexico. Their civilization was largely borrowed from the Mayas.

Then came the Spaniards under Cortez, who overthrew the powerful Aztecs under their chief, Montezuma, and captured Mexico City. Cortez sent so much treasure home to Spain that many nobles started at once to make their fortunes in the New World, and Mexico became a Spanish colony. Many Spaniards married native Indians and built up huge estates on which the *peons*, as the working-class Indians came to be called, did the work. These large estates were handed down from father to son and until lately the peon had little chance to better himself. But now the government feels that the best way to get rid of the evils of peonage is to break up the great estates and give the land in small farms to the Indians. This is being done and today more than twelve million acres have been given over to the people.

The Government. — Mexico is a Federal Republic consisting of 28 states, 2 territories, and a Federal District. A President is elected by the people for a term of four years, but there is no vice-president. The Congress consists of a Senate of 56, with a four-year term, and a Chamber of Deputies elected for two years.

After Mexico gained her independence in 1821 there were long and bloody civil wars, but in recent years, under the leadership of Presidents Calles and Cardenas, Mexico has had a more stable government and many reforms have been made. Better schools are being developed as rapidly as possible, newer methods are being introduced into all the industries, and the great estates are being divided into small farms for the peons.

Inland Cities of Mexico. — *Mexico City* is the capital of the Republic. It has nearly 1,000,000 people and is by far the largest city in the country. It is one of the oldest and most interesting cities in America. Some parts are very ancient, the buildings and

MEXICO CITY

The great Roman Catholic Cathedral stands in an open plaza where patriotic celebrations, military concerts, and other outdoor entertainments are held.

streets resembling cities in Spain. Other sections have buildings and avenues which are among the most modern and beautiful in the country. Its position high above sea level in a protected valley gives it a pleasant climate throughout the year.

It has beautiful boulevards, parks, museums, theaters, and castles. The Plaza Mayor is one of the most beautiful public squares in the New World. Here stands the famous old Cathedral, built on the site of a former Aztec temple. The official home of the President, the National Palace, was begun over two hundred years ago. Over its main entrance hangs the Liberty Bell of Mexico. The National Museum is famous for its ancient art; the National Theater, one of the finest in the country, cost millions of dollars. Few countries can boast a more interesting, beautiful, and imposing capital than Mexico.

Guadalajara, with about 206,000 people, is the second largest city. It is located near the western edge of the plateau, about 250 miles from Mexico City. It is a railroad center and lies in a rich farming section. A splendid road has recently been built direct from Mexico City. Many tourists go to

A PUBLIC SCHOOL AT HUITAHAC

Formerly church property, this little building was confiscated by the government for a school, one of the 4000 opened since 1920.

Guadalajara, and the late Dwight W. Morrow, when he was the American consul to Mexico, had his residence in this city.

Puebla is the third city and has about 115,000 inhabitants. It is an important commercial and distributing center, with numerous cotton mills. It is located a short distance southeast of the capital in the heart of the most productive part of the country.

San Luis Potosi is an important railroad center on the plateau west of the seaport of Tampico about halfway between the Atlantic and Pacific oceans. The location makes it a great distributing point for the mines, ranches, and farms in central Mexico. It has tanneries, flour and linen mills, cold-storage plants, ore smelters, and other manufacturing industries.

Monterrey, in the northeastern part of Mexico, has a population of about 153,000. It is a manufacturing as well as commercial center. Breweries, steel mills, flour and cotton mills, glass factories, and other manufacturing plants are here. A large American colony is located in Monterrey and many of the shops have signs in both Spanish and English. Monterrey in the interior and Tampico on the Gulf coast resemble our cities more than any others in Mexico.

Mining Towns. — There are many mining towns, for almost every section of the country does mining of some kind. Guanajuato and Pachuca are the most famous of these towns. These are very old mining centers northwest and northeast of Mexico City, one of the richest mining regions in America. Gold, silver, iron, lead, copper, tin, mercury, and sulfur come from this section. Guanajuato has about 18,000 inhabitants, and is one of the wealthiest, oldest, and most interesting mining towns in Mexico.

Education and Living Conditions. — Mexico is a country of extremes. Side by side we find wealth and poverty, culture and ignorance, old and new methods of farming and manufacturing. Education is improving, but many Mexicans are still illiterate. The farmers live near the farms in small villages of a few dozen houses. Most of the houses have one or two rooms with little furniture, small windows, and few modern conveniences.

In the past there has been friction between the United States and her southern neighbor, but now that Mexico has a stable government, is educating her people, and developing her great natural resources, the two countries are coming to understand each other better and good feeling prevails. Many believe that Mexico has a bright future, and we may look forward to the day when the United States and Mexico will settle all questions

HUASTECA CANYON

A typical Mexican hacienda (farm), close to the wild jumble of the Sierra Madre peaks. The flat spiny leaves of the nopal cactus look like the "Gingerbread Boy," caught at last.

TYPICAL NATIVES

Notice the picturesque jug of the woman and the quaint hat of the man.

TEXCO, MEXICO

Towering above the small and crowded stone houses is the fine old cathedral, dominating the life of the town.

of difference between them in the friendly spirit of good neighbors.

Activities and Questions

1. Compare Mexico and the United States in size and population.

2. What are some of the chief products of Mexico?

3. Who were the Mayas? the Aztecs?

4. Name the chief ports; the leading inland cities.

5. Why has Mexico such a small number of navigable rivers?

6. Describe the climate of the coastal plains; of the plateau country.

7. How do the Mexican farmers live?

THE TEMPLE OF THE SUN

Built many years ago by the Maya Indians, this temple to Kul-kul-can, the Sun God, rises 91 steep stone steps above the plain.

XVI. THE CENTRAL AMERICAN REPUBLICS

Sailing the Spanish Main. — "All aboard for Puerto Barrios!" The white fruit steamer blows a long blast from its whistle, we wave at our friends standing on the wharf, and our ship moves gracefully into the main stream of the Hudson River, picks up speed as we go down the harbor, and then proceeds southward, bound for Central America and our Spanish Main! We have heard strange stories of these seas; of pirates with fleet ships carrying the black flag; of buccaneers raiding coast towns and hiding their treasure on lonely islands; of Spanish nobles forcing the natives to give them gold and silver to load into their lofty ships.

We want to know more about these lands and these tropical seas. We are sailing in a southwesterly direction and are far out to sea as we pass our South Atlantic States. We round the tip of Florida, pass the island of Cuba, and sail west and south to the Gulf of Honduras, at the very head of which lies Puerto Barrios.

Bananas. — As we pull into port we know why we came to Puerto Barrios on a fruit steamer. Long trainloads of bananas are constantly being brought out from the plantations for shipment by steamer. This is the yellow gold that American fruit companies are bringing back to the United States. All of the Central American countries produce bananas. The United Fruit Company has nearly 30,000 acres of banana farms in Guatemala alone. Each plantation is divided into farms of 1,000 acres, and these into twenty-one-acre sections which are let out to native farmers. Each banana tree bears only one bunch of bananas a year and, strange as it may seem, they grow upside down. These bunches are cut when still green, but during shipment they ripen slowly so that when ready to sell they have turned a golden yellow.

chain of mountains known as the Cordilleras that runs the full length of it. Some of the great peaks are active volcanoes and throughout this land earthquakes are common. This range lies near the Pacific, and goes down to the sea in a series of sharp, rocky slopes; towards the Caribbean the slope is more gradual, often ending in wide coastal plains somewhat above sea level. These coastal plains are hot, moist jungles, and are very unhealthful except at the harbors where modern port facilities are improving these conditions.

Good natural harbors are scarce. On the Pacific Coast we note the Gulf of Fonseca and the Bay of Corinto. All of these countries, except Salvador and British Honduras, have ports on both coasts, an important fact in the development of Central America.

Climate and Seasons. — Most of the people live on the plateaus and highlands where there is a good rainfall, and the temperature seldom goes above 80 degrees. There are only two seasons here, the dry and the rainy. The dry season extends from about November to April; then comes the rainy season when there is nearly everywhere a daily downpour.

Courtesy United Fruit Company
YELLOW GOLD
Bananas are shipped by steamer to the New York, San Francisco, New Orleans, and Boston markets.

Coffee. — Coffee, however, is the leading product of the Central American countries. The coffee that is produced here from thousands of finkas or plantations is said to be the best in the world. Most of this coffee is shipped to the United States, although most of the Costa Rican coffee goes to England. Coffee trees grow on the slopes and higher lands back of the coastal lowlands where banana plantations are found.

Physical Features of Central America. — Central America is like an irregular triangle between the Caribbean Sea and the Pacific Ocean. It varies in width from 50 to 500 miles across.

One of the most interesting things about the land is the

Three Lions
COFFEE BEANS GET A BATH
After they are picked, coffee beans are put through a bath of running water, or sluice. The ripe berries float and any green ones sink to the bottom.

The People. — Many years ago, a remarkable people lived in Central America. They were the Maya Indians. They moved south from the Yucatan peninsula and settled in Guatemala and Honduras, where they built many beautiful temples, the ruins of which are still to be seen. The Mayas were overthrown by the Aztecs, whose center was Mexico City. Then came the Spanish, who were always looking for gold and silver. They made slaves of the Maya and Aztec Indians, and destroyed their towns and temples. In more recent years Negroes from the West Indies have been brought over to work on the plantations. Today there are between eight and nine million people in Central America.

The Government. — Central America includes the six republics of Guatemala, Honduras, Salvador, Nicaragua, Costa Rica, and Panama, and the colony of British Honduras. About 100 years ago the people of Central America revolted from Spain, just as the thirteen American colonies revolted from England, and gained their independence. Gradually they set up governments of their own and became small independent republics. Each of these republics elects a president, who is assisted by his Cabinet, and each republic sends a minister to Washington.

Education — The Central American republics are giving more and more attention to education. Everyone must go to the primary schools for six years. Many rural schools are held on the far-away coffee and banana plantations. Later on many of these pupils go to trade schools and schools of art and music. In the capitals we find colleges that train young people for law, medicine, engineering, agriculture, and the arts and sciences.

Guatemala. — Guatemala in area is about the size of our state of New York. It has a population of three and one-half million. More than half of them are Indians, who live in rather crude, thatch-roofed huts. A railroad connects Puerto Barrios with Guatemala City, the capital, which is 200 miles inland, and then goes on to San José on the Pacific coast. At Puerto Barrios the heat is intense, but at Guatemala City the climate is much more temperate, for it is nearly 5,000 feet above sea level. The inhabitants of this city number about 175,000 and live for the most part in one-story houses of faded pink or blue or yellow stucco.

Three Lions

A STREET SCENE IN GUATEMALA

Tourists find Guatemala very interesting. Guatemala City has many good hotels, interesting Indian markets, and a fine airport. The old capital, Antiqua, shaken many times by earthquakes, is one of the most beautiful and colorful spots in all Central America.

Honduras. — When Columbus made his famous voyage in 1502 along this coast, Cape Honduras was his first landing place. It is a country of deep valleys and high mountains. In area it is about the same as its neighbor, Guatemala. It has over a million people, the majority of whom are Indians.

The capital is Tegucigalpa, a city of about 47,000, in the highlands of the interior. The only port on the Pacific Coast is Amalpa, but the harbor is not very deep. Honduras exports, in addition to bananas and coffee, many tropical hardwoods, especially mahog-

LOGGING ACTIVITIES, LAKE NICARAGUA
Three Lions
A native and his ox team haul a heavy log to the mill.

any. It has several small silver and gold mines.

Salvador (El Salvador). — Salvador is the smallest of all the Central American republics. It is, however, the most thickly settled. The nearly two million of its population live in an area about the size of our state of Maryland, with 144 persons to every square mile of land. San Salvador is the capital with over 100,000 people.

There are many volcanoes and some of these are quite active. These frequent volcanic eruptions help as well as hurt, for the volcanic ash which spreads far and wide over the country adds richness to the soil. Some of the extinct volcanoes have crater lakes and one of them, Lake Ilopango, is used as a landing field for seaplanes.

Nicaragua. — There is a good reason why the United States should be interested in this country. If you look at the map, the first thing you note is a great lake near the Pacific. This is Lake Nicaragua, one hundred miles long and forty-five miles wide. A smaller lake, Lake Managua, thirty miles long and fifteen miles wide, is connected by a short river with Lake Nicaragua, and these two lakes drain into the Caribbean through the San Juan River. The United States has bought the right to build a canal here some day.

This country produces about the same kinds of products as Guatemala, and the United States takes over half of all its exports, and furnishes about three-fourths of its imports. Its jungles produce the beautiful mahogany wood which we use for our best furniture. Gold is mined and it is a leading export.

Nicaragua is the largest of all the central American republics. Its population, however, is just over a million people. There is an excellent port at Corinto on the Pacific.

Costa Rica. — This bright little country has many names. When Columbus sailed along its eastern shoreline he spoke of it as "a rich coast" — "Costa Rica." It has often been called "The Heart of the Americas," and many who have been there speak of it as "The Land of the Painted Oxcarts." In area it is

COSTA RICA, THE LAND OF THE PAINTED OXCARTS

about as large as two of our New England states, New Hampshire and Vermont.

Two mountain ranges run the length of this little country, and most of its inhabitants live on the fertile mountain table-land or plateau between the mountains. This central plateau is from 3,000 to 5,000 feet high, and its climate is delightful. Down on the coast, however, the weather is hot and humid. The mountains are volcanic, and some of the peaks are still active, like Mount Poas and Mount Irazu. Mount Irazu, far to the south, is over 11,000 feet high, and if one climbs the great ridge back of the crater he can see, without changing his position, three important bodies of water, the Caribbean Sea to the East, Lake Nicaragua to the North, and the Pacific Ocean to the West.

The chief products, in addition to bananas and coffee, are sugar, coconut, peanut oil, leather goods, cocoa, tiles and brick, and many varieties of beautiful tropical wood.

The capital is San José, a city of over 65,000 inhabitants. It is a beautiful, modern city with many fine buildings. One of the things you would be sure to see along nearly every street would be the slow-moving ox-carts with their brilliantly painted wheels in various colors. Some of these wheels are truly works of art. They used to be made of one solid piece of mahogany, but now slabs are cut and fitted to the rim of the wheel.

Panama and the Canal Zone. — In 1513 Balboa and his men forced their way through nearly fifty miles of thick jungle and across a rugged mountain range, to stand at last on the shore of a great calm sea that stretched far away before their amazed and wondering eyes. From that time on, men dreamed of the day when this narrow fifty-mile strip could be cut through by a canal, and so avoid the long, dangerous trip around Cape Horn.

Finally France, one of whose engineers, Ferdinand De Lesseps, had succeeded in build-

THE PANAMA CANAL

The boats are drawn into each lock by powerful electric locomotives running on tracks parallel to the canal, the gates are then closed, and the vessels raised or lowered to the next level.

ing the Suez Canal, said it would build a canal across this Isthmus. But the heat and the rain, the swampy jungles and the yellow fever overcame all efforts. The men died like flies; the money gave out; and De Lesseps had to abandon his project and go back to France. It seemed an impossible task, till a president of the United States, Theodore Roosevelt, undertook the work. The United States bought the claims of the French and in 1905 "the dirt began to fly." A great American engineer, Colonel George W. Goethals, was put in charge. He had many able assistants, but he, too, would have probably met defeat in this tropical land if it had not been for Colonel William C. Gorgas, who so safeguarded the health of the workmen that they did not suffer from tropical diseases as did the French. In 1914 the first steamer went through the canal, a distance of fifty miles.

The Panama Canal is known as a lock canal. Vessels cannot sail right out of the Caribbean Sea into the canal and out again into the Pacific. All ships have to be lifted or lowered by means of locks, for the canal was not dug down to sea level.

Nearly one-fourth of the people of Panama live in the famous old city of Panama. Dense forests cover much of the country and fully one-half of it is unsettled. Fruits and vegetables are raised for people who live in the Canal Zone and bananas, cacao and coconuts are exported. Fishing in the Bay of Panama for pearl oysters to obtain pearls and mother-of-pearl is one of Panama's oldest industries.

The United States now owns a strip ten miles wide across the Isthmus. This is called the Canal Zone, and although the United States allows all nations to use the canal, we control and operate it.

British Honduras. — British Honduras is a colony of the British Empire. It is a small district along the coast directly north of the Gulf of Honduras. The population is only 60,000. Belize is its capital. It is chiefly famous for its tropical woods like mahogany and cedar, and the natives are fine woodsmen. The rainfall has been known to exceed 150 inches a year. There are many ruins here of the former cities of the great Mayas.

Relations with the United States. — Our relations with these countries are steadily improving. We help them develop their resources; they supply us with articles we cannot grow. They are growing rapidly, more coffee and banana plantations are being laid out, more railroads are being built, more steamers are going back and forth, and more tourists are going on these steamers to see the interesting places. Soon the completed links of the new Pan-American Highway will run the whole length of Central America, and you and your family may enjoy an automobile trip through this colorful countryside. As we come to know these people better, we shall want to keep on friendly terms, for they are near neighbors, and each of us can be of great help to the other.

Activities and Questions

1. Study a map of the world carefully and note the great saving of time and distance made possible by the Panama Canal.
2. About how many miles are saved if one is sailing through the canal, (*a*) from New York to San Francisco, (*b*) from New York to Honolulu, (*c*) from New York to Manila, (*d*) from San Francisco to London, (*e*) from Boston to Valparaiso?
3. What are the two chief products of Central America?
4. About what proportion of the products of these countries is sent to the United States?
5. Tell about education in Central America.
6. Which countries touch both the Pacific Ocean and the Caribbean Sea?
7. List one outstanding thing about each one of the Central American countries.
8. If you were going to live for a year in Central America, which one of the countries would you select to live in? Why?
9. Do you think that the proposed canal through Nicaragua would have any advantages over the present canal at Panama?
10. Make a special report to the class on one of the following:
(*a*) The United Fruit Company
(*b*) George W. Goethals: Great Engineer
(*c*) William C. Gorgas: Great Doctor
(*d*) The Ancient Mayas
(*e*) A Coffee Plantation

From the top of Signal Hill one watches the light and shade on the coral peaks of Curaçao, island possession of the Netherlands.

XVII. THE WEST INDIES

The West Indies are divided into two groups according to their size and location. The largest four, Cuba, Haiti, Jamaica, and Puerto Rico, are known as the Greater Antilles. The smaller islands around the eastern end of the Caribbean Sea are called the Lesser Antilles. Cuba, the largest of all, is an independent republic. The next largest, Haiti, is divided between two republics, Haiti and the Dominican Republic. The rest belong to the United States, Great Britain, France, and Holland.

Land and Climate. — Most of the West Indies are mountainous and are noted for their beautiful scenery. Much of the rich soil has come from volcanoes, some of which are still active. On the island of Martinique, one of the Lesser Antilles belonging to France, Mont Pelée blew its head off in 1902 and the poison gases which swept down the mountain side killed 40,000 people in the city of Pierre on that island.

All the West Indies, except some of the Bahamas, are south of the Tropic of Cancer where it is hot in what is called the tropics. The lowlands are always warm and there is little change in temperature throughout the year such as we have in the northern United States. The trees hold their leaves the year round and the grass is always green. The winds known as the *trade winds* blow steadily from the northeast, tempering the heat and bringing plenty of rainfall. Severe storms called *hurricanes* sometimes sweep over these islands, killing many people and doing much damage to buildings, trees, and crops.

Crops. — The West Indies produce many crops, such as cacao, bananas, coffee, sugar cane, and coconuts, which cannot be grown in colder countries. What they do not use

297

MARTINIQUE *Publishers' Photo*

Squatting in the shadows of Mont Pelée is the town where the luckless Josephine was born — Josephine, wife of the great Napoleon of France.

they sell to northern countries and then buy other foods, such as wheat, meat, fish, and temperate zone fruits. Bananas, beans, and corn are common foods of the natives. A list of different products raised on these islands is a surprisingly long one, and includes, in addition to those already named, pineapples, oranges and grapefruit, rice, tropical fruits, and many kinds of vegetables. There are few farm animals and consequently little meat.

In addition to the food crops, cotton, sisal hemp, rubber, and tobacco are grown for sale. There is little manufacturing except that of sugar and tobacco. Forests furnish mahogany and other fine hardwoods for export. One of the most common trees is the royal palm, rows of which often line the streets and highways.

People of the West Indies. — When the Spaniards came to these islands, they found them peopled by Indian tribes, many of whom were engaged in farming. Later, Negro slaves were brought over from Africa to work on the Spanish plantations. The descendants of Indians, Negroes, and Spaniards make up most of the population of the West Indies today, but people from other parts of the world have also come to the West Indies to live so that one finds many different peoples living on the various islands. Most of the people in the West Indies speak Spanish.

Outside the cities the homes of the natives are often the simplest kind of thatched huts. In such warm regions, little shelter is needed, and scanty cotton clothing is enough to keep them comfortable.

Cuba, the Tropical Wonderland. — Cuba, whose capital city, Habana, is only ninety miles from our southern city of Key West, is a long narrow island between the Caribbean Sea and the Gulf of Mexico. Its length of 760 miles from east to west is about six times its greatest width from north to south. Thick forests cover the highlands, but there are beautiful valleys and fertile lowlands on which are grown the many tropical products for which this island is noted.

The trade winds sweep freely over the whole of Cuba and give it an even temperature and

KINGSTON, JAMAICA *Publishers' Photo*

In the golden valley, beneath the dark hills, are the Hope Gardens, where flowers of iridescent hues vie in color with the brilliant plumage of parrots.

TRINIDAD

As the winds blow softly through the cluster of tall bamboo stalks, they whisper of ancient things.

The natives — East Indian Hindus in this picture — live in thatched huts under the shade of sheltering palms.

BALANCED BURDENS

The women of the island of Santa Lucia work, as did the women of primitive races, at hard labor, while the men look on.

299

rainfall. Except on the highest lands, the thermometer seldom goes below sixty degrees or above ninety degrees. This makes it popular with winter tourists, who can travel either on the railroad or on good highways from one end of the island to the other to view its picturesque valleys and huge sugar plantations.

Cuba's great money crop is sugar, most of which comes to the United States. The soil is so fertile and the climate so mild that the cane, once planted, grows for eight or ten years without replanting. Cuba is also noted for its tobacco, and the making of cigars and cigarettes is one of its biggest industries. It also exports bananas, coconuts, cacao, pineapples, and coffee. Large quantities of fresh meats, dressed chickens, cheese, butter, eggs, and other products are shipped to Cuba which, in turn, sends to our country a variety of tropical and semi-tropical fruits and, in addition to these, green vegetables during the winter season.

But Cuba's wealth does not consist wholly of sugar and tropical products. There are many mines producing coal, asphalt, iron, copper, gold, silver, lead, zinc, and other metals. Much of the iron ore is shipped to our eastern cities to be made into iron and steel.

Habana, the capital and largest city, is an attractive, modern city with beautiful public buildings, good hotels, and shady parks. It is only an hour's ride by airplane from Key West, and many people from the United States make this short trip just to see this interesting old city. *Santiago*, another old city, is the next largest seaport. It is the center of the richest mining district in Cuba.

Haiti and the Dominican Republic. — The island of Haiti is all mountains and valleys with very little level land. An old legend tells of a sea captain, who, when he was asked to describe Haiti, crumpled up a piece of paper and threw it on the table, saying, "That is Haiti." Pine trees cover the highlands, while on the lower slopes are palms, mahogany, and logwood, which is used for making dye. Its products and exports are like those of the other West Indies.

The Republic of Haiti was once ruled by the French and the people now use French as their language. Most of them are Negroes. Spanish is used in the Dominican Republic. In the old city of Santo Domingo is the "House of the Admiral," a stone castle built by Diego, the son of Columbus, when he ruled over these Spanish possessions.

Jamaica, the Land of Bananas. — Jamaica is famed for its bananas. They form one of the chief foods of the people and large numbers are exported. Jamaica ginger is another well-known export. This island belongs to Great Britain. Many visitors go there during the winter season on account of its mild climate.

SWEET AS THE SUGAR CANE *Ewing Galloway*
Ox-drawn carts loaded with sugar cane, are drawn up in front of a sugar mill in Cuba, waiting to be unloaded.

"Citadel La Ferrière," Haiti — *Ewing Galloway*

A memorial to the "Black Napoleon," born a slave, but who rose to proclaim himself King Henry I of Haiti, in 1811.

Puerto Rico — *Publishers' Photo*

The military road winds across the country landscape, dotted by low-roofed houses amid fertile fields, and shut in by the mountains reaching to hazy distances.

Habana — *John Kabel*

The statue of Gomez stands amid the architectural loveliness of the President's palace and the Capitol.

JAMAICA

Ewing Galloway

The Negro women, balancing bunches of yellow fruit on their turbaned heads, march along like an army wearing golden helmets.

Puerto Rico. — As Americans we have a special interest in Puerto Rico because it belongs to the United States, and Puerto Ricans are citizens of our country. It is a small island, only a little over 100 miles long and about 35 miles wide, yet it contains over one and one-half millions of people. As most of them live in the country and depend on farming, it is hard to make a living, and many of them are very poor.

A range of mountains runs through the center of the island from east to west. Most of the forests have been cut and the land is cultivated on the slopes of the mountains as well as on the lowlands. The northern slope is well watered but the southern slope is so dry that the Government has had to build irrigation works. Puerto Rico has very fertile soil and large crops of sugar, tobacco, coffee, and fruits are grown for export.

When the island came into the possession of the United States in 1898, most of the people could neither read nor write. But now all children are required to attend school. Both English and Spanish are spoken.

The Virgin Islands. — Our country also owns the Virgin Islands, a group of small islands just east of Puerto Rico. The United States bought these islands from Denmark in 1917. Most of the people are colored. One of the islands, St. Thomas, has a very fine harbor at Charlotte Amalie, where the United States has a coaling and naval station. Here, as in Puerto Rico, nearly all of the people depend on agriculture for a living.

Activities and Questions

1. Which of the West Indies are independent countries?

2. Name the Greater Antilles. Which groups of islands are included in the Lesser Antilles?

3. Plan a cruise around the West Indies from Key West, naming the places at which you would stop and the things you would want to see on each island.

4. Compare the longitude of Habana with that of Washington, D.C. Which is farther west?

5. Make a list of products from the West Indies which would sell easily in European countries.

THE VIRGIN ISLANDS

Publishers' Photo

Charlotte Amalie is a commercial city, built around the curving shore of a beautiful landlocked harbor.

ON THE ROAD TO CAYAMBI — *James Sawders*
Three Indian children of Ecuador drive their flocks and herds along the Pan-American Highway.

OUR NEIGHBORS IN SOUTH AMERICA

GEOGRAPHY AND HISTORY

The countries of North, Central, and South America which lie south of the United States are called Latin America. This is because they have been settled by people from the Latin countries of Europe. We have already studied Mexico, Central America, and the West Indies. We come now to a study of South America proper. Its importance makes necessary a detailed treatment suited to the understanding of more advanced pupils, and this is given in a later book of this series. The following summary is meant only as an introduction to the later study.

The Continent of South America. — Let us look at this pear-shaped continent which is 5000 miles long and about 3000 miles wide at its broadest point. It is nearly as large as North America but has less than half as many inhabitants. North America at its most northwestern point almost touches Asia. South America at its most eastern point swings much closer to the Old World than most people realize. Brazil extends about 2600 miles east of a north-south line drawn through New York City. It thus brings South America about as close to Europe as it is to the United States. The most western point of South America is almost directly south of Miami, Florida.

South America is connected with Central America by the Isthmus of Panama. A highway is being built which will lead from our

ROAD BUILDING IN PERU
De Cou, from Sawders

The Pan-American Highway crosses and recrosses the steep, narrow gorge of the Rimac River as it makes its way up the almost perpendicular cliffs in the Andes.

state of Texas through Mexico and Central America into northwestern South America.

Within the past few years our country has given much attention to air lines between North and South American cities and airplane traffic between the Americas is increasing greatly and bids fair to increase much more in future years. Through such means, as well as through steamship travel, we hope that American people of the various countries will come to know one another better.

South America is considered much less fortunate than its northern neighbor both in its location and shape. Most of the continent lies within the southern, or water, hemisphere. It is thus cut off from the main east-west lines of travel. Its widest part, including about two thirds of its total area, lies within the tropics. Its southern tip reaches almost two thirds of the way from the Equator to the South Pole, to where it is only about 700 miles from Antarctica. This area runs into an extremely cold climate, exactly opposite from that of the tropics.

The Mountains. — The southern continent is much more rugged than the northern. Along its western side from north to south lie the Andes Mountains. They are a part of a great mountain chain which runs the entire length of South, Central, and North America. The Rocky Mountain, Cascade, and Coastal ranges of western United States are a part of this chain. In Bolivia and Peru they spread into a plateau four hundred miles in width. This plateau averages more than two miles above sea level in height.

The Andes rise almost out of the Pacific Ocean for much of their more than 4000 miles of length. They leave at most little but a ledge of coastal plain with few rivers or bays in which ships may find a harbor. There are few passes across them for more than 3000 miles which are not more than two miles above sea level at their lowest points.

Eastern South America also has mountain ranges. These ranges correspond to the eastern, or Appalachian, highlands of our United States. The Brazilian Highlands are a plateau varying from one to three thousand feet in height. This plateau is broken by many much higher, rounded, sloping mountain peaks.

There is also the Coast Range which runs southward from Rio de Janeiro. It rises abruptly from the Atlantic Ocean. Its peaks are very high and sharp, giving to this section of the country wild and rugged surface features.

Some distance from the north coast are the highlands of Venezuela and the Guianas. They are not as well known as the highlands

THE HIGH PLATEAU OF BOLIVIA
James Sawders
Indians and their packs crossing a lonely rocky stretch of the Altiplano.

of Brazil. In Colombia we find very high and rugged extensions of the Andes.

The Flat Lands. — The eastern slopes of the Andes break down into rough foothills which gradually merge into rolling plains.

Compare these plains and their border of mountains with the Appalachian mountains and plains.

The pampas of Argentina and the llanos of Venezuela and Colombia are such rolling, grass-covered plains. They are among the leading cattle-growing sections of the world. The plains of northern Argentina extend northward to join the great plains of the Amazon River basin in Brazil. The Amazon (the world's largest river) provides the greatest river drainage area in the world. Brazil itself is as large as the United States.

The valleys of the La Plata River in northern Argentina, Uruguay, and southwestern Brazil, and of the Orinoco River in northern Venezuela also provide great areas of grassy plains. The La Plata is the second largest river system of South America, the Orinoco the third.

HAY HARVEST
James Sawders
The hay grown on the high plateau of Bolivia near Lake Titicaca is being stacked in roofed piles which look like thatched houses.

Land of Contrasts. — South America is a continent of great contrasts in surface features and of extremes in temperature. We find in the tropical areas the high heat and humidity of the lowlands. We find also the thin air of the cool, high tablelands. The south temperate zone is the part of South America most favorable to human progress. Uruguay lies wholly within this zone. Nearly all of Argentina and Chile are found there also, as well as a long stretch of southern Brazil.

Great Undeveloped Resources. — South America is also a continent of abundant natural resources. The great mineral wealth of its mountain areas has been hardly more than touched. Its rich agricultural sections are being better farmed as more farm machinery comes into use. Railroads and highways are hard to build because of the high mountains and the swamps and jungles of many lowlands. Transportation and communication are still in their infancy in many sections of the country. Business interests outside of South America have often sought personal gain only in their dealing with South American countries. They are coming to realize, however, that South America is a continent of the future.

The History of South America. — We have all learned about the discovery of America by Columbus in 1492 upon his first voyage west to this New World, which he thought was India. He had really discovered several islands of the West Indies, — the Bahamas, Haiti, and Santo Domingo. Columbus made three more voyages to this region. He discovered the coast of Central America and, in 1498, the mouth of the Orinoco River in what is now Venezuela.

Columbus was followed by other explorers, who settled in Central America and upon some of the islands of the West Indies. One of them, Balboa, with a party of Spaniards crossed the Isthmus of Panama in 1513 and discovered the Pacific Ocean. Another discovered the coast of Brazil about where Recife is now located. He sailed northwest along the coast until he came to the mouth of the Orinoco River which, as we have seen, had already been discovered by Columbus.

Another leader and party of Spaniards sailed south along the South American east coast until they came to the mouth of the La Plata River, between the present states of Argentina and Uruguay.

In 1520 Magellan sailed south along this east coast of South America until he came to the southern tip, passed through the strait which now bears his name, and sailed on west across the Pacific Ocean until he came to the Philippine Islands. Here he was killed

The Amazon Valley, Brazil
James Sawders
Surveyors are working on a road to run through newly cleared rubber plantation land.

in a battle with the natives. One of his ships, however, made the voyage from the Philippines around Africa and back to Spain, thus making the first trip around the world. This has been called the greatest ocean voyage ever made.

Using the map of the world, trace this voyage from Spain around the world and back to Spain again. Estimate how far Magellan sailed after leaving the Strait of Magellan until he reached the Philippine Islands.

The Spaniards who had settled in Central America began to explore the country to the north and south of them. Some forced their way through Mexico into what is now southern United States. They went north as far as the present state of Arkansas and discovered the Arkansas and Mississippi Rivers. One party, led by Ponce de Leon, sailed from Puerto Rico in the West Indies in 1513 and landed on the coast of what is now our state of Florida. They explored much of the Florida peninsula.

Other parties went south from Panama and conquered the Indian tribes who ruled the mountain regions which are now Colombia, Ecuador, Bolivia, Peru, and northern Chile. This conquest of northwestern South America is discussed more fully in our studies of Ecuador, Peru, Bolivia, and Chile.

The Spaniards explored South America in a search for riches. They had heard stories of great amounts of silver and gold owned by some of the South American Indians. In "The Land of the Incas" they found Indians who used these two precious metals to adorn their temples, to make ornaments, and even to make dishes which they used in their homes. The Spaniards in many cases destroyed entire Indian villages, captured or killed many of the Indians and their leaders, and took their silver and gold back to Spain.

We can see how these groups of Spaniards, each under some leader, gradually came to discover and settle many parts of South America and to find out the size and shape of

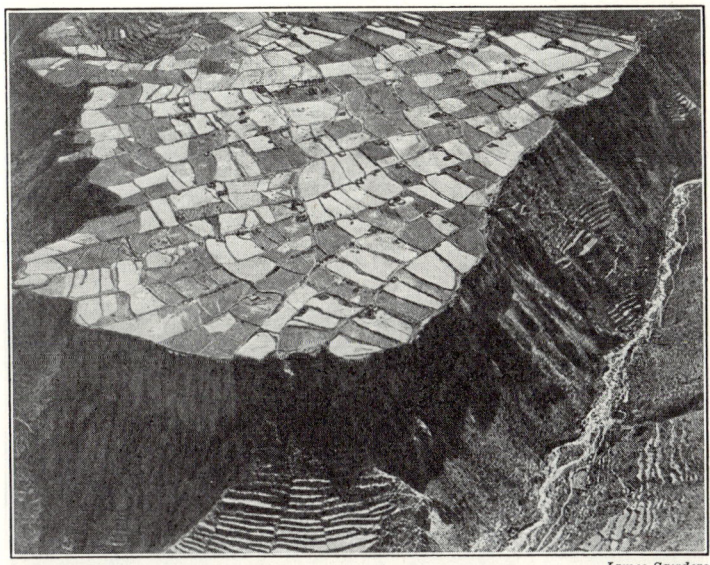

OLD INCA LANDS OF PERU *James Sawders*
The farmers of the South American highlands terrace their farms in order to take advantage of the drainage from mountain streams.

that continent. At the same time they explored and made settlements in Central America, the West Indian Islands, and in southern United States.

We must remember that four hundred years ago Spain and Portugal were both great world powers. Their ships sailed to all parts of the then known world, just as American and British ships and airplanes are going to all parts of the world today. Spain and Portugal were great rivals and each wished to gain control of South America. Spain finally won the greater number of sections of South America. The Portuguese, however, won Brazil, settled that great country, and ruled it until it became independent in 1822 (although Portugal did not recognize this independence until 1825). The Portuguese are still the leading European race found there.

South America Becomes Independent. — Nearly all of South America came to be ruled by the Spanish and Portuguese and was under the rule of these countries for about 300 years. The various countries had developed their own leaders by that time, however, and wished to secure freedom to govern themselves. Just as the United States fought the Revolutionary War to gain freedom from British rule, the countries of South America fought for and gained their freedom from Spain and Portugal.

The United States, which were British colonies at the time, gained their freedom in the latter part of the eighteenth century, 1783 to be exact. The South American countries gained their freedom during the first part of the nineteenth century, the majority of them having become free by the end of the eighteen-twenties.

Just as George Washington led the British colonies to freedom and became a national hero, two great South American leaders, Simon Bolivar and José de San Martín, led the Spanish and Portuguese colonies of South America in their successful fight for freedom. Simon Bolivar is still known as the George Washington of South America.

The People of South America. — We have mentioned the fact that when the Spanish and Portuguese began to settle Latin America they fought with Indian tribes who were living there. The Aztec Indians inhabited parts of Mexico and Central America. The Incas had become happy and prosperous among the Andes Mountains in western and northwestern South America. There were also the Indian natives of the Amazon Valley. There were Indians dwelling in southern South America, even in the cold, damp regions near the southern tip. The early Spaniards and Portuguese fought with these Indians just as did our ancestors with the Indian tribes of North America. In many cases the Indians were massacred or thrown into slavery. Their wealth in silver and gold was sent back to the European kings of their conquerors.

The Spanish and Portuguese, however, did not completely overcome the Indians and force them to live on Indian reservations as was done here in the United States. They made slaves of many of them, forced others to live in cut-off mountain regions, and allowed many who yielded to them to live in the same communities with the white men. This is why the population of South America today contains so many Indians and Mestizoes, or people of mixed white and Indian blood.

During the days of the slave trade, at the

NEAR AREQUIPA, PERU *De Cou, from Sawders*
The snow-capped El Misti, the favorite volcanic peak of Peru, is a beautiful back drop for an Indian corral.

same time that slaves were being brought from Africa to the United States, many Negro slaves were brought into various parts of South America. We now find among the population whites, Indians, Negroes, and people who have mixed white and Indian, white and Negro, and Indian and Negro blood. There has been much intermarrying among these three different races.

In South America, just as with our British ancestors here, wealthy Spanish and Portuguese families came to control large areas of land, to own many slaves, and practically to control the governments of the various countries. As a result many of the poorer people became peasants, or peons, who lived almost in slavery and who depended entirely upon the wealthy for the work which gave them a living. Some countries of South America have been slow to realize that these poorer classes of people should be educated and given a chance to raise their standard of living. Slowly, however, the welfare of the masses is coming to be considered, as we shall see when we take up the individual countries.

South American People Today. — In recent times many British, German, Italian, Russian, Japanese, and North American people have settled in Latin America and have become citizens of their adopted countries. All of these have helped to increase the amount and kinds of crops grown where they settled on the land. They have also helped to build up new industries and increase commerce.

In order to know South Americans well we must know the people of each individual country. They differ in many ways as we go from country to country. Each country has much national pride. A citizen of Brazil, for example, wishes to be known first as a Brazilian. The same is true of the citizens of Argentina, Chile, Peru, or any of the other countries.

The people of the different countries do not know each other well. The scarcity of railroads and improved highways and the great distances tend to cut off these peoples from each other. The mountain barriers, heat of the tropics, and the marshy lowlands have the same effect.

These people of the various South American countries do have certain things in common, however. They speak the Spanish language with the exception of the people of Brazil,

VALLE DEL CAUCA

A picturesque place — this market square in a busy town in the Cauca Valley, Colombia.

who speak Portuguese, and a few groups who speak French. The great majority of the people are either Indian or white or a mixture of Indian and white. In the tropical regions there are many Negroes. In Argentina, Uruguay, Chile, and southern Brazil most of the people are white. Almost all South Americans are members of the Roman Catholic church. All of the countries, with the exception of British, French, and Dutch Guiana, have established governments much like our own.

Countries. — There are about a dozen countries in South America, of which Argentina, Brazil, and Chile are the most important. All these countries, except the Guianas, are republics, but in some the president has full powers.

Argentina is the most advanced state, with an area of more than a million square miles and a population of over 13,000,000. Its most important products are livestock, especially cattle and sheep, and grain, especially wheat. The capital, Buenos Aires, is the third largest city in the Americas and the largest Latin American city.

Brazil has well over 3,000,000 square miles of territory and an estimated population of nearly 45,000,000. The capital, Rio de Janeiro, with nearly two million people, is noted for its beautiful harbor and is one of the most striking cities in the world. Brazil produces about two thirds of the world's supply of coffee and much stock for export. It is the largest supplier of rubber in the Americas. It touches every country in South America except Chile and Ecuador.

Chile has an area of about 300,000 square miles, and it has nearly five million inhabitants. It produces most of the world's nitrate and iodine and is the second largest producer of copper.

Bolivia has all kinds of mining, especially tin, of which it exports about 16% of the world supply. It also ranks next to Brazil in rubber.

Paraguay is an inland state with fewer than a million people. Meat packing is the chief industry.

Uruguay, though half as large as Paraguay, has twice as many people. It has the most advanced social legislation in South America. Grain and livestock are the leading products.

Peru (area about 500,000 square miles, population nearly 7,000,000) is especially rich in valuable minerals. It was the home of the early Incas and has a university older than Harvard.

Ecuador, so called because its capital, Quito, lies almost on the equator, averages ten people for each of its 275,000 square miles. It is rich in minerals and has some of the highest peaks in the Andes. Cotopaxi is just under, and Chimborazo just over, four miles above sea level. Besides minerals, Ecuador exports "Panama" hats.

Colombia, with about 450,000 square miles and nearly 9,000,000 people, is rich in gold, silver, and precious stones, as well as other minerals. But it is also an agricultural country with very rich soil. Of its five universities, the oldest, at Bogota, though twenty-one years younger than the one at Lima, is seventy-six years older than Harvard.

Venezuela has about 350,000 square miles and 3,500,000 people. It is especially rich in gold, petroleum, and asphalt, but agriculture and stock raising are its leading occupations. It is one of the few countries in the world with no public debt.

The *Guianas*, British, Dutch, and French, lie to the east of Venezuela. British Guiana

James Sawders

GLACIAL PEAKS

Airmen flying over the Andes look down on miles and miles of snow-capped mountain peaks like these. The thin clouds that hang in the depressions are like misty scarves wrapping the peaks around.

RIO DE JANEIRO

From the humpback mountain of Corcovado one looks down on the harbor and houses of Brazil's biggest and busiest city. To sail into this bay from the wide ocean outside is to sail into the most beautiful harbor in the world.

Photos by James Sawders

MONTEVIDEO

The capital and principal seaport of Uruguay is one of the cleanest and most healthful cities in the world. The statue in the plaza is of Artigas, the George Washington of Uruguay.

BUENOS AIRES

The capital of Argentina is known as the "Paris of America" because it is so beautiful, so fashionable, and so gay. Around Plaza Congreso are many fine buildings.

PERU

Aerial Explorations.

In a land famed for its riches, its romantic history, and its beautiful scenery, this petroleum tank farm looks bare and ugly. But in this modern world, oil is in great demand everywhere.

James Sawders

BOLIVIA

The Indians of Bolivia are descendants of the old Inca Empire. In the village of Sarata, at the foot of Bolivia's giant mountain Illimani, these Indians are preparing for a fiesta dance.

© *William LaVarre from Gendreau*

BRITISH GUIANA

Protected from the hot sun by huge leaves of some jungle plant, three Indian natives rest at the edge of a chasm into which pour the waters of Kaieteur Falls.

is largely jungle, but it has some mines and much beautiful scenery. Dutch Guiana, now called Surinam, has more agriculture and fewer minerals than British Guiana. French Guiana is famous chiefly for its former penal colony, Devil's Island. The capital is Cayenne, from which our red pepper gets its name.

AREQUIPA, PERU
De Cou, from Sawders
This is the Plaza d'Armes in front of the Cathedral.

Our Relations with South America. — The people of South America have in the past had little contact with the United States. They were too far away, and they seemed to have more in common with European nations than with us. The policies of our business interests, and even of our government, have not always been such as to promote friendly feeling between us and the South American nations. Too often we have failed to understand their customs and traditions. Our money has been so much more valuable than theirs that it has been hard for them to trade profitably with us.

In recent years, however, our government and our better business firms have sought to promote the good-neighbor policy toward all of Latin America. Both President Roosevelt and President Truman have carried out such a policy. The airplane is rapidly making it easier to travel the great distances from our country to theirs. Many of our people are visiting South America and are learning of the good things which exist there. When World War II closed many of their markets in Europe and Asia, South American countries came to realize the advantages to them of trading more with the United States. The increasing use of motor vehicles is causing new roads to be built where once there were only mule trains. The day is coming, soon, when it will be possible to drive a car from New York to Buenos Aires!

We are coming to realize that the twenty-one American republics have many things in common. All have formed governments based upon the free will of the people. In them "government of the people, by the people, for the people," as Abraham Lincoln said, has flourished and prospered. In them the rights of the individual citizen are respected and upheld by law. In them man is guaranteed freedom in "life, liberty, and the pursuit of happiness," as Thomas Jefferson expressed it in writing our Declaration of Independence. They are imbued with the spirit that combines faith in material progress with concern for human welfare.

These American democracies depend for their existence upon reason rather than upon force. Each has had to use force at times to preserve the things in which it believes. Each has always kept in mind, however, the fact that man should so develop his mind and character that free men may make and carry out the laws which govern themselves. Such government may depend in the long run upon the honesty, intelligence, education, and sense of justice and fair play of the masses of people. It may also depend upon those people taking an active interest in the affairs of government.

Unity and Friendship among the Americas. — How do the things we have in common affect our dealings with the other countries of the Americas? How can a group of American nations, the twenty-one American republics, live peacefully together? How can we assure among the Americas a growing feeling of respect for each other? Certainly each nation can come to understand the problems the others face. Each can try to deal fairly and honestly with all the others.

In the long run, friendship between two countries depends more upon a profitable exchange of goods between them than upon any other single thing. Trade cannot flourish when it helps one country and injures the other. It cannot take place in goods which each produces in abundance. It can take place only in goods which one or the other does not produce in large enough quantities for its needs. An honest attempt to find things in each which the other can use will often result in profitable trade where no trade was thought possible.

Brazil exports coffee and rubber, which we do not produce. It is easy therefore for us to trade with Brazil, for that country needs machinery, money, iron and steel products, wheat, and textiles from us. Brazil has always been and is now one of our best friends in Latin America. Chile exports nitrates, copper, iodine, and wool. We also produce some of each of these things but can use a part of Chile's supply in return for the textiles, oil, sugar, and automobiles which Chile imports and we export. We are now taking all of her export copper. Our friendship with Chile seems to be growing stronger.

Argentina competes with our leather and meat industries. She also exports wheat, corn, linseed, and wool, all of which we produce in large amounts. She imports, however, textiles, oils, iron and steel products, and various foodstuffs that we export.

In the past Argentina has traded chiefly with European nations who could use her exports as well as send to her the supplies she needed. The fact that she owns minerals which may be of use to us, that we can use some of her high-grade meat and leather products in addition to our own, and that she needs money which we have should greatly increase our trade with her. These facts led to trade agreements, in October, 1941, between the United States and Argentina.

A NATIONAL SPORTS TOURNAMENT
James Sawders
Girls and boys from all over Bolivia took part in this tournament at the La Paz Stadium.

COLOMBIA
James Sawders

Here in the north, at Tolima, coffee is being dried on sliding trays. In bad weather the trays slide in under cover so that the beans will be protected. Tolima is in the heart of the coffee district. This part of the state is mostly high tablelands with a temperate climate all the year round.

More and more, as foreign markets have been closed to our commerce, we have turned to South America for an exchange of products. A look at the labels on the canned goods on any grocer's shelves will show this. Many of them state that the contents were grown in the Argentine or Brazil or some other South American country. On the other hand, American farm machinery is widely used in these southern countries.

Many American firms own interests in factories in Argentina, Brazil, and Chile. American money and American experience have contributed largely to the widespread use of electricity and the successful operation of air lines as a means of communication. Many billions of American dollars are invested in South American oil fields, mines, railways, and other industries.

The United States has another important contact with South America over its 27,000 miles of cables and its invisible radio paths. Press associations receive and send news constantly; the National Broadcasting Company, and others, broadcast many of their entertainment programs. Business is carried on from North American offices to South American branches by telephone quite as easily as from state to state. Today, South American countries can talk with one another and with nearly all the telephones scattered around the world.

The fact that airplanes carry mail and express so swiftly has speeded up trade between North and South America tremendously. Fresh fruits from the United States can be flown to Colombia. Gold, live chicks, orchids, tobacco products — all these and many other items can be shipped with great speed and safety.

Since the adoption by the United States of a "good neighbor" policy toward South America, social and political relations have been more friendly than in former times, and our trade with our southern neighbor has shown marked improvement. There has also been an increase in the exchange of professors and students between the universities of North and South America. American universities now have students from Argentina, Brazil, Chile, Ecuador, and Peru.

President Roosevelt raised our legations in Bolivia, Ecuador, and Paraguay to the status of embassies.

The United States is continuing the efforts which for nearly twenty years it has been making toward better understanding among the nations of the Western Hemisphere and it is bringing results.

We are coming to know South American people better. We must come to know them better still if we are to have the friendship among all the American nations which is necessary for their safety and prosperity.

James Sawders

LAKE TITICACA

As the sunset deepens and the tired winds rest, the Indian fisherman paddles his balsa wood boat toward home. The mountains all around this great Andean lake grow black with shadows, and the waters reflect only the faint colors of a setting sun

PETERSBURG, ALASKA
Shrimp boats tied up in harbor for the night.

John Kabel

XIX. SUMMARY OF NORTH AMERICA

Size and Extent. — North America is one of the most fortunate of the continents. With an area of about 8,000,000 square miles, it is smaller than Asia and Africa, but larger than the other continents. It is located entirely in the Northern Hemisphere, mostly in the North Temperate Zone, although it ranges through about 75 degrees of latitude (north and south extent) from about 8 degrees north of the equator to about 7 degrees short of the North Pole. It also has a wide range of longitude (east and west extent) from about 20 degrees to about 170 degrees West Longitude. In giving these figures, Greenland is included as a part of North America.

Favorable Commercial Position. — With such a wide range north and south as well as east and west, North America has a very favorable position for world trade because of its long frontage on the two great oceans of commerce. On the Atlantic side, it faces the leading nations of Europe, while on the Pacific, it faces the countries of Asia. To the southeast are the rich and growing countries of South America. It is fortunate in having many good harbors along both oceans and on the Gulf of Mexico.

Relief of the Land and Drainage. — The continent, as a whole, is shaped somewhat like a triangle, with the base bordering on the Arctic Ocean and the southern apex or point at the Isthmus of Panama. The mountains are at the sides of the triangle, east and west, and they seem to come together on the high Mexican Plateau, forming a single highland from there south to Panama. Between the relatively low, forest-covered Appalachian Mountains on the east and the higher, rugged, snow-capped Rocky and Sierra Nevada-Cascade Mountains on the west, there are vast, fertile plains. These are drained mainly by three great river systems: the Missouri-Mississippi which flows southward into the Gulf of Mexico; the Great Lakes-St. Lawrence which drains eastward into the Gulf of St.

THE "SOO" CANAL *Ewing Galloway*
Endless lines of freight-carrying barges file through the large locks of this famous canal, carrying the cargoes of the world between Lake Superior and Lake Huron.

Lawrence and the Atlantic; and the Mackenzie which reaches northward to the Arctic Ocean. The Yukon, Columbia, and Colorado rivers drain the plateau and mountains westward into the Pacific Ocean.

Climate and Vegetation. — North America has most every type of climate to be found anywhere on earth. In the extreme south, we find low latitude or tropical climates with their rain forests, grasslands, and jungles. In the extreme north, are the high latitude or polar climates, with islands capped with snow and ice the year round making glaciers which extend down to the oceans — a truly cold desert with very little plant life. Between these two extremes are nearly all of the climates of the middle latitudes or temperate zone with vast forests of cone-bearing trees and trees which shed their leaves each year, as well as grassy prairies and plains. On the high western plateaus there are also real dry deserts.

Soil and Agriculture. — With such a wide variety of climate and land forms, there is naturally much fertile soil and a large agricultural production, due to the energetic population and wide use of agricultural machinery such as one finds there. North America leads the world in the production of corn, cotton, and tobacco.

Transportation and Communication. — There are thousands of miles of navigable waterways in North America and some of them, such as the Great Lakes, are very widely used. In addition, the continent has a railway mileage almost as great as all of the others taken together. In fact, the United States alone has over one-third of the world's railway mileage. There are more automobiles and good motor highways in North America than in all the rest of the world. The telephone and

NORTH AMERICA

Map Questions and Activities

1. Measure the airline distance across the United States from New York to Los Angeles.
2. What direction is St. John's, Newfoundland, from the North Pole?
3. How much of continental United States is in the tropical zone?
4. How many different countries are shown on this map? Name them.
5. How are the highlands shown? the lowlands? the water depths?
6. How are the directions indicated on this map? the distances?
7. Compare the area of Canada with that of the United States.
8. What is the third largest country in North America?

NORTH AMERICA

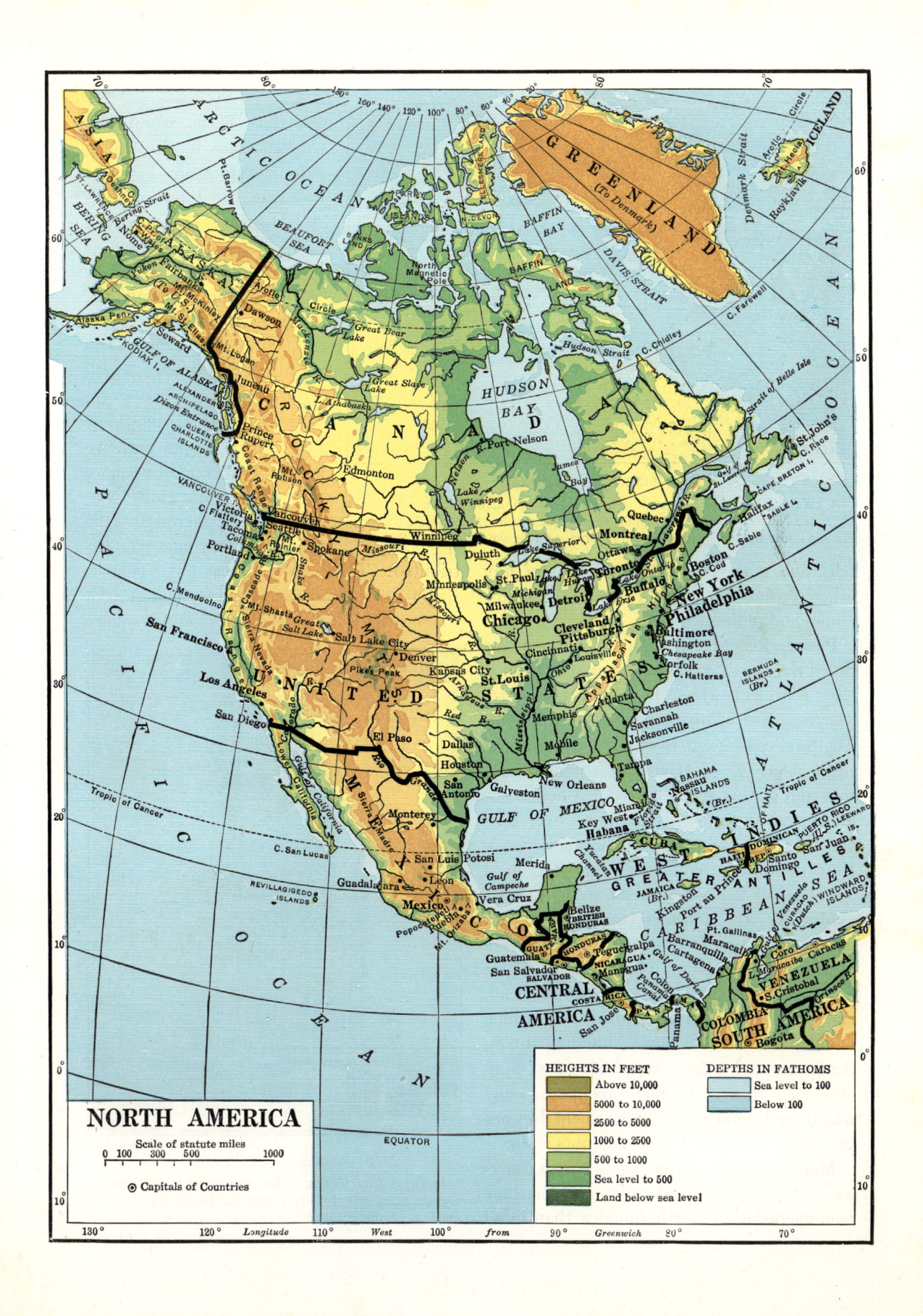

PORT ARTHUR BRIDGE, TEXAS
A mile and a half of bridge rises from a flat marshland to tower 230 feet above the Neches River — the highest span in the south. Ocean-going steamers slip under its steel framework unhindered, on their way up or down the river.

telegraph mileage also exceeds that of any other continent by far. It also leads in airplanes and radios.

Power Resources. — This is sometimes called the Power Age, and fortunate indeed is that continent which has large power resources. North America is such a continent. The total coal resources of the world are said to be about 7,000,000,000,000 (seven trillion) tons and of this amount, North America has about five-sevenths. It produces over one-third of the world's coal; and has more petroleum, natural gas, artificial gas, and developed water power than any other continent.

Mineral Resources. — In addition, our continent is very fortunate in the possession of nearly every mineral used by man. There are vast deposits of iron ore, copper, lead, zinc, nickel, gold, silver, bauxite from which aluminum is made, asbestos, building stones, fertilizers, and other extensively used minerals and rocks. In fact, about the only widely used metal which our continent does not produce in any considerable amounts is tin.

Manufacturing. — Here again North America leads. There is said to be more machine manufacturing in North America than in all the rest of the world. Of course, there is also much manufacturing by hand in countries like those of Central America and Mexico, but even there, the machine is beginning to make itself felt.

Distribution of Population. — There are about 2,000,000,000 people in the entire world. Of this number, North America has barely one-tenth. Both Asia and Europe have many more people than we have. However, in area we rank third among the continents. Furthermore, the people are very unevenly distributed. There are vast areas in Greenland, Baffin Land, northern Canada, and Alaska where there is less than one person per square

Courtesy Monsano Chemical Co.
A DISTILLATION TOWER
In Texas City, Texas, is this styrene producing plant — styrene being one of the raw materials required for making Buna-S synthetic rubber.

BLUE LAKE IN THE ROCKY MOUNTAINS, MONTANA — *Courtesy Northern Pacific Railway*
Along the east coast and the west stretches the long, ragged line of mountains — source of stream and waterfall and fertile valleys — in whose captive lakes of crystal clearness are reflected the glories of sunrise and sunset.

TEXAS FIELDS
Where all one sees are a tufted sky and a great smooth blanket of golden grain.

WASHINGTON STATE
Dam and water wheels harness the river's might to do the work and will of man.

mile. Even our own United States has some parts in the western plateaus and mountains where this is true. The most people are to be found in southeastern Canada, eastern United States, and on the high plateau of Mexico around Mexico City. Then there are scattered areas of dense population around the great cities of the west.

Activities and Questions

1. Compare North America with the other continents in size.

2. In what agricultural products does it excel?

3. How do North America's transportation and communication facilities compare with those of other continents?

4. Describe the varieties of climate in this continent.

5. What important mineral does North America produce only in small amounts?

6. Compare its sources of power with those of other continents.

7. Where are the most people to be found?

DERIVATIONS OF NAMES OF THE STATES OF THE UNITED STATES

Alabama, from the Indian tribe Alibamu ("I open or clear the thicket").
Arizona, from the Aztec "Arizonac" ("small springs" or "few springs").
Arkansas, from the Arkansas tribe of Indians.
California, from a fabled island of gold and gems in an early romantic tale, *Las Gergas de Esplandian*, by Garci Ordonez de Montalvo, a Spanish author.
Colorado, from the Spanish "colorado" ("ruddy"), in allusion to the color of the Colorado River.
Connecticut, from the Indian for "at the long tidal river," *i.e.* Connecticut River.
Delaware, from Lord Delaware (1577–1618), a colonial governor of Virginia.
Florida, from the Spanish "Pascua de Flores" ("Feast of Flowers"), the day in 1513 in which Ponce de Leon took possession of it.
Georgia, named after King George II of England.
Idaho, from the Indian for "gem of the mountains."
Illinois, from the Indian "Illinwek" ("men"), with a French termination.
Indiana, meaning "Indian land."
Iowa, from the Iowa tribe ("sleepy ones").
Kansas, from the Kansa tribe.
Kentucky, from an Indian word of uncertain meaning: perhaps, "Dark and Bloody Ground."
Louisiana, named after King Louis XIV of France.
Maine, so named as being the main land of New England, as distinguished from the islands.
Maryland, named after Henrietta Maria, wife of Charles I of England.
Massachusetts, from the Massachusetts tribe ("at or about the great hill").
Michigan, from the Michigamea tribe ("great water").
Minnesota, from the Sioux for "cloudy water" or "sky-tinted water."
Mississippi, from the Indian "father of waters," alluding to the Mississippi River.
Missouri, from the Missouri tribe ("great muddy"), alluding to the Missouri River.
Montana, from the Latin for "mountainous."
Nebraska, from the Indian for "shallow water."
Nevada, from the Spanish for "snow-covered."
New Hampshire, named after Hampshire in England.
New Jersey, named after Jersey Island, in commemoration of the governorship there of Sir George Carteret, one of the original grantees.
New Mexico, named after Mexico.
New York, named after the Duke of York (afterward James II of England), to whom it was granted by Charles II.
North Carolina, named after King Charles II of England.
North Dakota, from the Dakota Indians ("allies").
Ohio, from the Iroquois for "beautiful river," alluding to the Ohio River.
Oklahoma, from the Choctaw for "red people."
Oregon, derivation uncertain, perhaps from the Spanish "oregano" ("wild majoram"), or Oregones ("big-eared men").
Pennsylvania, named after William Penn, to whom the original charter was granted, and meaning "Penn's wooded country" (from the Latin "silva," meaning "wood").
Rhode Island, named after the island of Rhodes in the Aegean Sea.
South Carolina. See *North Carolina*.
South Dakota. See *North Dakota*.
Tennessee, derivation uncertain; perhaps, "river with the great bend."
Texas, from Texas Indians ("allies").
Utah, from Ute Indians.
Vermont, from the French "vert mont" ("green mountain").
Virginia, from the "Virgin Queen," Elizabeth of England.
Washington, named after George Washington.
West Virginia, formerly the western section of Virginia.
Wisconsin, from the Wisconsin Indians.
Wyoming, from the Delaware Indian for "upon the great plain."

REFERENCE MAPS
TO
OTHER CONTINENTS
PHYSICAL-POLITICAL

NORTH AMERICA

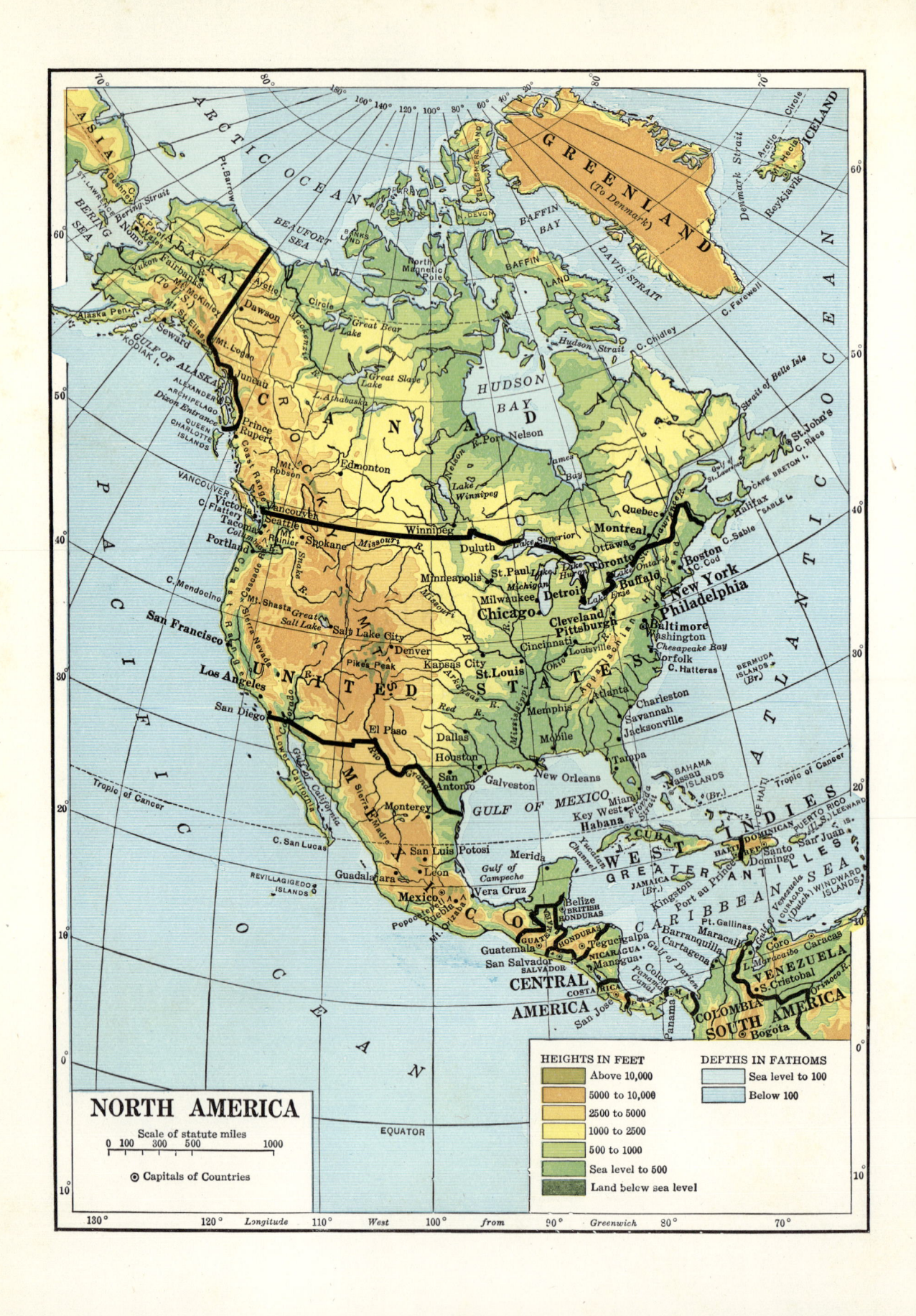

SOUTH AMERICA
Scale of statute miles
0 100 200 300 400 500 750 1000
HEIGHTS IN FEET
Above 10,000
5000 to 10,000
2500 to 5000
1000 to 2500
500 to 1000
Sea level to 500
DEPTHS IN FATHOMS
Sea level to 100
Below 100
Capitals of Countries
GALAPAGOS ISLANDS (To Ecuador) Same scale as main map
CARIBBEAN SEA
ATLANTIC OCEAN
PACIFIC OCEAN
BRAZIL
PERU
BOLIVIA
COLOMBIA
VENEZUELA
ECUADOR
PARAGUAY
URUGUAY
BRITISH GUIANA
SURINAM (Dutch)
FRENCH GUIANA
ANDES MTS.
Buenos Aires
Rio de Janeiro
Tropic of Capricorn
EQUATOR
Longitude West from Greenwich

ASIA

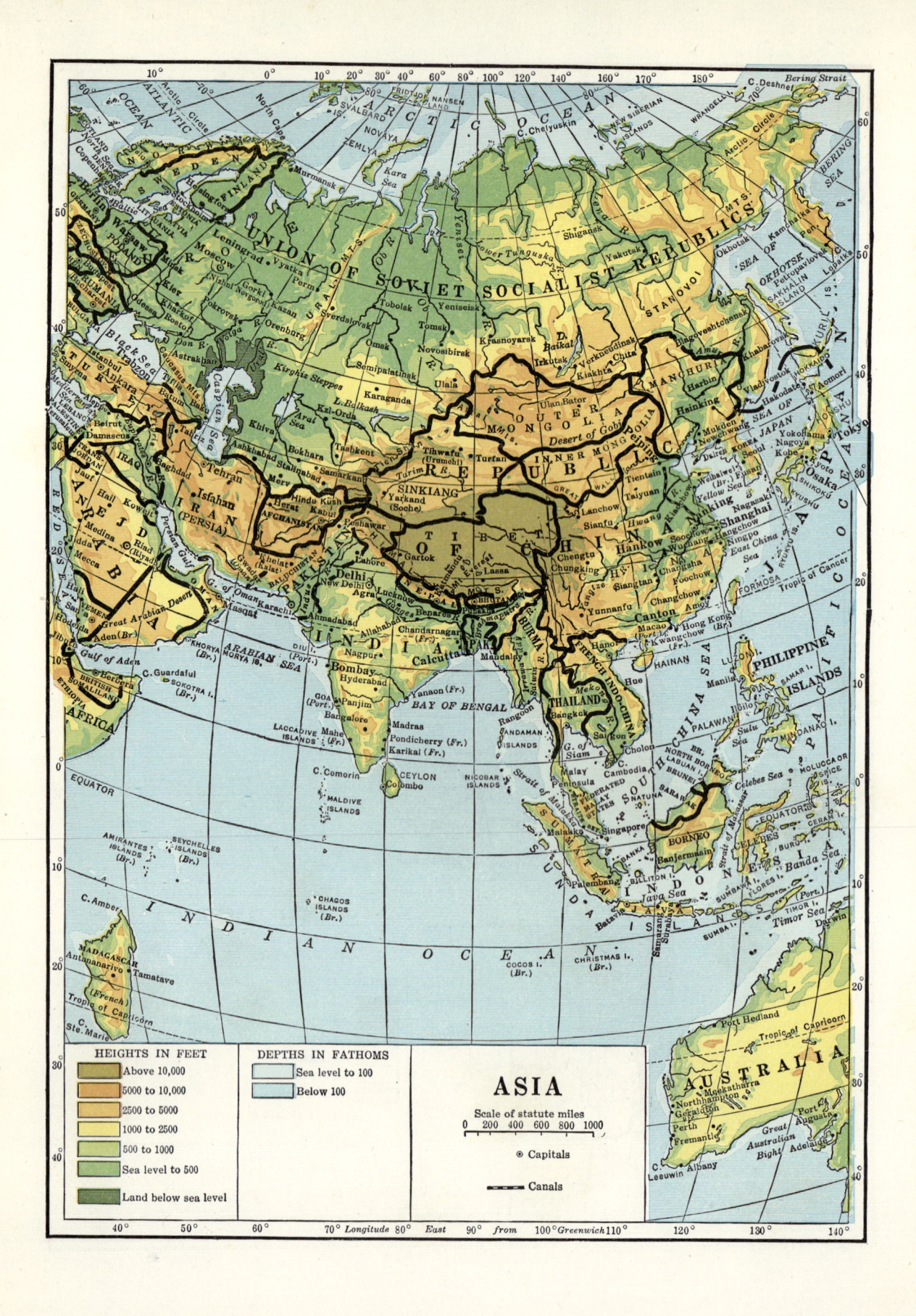

Scale of statute miles
0 200 400 600 800 1000

⊙ Capitals
╌╌╌ Canals

HEIGHTS IN FEET
- Above 10,000
- 5000 to 10,000
- 2500 to 5000
- 1000 to 2500
- 500 to 1000
- Sea level to 500
- Land below sea level

DEPTHS IN FATHOMS
- Sea level to 100
- Below 100

EUROPE
Scale of statute miles
0 100 200 300 400 500
Capitals of Countries
Railroads
Canals
HEIGHTS IN FEET
Above 10,000
5000 to 10,000
2500 to 5000
1000 to 2500
500 to 1000
Sea level to 500
Land below sea level
DEPTHS IN FATHOMS
Sea level to 100
Below 100
ARCTIC OCEAN
ATLANTIC OCEAN
NORTH SEA
BALTIC SEA
BLACK SEA
CASPIAN SEA
MEDITERRANEAN SEA
BAY OF BISCAY
UNION OF SOVIET SOCIALIST REPUBLICS
URAL MTS.
ASIA
AFRICA
TURKEY
ICELAND
NORWAY
SWEDEN
FINLAND
BRITISH ISLES
IRELAND (EIRE)
FRANCE
SPAIN
PORTUGAL
GERMANY
POLAND
CZECHOSLOVAKIA
AUSTRIA
HUNGARY
RUMANIA
YUGOSLAVIA
BULGARIA
ITALY
GREECE
ALBANIA
Longitude West from Greenwich
Longitude East from Greenwich

AFRICA
Scale of statute miles
0 200 400 600 800 1000
Capitals of Independent Countries
Capitals of Foreign Possessions
Canals
HEIGHTS IN FEET
Above 10,000
5000 to 10,000
2500 to 5000
1000 to 2500
500 to 1000
Sea level to 500
Land below sea level
DEPTHS IN FATHOMS
Sea level to 100
Below 100
ATLANTIC OCEAN
ATLANTIC OCEAN
INDIAN OCEAN
EQUATOR
Tropic of Cancer
Tropic of Capricorn
EUROPE
SPAIN
ITALY
TURKEY
Caspian Sea
Tehran
IRAN (PERSIA)
Strait of Gibraltar
Tangier (Neutral Zone)
Tetuan
Melilla
Oran
Algiers
Constantine
Bone
Tunis
C. Bon
Sicily
Athens
Crete
Cyprus
Aleppo
Syria
Beirut
Damascus
Bagdad
IRAQ
Basra
Kuwait
Persian Gulf
MADEIRA IS. (Port.)
Rabat
Casablanca
Fez
Mekinez
(Marrakech) Morocco
Mogador
MOROCCO (Fr.)
NORTHERN ALGERIA
Biskra
Ain Sefra
Tuggurt
Wargla
Colomb Beshar
Susa
Sfax
G. of Gabes
Tripoli
TUNISIA
TRIPOLITANIA
G. of Sidra
Bengasi
Derna
CYRENAICA
Alexandria
Port Said
Suez Canal
Suez
PALESTINE
TRANS-JORDAN
Mt. Sinai
Cairo
CANARY IS. (Span.)
IFNI (Sp.)
ALGERIA
SOUTHERN ALGERIA
(French)
Ghadames
Ghat
Ideles
LIBYA
Murzuk
Tummo
Oases of Kufra
Siwa Oasis
Libyan Desert
Assiut
EGYPT
Kharga
Aswan
RED SEA
NEJD
Medina
Riyadh
Mecca
ARABIA
OMAN
Villa Cisneros
RIO DE ORO (Sp.)
C. Blanco
MAURITANIA
Wadan
Taudeni
SAHARA
Arawan
FRENCH WEST AFRICA
Tombouctou
FRENCH SUDAN
NIGER
Agades
Wady Halfa
Port Sudan
Dongola
Suakin
Berber
Asmara
Hali
ASIR
YEMEN
Massaua
Sana
Hodeida
Aden
Gulf of Aden
SOKOTRA I. (Br.)
Djibouti
Guardafui
St. Louis
Senegal R.
Dakar
SENEGAL
Kayes
Segu
Bamako
Niger R.
UPPER VOLTA
GAMBIA (Br.)
Bathurst
PORT. GUINEA
Bolama
Timbo
FRENCH GUINEA
Kurussa
Konakry
Freetown
SIERRA LEONE (Br.)
Monrovia
Grand Bassa
LIBERIA
C. Palmas
Kong
IVORY COAST
Kumasi
ASHANTI
GOLD COAST
NORTHERN TERRS.
DAHOMEY
Bingerville
Sekondi
Akkra
Lome
Porto Novo
Lagos
GULF OF GUINEA
Sokoto
Kano
Zaria
NIGERIA
Zungeru
Bida
Yola
Ibadan
Binue R.
Assaba
Buea
Kuka
L. Chad
Ft. Lamy
CHAD
FRENCH EQUATORIAL AFRICA
Shari R.
ANGLO-EGYPTIAN SUDAN
El Fasher
El Obeid
Omdurman
Khartum
White Nile R.
Blue Nile R.
Sennar
Gondar
L. Tsana
Kodok
(British)
FRENCH SOMALI COAST
Berbera
BRITISH SOMALILAND
Dire Dawa
Addis Ababa
ETHIOPIA
Bari
Obbia
SOMALILAND
Juba R.
Bardera
Mogadisho
Ngaundere
CAMEROON
Yaunde
Bangui
UBANGI-SHARI
Zemio
Mbomu R.
FERNANDO PO I. (Sp.)
PRINCES I. (Port.)
ST. THOMAS I. (Port.)
ANNOBON I. (Sp.)
SPANISH GUINEA
Libreville
Franceville
GABUN
MIDDLE CONGO
Upoto
Coquilhatville
Stanley Falls
Stanleyville
Ruwenzori Mts.
Albert Nyanza
L. Rudolf
UGANDA
KENYA
BRITISH EAST AFRICA
Entebbe
Kisumu
Victoria Nyanza
Mt. Kenya
Nairobi
Lamu
Mombasa
PEMBA I.
Zanzibar
Dar es Salaam
Kilwa
Mt. Kilimanjaro
Tabora
Ujiji
TANGANYIKA
BELGIAN CONGO
Congo R.
Kasai R.
Kindu
Kongolo
Lake Tanganyika
Mpweto
L. Moero
L. Bangweolo
Mayumba
Brazzaville
Leopoldville
Kabinda
Matadi
Boma
Luluaburg
Ambriz
Loanda
Malanje
Novo Redondo
Benguela
Lobito
Bihe
ANGOLA (Portuguese)
Kubango R.
Elizabethville
(British)
NORTHERN RHODESIA
Ft. Jameson
Zomba
Blantyre
NYASALAND
Lake Nyasa
Rovuma R.
MOZAMBIQUE (Portuguese)
Mozambique
Mozambique Channel
ASCENSION I. (Br.)
ALDABRA IS. (Br.)
FARQUHAR IS. (Br.)
COMORO IS. (Fr.)
C. Amber
Majunga
MADAGASCAR (French)
Tamatave
Antananarivo
Fianarantsoa
Tulear
C. Ste. Marie
Mossamedes
Porto Alexandre
ST. HELENA I. (Br.)
C. Frio
Grootfontein
SOUTHWEST AFRICA (To Union of South Africa)
Livingstone
Zambezi R.
Salisbury
SOUTHERN RHODESIA
Bulawayo (Br.)
Sena
Beira
Swakopmund
Walvis Bay
Windhoek
BECHUANALAND PROTECTORATE
Kalahari Desert
Limpopo
Mafeking
TRANSVAAL
Pretoria
Johannesburg
Inhambane
Delagoa Bay
Lourenço Marques
SWAZILAND
Angra Pequena (Luderitz)
Orange R.
Kimberley
ORANGE FREE STATE
NATAL
BASUTOLAND
Bloemfontein
Pietermaritzburg
Durban
Port Nolloth
UNION OF SOUTH AFRICA
CAPE OF GOOD HOPE (British)
East London
Port Elizabeth
Cape Town
C. of Good Hope
C. Agulhas
CAPE VERDE ISLANDS (Port.)
Praia
C. Verde
Dakar
SEYCHELLES IS. (Br.)
MAHÉ I.
AMIRANTES IS. (Br.)
FARQUHAR IS. (Br.)
AGALEGA IS.
C. Amber
MADAGASCAR
TROMELIN I.
I. STE. MARIE (Fr.)
CARGADOS IS. (Br.)
MAURITIUS I. (Br.)
RÉUNION I. (Fr.)
Longitude West 0° Longitude East from Greenwich

AUSTRALASIA

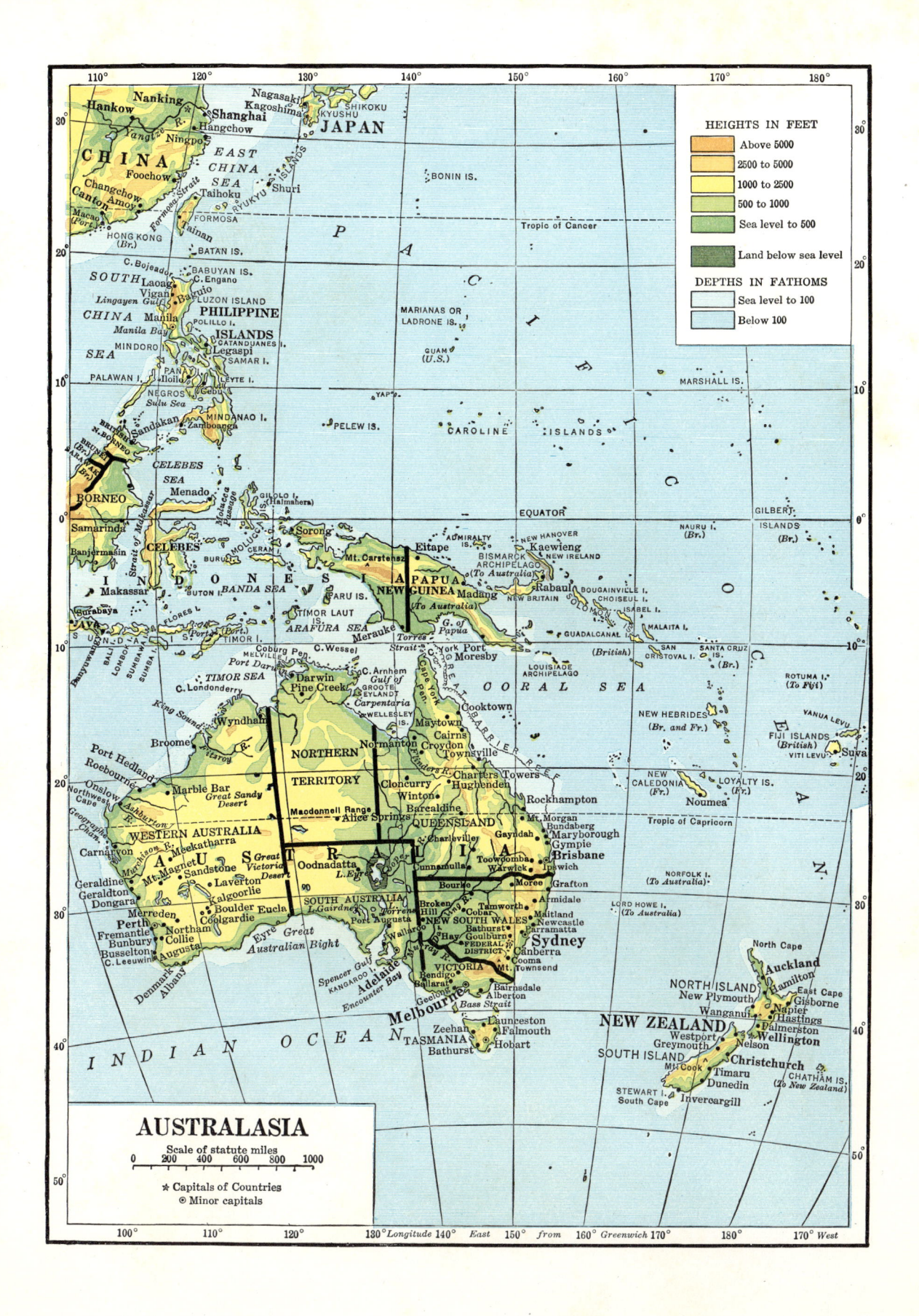

APPENDIX A

THE EARTH

How do we know that the earth is round? Here are three of the best proofs.

1. **Eclipse Proof.** — Sometimes the earth gets between the sun and the moon in such a way that it casts a shadow on the moon. This is called the eclipse of the moon. The shape of this shadow is always circular and the only object that always casts a circular shadow is a sphere. This is probably the best proof that the earth is round.

2. **Ship Proof.** — When a ship goes out to sea the lowest part above the water line disappears first and when it is approaching land the highest part appears first. Over all the oceans, larger lakes, and seas, the rate of appearance and disappearance is the same in all directions for the same rate of travel of the ship. This proves that the earth is equally curved in all directions. A sphere is the only object which has equal curvature in all directions.

3. **Measurement Proof.** — Surveyors, by careful measurements, have proved that the actual curvature of the surface of the earth is eight inches per mile in any direction.

The airplane, rising above the land and the water, and flying across the polar regions between countries and in all other directions, is giving us further proofs of the shape and size of our earth as calculated by scientists. Photographs taken from high up in the air show that the surface of the earth is curved.

The circumference, or distance around the earth, along the Equator is known to be nearly 25,000 miles. Since the earth is round, the circumference through the poles is about the same. Knowing the circumference, it is easy to calculate the diameter of the earth and its total area.

MEASURING DISTANCES

When men began to travel over the earth and make maps of the areas they had visited, they had to have some way of locating places on their maps so that others would know where these places were on the earth. So they planned our location scheme known as *latitude* and *longitude*. This scheme helps us not only to find the locations of places but also distances north and south and east and west between places.

Latitude. — On most of the maps which you study, you will find lines running across the map showing east-west directions and other lines crossing these showing north and south directions. Lines running east and west are parallels of latitude. They are all parallel to the Equator and to each other. This means that each parallel is the same distance from the Equator and from every other parallel at all points.

Trace one of these parallels on the globe and you will find that it is a complete circle. They get smaller and smaller as they near the poles. They also appear as circles on a polar projection map where the pole is in the center of the map.

Parallels of latitude show east-west directions and distances north and south of the Equator. Every circle is divided into 360 equal parts or degrees. From the Equator to either pole is one-fourth of a circle. Therefore, the distance in degrees from the Equator to either pole is one-fourth of 360 degrees or 90 degrees. The symbol for a degree is a small circle.

As the Equator is the starting point for measuring latitude, it is numbered 0°. The latitude of the north pole is 90° North Latitude or Lat. 90° N. The latitude of the south pole is 90° South Latitude. The greatest latitude any place can have is 90° and this is found only at the poles. A degree of latitude equals nearly 70 miles. On most maps, only a few of the parallels are shown, usually those 5°, 10°, or 15° apart.

All places south of the Equator are in south latitude and all places north of the Equator are in north latitude. Places between the Tropic of Cancer and the Tropic of Capricorn are said to be in low latitudes. Those within the Arctic Circle or the Antarctic Circle are said to be in high latitudes. Places between the Tropic of Cancer and the Arctic Circle, or between the Tropic of Capricorn and the Antarctic Circle are said to be in middle latitudes. This is where we live.

Longitude. — The lines indicating north and south directions on maps are called meridians of longitude. Longitude is distance in degrees east or west of a chosen meridian. The meridian generally used is the one passing through Greenwich, near London, England. This is called the *Prime Meridian*. The greatest longitude a place may have is 180°, or half way around the world from the Prime Meridian.

The meridians come closer and closer together as they near the poles where they all meet as they pass through the poles. Like the parallels of latitude, the meridians of longitude are usually curved lines on the map. Most maps show only a few meridians, usually those of 5°, 10°, or 15° apart.

Directions and Location. — Places are located in many cities by means of a scheme like the one shown in this diagram.

A street running east and west (Main Street) is selected from which to reckon distances north and south. Similarly, a street running north and south (Front Avenue) is selected from which to reckon distances east and west.

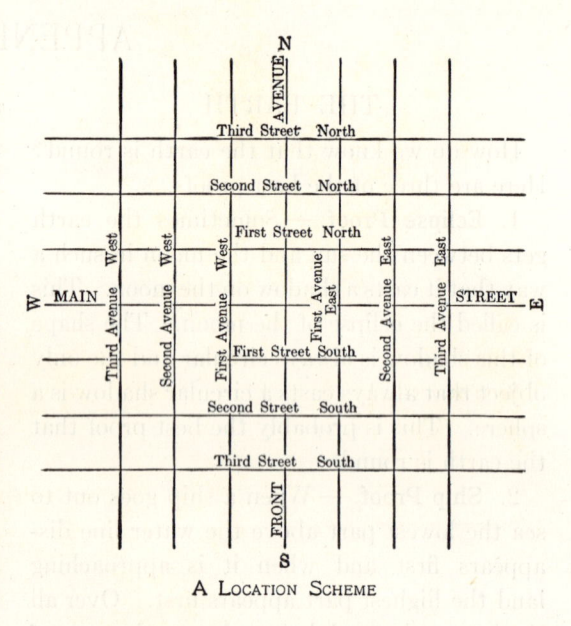

A LOCATION SCHEME

The earth may be likened to a huge city, with the Equator as Main Street and the Prime Meridian as Front Avenue. For example, 1° North Latitude corresponds to First Street North in the diagram, while 1° South Latitude corresponds to First Street South. In like manner, 1° East Longitude means 1° east of the Prime Meridian and corresponds to First Avenue East in the diagram.

These schemes of measurements are useful both on land and sea, and also in the air. The captain on the sea, knowing his own position, and hearing an SOS giving the latitude and longitude of the sender, knows in what direction to steer his vessel in order to reach the stricken one. Land travelers, using instruments, can find their location and proceed in the right direction. An aviator, using charts and tables, may plot his course, set his speedometer, and guiding his plane by the compass, tell when he is over his objective by looking at his watch.

APPENDIX B

STATISTICS

TABLE I

THE SIZE OF THE EARTH

Diameter of the earth at equator (miles)	7,926.67
Distance around the earth at equator (miles)	24,901.96
Land area (square miles)	57,000,000
Water area (square miles)	140,000,000
Total area (square miles)	197,000,000

TABLE II

AREA AND POPULATION OF NORTH AMERICA

Round figures are approximate only. Density is computed on basis of latest population figures even when these are estimates. Asterisk (*) indicates the capital of the country. The world totals are published by the League of Nations.

Country	Area Square Miles	Last Census Year	Last Census Population (thousands)	Official Estimates Year	Official Estimates Population (thousands)	Density per Square Mile	Largest City	Estimated Population (Thousands)
Total world	51,177,000	—	—	1937	2,115,800	41.3		
North America								
United States (continental)	2,973,776	1940	131,669			44.1	New York	7,455
Per cent of world total	5.8				6.2			
Alaska	586,400	1939	73			.1	*Juneau	5
Hawaii	6,407	1940	423			64.7	*Honolulu	146
Canada	3,466,793	1931	10,377	1939	11,315	3.2	Montreal	900
Newfoundland and Labrador	152,734	1935	290	1938	295	1.9	*St. John's	42
Mexico	760,290	1930	16,553	1939	19,478	25.6	*Mexico	1,029
Central America								
British Honduras	8,598	1931	51	1938	57	6.7	*Belize	17
Costa Rica	23,000	1927	472	1939	623	27.0	*San Jose	71
Guatemala	42,364	1927	2,005	1937	3,008	71.0	*Guatemala	167
Honduras	46,250	1935	962	—	—	20.8	*Tegucigalpa	43
Nicaragua	49,500	1920	638	1938	1,172	23.7	*Managua	115
Panama	32,380	1930	467	1936	535	16.5	*Panama	128
El Salvador	13,176	1933	1,550	1939	1,704	129.3	*San Salvador	102
West Indies								
Cuba	44,164	1931	3,962	1938	4,228	95.7	*Habana	569
Dominican Republic	19,332	1935	1,478	1937	1,581	81.8	*Ciudad Trujillo	71
Haiti	10,204	1918	1,631	1937	2,700	264.6	*Port-au-Prince	105
Puerto Rico	3,435	1940	1,869			525.8	*San Juan	137
Bermuda	19	1931	28	1937	32	1,684.2	*Hamilton	4
British West Indies	12,611	1931	2,023	1937	2,204	174.8	Kingston (and suburb)	141
French West Indies	1,114	1936	551	—	—	494.6	Fort-de-France	52
Netherland West Indies (islands)	403	1938	101	—	—	250.6	*Willemstad	30

TABLE III

AREA AND POPULATION OF THE UNITED STATES AND POSSESSIONS

State	Area in Square Miles	Population 1940	State	Area in Square Miles	Population 1940
Alabama	51,609	2,832,961	Maine	33,215	847,226
Arizona	113,909	499,261	Maryland	10,577	1,821,244
Arkansas	53,102	1,949,387	Massachusetts	8,257	4,316,721
California	158,693	6,907,387	Michigan	58,216	5,256,106
Colorado	104,247	1,113,296	Minnesota	84,068	2,792,300
Connecticut	5,009	1,709,242	Mississippi	47,716	2,183,796
Delaware	2,057	266,505	Missouri	69,674	3,784,664
District of Columbia	69	663,091	Montana	147,138	559,456
Florida	58,560	1,897,414	Nebraska	77,237	1,315,834
Georgia	58,876	3,123,723	Nevada	110,540	110,247
Idaho	83,537	524,873	New Hampshire	9,304	491,524
Illinois	56,400	7,897,241	New Jersey	7,836	4,160,165
Indiana	36,291	3,427,796	New Mexico	121,666	531,818
Iowa	56,280	2,538,268	New York	49,576	13,479,142
Kansas	82,276	1,801,028	North Carolina	52,712	3,571,623
Kentucky	40,395	2,845,627	North Dakota	70,665	641,935
Louisiana	48,523	2,363,880	Ohio	41,222	6,907,612

APPENDIX B

TABLE III — Continued

State	Area in Square Miles	Population	Outlying Possessions	Area in Square Miles	Population
Oklahoma	69,919	2,336,434	Alaska	586,400	72,524
Oregon	96,981	1,089,684	American Samoa	76	12,908
Pennsylvania	45,333	9,900,180	Guam	206	22,290
Rhode Island	1,214	713,346	Hawaii	6,454	423,330
South Carolina	31,055	1,899,804	Panama Canal Zone	553	51,827
South Dakota	77,047	642,961	Puerto Rico	3,435	1,869,255
Tennessee	42,246	2,915,841	Virgin Islands of the United States	132	24,889
Texas	267,339	6,414,824	Total for Outlying Possessions	597,256	2,595,956
Utah	84,916	550,310	Total United States	3,619,643	150,621,231
Vermont	9,609	359,231			
Virginia	40,815	2,677,773			
Washington	68,192	1,736,191			
West Virginia	24,181	1,901,974			
Wisconsin	56,154	3,137,587			
Wyoming	97,914	250,742			
Total for continental United States	3,022,387	131,669,275			

TABLE IV

Population of Cities of 100,000 or More — Final Figures: 1940 [1]

City	Population 1940	Population 1930	City	Population 1940	Population 1930
Total	37,987,989	36,195,171	Minneapolis, Minn.	492,370	464,356
Akron, Ohio	244,791	255,040	Nashville, Tenn.	167,402	153,866
Albany, N. Y.	130,577	127,412	Newark, N. J.	429,760	442,337
Atlanta, Ga.	302,288	270,366	New Bedford, Mass.	110,341	112,597
Baltimore, Md.	859,100	804,874	New Haven, Conn.	160,605	162,655
Birmingham, Ala.	267,583	259,678	New Orleans, La.	494,537	458,762
Boston, Mass.	770,816	781,188	New York, N. Y.	7,454,995	6,930,446
Bridgeport, Conn.	147,121	146,716	Norfolk, Va.	144,332	129,710
Buffalo, N. Y.	575,901	573,076	Oakland, Calif.	302,163	284,063
Cambridge, Mass.	110,879	113,643	Oklahoma City, Okla.	204,424	185,389
Camden, N. J.	117,536	118,700	Omaha, Nebr.	223,844	214,006
Canton, Ohio	108,401	104,906	Paterson, N. J.	139,656	138,513
Charlotte, N. C.	100,899	82,675	Peoria, Ill.	105,087	104,969
Chattanooga, Tenn.	128,163	119,798	Philadelphia, Pa.	1,931,334	1,950,961
Chicago, Ill.	3,396,808	3,376,438	Pittsburgh, Pa.	671,659	669,817
Cincinnati, Ohio	455,610	451,160	Portland, Oreg.	305,394	301,815
Cleveland, Ohio	878,336	900,429	Providence, R. I.	253,504	252,981
Columbus, Ohio	306,087	290,564	Reading, Pa.	110,568	111,171
Dallas, Texas	294,734	260,475	Richmond, Va.	193,042	182,929
Dayton, Ohio	210,718	200,982	Rochester, N. Y.	324,975	328,132
Denver, Colo.	322,412	287,861	Sacramento, Calif.	105,958	93,750
Des Moines, Iowa	159,819	142,559	St. Louis, Mo.	816,048	821,960
Detroit, Mich.	1,623,452	1,568,662	St. Paul, Minn.	287,736	271,606
Duluth, Minn.	101,065	101,463	Salt Lake City, Utah	149,934	140,267
Elizabeth, N. J.	109,912	114,589	San Antonio, Texas	253,854	231,542
Erie, Pa.	116,955	115,967	San Diego, Calif.	203,341	147,995
Fall River, Mass.	115,428	115,274	San Francisco, Calif.	634,536	634,394
Flint, Mich.	151,543	156,492	Scranton, Pa.	140,404	143,433
Fort Wayne, Ind.	118,410	114,946	Seattle, Wash.	368,302	365,583
Fort Worth, Texas	177,662	163,447	Somerville, Mass.	102,177	103,908
Gary, Ind.	111,719	100,426	South Bend, Ind.	101,268	104,193
Grand Rapids, Mich.	164,292	168,592	Spokane, Wash.	122,001	115,514
Hartford, Conn.	166,267	164,072	Springfield, Mass.	149,554	149,900
Houston, Texas	384,514	292,352	Syracuse, N. Y.	205,967	209,326
Indianapolis, Ind.	386,972	364,161	Tacoma, Wash.	109,408	106,817
Jacksonville, Fla.	173,065	129,549	Tampa, Fla.	108,391	101,161
Jersey City, N. J.	301,173	316,715	Toledo, Ohio	282,349	290,718
Kansas City, Kans.	121,458	121,857	Trenton, N. J.	124,697	123,356
Kansas City, Mo.	399,178	399,746	Tulsa, Okla.	142,157	141,258
Knoxville, Tenn.	111,580	105,802	Utica, N. Y.	100,518	101,740
Long Beach, Calif.	164,271	142,032	Washington, D. C.	663,091	486,869
Los Angeles, Calif.	1,504,277	1,238,048	Wichita, Kans.	114,966	111,110
Louisville, Ky.	319,077	307,745	Wilmington, Del.	112,504	106,597
Lowell, Mass.	101,389	100,234	Worcester, Mass.	193,694	195,311
Memphis, Tenn.	292,942	253,143	Yonkers, N. Y.	142,598	134,646
Miami, Fla.	172,172	110,637	Youngstown, Ohio	167,720	170,002
Milwaukee, Wis.	587,472	578,249			

[1] Sixteenth Census of the United States, 1940.

APPENDIX B

TABLE V
Mountains and Rivers in North America

Mountain	Location	Height (Ft.)	River	Length	Outflow
Mt. McKinley	Alaska	20,300	Missouri-Mississippi	4,200	Gulf of Mexico
Mt. Logan	Canada	19,850	Mackenzie	2,400	Arctic Ocean
Mt. Orizaba	Mexico	18,500	Yukon	2,100	Bering Sea
Mt. St. Elias	Alaska-Canada	18,000	Rio Grande	2,200	Gulf of Mexico
Mt. Popocatepetl	Mexico	17,800	Saint Lawrence	2,100	Gulf of St. Lawrence

TABLE VI
Largest Lakes in North America

Lake	Location	Area (Sq. Mi.)	Altitude (Ft.)	Depth (Ft.)
Superior	U. S.-Canada	31,200	602	1,000
Huron	U. S.-Canada	23,000	580	800
Michigan	U. S.	22,400	580	870
Great Bear	Canada	11,500	300	250
Erie	U. S.-Canada	10,000	570	200

REFERENCES

Stars indicate books for more advanced pupils, or for the teacher.

Aitchison, Alison E., and Uttley, Marguerite. *North America by Plane and Train.* Bobbs-Merrill Co., Indianapolis.

*Allen, Nellie B. *Geographical and Industrial Studies. Africa, Australia, and the Islands of the Pacific.* Ginn and Co., Boston.

*———. *Geographical and Industrial Studies. Asia.* Ginn and Co., Boston.

*———. *Geographical and Industrial Studies. The New Europe.* Ginn and Co., Boston.

———. *Geographical and Industrial Studies. North America.* Ginn and Co., Boston.

*———. *Geographical and Industrial Studies. South America.* Ginn and Co., Boston.

———. *Geographical and Industrial Studies. United States.* Ginn and Co., Boston.

*Bealby, J. T., and Fairford, F. *Peeps at Many Lands: Canada and Newfoundland.* The Macmillan Co., New York.

*Bowman, Isaiah. *South America. A Geography Reader.* Rand McNally and Co., Chicago.

*Browne, Edith A., Forrest, A. S., and Christmas, E. W. *Peeps at Many Lands: South America.* The Macmillan Co., New York.

*Browne, Edith A., and Goodall, A. M. *Peeps at Many Lands: Spain and Portugal.* The Macmillan Co., New York.

*Carpenter, Frank G. *Carpenter's New Geographical Reader. Africa.* American Book Co., New York.

*———. *Carpenter's New Geographical Reader. Asia.* American Book Co., New York.

*———. *Carpenter's New Geographical Reader. Australia.* American Book Co., New York.

*———. *Carpenter's New Geographical Reader. Europe.* American Book Co., New York.

———. *Carpenter's New Geographical Reader. North America.* American Book Co., New York.

*———. *Carpenter's New Geographical Reader. South America.* American Book Co., New York.

Castillo, Carlos. *Mexico. Burton Holmes Travel Stories.* Wheeler Publishing Co., Chicago.

*Chamberlain, J. F. and A. H. *The Continents and Their People. Africa. A Supplementary Geography.* The Macmillan Co., New York.

*———. *The Continents and Their People. Asia. A Supplementary Geography.* The Macmillan Co., New York.

*———. *The Continents and Their People. Europe. A Supplementary Geography.* The Macmillan Co., New York.

———. *The Continents and Their People. North America. A Supplementary Geography.* The Macmillan Co., New York.

*———. *The Continents and Their People. Oceania. A Supplementary Geography.* The Macmillan Co., New York.

REFERENCES

*Chamberlain, J. F. and A. H. *The Continents and Their People. South America. A Supplementary Geography.* The Macmillan Co., New York.

*Clark, Vinnie B. *Europe.* Silver, Burdett and Co., New York.

Compton's Pictured Encyclopedia. F. E. Compton and Co., Chicago.

Dakin, Wilson S. *Great Rivers of the World.* The Macmillan Co., New York.

*Della Chiesa, Carol. *Children of the World. The Three of Salu. Around the Year in Northern Italy.* World Book Co., Yonkers-on-Hudson, New York.

Eisen, Edna E. *Our Country from the Air.* Wheeler Publishing Co., Chicago.

Fairgrieve, James, and Young, Ernest. *Human Geography by Grades. The United States.* D. Appleton and Co., New York.

*Ferryman, A. F. M., and Thomson, M. P. *Peeps at Many Lands: Norway and Denmark.* The Macmillan Co., New York.

*Finnemore, John, and Browne, Edith A. *Peeps at Many Lands: Italy and Greece.* The Macmillan Co., New York.

*Finnemore, John, Lewis, J. H., and McCormick, A. D. *Peeps at Many Lands: Switzerland.* The Macmillan Co., New York.

*Fox, F., and Vaile, P. A. *Peeps at Many Lands: Australia and New Zealand.* The Macmillan Co., New York.

*Franck, Harry A. *Travels in Many Lands. China.* F. A. Owen Publishing Co., Dansville, N. Y.

*——. *Travels in Many Lands. South America.* F. A. Owen Publishing Co., Dansville, N. Y.

*Gregory, J. W. *Africa. A Geographical Reader.* Rand McNally and Co., Chicago.

Harris, Leila G. and Kilroy. *Canadian Ways.* McKnight and McKnight, Bloomington, Illinois.

Henderson, Rose. *Little Journeys in America.* The Southern Publishing Co., Dallas.

*Hoke, G. W. *Lands and Life, Book I. Russia and the Old East.* Johnson Publishing Co., Richmond.

Hotchkiss, Caroline W. *Representative Cities in the United States.* Houghton Mifflin Co., Boston.

*Huntington, Ellsworth. *Asia. A Geographical Reader.* Rand McNally and Co., Chicago.

*Johnston, L. E., and Finnemore, John. *Peeps at Many Lands: China and Japan.* The Macmillan Co., New York.

*Jungman, Beatrice and Nico. *Peeps at Many Lands: Holland.* The Macmillan Co., N. Y.

*Kelly, R. F., and Finnemore, John. *Peeps at Many Lands: Egypt and the Holy Land.* The Macmillan Co., New York.

Koch, Felix J. *Little Journeys through the Great Southwest.* A. Flanagan and Co., Chicago.

——. *Little Journeys to Our Western Wonderland.* A. Flanagan and Co., Chicago.

——. *A Little Journey to Northern Wilds.* A. Flanagan and Co., Chicago.

Lands and Peoples. The Grolier Society, N. Y.

Lefferts, Walter. *Our Neighbors, North and South.* J. B. Lippincott Co., Philadelphia.

——. *Our Own United States.* J. B. Lippincott Co., Philadelphia.

*Lewin, Evans. *Africa.* Oxford University Press, New York.

*McDonald, Etta Blaisdell, and Dalrymple, Julia. *Hassan in Egypt.* Little, Brown and Co., Boston.

*——. *Marta in Holland.* Little, Brown and Co., Boston.

*——. *Josepha in Spain.* Little, Brown and Co., Boston.

*——. *Rafael in Italy.* Little, Brown and Co., Boston.

Pack, Charles L. *The Forestry Primer.* American Tree Association, Washington, D. C.

*Perry, Walter Scott. *With Azir Girges in Egypt.* Mentzer, Bush and Co., Chicago.

Pitkin, Walter B., and Hughes, Harold F. *Seeing America. Book I — Farm and Field.* The Macmillan Co., New York.

——. *Seeing America. Book II — Mill and Factory.* The Macmillan Co., New York.

Sauer, Carl. *Man in Nature. America before the Days of the White Man.* Charles Scribner's Sons, New York.

*Schwatka, Frederick. *The Children of the Cold.* Educational Publishing Co.

*Stefansson, Vilhjalmur, and Schwartz, Julia A. *Northward Ho!* The Macmillan Co., N. Y.

Tappan, Eva M. *Diggers in the Earth.* Houghton Mifflin Co., Boston.

*Taylor, Griffith. *Australia. A Geographical Reader.* Rand McNally and Co., Chicago.

Thompson, Ruth. *Comrades of the Desert. Stories of the Adventures of Four Boys on Sagebrush Land.* Harr Wagner Publishing Co., San Francisco.

*Tietjens, Eunice. *China. Burton Holmes Travel Stories.* Wheeler Publishing Co., Chicago.

*Whitcomb, Clara E., and George, Marian M. *A Little Journey to Italy, Spain, and Portugal.* A. Flanagan and Co., Chicago.

*Wilbur, Susan. *Egypt and the Suez Canal. Burton Holmes Travel Stories.* Wheeler Publishing Co., Chicago.

INDEX

Key to Pronunciation: — ā, as in āle; ă, as in senăte; â, as in câre; ă, as in ăm; ă, as in finăl; ä, as in ärm; ȧ, as in ȧsk; *a*, as in sof*a*; ē, as in ēve; ĕ, as in crĕate; ĕ, as in ĕnd; ẽ, as in novẽl; ẽ, as in cindẽr; ī, as in īce; ĭ, as in Ill; ō, as in ōld; ŏ, as in ŏbey; ô, as in lôrd; ŏ, as in ŏdd; *o*, as in c*o*nnect; ōō, as in fōōd; ŏŏ, as in fŏŏt; ou, as in thou; th, as in thin; ᴛʜ, as in this; ū, as in pūre; ů, as in ůnite; û, as in ûrn; ŭ, as in stŭdy; *u*, as in circ*u*s; ᴋ for ch, as in chorus; ŋ (like ng), for n before the sound k or hard g, as in baŋk; ɴ indicates that the preceding vowel is pronounced as a nasal; g, as in go.

The principal map references are in **boldfaced** type.

Aberdeen (ăb′ẽr-dēn′), South Dakota, 12, 95; maps, 2, **81.**
Acapulco (ä′kä-pōōl′kō), Mexico, 282; map, **280.**
Adams, John, 170, 241.
Adirondack (ăd′ĭ-rŏn′dăk) Mountains, 178, 180, 181, 186, 190; map, **177.**
Adler Planetarium, Chicago, 216.
Adobe huts, 26.
Africa (ăf′rĭ-kȧ), 194, 317.
Agricultural Experiment Stations, 156.
Agricultural machinery: in Canada, 258; in the United States, 8, 80, 82, 83, 84, 85, 95, 96, 129, 148, 182, 203, 207, 210, 213, 214, 216, 221, 234.
Agricultural regions of the United States, 82; map, **82.**
Agriculture: in Canada, 245, 247; in Mexico, 282, 283; in North America, 318; in the United States, 82, 147; in the Virgin Islands, 302.
Agriculture, Department of, 82.
Airplanes, 1, 5, 30, 96, 97, 104, 132, 152, 154, 158, 193, 198, 216, 220, 260, 261, 266, 300, 320.
Airport, Kansas City, 97.
Akron (ăk′rŭn), Ohio, 220, 221; maps, 29, **205, 215.**
Alabama (ăl′ȧ-băm′ȧ), 126, 127, 128, 129, 132, 134, 135, 136, 137, 138, 142, 143, 160, 162, 175; maps, 29, 34, **131, 139.**
Alabama River, 19, 140, 142; maps, **131, 139.**
Alamo (ä′lä-mō), The, 120.
Alaska (ȧ-lăs′kȧ), 48, 273–277, 320; climate, 273; glaciers, 275; location, 273; physical characteristics, 273; population, 273–274; products, 274, 277; travel in, 274; maps, 2, **319.**
Alaska Railroad, 276.
Albany (ôl′bȧ-nĭ), New York, 3, 14, 176, 196, 199; maps, 2, 29, **177, 191.**
Alberta (ăl-bûr′tȧ), Canada, 247, 257, 258; maps, 28, **248.**
Albuquerque (ăl′bŭ-kûr′kĕ), New Mexico, 57, 76; maps, 28, **59, 73.**
Alcott, Louisa M., 241.
Aleutian (ȧ-lū′shăn) Islands, 273, 277.

Alfalfa, 40, 57, 58, 60, 62, 86, 87, 129, 132, 207.
Allegheny (ăl′ĕ-gā′nĭ) **Mountains,** 165, 176; maps, **29,** 149.
Allegheny Plateau, 178, 186, 187, 188, 198; maps, **29,** 149.
Allegheny River, 186, 187, 188, 194, 196; map, **177.**
Allen, Ethan, 240.
Allentown, Pennsylvania, 196; maps, **177, 191.**
Alligators, 151, 152.
Altoona (ăl-tōō′nȧ), Pennsylvania, 176, 178, 196; maps, 29, **177, 191.**
Aluminum, 47, 117, 118, 170, 190, 201, 252, 320.
Amarillo (ăm′ȧ-rĭl′ō), Texas, 122; maps, 29, **103, 119.**
America (ȧ-mĕr′ĭ-kȧ), 1, 71, 204, 235, 236, 262.
American Colonies, 293.
American Government, 170.
American Revolution, 99, 234.
Americans, 27, 68, 262, 284, 296, 302.
Ammonoosuc (ăm′ō-nōō′sŭk) River, 227.
Amsterdam (ăm′stẽr-dăm), 196; maps, **177, 191.**
Anaconda (ăn′ȧ-kŏn′dȧ), Montana, 12, 64; maps, 29, **60, 73.**
Androscoggin (ăn′drŏs-kŏg′ĭn) River, 240; map, **225.**
Angora goats, 19, 42.
Animal industries in the East North Central States, 207.
Animals (farm): in Labrador, 270; in Newfoundland, 269; in the United States, 71, 74, 80, 84, 86, 87, 92, 93, 134, 135, 163, 206; in the West Indies, 298.
Animals (fur-bearing): in Canada, 251, 254, 260; in Labrador, 270; in the United States, 35, 92, 104, 250.
Animals (wild): in Canada, 251, 257; in Newfoundland, 265; 269; in the United States, 35, 113, 114, 129, 152.
Annapolis (ȧ-năp′ō-lĭs), Maryland, 147, 164, 170; maps, 29, **149, 169.**
Annapolis Valley, 247.
Antarctic Circle, 324.
Antelope in the Black Hills, 90.

Anticosti (ăn′tĭ-kŏs′tĭ) Island, 252; map, **249.**
Antilles (ăn-tĭl′ēz), Greater and Lesser, 297; map, **281,** 319.
Apalachicola (ăp′ȧ-lăch′ĭ-kō′lȧ) Bay, 153.
Apiary at Mount Vernon, Ind., 209.
Appalachian (ăp′ȧ-lā′chĭ-ăn) Highlands, 126, 136, 144, 162, 175.
Appalachian Mountains, 148, 150, 168, 197, 251, 317; map, **29,** 149.
Apples: in Canada, 247, 256; in the United States, 5, 32, 40, 41, 44, 48, 92, 113, 156, 162, 163, 184, 185, 207, 232.
Aquarium, The John G. Shedd, Chicago, 216.
Aqueduct, Los Angeles, 50, 51, 52.
Arctic (ärk′tĭk) Circle, 273, 324.
Arctic Ocean, 273, 317, 318; maps, **248, 319.**
Arizona (ăr′ĭ-zō′nȧ), 17, 54, 56, 57, 58, 59, 60, 64, 66, 68, 74, 76, 118; maps, 2, 28, 34, **60, 73.**
Arkansas (är′kăn-sô), 92, 99, 100, 101, 110, 113, 116, 117, 118, 122, 126, 143; maps, 2, 29, 34, **103, 119.**
Arkansas River, 56, 61, 122; map, **103.**
Arkansas Valley, 61.
Arlington (är′lĭng-tŭn) Bridge, 173.
Arlington Cemetery, 172.
Aroostook (ȧ-rōōs′tŏŏk) County, 232.
Arrowrock Dam, 61, 62.
Art Museum, Nashville, 141.
Asbestos, 193, 247, 256, 320.
Asheville (ăsh′vĭl), North Carolina, 168, 170, 171; maps, 29, **149, 169.**
Ashland (ăsh′lănd), Kentucky, 142; maps, **131, 139.**
Ashtabula (ăsh′tȧ-bū′lȧ), Ohio, 6; maps, **205, 215.**
Asia (ā′shȧ), 273, 317, 320.
Asparagus, 108.
Asphalt, 300.
As the Airman Sees Our United States, 1–24; map, **2.**
Astor, John Jacob, 35.
Astoria (ăs-tō′rĭ-ȧ), Oregon, 35, 45, 46, 50; maps, 28, **37, 49.**
Athens (ăth′ĕnz), Greece, 140.

1

INDEX

Atlanta (ăt-lăn'tȧ), Georgia, 20, 21, 147, 168; maps, 2, 29, **149**, **169**.
Atlantic (ăt-lăn'tĭk) City, New Jersey, 182, 183; maps, 29, **177**, **191**.
Atlantic Coast, 130, 210.
Atlantic Coastal Plain, 148, 150, 223.
Atlantic Ocean, 3, 24, 25, 35, 97, 153, 175, 190, 244, 251, 265, 270, 288, 317.
Augusta (ô-gŭs'tȧ), Maine, 224, 240; maps, 29, **225**, **238**.
Austin (ôs'tĭn), Texas, 99, 122; maps, 28, **103**, **119**.
Australia (ôs-trā'lĭ-ȧ), 234.
Automobiles, 5, 8, 9, 10, 22, 46, 82, 95, 96, 182, 198, 203, 212, 214, 216, 218, 220, 221, 247, 261, 318.
Avalon (ăv'ȧ-lŏn), 264, 265.
Avocado, 153.
Aztec (ăz'tĕk) Calendar Stone, 286.
Aztecs, 284, 287, 293.

Baffin (băf'ĭn) Land, 320; map, **319**.
Bagasse, 108, 110.
Bahamas (bȧ-hā'mȧz), 297; maps, **281**, 319.
Bakersfield (bāk'ērz-fēld), California, 15, 42, 47; maps, 2, **37**, **49**.
Balboa (bäl-bō'ȧ), 295.
Baltimore (bôl'tĭ-mōr), Maryland, 22, 23, 147, 164, 167, 168, 170; maps, 2, 29, **149**, **169**.
Bamboo, 299.
Bananas: imported into the United States, 19, 125; in Central America, 291–293, 295–296; in Mexico, 279, 283; in the West Indies, 297, 298, 300, 302.
Banff (bămf), Canada, 257, 258; maps, 2, **248**.
Bangor (băn'gôr), Maine, 239, 240; maps, 29, **225**, **238**.
Bar Harbor, Maine, 239; map, **238**.
Barley: in Canada, 256, 258; in Newfoundland, 269; in the United States, 40, 44, 62, 84, 88, 206.
Barnegat (bär'nĕ-găt') Bay, 185.
Barre (băr'ĕ), Vermont, 236, 240; maps, **225**, **238**.
Bass, 182, 232.
Bath (báth), Maine, 240; maps, **225**, **238**.
Baton Rouge (băt'un rōōzh'), Louisiana, 19, 99, 116, 124, 125; maps, 2, 29, **103**, **119**.

Battle Harbor, Labrador, 271.
Bauxite, 99, 114, 117, 118, 320.
Bay of Corinto, 292.
Bay D'East River, 268.
Bay of Fundy (fŭn'dĭ), 245, 250; map, **249**.
Bay of Islands, 264.
Bayonne (bāy'ōn'), New Jersey, 22, 193; map, **191**.
Bayous, 104.
Bay St. Louis, Mississippi, 140; maps, **131**, **139**.
Beans: in Canada, 247; in Mexico, 283; in the United States, 26, 76, 108, 160, 185, 207, 232; in the West Indies, 298.
Beaumont (bō'mŏnt), Texas, 115; maps, 29, **103**, **119**.
Bees, 135, 209.
Beets, 86, 232.
Belgium (bĕl'jĭ-ŭm), 278.
Belle Isle (bĕl' īl'), 268.
Bellingham (bĕl'ĭng-hăm), Washington, 42, 48; maps, 28, **37**, **49**.
Bennington Battle Monument, 242.
Berkshire (bûrk'shĭr) Hills, 3, 223, 239; map, **225**.
Berlin (bûr'lĭn'), Germany, 214.
Berries, 40, 41, 42, 48, 86, 265.
Bethlehem (bĕth'lĕ-hĕm), Pennsylvania, 196; maps, **177**, **191**.
Billings (bĭl'ĭngz), Montana, 10, 12, 76; maps, 2, 28, **60**, **73**.
Biloxi (bĭ-lŏk'sĭ), Mississippi, 140; maps, **131**, **139**.
Bingham (bĭng'ăm), Utah, 65, 66.
Binghamton (bĭng'ăm-tŭn), New York, 198; maps, 29, **177**, **191**.
Birds, wild, 104.
Birmingham (bûr'mĭng-ăm), Alabama, 127, 137, 138, 140; maps, 29, **131**, **139**, 149, 169.
Birmingport (bûr'mĭng-pōrt), Alabama, 138.
Bisbee (bĭz'bē), Arizona, 17, 64; maps, 2, **60**, **73**.
Bishop's Falls, 268.
Bismarck (bĭz'märk), North Dakota, 79, 95; maps, 28, **81**, **94**.
Bison (buffalo), 25, 30, 72, 90.
Bivalve, 182.
Black bass, 210.
Black Belt, 129, 130.
Blackberries, 42.
Blackfish, 163.
Black Hills, 78, 90, 92; map, **81**.
Black Mountains, 171.
Black Warrior River, 138.
Blewitt Falls, 150.
Blueberries, 186, 232, 265.
Blue grass, 162.
Blue-Grass Region, 135, 140, 142.
Blue Lake, 321.
Blue Ridge Mountains, 21, 148, 162, 171.

Boise (boi'zȧ), Idaho, 57, 61, 76; maps, 28, **60**, **73**.
Boll weevil, 129, 130, 132, 156, 158.
Bonnet Carre Spillway, 125.
Boots and shoes, 214, 236, 240.
Borax, 47, 63.
Boston (bŏs'tŭn), Massachusetts, 1, 3, 4, 22, 208, 224, 226, 229, 232, 239, 241, 292; maps, 2, 29, 34, **225**, **238**.
Boulder Dam. See *Hoover Dam*.
Bowie, James, 120.
Bow River Valley, 258.
Bradford, William, 226.
Brass, 193, 212, 224, 236.
Brazil (brȧ-zĭl'), 125, 252.
Bridgeport (brĭj'pōrt), Connecticut, 24, 228, 242; maps, 29, **225**, **238**.
British Columbia, 247, 258, 260; map, **248**.
British Commonwealth of Nations, 262.
British Empire, 244.
British Honduras, 296.
British Isles, 269.
Brockton (brŏk'tŭn), Massachusetts, 235; maps, **225**, **238**.
Bronze, 236.
Brooklyn (brŏŏk'lĭn), New York, 192; map, **191**.
Brooks Mountains, Alaska, 273.
Brook trout, 210.
Broom corn, 112, 113.
Brownsville (brounz'vĭl), Texas, 108; maps, **103**, **119**.
Brown University, 242.
Brunswick (brŭnz'wĭk), Georgia, 167; maps, **149**, **169**.
Bryce (brīs) Canyon, 68, 70.
Buckwheat: in Canada, 245; in the United States, 135, 163.
Buffalo, 1, 3, 5, 6, 7, 88, 93, 175, 190, 198; maps, 2, 29, **177**, **191**.
Building materials, 74, 170, 188, 212, 228.
Building stone, 236, 240, 320.
Bunch grass, 78.
Burlington (bûr'lĭng-tŭn), Vermont, 224, 240; maps, **225**, **238**.
Burr, Aaron, 171.
Butte (būt), Montana, 12, 13, 57, 64; maps, 2, 28, **60**, **73**.
Buzzards (bŭz'ȧrdz) Bay, 223; map, **225**.
Byrd, Admiral, 234.
Byrd Antarctic Expedition, 234.

Cabbage: in Newfoundland, 269; in the United States, 108, 132, 160, 185, 207.
Cabinet woods: in Guatemala, 294; in Mexico, 279.
Cabot, John, 262.
Cabot Strait, 262.

INDEX

Cacao in the West Indies, 297, 300.
Cactus, 54, 55, 107.
Cactus Flat, 62.
Calgary (kăl′ga-rĭ), Canada, 247, 258; maps, 2, **248**.
California (kăl′ĭ-fôr′nĭ-*a*), 15, 30, 32, 34, 40, 42, 44, 45, 46, 47, 48, 50, 52, 59, 61, 63; maps, 28, 34, **37**, **49**.
Calles, General, 287.
Calumet (kăl′ū-mĕt), Michigan, 210; maps, **205**, **215**.
Cambridge (kām′brĭj), Massachusetts, 239; maps, **225**, **238**.
Camden (kăm′dĕn), New Jersey, 185, 194; maps, 29, **177**, **191**.
Campbellton (kăm′bĕl-tŭn), Canada, 246.
Campobello (kăm′pō-bĕl′ō) Island, 239.
Canada (kăn′*a*-d*a*), 6, 7, 198, 216, 239, 244–261, 262, 270, 274, 320; agriculture, 245, 247, 254, 255, 256, 257, 258, 260; animals, 251, 254, 260; cities, 250, 254, 255, 256, 257, 258, 260, 261; fishing, 245, 246, 251, 252, 257, 260; forests, 250, 251, 254, 620, 261; fur farming, 250; hunting, 251, 252, 257; important products, 247; lumbering, 252, 254, 260; manufacturing, 252, 255, 260; Maritime Provinces, 244; minerals, 250, 256, 260; mountains, 251, 254, 258; people, 252, 255, 261; provinces, 244; shipping, 244, 254, 258, 260; water power, 252, 254, 256; maps, 2, **248**–**249**, 319.
Canadian Bridge, 256.
Canadian Horseshoe Falls, 256.
Canadian National Railways, 257.
Canadian Pacific Railway, 257.
Canadian Rockies, 258, 259, 260; map, **248**.
Canal Zone, 295, 296; map, **281**.
Canning industry: in the Maritime Provinces, 42; in the United States, 42, 45, 46, 50, 92, 136, 167, 168, 185, 194.
Cantaloupes, 58, 59, 160.
Canton (kăn′tŏn), Ohio, 221; maps, 29, **205**, **215**.
Canyons, 54, 55.
Cape Breton (brĕt′ŭn) Island, 251; map, **249**.
Cape Cod, 223, 232; map, **225**.
Cape Cod Bay, 239; map, **225**.
Cape Eternity, 252.
Cape Fear River, 167; map, **149**.
Cape Hatteras (hăt′ĕr-*a*s), 150; maps, **149**, **169**.
Cape Horn, 295.
Cape May, 182; maps, **177**, **191**.
Cape St. Anthony, 263.

Caribbean (kăr′ĭ-bē′ăn) Sea, 292, 294, 295, 296, 298; maps, **281**, 319.
Caribou, 251, 260, 264, 265.
Carlsbad (kärlz′băd) Caverns, 68, 70.
Carpenter's Hall, 194.
Carpets and rugs, 194, 196.
Carrara (kär-rä′rä) marble, 137.
Carrots, 86, 184, 232.
Carson (kär′sŭn) City, Nevada, 57, 61; maps, 28, 37, 49, **60**, **73**.
Carson River, 61.
Cartier, Jacques, 252.
Cascade Mountains, 13, 15, 34, 40, 41, 317; maps, 28, **37**.
Casco (kăs′kō) Bay, 240; map, **225**.
Catskills (kăts′kĭlz), 178, 179, 180; map, **177**.
Catskill State Park and Forest Preserve, 178.
Cattle, 5, 10, 12, 15, 17, 19, 22, 30, 67, 71, 72, 76, 78, 87, 96, 107, 108, 118, 120, 132, 152, 162, 163, 184, 206, 207, 269; map, 113.
Cattle, beef, 40, 57, 72, 74, 88, 112, 114, 134, 135.
Cattle, dairy, 40, 57, 72, 88, 112, 114, 134, 135, 182, 184.
Cedar Rapids, Iowa, 96; maps, 29, **81**, **94**.
Cedar River, 96; map, **81**.
Celery, 108, 207, 221.
Celotex, 108, 109.
Central America, 19, 125, 320; maps, **280**–**281**, 319.
Central American Republics, 291–296; bananas, 291, 292; British Honduras, 296; climate, 292; coffee, 292; Costa Rica, 294; education, 293; government, 293; Guatemala, 293; Honduras, 293, 294; Nicaragua, 294; Panama Canal, 295–296; people, 293; physical features, 292; relations with the United States, 296; Salvador, 294; seasons, 292; maps, **280**–**281**, 319.
Champlain (shăm-plān′) Valley, 182.
Charles River, 224, 235, 239.
Charleston (chärlz′tŭn), South Carolina, 20, 21, 147, 167; maps, 2, 29, **149**, **169**.
Charleston, West Virginia, 147, 170; maps, 29, **149**, **169**.
Charlotte (shär′lŏt), North Carolina, 147, 168; maps, 29, **149**, **169**.
Charlottetown, 247, 250, 251; maps, 2, **249**.
Chattahoochee (chăt′*a*-hōō′chē) River, 20; map, **149**.

Chattanooga (chăt′*a*-nōō′g*a*), Tennessee, 137, 140, 141; maps, 29, **131**, **139**, 149, 169.
Chemicals, 5, 147, 168, 170.
Cherries, 40, 42, 184, 247, 256.
Chesapeake (chĕs′*a*-pēk) Bay, 22, 162, 163, 164, 167, 170; map, **149**.
Cheyenne (shī-ĕn′), Wyoming, 57, 76; maps, 28, **60**, **73**.
Chicago (shĭ-kô′gō), Illinois, 1, 6, 8, 10, 66, 95, 152, 203, 204, 206, 207, 210, 212, 214, 216, 218, 220; maps, 2, 29, **205**, **215**.
Chicago River, 214.
Chicago River Ship Canal, 216.
Chickasaw (chik′*a*-sô) Ridge, 128.
Chickens, 87, 88, 112, 114, 132, 134, 184, 186, 206, 208; map, 208.
Chicoutimi (shē′kōō′tē′mē′), Canada, 252; maps, 2, **249**.
Childs Glacier, 275.
Chile (chĭl′ĭ), 125, 167, 218.
China (chī′n*a*), 50, 51, 52, 153, 194, 228.
Chinatown, 50, 51.
Christ, 284.
Christmas greens, 39.
Churchill (chûrch′ĭl), Canada, 258, 260; maps, 2, **248**.
Cigars, 156, 157, 158, 192, 193, 196, 221, 242.
Cincinnati (sĭn′sĭ-năt′ĭ), Ohio, 207, 214, 218, 219; maps, 29, **205**, **215**.
Cities: in Alaska, 273, 274; in Canada, 250, 254, 255, 256, 257, 258, 260, 261; in Mexico, 282, 284, 287, 288; in North America, 252; in the United States, 1, 5, 6, 12, 17, 20, 24, 48, 74, 80, 88, 93, 95, 96, 107, 116, 118, 126, 127, 140, 142, 143, 150, 152, 158, 168, 175, 193, 196, 198, 202, 203, 204, 206, 208, 212, 214, 220, 235, 239, 242, 273, 300; in the West Indies, 298.
Citrus fruits, 108, 147, 152, 156; map, 44.
Civil War, 74.
Clams, 153, 230, 232.
Cleveland (klēv′lănd), Ohio, 1, 6, 8, 203, 204, 206, 212, 216, 217, 218, 221; maps, 2, 29, **205**, **215**.
Cliff dwellings, 55, 71, 75.
Climate: in Alaska, 273; in Central America, 292; in Mexico, 279, 287; in Newfoundland, 269; in North America, 318; in the United States: East North Central States, 207; Mountain States, 74; New England States, 226, 227; Pacific

States, 17, 40, 42, 44, 48, 52; South Atlantic States, 140, 147, 150, 152, 153, 154; West North Central States, 78, 84, 92; West South Central States, 17, 100, 101, 108, 120; in the West Indies, 297, 300.
Clothing, 147, 167, 176, 192, 203, 218, 221, 284.
Clover, 84, 129, 132, 135, 245.
Coachella (kō'á-chĕl'là) Valley, 40, 44.
Coal: in Alaska, 274; in Canada, 250; in Cuba, 300; in Mexico, 284; in Newfoundland, 269; in North America, 320; in the United States, 6, 10, 57, 66, 74, 76, 90, 95, 96, 116, 127, 136, 138, 140, 147, 158, 167, 170, 176, 187, 188, 196, 198, 203, 204, 210, 214, 216, 218, 221, 247, 250.
Coal, anthracite, 187, 196, 210.
Coal, bituminous, 137, 166, 187, 210.
Coal mines and mining, 122, 135, 136, 137, 140, 142, 163, 189, 211.
Coastal plain, 20.
Coast Ranges, 13, 34; map, **37**.
Cobalt in Canada, 256.
Cocoa in Mexico, 279.
Coconuts in the West Indies, 297, 300.
Cod, 163, 226, 232, 245, 252, 265, 272.
Cody, William F. (Buffalo Bill), 74.
Coeur d'Alene (kûr dá-lān'), Idaho, 13, 76; maps, **60**, **73**.
Coffee, 19, 125, 279, 292, 293, 295, 297, 300.
Coke, 187, 188, 221.
Colorado (kŏl'ō-rä'dō), 54, 56, 57, 59, 61, 62, 63, 64, 66, 68, 71, 74, 75, 86, 107; maps, 28, 34, **60**, **73**.
Colorado Plateau, 68; map, **60**.
Colorado River, 17, 18, 44, 45, 56, 58, 59, 61, 68, 122, 318; map, **60**.
Colorado Springs, 68, 74; maps, 28, **60**, **73**.
Columbia (kŏ-lŭm'bĭ-á), 147, 168; maps, **149**, **169**.
Columbia River, 13, 35, 45, 46, 48, 50, 56, 304; maps, 28, **37**.
Columbus (kŏ-lŭm'bŭs), Ohio, 203, 214, 219, 220; maps, 29, **205**, **215**.
Columbus, Christopher, 283, 284, 300.
Combine, 84, 85.
Comstock Lode, 64.
Concord (kŏŋ'kŏrd), New Hampshire, 224, 240; maps, 29, **225**, **238**.

Coney (kō'nĭ) Island, 182; map, **177**.
Congress, 170, 173.
Congressional Library, 23, 172.
Conneaut (kŏn'ē-ôt'), Ohio, 6; map, **215**.
Connecticut (kŏ-nĕt'ĭ-kŭt), 24, 182, 192, 224, 228, 231, 233, 235, 236, 242; maps, 29, 34, **225**, **238**.
Connecticut River, 3, 24, 224, 240; map, **225**.
Connecticut Valley, 3, 232.
Continental Congress, 22, 194.
Coolidge Dam, 17, 58, 59.
Copper, 12, 17, 47, 57, 63, 64, 65, 66, 74, 167, 176, 193, 198, 210, 212, 236, 247, 256, 268, 274, 288, 300, 320.
Corcoran Art Gallery, 23, 172.
Cordilleras, 292.
Cordova (kôr'dō-vá), Alaska, 274.
Corn: in Mexico, 279, 283; in the United States, 20, 26, 40, 84, 86, 87, 88, 92, 112, 113, 114, 122, 127, 128, 132, 134, 135, 140, 144, 147, 160, 163, 184, 206, 207, 208, 221, 224, 232, 318; map, 85.
Corn Belt, 72, 85, 86, 87, 88, 206, 207, 208, 220.
Corn and Winter Wheat Belt, 84, 85, 184, 206.
Corner Brook, 268.
Cortez, 287.
Costa Rica (kŏs'tá rē'ká), 292–295; maps, **281**, 319.
Cotton: in Mexico, 279, 283; in North America, 318; in the United States, 19, 20, 57, 58, 86, 87, 99, 100, 110, 111, 112, 113, 114, 120, 122, 125, 126, 127, 128, 129, 130, 132, 137, 138, 140, 142, 147, 148, 156, 158, 159, 167; in the West Indies, 298.
Cotton Belt, 110, 112.
Cotton gin, 111, 112, 138, 148, 156, 159, 168.
Cotton goods, 97, 140, 142, 167, 168, 193, 196, 235.
Cotton manufacturing and mills, 5, 111, 112, 121, 122, 137, 138, 140, 156, 158, 159, 168, 234, 235, 240, 288.
Cottonseed mills, 122, 138, 142, 156.
Cottonseed products, 99, 112, 127, 134, 140, 167.
Council Bluffs, Iowa, 96; maps, **81**, **94**.
Covington (kŭv'ĭng-tŭn), Ohio, 142; maps, **205**, **215**.
Cowboys, 113.
Cowpeas, 132, 134.
Cow-sow-hen method of farming, 132.

Crabs, 107.
Cranberries, 185, 232.
Crater (krā'tĕr) Lake, 33, 34.
Creameries, 42, 93, 95, 96, 122.
Creoles, 19.
Cripple Creek, Colorado, 64; maps, **60**, **73**.
Crockett, Davy, 120.
Crops: in the Cotton Belt, 112; on the Mississippi Lowlands, 128; in the South Atlantic States, 147, 148; in the West Indies, 297; in the West South Central States, 100, 101, 113.
Cuba (kū'bá), 108, 125, 156, 291, 297, 298, 300; maps, 2, **281**, 319.
Cumberland (kŭm'bĕr-lănd) Plateau, 141; map, **131**.
Cumberland River, 140; map, **131**.
Curaçao (kōō'rä-sä'ō), 297.
Cutlery, 242.
Cuyahoga (kĭ'á-hō'gá) River, 217.
Cypress, 102, 104, 129, 164.

Dacotah Indians, 11.
Dairying, 5, 10, 42, 72, 88, 92, 96, 182, 184, 207, 256.
Dairy products, 32, 42, 79, 163, 176, 203, 224, 247, 255.
Dakotas (dá-kō'táz), The, 95; maps, 28, 34, **81**, **94**.
Dallas (dăl'ás), Texas, 19, 116, 120, 121; maps, 2, 29, **103**, **119**.
Danvers (dăn'vẽrs), Massachusetts, 235.
Dark Ages in Europe, 284.
Dartmouth College, 240.
Dates, 42, 44, 58.
Davenport (dăv'ĕn-pōrt), Iowa, 96; maps, 29, **81**, **94**.
Davis, Jefferson, 171.
Dawson (dô'sŭn), Canada, 247; map, **248**.
Dayton (dā'tŭn), Ohio, 220; maps, 29, **205**, **215**.
Daytona Beach, 154, 156; maps, **149**, **169**.
Dead Sea, 63.
Death Valley, 47, 48; map, **37**.
Decker, Indiana, 209.
Declaration of Independence, 194.
Delaware (dĕl'á-wâr), 22, 147, 168; maps, 29, 34, **149**, **169**.
Delaware Bay, 175, 182; map, **177**.
Delaware River, 22, 168, 175, 180, 185, 193, 194; map, **177**.
Delaware Water Gap, 180.
De Lesseps, Ferdinand, 295.
Delta, The, 128, 129, 142.
Denmark (dĕn'märk), 273, 302.
Denver (dĕn'vẽr), Colorado, 57, 74; maps, 28, **60**, **73**.
Deserts, 47, 48, 54, 318.
Des Moines (dē moin'), Iowa, 79, 88, 96; maps, 29, **81**, **94**.

Des Moines River, 96; map, **81.**
Detroit (dĕ-troit'), Michigan, 203, 206, 212, 213, 216, 217, 220, 256; maps, 29, **205, 215.**
Detroit River, 216.
Dewey, Admiral, 173.
Diego (Son of Columbus), 300.
Dismal Swamp, 164, 165.
District of Columbia, 170; maps, 29, **149, 169.**
Dogs: in Alaska, 274; in Labrador, 272; (huskies) in New Hampshire, 234.
Dominican (dŏ-mĭn'ĭ-kăn) Republic, 297, 300; maps, **281,** 319.
Dover (dō'vẽr), Delaware, 147; maps, 29, **149, 169.**
Dried fruit in California, 45.
Dry farming, 62, 100.
Dry Valley, 62.
Dubuque (dōō-būk'), Iowa, 96; maps, 29, **81, 94.**
Ducks, 186, 208.
Duluth (dōō-lōōth'), Minnesota, 90, 91, 93, 95, 204, 212; maps, 29, **81, 94.**
Durham (dûr'ăm), North Carolina, 158; maps, 29, **149, 169.**
Dynamos, 140.

Earth, 323–324.
Earthquakes in Central America, 292.
East Boston, Massachusetts, 229.
East Liverpool, Ohio, 214, 221; map, **215.**
East North Central States, 202–222; important products, 203; statistics, 203; maps, **205, 215.**
Eastport, Maine, 232, 239; maps, **225, 238.**
East River, 22, 192.
East St. Louis, Illinois, 221; maps, 29, **205, 215.**
East South Central States, 126–146; important products, 127; statistics, 127; maps, **131, 139.**
Edmonton (ĕd'mŭn-tŭn), Canada, 247, 258; maps, 2, **248,** 319.
Education: in Central America, 293; in Mexico, 288.
Edwards Plateau, 114.
Egypt (ē'jĭpt), 58, 107.
Electricity, 6, 20, 34, 52, 58, 59, 61, 62, 64, 80, 93, 95, 116, 118, 140, 142, 143, 190, 198, 256, 268.
Elephant Butte Dam, 59, 62, 120.
Elizabeth, New Jersey, 22, 193; map, **191.**
Elizabethtown, Pennsylvania, 184.
Elm trees in New England, 230, 231.
El Paso (ĕl păs'ō), Texas, 17, 118, 120; maps, 2, 28, **103, 119,** 319.

Emerson, 239.
Emperor Falls (Canadian Rockies), 259.
England (ĭŋ'glănd), 158, 194, 228, 244, 262, 278, 293.
Equator, 100, 317, 323–324.
Erie (ē'rĭ), Pennsylvania, 6, 196; maps, 29, **177, 191.**
Erie Canal, 3, 5, 202.
Eskimos: in Alaska, 273, 274; in Labrador, 270.
Estuaries, 150.
Euclid, 6.
Eugene, 42.
Europe (ū'rŭp), 99, 135, 192, 203, 206, 228, 245, 258, 262, 264, 266, 317, 320.
Europeans, 25, 26, 27.
Evansville (ĕv'ănz-vĭl), Indiana, 214, 220; maps, 29, **205, 215.**
Everett (ĕv'ẽr-ĕt), Washington, 13, 42, 48; maps, 28, **37, 49.**
Everglades, 152; map, **149.**
Exploits (ĕks'ploits) River, 268.
Exports: from Guatemala, 294; from Haiti, 300; from Los Angeles, 52; from Mexico, 284; from New Orleans, 125; from Nicaragua, 294; from Seattle, 48.

Factories: in Canada, 252; in Newfoundland, 268; in the United States, 20, 22, 34, 40, 50, 95, 108, 126, 144, 148, 156, 188, 216, 221, 234, 235, 242.
Fairbanks (fâr'băŋks), Alaska, 273; map, **319.**
Fall line, 150.
Fall River, Massachusetts, 239; maps, **225, 238.**
Faneuil Hall, 241.
Fargo (fär'gō), North Dakota, 79, 95; maps, 29, **81, 94.**
Farming: in Canada, 254; in Mexico, 288; in Newfoundland, 269; in the United States, 74, 80, 82, 107, 147, 152, 158, 178, 182, 206, 226, 227, 232; in the West Indies, 298, 302.
Farms: in Canada, 255, 256, 260; in Mexico, 288, 289; in Newfoundland, 265; in the United States, 5, 8, 19, 24, 80, 82, 87, 90, 114, 129, 134, 135, 143, 150, 202.
Fertilizers, 64, 66, 181, 128, 137, 140, 142, 143, 153, 164, 167, 168, 184, 320.
Field Museum of Natural History, Chicago, 216.
Figs, 42, 45.
Films, 52.
Finger Lakes, New York, 178, 179, 185, 198.

Fiords: of Alaska, 273; of Labrador, 270.
Fisheries: of the East South Central States, 135–136; of Florida, 153–154; of New England, 230–232; of the Pacific States, 45–46; of the South Atlantic States, 163–164; of the West South Central States, 107.
Fishing: in Alaska, 273, 274, 276; in Canada, 245, 246, 251, 252, 257; in Labrador, 270, 271, 272; in Newfoundland, 264, 265, 266, 267, 269; in the United States, 50, 92, 95, 126, 140, 155, 156, 163, 182, 183, 208, 226, 240.
Flagstaff, Arizona, 76; maps, **60, 73.**
Flax, 42, 79, 84, 93, 133; map, 132.
Flint, Michigan, 212, 220, 221; maps, 29, **205, 215.**
Florida (flŏr'ĭ-dà), 1, 20, 44, 101, 107, 147, 150–156, 158, 162, 164; maps, 2, 29, 34, **149, 169.**
Florida Keys, 156; maps, **149, 169.**
Flour and flour milling, 5, 6, 10, 12, 13, 40, 48, 74, 76, 88, 89, 93, 95, 96, 97, 122, 125, 140, 198, 206, 216, 220, 221, 247, 288.
Flowers in Alaska, 273.
Ford Automobile Plant, Detroit, 213.
Forests: in Canada, 245, 250, 251, 254, 258, 259, 260, 261; in Labrador, 270, 272; in Mexico, 278, 283; in Newfoundland, 264, 265, 266, 269; in North America, 318; in the United States, 1, 13, 17, 19, 20, 25, 26, 35, 38, 39, 50, 66, 67, 74, 76, 90, 92, 93, 95, 100, 101, 102, 104, 118, 120, 122, 126, 129, 136, 137, 140, 142, 144, 156, 163, 164, 165, 166, 170, 178, 180, 186, 202, 210, 214, 223, 224, 226, 227, 228, 230, 236; in the West Indies, 298, 302.
Fort McHenry (măc-hĕn'rĭ), Maryland, 23.
Fort Orange (ŏr'ĕnj), New York, 4.
Fortress Monroe (mŏn-rō'), Virginia, 167.
Fort Smith, Arkansas, 122; maps, 29, **103, 119.**
Fort Wayne (wān), Indiana, 221; maps, 29, **205, 215.**
Fort William, Canada, 258; map, **249.**
Fort Worth, Texas, 19, 116, 120, 121; maps, 2, 29, **103, 119.**
Foundry products, 236.
Fox farms, 250.
France (frȧns), 99, 202, 252, 262, 278, 295, 297.
Frankfort, Kentucky, 127; maps, 29, **131, 139.**

Franklin, New Hampshire, 235; maps, **225, 238**.
Fredericton (frĕd′ẽr-ĭk-tŭn′), New Brunswick, 247, 251; maps, 2, **249**.
French, The, 99, 251, 252.
French and Indian War, 252.
Fresno (frĕz′nō), California, 44; maps, 28, **37, 49**.
Fruit: in Alaska, 273; in Canada, 256, 260; in Central America, 291; in Mexico, 279, 283; in the United States, 5, 6, 15, 30, 32, 40, 42, 44, 45, 48, 50, 57, 58, 61, 62, 74, 86, 92, 101, 132, 147, 152, 153, 160, 162, 163, 167, 168, 170, 176, 184, 185, 203, 207, 208, 224, 245, 247; in the West Indies, 298, 302.
Fur, 35, 247; farming, 250; trading, 252; trapping, 260.
Furniture, 38, 50, 122, 136, 140, 147, 148, 166, 167, 168, 203, 210, 214, 216, 220, 221, 242, 294.

Galveston (gắl′vĕs-tŭn), Texas, 116, 120, 122; maps, 29, **103, 119**.
Garden of the Gods, 68, 71.
Gary (gā′rĭ), Indiana, 8, 10, 212; maps, 29, **205, 215**.
Gas, natural, 90, 114, 116, 120.
Gasoline, 74.
Gaspé (gȧs′pā′), Canada, 251, 252; map, **2**.
Gaspé Peninsula, 251; map, **249**.
Geese, 208.
General Grant National Park, 34.
Genesee (jĕn′ĕ-sē′) Falls, 200.
Genesee River, 5, 198, 200; map, **177**.
George Washington Bridge, 22, 193.
Georgia (jôr′jȧ), 20, 44, 147, 156, 158, 159, 160, 161, 164, 166, 167, 168, 175, 214; maps, 2, 29, 34, **149, 169**.
Germany (jûr′mȧ-nĭ), 167, 278, 284.
Geysers, 68.
Gila (hē′lȧ) River, 17, 58; map, **60**.
Gilford (gĭl′fẽrd), New Hampshire, 233.
Glacier (glā′shẽr) Bay, 275.
Glacier (ice sheet), 83, 178, 182, 223.
Glacier National Park, 68, 69.
Glaciers: in Alaska, 273; in Canada, 258; in the United States, 68.
Glass, 147, 196, 212, 221, 288.
Glass Mountain, 68.
Globe, Arizona, 64; maps, **60, 73**.
Gloucester (glŏs′tẽr), Massachusetts, 230, 232; maps, **225, 238**.

Gloversville (glŭv′ẽrz-vĭl), New York, 198; maps, **177, 191**.
Goats, 19, 42, 114, 118.
Goethals, Colonel George W., 295.
Gold: in Alaska, 274; in Canada, 247, 250, 256, 260; in Central America, 291, 293, 294; in Cuba, 300; in Mexico, 283, 285, 288; in Newfoundland, 268; in North America, 320; in the United States, 30, 46, 47, 57, 63, 64, 66, 74, 79, 90, 212.
Golden Gate, 16, 45, 50.
Goldfield, Nevada, 64; maps, **60, 73**.
Goldfish farm, 210.
Gold Rush of 1849, 46, 295.
Gorgas, Colonel, 295.
Gosnold, Captain, 226.
Government Buildings of Canada, Ottawa, 255.
Government of Mexico, 287.
Grain, 6, 13, 15, 42, 57, 74, 76, 79, 80, 92, 95, 96, 99, 108, 113, 121, 125, 126, 127, 134, 140, 142, 147, 163, 203, 204, 206, 207, 208, 216, 218, 220, 232, 247, 258.
Grain elevators, 13, 95, 120, 140.
Grand Bank, Newfoundland, 264, 265.
Grand Canyon, 68, 76; map, **60**.
Grand Canyon National Park, 70.
Grand Falls, Newfoundland, 268, 272.
Grand Forks, North Dakota, 95; maps, 29, **81, 94**.
Grand Rapids, Michigan, 214, 220; maps, 29, **205, 215**.
Grand River, 61; map, **60**.
Granite, 166, 212, 236, 240.
Grant, General U. S., 173.
Grapefruit, 44, 45, 58, 108, 152, 298.
Grapes, 42, 44, 184, 185, 207, 256; map, 44.
Grasslands in Canada, 260.
Grazing, 13, 67, 100.
Great American Desert, 58.
Great Appalachian Valley, 162, 163.
Great Basin, The, 62, 63, 282.
Great Britain, 244, 262, 284, 297, 300.
Great Falls, 59, 76.
Great Lakes, 5, 184, 192, 196, 198, 202, 203, 204, 206, 207, 208, 210, 212, 216, 218, 252, 256, 258, 260, 318; map, **177, 205**.
Great Plains, 12, 17, 113.
Great Republic, 229.
Great Salt Lake, 63, 76; map, **60**.
Great Smoky Mountain National Park, 144, 148.
Great Smoky Mountains, 144, 145, 171; map, **148**.
Great Valley of California, 15, 40, 42, 47, 50.

Greece (grēs), 140, 141.
Greek divers, 154, 155.
Greene, Mrs. Nathanael, 112.
Greenfield, Canada, 245.
Greenland, 317, 320; maps, 249, **319**.
Green Mountains, 223, 236; map, **225**.
Greensboro (grēnz′bŭr-ō), North Carolina, 168; maps, **149, 169**.
Greenville, South Carolina, 142; maps, 29, **149, 169**.
Greenwich, England, 324.
Grenfell Mission, 263.
Growing season: in Alaska, 273; in Mexico, 282; in Newfoundland, 269; in the United States, 83, 86, 100, 101, 156.
Guadalajara (gwä′thä-lä-hä′rä), Mexico, 288; maps, **280**, 319.
Guadalupe (gô′dĕ-lōōp′) Mountains, 17.
Guanajuato (gwä′nä-hwä′tō), Mexico, 288; map, **280**.
Guatemala (gwä′tȧ-mä′lȧ), 291, 293, 294; maps, **280, 319**.
Guatemala City, 293; maps, **280, 319**.
Gulf of California, 44; maps, **280, 319**.
Gulf of Campeche (käm-pā′chā), 282; maps, **280**, 319.
Gulf of Fonseca (fŏn-sā′kä), 292; map, **280**.
Gulf of Honduras (hŏn-dōō′rȧs), 291; map, **280**, 319.
Gulf of Mexico, 25, 100, 101, 104, 107, 120, 126, 127, 136, 153, 154, 298, 317, 318; maps, 2, 29, 280, **319**.
Gulf of St. Lawrence, 251, 318; map, **249**.
Gulf of Tehuantepec (tȧ-wän′tȧ-pĕk′), 282; map, **280**.
Gulfport, Mississippi, 140; maps, **131, 139**.
Gulf Stream, 154, 266.
Gypsum, 250.

Habana (hȧ-bän′ȧ), Cuba, 156, 298, 300, 301; maps, **281**, 319.
Haddock, 163, 232, 245, 265.
Haiti (hā′tĭ), 297, 300, 301; maps, **281, 319**.
Haiti, Republic of, 300; maps, **281**, 319.
Halibut, 45, 245, 265.
Halifax (hăl′ĭ-făks), Nova Scotia, 244, 245, 247, 251; maps, 2, **249**, 319.
Hamilton, Canada, 256; maps, 2, **249**.
Hamilton River, 268, 272; map, **249**.
Hampton Roads, Virginia, 167.

INDEX

Hancock, John, 241.
Hanover (hăn'ō-vẽr), New Hampshire, 240.
Hardware, 242.
Hardwoods, 166, 298.
Harney Peak, 90.
Harpers Ferry, West Virginia, 171.
Harrisburg (hăr'ĭs-bûrg), Pennsylvania, 176, 196, 197; maps, 29, **177, 191**.
Hartford (härt'fẽrd), Connecticut, 24, 224, 242; maps, 29, 34, **225, 238**.
Harvard University, 239, 241.
Harvesting: corn, 85; grain, 321; hemp, 134; potatoes, 184; rice, 110; tobacco, 133; wheat, 40, 83, 257.
Haverhill (hā'vẽr-ĭl), Massachusetts, 235, 239; maps, **225, 238**.
Hawaii (hä-wī'ē), 108.
Hawkinsville (hô'kĭnz-vĭl), Georgia, 159; map, **169**.
Hay, 42, 61, 76, 79, 86, 87, 88, 128, 129, 134, 163, 182, 184, 185, 206, 207, 208, 224, 232, 245, 256, 269.
Hay and Pasture Region, 206.
Helena (hĕl'ē-nȧ), Montana, 57, 62, 76; maps, 28, **60, 73**.
Hemp, 133, 134, 206.
Henequen (sisal), 282, 283.
Herring, 163, 230, 232, 245.
High plains, 78, 79.
Hill farmers, 143.
Hoboken (hō'bō-kĕn), New Jersey, 22, 193; map, **191**.
Holland (hŏl'ănd), 278, 297.
Hollywood (hŏl'ĭ-wŏŏd'), California, 52.
Holyoke (hōl'yōk), Massachusetts, 239; maps, **225, 238**.
Homestake Mine, 90.
Honduras (hŏn-dōō'rȧs), 291, 293, 294; maps, **280**, 319.
Honey, 135, 209.
Hood River Valley, 40.
Hoover Dam, 58, 62.
Hopedale (hōp'dāl), Massachusetts, 270, 271; map, **238**.
Hops, 42.
Horses, 44, 78, 83, 84, 85, 86, 87, 102, 110, 114, 118, 135, 162, 164, 184, 208, 269; map, 134.
Horseshoe Curve, 176, 178.
Hot springs, 68.
Hot Springs Mountain, 118.
Hot Springs National Park, 118.
Houghton (hō'tŭn), Michigan, 210; map, **215**.
Housatonic (hōō'sȧ-tŏn'ĭk) River, 224, 239; map, **225**.
Houston (hūs'tŭn), Texas, 19, 99, 111, 112, 116, 120, 121; maps, 2, 29, **103, 119**.

How Our Country Grew, 25–30.
Huasteca Canyon, 289.
Hudson Bay (hŭd'sŭn), 258, 260; maps, **248–249**, 319.
Hudson, Henry, 190.
Hudson-Mohawk Valley, 196.
Hudson River, 3, 22, 190, 192, 193, 199, 291; map, **177**.
Hudson Strait, 270.
Humber (hŭm'bẽr) River, 263, 268.
Humboldt (hŭm'bōlt) River, 61; map, **60**.
Humus, 80, 152.
Hunting: in Alaska, 273; in Canada, 251, 252, 257; by the Indians, 26; in Labrador, 270; in Minnesota, 95; in the Mississippi marshes, 106.
Huntington (hŭn'tĭng-tŭn), Indiana, 208; maps, **205, 215**.
Huntington, West Virginia, 147, 170; maps, **149, 169**.
Hurricanes, 297.
Hydro-electric plants, 58, 61, 188, 190, 201, 256.
Hydroplanes in Alaska, 274.

Icebergs, 265, 266, 273.
Ice sheet, The great, 92.
Idaho (ī'dȧ-hō), 13, 54, 56, 57, 61, 62, 66, 67, 71, 74, 76; maps, 2, 29, 34, **60, 73**.
Illinois (ĭl-ĭ-noi'), 85, 202, 203, 204, 206, 210, 212, 214, 220, 221; maps, 2, 29, 34, **205, 215**.
Illinois River, 216, 221; map, **205**.
Imperial Valley, 17, 18, 40, 44, 45, 59.
Imports: of Los Angeles, 52; of Nicaragua, 294; of New Orleans, 125; of Seattle, 48; of South America, 314.
Independence Hall, 194.
Indiana (ĭn-dĭ-ăn'ȧ), 8, 9, 85, 202, 203, 204, 206, 207, 208, 209, 210, 211, 214, 216, 218, 220, 221; maps, 2, 29, 34, **205, 215**.
Indiana Harbor, 212.
Indiana limestone, 212.
Indianapolis (ĭn-dĭ-ăn-ăp'ŏ-lĭs), Indiana, 203, 206, 207, 218, 220; maps, 29, **205, 215**.
Indian River, 150; map, **149**.
Indians: in Alaska, 273, 274; in Guatemala, 293; in Labrador, 270; in Mexico, 284, 286, 287; in the United States, 26, 27, 31, 59, 71, 100, 129, 180, 192, 228; in the West Indies, 298.
Indian Territory, 27.
Indian totems, Alaska, 274.
Inland Empire, 40.
Inland Passage, 274.
International Peace Bridge, 7.

Interoceanic Railroad, 282.
Iowa (ī'ō-wȧ), 78, 79, 86, 87, 88, 96, 206; maps, 2, 29, 34, **81, 94**.
Ireland (īr'lănd), 262.
Iron and steel, 6, 8, 90, 95, 96, 127, 137, 138, 140, 147, 148, 167, 170, 176, 187, 194, 196, 198, 210, 212, 214, 218, 300.
Iron ore, 6, 8, 63, 66, 74, 76, 79, 90, 91, 95, 137, 138, 142, 170, 188, 196, 198, 203, 204, 212, 250, 268, 288, 300, 320.
Irrigation, 12, 13, 17, 40, 41, 42, 56, 57, 58, 59, 61, 62, 76, 86, 87, 107, 108, 110, 120, 260.
Isthmus of Panama (păn-ȧ-mä'), 295, 317; maps, **281**, 319.
Isthmus of Tehuantepec (tā-wän-tȧ-pĕk'), 278.
Italy (ĭt'ȧ-lĭ), 137, 252.

Jackson, Mississippi, 127, 142, 212; maps, 29, **131, 139**.
Jacksonville, Florida, 1, 19, 20, 147, 156, 166; maps, 2, 29, **149, 169**.
Jamaica (jȧ-mā'kȧ), 297, 298, 300, 302, 317; maps, **281**, 319.
Jamaica ginger, 300.
James Bay, 260.
James River, 20; map, **149**.
Japan (jȧ-păn'), 50.
Jaurez, 23; map, **280**.
Java (jä'vȧ), 108.
Jefferson City, Missouri, 79; maps, 29, **81, 94**.
Jefferson, Thomas, 170, 171.
Jenks, Joseph, 236.
Jersey City, New Jersey, 22, 193; maps, 29, **177, 191**.
Jewelry, 224, 242.
Johnstown, Pennsylvania, 196, 198; maps, 29, **177, 191**.
Juneau (jōō'nō), 274, 276; maps, **248**, 319.
Juniata (jōō-nĭ-ăt'ȧ) River, 176; map, **177**.

Kalamazoo (kăl-ȧ-mȧ-zōō'), Michigan, 221; maps, **205, 215**.
Kanawha (kȧ-nô'whȧ) Valley, 170.
Kansas (kăn'zȧs), 78, 79, 83, 84, 86, 87, 90, 92, 96, 101, 107, 114; maps, 2, 28, 34, **81, 94**.
Kansas City, 79, 88, 89, 95, 96, 97, 127; maps, 29, **81, 94**.
Kaolin, 170, 193.
Kearney (kär'nĭ), New Jersey, 188.
Keeweenaw Peninsula, 210; map, **205**.
Kennebec (kĕn-ē-bĕk') River, 224, 240; map, **225**.
Kennecott, Alaska, 274.
Kensico Dam and Reservoir, 179.

INDEX

Kentucky (kĕn-tŭk'ĭ), 126, 127, 128, 132, 133, 134, 135, 136, 137, 140, 142, 144, 206; maps, 2, 28, 34, **131**, **139**.
Kentucky Derby, 135.
Ketchikan (kĕch-ĭ-kän'), Alaska, 274.
Key, Francis Scott, 23.
Key West, Florida, 152, 156, 298, 300; maps, 29, **149**, **169**.
Kingston, Canada, 255, 298, 317; maps, 2, **249**.
Klamath (klăm'áth) Mountains, 15, 34.
Knoxville (nŏks'vĭl), Tennessee, 138, 140; maps, 29, **131**, **139**.
Kodaks, 5, 7.
Kumquat, 152.

Labrador (lăb-rá-dôr'), 262, 270–272; coast of, 270; fishing, 272; forests, 272; land of, 270; people, 270; water power, 272; maps, 2, **248**–**249**.
Labrador Current, 266.
Lackawanna (lăk-á-wŏn'á), New York, 6, 198; maps, **177**, **191**.
Lake Champlain, 180, 240; maps, **177**, **225**.
Lake District of Florida, 152.
Lake Drummon, Dismal Swamp, 165.
Lake Erie (ē'rĭ), 5, 6, 8, 95, 178, 185, 192, 196, 198, 207, 216, 217, 218, 219, 256; maps, **177**, **205**.
Lake Huron (hū'rŏn), 216, 256; map, **205**.
Lake Louise, 258, 260.
Lake Managua (mä-nä'gwä), 294; map, **280**.
Lake Michigan, 8, 9, 10, 90, 207, 214, 216, 218; map, **205**.
Lake Nicaragua (nĭk-á-rä'gwá), 294; map, **280**.
Lake Okechobee (ō-kĕ-chō'bē), 152; map, **149**.
Lake Ontario (ŏn-tā'rĭ-ō), 3, 5, 175, 178, 185, 198, 200, 255, 256; map, **177**.
Lake Placid, 180, 181.
Lake Pontchartrain (pŏn'chár-trān), 125; map, **103**.
Lake St. Clair, 216, 217; map, **205**.
Lake St. John, 252; map, **249**.
Lake Superior, 6, 8, 90, 93, 95, 204, 212, 256; map, **205**.
Lake Superior District, 137, 196.
Lake trout, 210.
Lake Washington, Seattle, 48.
Lakewood, Ohio, 8; maps, **205**, **215**.
Lancaster (lăŋ'kás-tēr), Pennsylvania, 196; maps, **177**, **191**.
Land of Ten Thousand Lakes, 92.

Lansing (lăn'sĭng), Michigan, 203, 212; maps, 29, **205**, **215**.
Latitude, 36, 323–324.
Laurentian (lô-rĕn'shĭ-ăn) Mountains, 254.
Lawrence (lô'rĕns), Massachusetts, 235, 239; maps, **225**, **238**.
Lead, 13, 47, 57, 63, 64, 66, 74, 79, 88, 90, 97, 211, 247, 256, 268, 284, 300, 320.
Leadville, Colorado, 64; maps, **60**, **73**.
Leather, 10, 97, 118, 214, 218, 224, 235, 266.
Lemons, 42, 44, 45, 152.
L'Enfant, Major, 170.
Lettuce, 58, 160, 232.
Levees, 104, 105, 110, 127, 128.
Lewis and Clark Highway, 320.
Lewiston (lū'ĭs-tŭn), Maine, 240; maps, **225**, **238**.
Lexington (lĕk'sĭng-tŭn), Kentucky, 133, 142; maps, **131**, **139**.
Liberty Bell, Philadelphia, 22.
Liberty Bell of Mexico, 287.
Lignite, 210.
Lincoln (lĭŋ'kŭn), Nebraska, 79, 96; maps, 29, **81**, **94**.
Lincoln, Abraham, 172, 221.
Lincoln Memorial, 172.
Lindbergh, Colonel, 35, 97.
Linen, 42, 288.
Little Rock, Arkansas, 99, 118, 122; maps, 29, **103**, **119**.
Live stock, 32, 57, 76, 79, 93, 96, 99, 127, 142, 147, 203, 206, 207, 216, 247, 254, 255, 283.
Lobsters, 230, 232, 245.
Lockport, Canada, 246.
Locomotives, 5, 170.
Lode mining, 64.
Loganberries, 42.
Logging, 38, 67, 294.
Logwood, 300.
London (lŭn'dŭn), 214.
Longfellow, Henry W., 240, 241.
Long Island, 22, 182, 185, 186, 190, 192, 244; maps, 29, **177**, **191**, **225**, **238**.
Long Island Sound, 22, 182, 183, 192, 223, 232, 236.
Longitude, 36, 323–324.
Long Range, 264.
Longview, Washington, 48; maps, **37**, **49**.
Lookout Mountain, 141; map, **131**.
Loon Lake, 181.
Lorain (lô-rān'), Ohio, 8; maps, **205**, **215**.
Los Angeles (lŏs ăŋ'gĕl-ĕs), California, 15, 17, 32, 45, 47, 50, 51, 52; maps, 2, 28, **37**, **49**.
Los Angeles River, 52.
Louisiana (lōō-ē'zē-ăn'á), 19, 99, 100, 101, 102, 104, 107, 108, 110, 112, 113, 114, 116, 125, 126, 132, 134, 135, 210; maps, 2, 28, 34, **103**, **119**.
Louis XIV, 99.
Louisville (lōō'ĭ-vĭl), Kentucky, 127, 133, 142; maps, 29, **131**, **139**.
Lowell (lō'ĕl), Massachusetts, 235, 239, 241; maps, 29, **225**, **238**.
Lowell, F. C., 235.
Lower California, 278, 283.
Lucin cut-off, 76.
Lumber, 13, 35, 38, 40, 48, 50, 66, 74, 92, 93, 95, 99, 120, 122, 125, 136, 138, 140, 142, 147, 148, 156, 164, 167, 168, 196, 203, 204, 210, 216, 218, 228, 240, 247, 268.
Lumbering: in Alaska, 274, 277; in Canada, 252, 254, 260; in the United States, 35, 38, 39, 66, 74, 76, 93, 101, 102, 126, 136, 164, 165, 180, 186, 210, 227, 228.
Lunenberg (lōō'nĕn-bûrg), Nova Scotia, 246.
Luray (lû-rā') Caverns, 162, 163.
Lynn (lĭn), Massachusetts, 235, 236; maps, **225**, **238**.

MacArthur, General Douglas, 122.
Machinery, 10, 97, 125, 133, 138, 140, 148, 158, 168, 196, 203, 216, 218, 224, 234, 235, 236, 270, 283, 320.
Mackenzie (má-kĕn'zĭ) River, 260, 318; maps, **248**, 319.
Mackerel, 45, 163, 182, 230, 232, 245.
Madison, Wisconsin, 203; maps, 29, **205**, **215**.
Magnesium, 125.
Maguey (Sisal hemp), 283.
Mahogany, 125, 283, 293, 294, 298, 300.
Maine (mān), 175, 223, 224, 228, 232, 233, 234, 236, 239; maps, 2, 29, 34, **225**, **238**.
Maine Forestry District, 228.
Mammoth Cave, 144, 145.
Manchester (măn'chĕs-tēr), New Hampshire, 224, 235, 240; map, **238**.
Manganese, 250.
Mango, 153.
Manhattan Island, 22, 31, 190, 192.
Manitoba (măn-ĭ-tō'bá), Canada, 247, 257; map, **248**.
Manufacturing: in Canada, 254, 255, 260; in Mexico, 284, 288; in North America, 320; in the United States, 8, 10, 20, 22, 24, 40, 76, 96, 120, 136, 137, 138, 140, 142, 150, 156, 167, 168, 192, 193, 198, 218, 221, 234, 236, 239, 240, 242; in the West Indies, 298.

INDEX

Manzanillo (män-sä-nēl′yō), Mexico, 282; map, **280**.
Maple sugar and syrup, 224, 230, 231.
Marble, 137, 140, 166, 236, 240.
Marblehead, Massachusetts, 223, 232; map, **238**.
Marble Head, 263.
Marconi, 269.
Marie Antoinette, 202.
Marietta, Ohio, 202; map, **215**.
Maritime Provinces, 244, 245, 247, 250, 251; map, **249**.
Marshall, John, 46.
Martinique (mär-tĭ-nēk′), 297, 298; map, **281**.
Martinsville, Indiana, 210; map, **215**.
Maryland (měr′ĭ-lănd), 23, 147, 150, 158, 167, 170; maps, 2, 29, 34, **149, 169**.
Massachusetts (măs-á-chōō′sĕts), 3, 24, 158, 185, 208, 223, 224, 228, 229, 232, 235, 236, 239; maps, 2, 29, 34, **225, 238**.
Matamoras (măt-á-mō′ras), Mexico, 108; maps, 29, **280**.
Maya (mä′yä) Monuments, 291, 293.
Mayas, 284, 287, 293.
Mayflower, 244.
McGill University, 254.
McKay, Donald, 229.
McKeesport, Pennsylvania, 196; maps, **177, 191**.
McKinley National Monument, 221.
McKinley, William, 221.
Meat packing, 10, 40, 74, 76, 88, 93, 95, 96, 97, 121, 122, 192, 193, 196, 198, 207, 208, 214, 216, 218, 220, 221.
Medford, Massachusetts, 228; maps, **225, 238**.
Meeker, Ezra, 216.
Mediterranean countries, 44, 245.
Mediterranean regions, 42.
Mediterranean Sea, 154.
Memphis (měm′fĭs), Tennessee, 127, 128, 142, 143; maps, 29, **131, 139**.
Mercury in Mexico, 288.
Merida (mā′rĕ-thä), Mexico, 282; map, **280**.
Meriden, Connecticut, 236, 242; maps, **225, 238**.
Meridians, 324.
Merrimack River, 224, 235, 240; maps, **225, 238**.
Mesabi iron mines, 95, 212.
Mesas, 17.
Mesa Verde National Park, 68, 75.
Mestizos, 284.
Mexican Plateau, 317; map, **230**.

Mexicans, 108, 112.
Mexico (měk′sĭ-kō), 17, 30, 99, 118, 120, 130, 153, 306, 309; maps, **280–281**, 319.
Mexico City, 282, 284, 287, 288, 292; maps, **280**, 319.
Mexico, Our Southern Neighbor, 278–290: agriculture, 282, 283; area, 278; inland cities, 287, 288; climate, 279; commerce, 284; education, 288, 290; government, 287; harbors, 279, 282; livestock, 283; living conditions, 283; manufacturing, 284; minerals and mining, 283, 284, 285; people, 284, 287; petroleum in, 284; physical characteristics, 278, 279; rivers, 279, 282; shape, 278; towns, 288; transportation, 281; wealth, 278; maps, **280–281**, 319.
Miami (mī-ăm′ĭ), Florida, 154, 166; maps, 29, **149, 169**.
Miami Beach, 154; maps, **149, 169**.
Michigan (mĭsh′ĭ-găn), 90, 203, 204, 206, 207, 209, 210, 212, 214, 216, 217, 220, 221, 256; maps, 2, 29, 34, **205, 215**.
Michigan Central Railroad, 216.
Middle Atlantic States, 54, 175–201, 202; important products, 175; statistics, 175; maps, **177, 191**.
Midnight Sun, 273.
Milwaukee (mĭl-wô′kê), Wisconsin, 10, 203, 206, 207, 214, 217, 218; maps, 2, 29, **205, 215**.
Minerals: in Canada, 250, 256, 260; in Mexico, 283; in Newfoundland, 266, 268; in North America, 320; in the United States, 26, 46, 47, 63, 64, 66, 90, 118, 126, 137, 166, 186, 187, 203.
Mining: in Canada, 260; in Cuba, 300; drift and shaft mining, 187; in Mexico, 283, 285, 288; in the United States, 13, 46, 63, 64, 65, 66, 74, 76, 136, 137, 187, 210.
Minneapolis (mĭn-ê-ăp′ô-lĭs), Minnesota, 10, 11, 12, 79, 88, 89, 92, 93; maps, 2, 29, **81, 94**.
Minnehaha Falls, 11.
Minnesota (mĭn-ê-sō′tá), 10, 11, 12, 78, 79, 82, 83, 84, 88, 90, 92, 93, 95, 96, 204, 206, 212, 216; maps, 2, 29, 34, **81, 94**.
Mission Station in Labrador, 271.
Mississippi (mĭs-ĭ-sĭp′ĭ), 19, 126, 127, 128, 129, 132, 134, 135, 136, 138, 140, 142; maps, 2, 29, 34, **131, 139**.

Mississippi Delta, 104, 105, 108, 127; maps, **103, 131**.
Mississippi River, 11, 12, 19, 30, 78, 89, 91, 93, 96, 97, 99, 100, 104, 105, 106, 108, 110, 122, 124, 125, 126, 127, 128, 136, 142, 202, 216, 221, 318; maps, **29, 103, 131, 319**.
Mississippi Valley, 19, 30, 54, 78; maps, **29**, 319.
Mississippi-Yazoo Basin, 142.
Missoula (mĭ-zōō′lá), Montana, 13, 76; maps, 2, 28, **60, 73**.
Missouri (mĭ-zōō′rĭ), 78, 79, 86, 87, 90, 92, 113, 126, 221; maps, 2, 29, 34, **81, 94**.
Missouri River, 12, 56, 62, 76, 86, 95, 96, 97, 127, 304; maps, **81, 94**.
Mixed farming, 86, 126, 132, 135, 140, 156, 163, 184, 256.
Mobile (mô-bēl′), Alabama, 19, 20, 136, 138, 140, 142; maps, 2, 29, **131, 139**.
Mobile Bay, 19, 140; maps, **131, 139**.
Mobile River, 19; maps, **131, 139**.
Mohair, 19, 42, 114.
Mohave (mô-hä′vä) Desert, 15, 47; maps, **37**, 49.
Mohawk (mō′hôk) River, 196; map, **177**.
Mohawk Valley, 3, 175, 180; map, **177**.
Moline (mô-lēn′), Illinois, 214; maps, **205, 215**.
Moncton (mŭŋk′tăn), Canada, 251; maps, 2, **249**.
Money crops and supply crops, 83.
Monongahela (mô-nŏŋ-gá-hē′lá), 194, 196; map, **177**.
Montana (mŏn-tăn′á), 12, 54, 56, 57, 59, 61, 62, 63, 64, 66, 68, 71, 72, 74, 76, 307; maps, 2, 28, 34, **60, 73**.
Montauk Point, 183; map, **225**.
Monterey (mŏn-tĕ-rā′), Mexico, 282, 288; maps, **280**, 319.
Montezuma, 287.
Montgomery, Alabama, 127, 142; maps, 29, **131, 139**.
Mont Pelée, 297, 298.
Montpelier (mŏnt-pēl′yĕr), Vermont, 224, 240; maps, 29, **225, 238**.
Montreal (mŏnt-rê-ôl′), Canada, 247, 251, 253, 254, 255, 257, 261; maps, 2, 29, **249**, 319.
Moose, 251.
Moosehead Lake, 236; maps, **225, 238**.
Mormons, 56.
Morrow, Dwight W., 288.
Motion pictures, 32, 50, 52, 168.

INDEX

Mount Adams, 224.
Mount Chocorua (chŏ-kŏr′ōō-á), 237.
Mount Desert Island, 239; map, **225**.
Mount Greylock, 223; map, **225**.
Mount Hood, 14, 15, 32; maps, 28, **37**.
Mount Jefferson, 224.
Mount Lassen (lăs′ĕn), 33; maps, 28, **37**.
Mount Lassen National Park, 34.
Mount Le Conte, 144.
Mount Madison, 224.
Mount Marcy, 180; map, **177**.
Mount McKinley, 273, 274, 275; map, **319**.
Mount Mitchell, 148; map, **149**.
Mount Orizaba (ō-rē-sä′bä), 279; map, **280**.
Mount Rainier (rā-nēr′), 13, 15, 32; maps, 28, **37**.
Mount Rainier National Park, 34, 35.
Mount Royal, 253.
Mount Royal Park, 254.
Mount Shasta (shăs′tá), 15, 32; maps, 28, **37**.
Mount Stanton, Glacier National Park, 69.
Mount St. Elias (ĕ-lī′ăs), 273; map, **248**.
Mount Vernon, Indiana, 209; map, **215**.
Mount Vernon, Virginia, 20.
Mount Washington, 224; map, **225**.
Mountaineers of Kentucky and Tennessee, 143.
Mountain passes, 72.
Mountains: in Alaska, 273; in Canada, 251, 258, 260; in Central America, 292; in Mexico, 278, 279; in North America, 317, 318; in the United States, 1, 15, 17, 24, 25, 27, 32, 34, 40, 46, 54, 55, 56, 57, 58, 62, 71, 72, 76, 126, 143, 144, 148, 168, 223, 236; in the West Indies, 300, 302.
Mountain States, The, 54–77, 78; important products, 57; statistics, 57; maps, **60**, **73**.
Mules, 74, 85, 87, 110, 114, 118, 129, 135, 144, 164, 208, 294; map, 134.
Mullet, 135, 153, 163.
Muscle Shoals, 143.
Muskmelons, map, 160.
Muskrats, 104.

Napoleon, 99, 298.
Narragansett Bay, 242; maps, **225**, **238**.
Narrows, The, 190, 192.

Nashua (năsh′ú-á), New Hampshire, 240; maps, **225**, **238**.
Nashville (năsh′vĭl), Tennessee, 127, 140; maps, **131**, **139**.
Nashville Basin, 140.
Natchez (năch′ĕz), Mississippi, 142; maps, **131**, **139**.
National Forests, 38, 40, 67, 90, 136.
National Monuments, 68.
National Parks, 34, 68, 144.
Natural gas, 47, 76, 137, 147, 166, 170, 188, 196, 212, 320.
Naval stores, 140, 147, 164, 166, 167.
Nebraska (nē-brăs′ká), 78, 79, 84, 86, 87, 90, 95, 96, 101; maps, 2, 28, 34, **81**, **94**.
Negroes, 110, 112, 129, 293, 298, 300, 302.
Netherlands (nĕth′ēr-lăndz), The, 297.
Nevada (nē-vä′dá), 54, 56, 57, 58, 61, 62, 64, 66, 74; maps, 2, 28, 34, **60**, **73**.
Newark (nū′ērk), New Jersey, 22, 176, 193; maps, 29, **177**, **191**.
Newark Airport, 22, 193, 195.
New Bedford (bĕd′fẽrd), Massachusetts, 228, 239; maps, 29, **225**, **238**.
New Britain (brĭt′′n), Connecticut, 242; maps, **225**, **238**.
New Brunswick, 22, 193, 239, 244, 247, 250, 251; map, **249**.
Newburyport (nū′bēr-ĭ-pōrt), Massachusetts, 235; maps, **225**, **238**.
New Castle (nū′cas′l), Pennsylvania, 196; maps, **177**, **191**.
New England, 3, 31, 150, 202, 244; maps, **225**, **238**.
New England Church, 231.
New England States, The, 223–243, 245; important products, 223; statistics, 224; maps, **225**, **238**.
Newfoundland (nū′fŭnd-lănd), 250, 262–270; animals, 264, 265, 269; climate, 269; farming in, 269; fishing, 264, 265, 266, 267; forests, 264, 266, 268; land of, 264; minerals, 266, 268, 269; nearness to Canada and Europe, 262; people, 262, 264, 265, 266, 269; plants, 264, 265, 269; seal fisheries, 266; tourist attractions, 269; water power, 266, 268; map, **249**, 319.
Newfoundland and Labrador, 262–272; maps, **249**, 319.
Newfoundland Banks, 232.
New Hampshire (hămp′shĭr), 175, 223, 224, 227, 228, 233, 234, 235, 236, 237, 239, 240; maps, 2, 29, 34, **225**, **238**.

New Haven (hā′v′n), Connecticut, 24, 242; maps, 29, **225**, **238**.
New Jersey (jûr′zĭ), 22, 175, 176, 180, 182, 185, 186, 188, 190, 192, 193, 195; maps, 2, 29, 34, **177**, **191**.
New Mexico (mĕk′sĭ-cō), 54, 56, 57, 62, 68, 74, 76, 107, 118; maps, 2, 28, 34, **60**, **73**.
New Orleans (ôr′lĕ-ănz), Louisiana, 17, 19, 97, 99, 100, 107, 108, 112, 116, 117, 122, 124, 125, 126, 127, 203, 292; maps, 2, 29, **103**, **119**.
Newport (nū′pōrt), Rhode Island, 242; maps, **225**, **238**.
Newport News, Virginia, 167; maps, **149**, **169**.
New York (State), 3, 35, 118, 162, 175, 176, 178, 179, 180, 182, 184, 185, 188, 193, 198, 199, 200, 202; maps, 2, 29, 34, **177**, **191**.
New York Barge Canal, 5, 192, 198.
New York Bay, 190, 192, 193; maps, **177**, **191**.
New York Central Railroad, 220.
New York City, 5, 22, 31, 152, 175, 176, 178, 179, 182, 185, 186, 190, 192, 193, 194, 196, 208, 214, 244, 261, 262, 269, 294; maps, 2, 29, 34, **177**, **191**.
New Zealand (zē′lănd), 234.
Niagara Falls (nī-ăg′á-rá), 5, 6, 125, 188, 190, 198, 200, 201, 256, 272; maps, 2, 29, **177**, **191**.
Niagara River, 15, 198; map, **177**.
Nicaragua (nĭk-á-rä′gwá), 293, 294, 296; maps, **280–281**.
Nicaraguan Canal, 294.
Nickel, 256, 268, 320.
Nile (nīl) **River,** 58, 107.
Nitrates, 125, 143, 167.
Nome (nōm), Alaska, 273; map, **319**.
Norfolk (nôr′fŏk), Rhode Island, 228.
Norfolk, Virginia, 159, 167; maps, 29, **149**, **169**.
North America, 252, 262, 273; summary of, 317–322; agriculture, 318; climate, 318; communication, 318, 320; drainage, 317, 318; favorable commercial position, 317; manufacturing, 320; mineral resources, 320; population, distribution of, 320, 322; power resources, 320; relief, 317, 318; size and extent, 317; soil, 318; transportation, 318, 320; vegetation, 318; map, **319**.
North Atlantic Ocean, 136.

INDEX

North Atlantic States (New England), 175; maps, **225, 238**.
North Bay, 256; maps, 2, **249**.
North Carolina (kăr-ō-lī′nȧ), 20, 144, 147, 148, 150, 156, 158, 159, 160, 164, 167, 168, 171; maps, 2, 29, 34, **149, 169**.
North Dakota (dȧ-kō′tȧ), 78, 79, 83, 87, 95, 101; maps, 2, 28, 34, **81, 94**.
Northern Hemisphere, 317.
North Platte River, 86, 87; map, **81**.
North Pole, 273, 317, 323–324.
North Temperate Zone, 317.
Northwest Territory, 247, 260.
Nova Scotia (nō-vȧ skō′shȧ), 200, 244, 245, 247, 251, 262, 268; map, **249**.
Norway (nôr′wā), 167, 252.
Nuts, 42, 127, 132.

Oats: 40, 83, 84, 86, 87, 88, 112, 163, 184, 206, 208, 245, 256, 269; map, 208.
Obregon, General, 287.
Ogden (ŏg′dĕn), Utah, 74, 76; maps, 28, **60, 73**.
Ogden Cut-off, 76.
Ohio (ō-hī′ō), 6, 85, 202, 203, 204, 206, 207, 210, 212, 213, 214, 217, 218, 219, 220, 221; maps, 2, 29, 34, **205, 215**.
Ohio River, 27, 127, 135, 142, 163, 170, 194, 202, 214, 218, 219; maps, 29, **205**.
Ohio Valley, 170, 218.
Oil. See *Petroleum*.
Oil City, Pennsylvania, 188; maps, **177, 191**.
Oil Creek, 188.
Oil (petroleum) refineries, 19, 22, 47, 114, 115, 116, 120, 122, 125, 166, 188, 193, 194, 211.
Oil shale, 66, 250, 269.
Oklahoma (ō-klȧ-hō′mȧ), 27, 92, 99, 100, 101, 112, 113, 114, 116, 122, 193; maps, 2, 29, 34, **103, 119**.
Oklahoma City, Oklahoma, 99, 115, 116, 122; maps, 29, **103 119**.
Old Boston Statehouse 24.
Old Faithful (Geyser), 68.
"Old Ironsides" (The Constitution), 228, 229.
Old Point Comfort, Virginia, 167.
Old World, 42.
Olives, 15, 42, 44, 153.
Olympia (ō-lĭm′pĭ-ȧ), Washington, 13, 32, 42; maps, 28, **37, 49**.
Omaha (ō-mȧ-hô), 79, 88, 95, 96, 207; maps, 29, **81, 94**.
Onions, 207; map, 160.
Ontario (ŏn-tā′rĭ-ō), 245, 247, 254, 255, 256, 261; maps, 29, **248–249**.

Oranges, 15, 32, 42, 44, 45, 58, 101, 108, 152, 298; map, 44.
Orchards, 5, 6, 15, 40, 42, 57, 86, 132, 184, 185, 207, 256.
Ore, defined, 63.
Oregon (ŏr′ĕ-gŏn), 13, 15, 30, 32, 34, 40, 42, 45, 48, 210, 260; maps, 2, 28, 34, **37, 49**.
Oregon Trail, The, 14, 216.
Orilia (ō-rĭl′ĭ-ȧ), Canada, 256; map, **2**.
Orizaba (ō-rĕ-sä′bä), Mexico, 278; map, **280**.
Orr, Hugh, 236.
Ottawa (ŏt′ȧ-wȧ), 255; maps, 2, **249**.
Ottawa River, 254; map, **249**.
Oxen, 74, 228, 245, 294, 300.
Oysters, 46, 107, 136, 147, 153, 162, 164, 168, 170, 182, 230, 232.
Ozark (ō′zärk) Mountains, 78, 92, 100, 118, 122; map, **103**.

Pachuca (pä-chōō′kä), Mexico, 285, 288; map, **280**.
Pacific (pȧ-sĭf′ĭk) Coast, 260.
Pacific Ocean, 13, 14, 15, 24, 25, 45, 46, 48, 258, 259, 273, 274, 288, 291, 292–296, 317, 318.
Pacific States, The, 32–53, 54, 67, 83; important products, 32; statistics, 32; maps, **37, 49**.
Paducah (pȧ-dū′kȧ), Kentucky, 142; maps, **131, 139**.
Palestine (păl′ĕs-tīn), 63.
Palm Beach, Florida, 156; maps, **149, 169**.
Panama (păn-ȧ-mä′), 293, 295, 317.
Panama Canal, 47, 48, 218, 295, 296; maps, **281**, 319.
Panama, Isthmus of, 46; maps, **281**, 319.
Pan-American Building, Washington, D. C., 172.
Panhandle, The, Texas, 122; Alaska, 274.
Panuco River, 282, 284.
Papaua, 153.
Paper, 35, 38, 140, 203, 210, 221, 224, 228, 230, 239, 247, 252, 254, 268, 272.
Parliament Building; Ottawa, Canada, 255; Victoria, Canada, 260.
Parsnips, 814.
Parthenon, The, 140, 141.
Pascagoula (păs-kȧ-gōō′lȧ), Mississippi, 140; maps, **131, 139**.
Passaic (pȧ-sā′ĭk), New Jersey, 193; map, **191**.
Passaic River, 193, 195.
Passamaquoddy (păs-ȧ-mȧ-kwŏd′ĭ) Bay, 239.
Pass Christian, 106.

Paterson (păt′ĕr-sŭn), New Jersey, 193; maps, **177, 191**.
Pawtucket (pô-tŭk′ĕt), Rhode Island, 234, 242; maps, **225, 238**.
Peaches, 5, 20, 40, 44, 92, 112, 156, 160, 161, 163, 184, 185, 207, 209, 232, 256.
Peanuts, 112, 127, 132, 134, 147, 156, 158, 160.
Pears, 5, 40, 44, 92, 112, 184, 185, 207, 209.
Peas, 41, 129, 185, 207.
Pecans, 20, 112, 160, 161.
Pennsylvania (pĕn-sĭl-vā′nĭ-ȧ), 6, 175, 176, 180, 182, 184, 186, 187, 188, 189, 194, 196, 197, 200, 218, 292; maps, 2, 29, 34, **177, 191**.
Pennsylvania Avenue, Washington, D. C., 170.
Pennsylvania Railroad, 175, 220.
Penn, William, 194.
Penobscot (pĕ-nŏb′skŏt) River, 224, 240; map, **225**.
Pensacola (pĕn-sȧ-kō′lȧ), Florida, 152, 153, 156; maps, 29, **149, 169**.
Peons in Mexico, 284.
People: in Canada, 251, 252, 255, 261; in Central America, 293; in Labrador, 270; in Mexico, 284, 288; in Newfoundland, 264, 265, 266, 269; in North America and other continents, 320, 322; in the United States, 10, 13, 25, 27, 30, 42, 46, 47, 54, 61, 76, 120, 125, 126, 127, 134, 143, 144, 153, 168, 175, 182, 192, 196, 204, 206, 208, 235; in the West Indies, 298, 299, 302.
Peoria (pĕ-ō′rĭ-ȧ), Illinois, 221; maps, 29, **205, 215**.
Peppermint, 207, 221.
Perch, 232.
Pershing, General, 173.
Petersburg, Alaska, 274.
Petitcodiac River, 245.
Petroleum (oil): in Alaska, 274; in Mexico, 279, 282, 283, 284; in Newfoundland, 269; in North America, 320; in the United States, 15, 17, 19, 32, 46, 47, 57, 66, 74, 76, 79, 90, 96, 99, 114, 115, 116, 120, 125, 135, 166, 170, 188, 210, 220, 247.
Petroleum products, 32, 48, 99, 114, 116, 125, 166, 167, 170, 176, 193, 210.
Philadelphia (fĭl-ȧ-dĕl′fĭ-ȧ), Pennsylvania, 22, 175, 176, 185, 186, 194, 208; maps, 2, 29, **177, 191**.
Phoenix (fē′nĭks), Arizona, 17, 57, 76; maps, 2, 28, **60, 73**.
Phosphate Rock, 64, 66, 137, 147, 153, 156, 157, 167.
Pickerel, 232.

INDEX

Piedmont, 20, 148, 150, 158, 166, 171, 175.
Pierre, Martinique (mär-tĭ-nēk′), 297.
Pierre (pēr), South Dakota, 79, 95; maps, 28, **81**, **94**.
Pig iron, 212.
Pikes Peak, 68; maps, 28, **60**.
Pike, Zebulon, 11.
Pilgrims, 226.
Pima cotton, 58.
Pineapples, 279, 298, 300.
Pinnacle Peak, 35.
Pioneers, 27.
Pipe lines, 47, 114, 188, 193, 210.
Pittsburgh (pĭts′bûrg), Pennsylvania, 138, 175, 178, 187, 194, 196, 218; maps, 29, **177**, **191**.
Pittsfield (pĭts′fēld), Massachusetts, 3, 235, 239; maps, **225**, **238**.
Platte (plăt) River, 86; map, **81**.
Plums, 5, 40, 44, 112, 207, 256.
Plymouth (plĭm′ŭth), Massachusetts, 226; map, **238**.
Plymouth Bay, 226.
Plywood, 38.
Pocatello (pō-ká-tĕl′ō), Idaho, 76; maps, 28, **60**, **73**.
Pocono (pō′kō-nō) Hills, 180.
Point Barrow, 273, 274; map, **319**.
Pompano, 107, 135, 163.
Ponce de Leon, 150, 154.
Pontiac (pŏn′tĭ-ăk), Michigan, 212; maps, **205**, **215**.
Pony Express, 72, 74.
Popocatepetl (pō-pō-kä-tā′pĕt′l), 279; map, **280**.
Port Angeles, Washington, 48; maps, **37**, **49**.
Port Arthur, Texas, 19, 116, 258; maps, **103**, **119**.
Port-aux-Basques, 265; map, **249**.
Port Huron, Michigan, 256; maps, 29, **205**, **215**.
Portland, Maine, 50, 224, 228, 240; maps, 29, **225**, **238**.
Portland, Oregon, 13, 14, 15, 32, 45, 48, 50; maps, 2, 28, **37**, **49**.
Portsmouth (pōrts′mŭth), Virginia, 167, 228, 240; maps, 29, **149**, **169**.
Portugal (pōr′tū-găl), 262, 278.
Potash, 47, 63, 167.
Potatoes, 40, 48, 84, 86, 108, 184, 206, 224, 232, 233, 247, 256, 269.
Potomac (pō-tō′măk) River, 20, 170, 171; map, **149**.
Pottery, 22, 26, 170, 193, 212, 213, 214, 284.
Poughkeepsie (pō-kĭp′sĭ), New York, 196, 199; maps, **177**, **191**.
Poultry, 40, 92, 208.
Prairie fires, 78, 79.
Prairie plains, 78, 79, 80.

Prairie Provinces of Canada, 257.
Prairies, 72, 202, 318.
President, The, 170.
Presidential Range, White Mountains, 224.
Pribilof (prē-bē-lŏf′) Islands, 276, 277.
Prime Meridian, 324.
Prince Edward Island, 244, 245, 247, 250, 251; map, **249**.
Proctor (prŏk′tēr), Vermont, 236, 240; map, **238**.
Progreso (prô-gra′sō), Mexico, 282; map **280**.
Prospecting for gold, 63.
Providence (prŏv′ĭ-dĕns), Rhode Island, 224, 235, 240, 242; maps, 29, **225**, **238**.
Providence River, 240.
Prunes, 42, 44.
Puebla (pwä′blä), Mexico, 288; map, **280**.
Pueblo (pwĕb′lō), Colorado, 66, 74; maps, 28, **60**, **73**.
Pueblos, 26.
Puerto Barrios (pwĕr′tō bär′rē-ōs), 291, 293; map, **280**.
Puerto Rico (rē′kō), 297, 301, 302; map, **281**.
Puget (pū′jĕt) Basin, 13, 40, 42.
Puget Sound, 13, 45, 46, 48.
Pulaski (pû-lăs′kĭ) Bridge, 195.
Pullman (pŏŏl′măn), 10.
Pumice, 90.
Puritans, 4.
Put-in-Bay, Lake Erie, 219.
Putnam, General Rufus, 202.
"Pyramid of the Sun" (Aztec temple), 286.

Quarrying in New England, 236.
Quebec (kwē-bĕk′), (City) Canada, 245, 247, 251, 252, 253, 255; maps, 2, 29, **248–249**.
Quebec (Province), 245, 247, 251, 254, 255, 261; maps, 2, 29, **248–249**.
Quebec Bridge, 253.
Queens Park, Toronto, 255.
Quincy (kwĭn′sĭ), Illinois, 221, 236; maps, **205**, **215**.

Radios, 82, 144, 194, 320.
Radium in Canada, 260.
Railroads: in Alaska, 274; in Canada, 244, 251, 258; in Mexico, 282, 288; in Newfoundland, 265; in the United States, 1, 5, 6, 8, 10, 19, 20, 22, 24, 26, 30, 34, 40, 47, 72, 74, 80, 88, 95, 97, 102, 108, 120, 122, 127, 129, 140, 142, 150, 156, 164, 166, 167, 168, 176, 178, 182, 186, 188, 194, 196, 202, 203, 204, 207, 212, 216, 218, 220.

Railway mileage in North America, 318.
Rainbow Natural Bridge, 71.
Rainfall, 13, 86, 100, 101, 108, 147, 156, 182, 273, 282, 283, 297, 300; map, 56.
Raleigh (rô′lĭ), North Carolina, 20, 147, 168; maps, 2, 29, **149**, **169**.
Raleigh, Sir Walter, 158, 168.
Ranches, 114, 118, 134, 288.
Rangeley (rānj′lĭ) Lakes, 239; maps, **225**, **238**.
Raspberries, 41, 42, 232.
Rayon, 35, 148, 168.
Reading (rĕd′ĭng), Pennsylvania, 196; maps, **177**, **191**.
Red Desert in Wyoming, 54.
Red fish, 107.
Red gum, 136.
Red River, 125; map, **103**.
Red River Valley of the North, 83; map, **81**.
Red snappers, 135, 153, 163.
Regina (rĕ-jī′ná), Canada, 247, 258; maps, 2, 28, **248**.
Reindeer, 247, 270, 273, 274.
Reno (rē′nō′), Nevada, 57, 61; maps, 28, **60**, **73**.
Resorts: in Florida, 156; on Long Island, 182; in New Jersey, 182; along the Great Lakes, 204, 206; on the Gulf of Mexico, 140; in New England, 236, 239; in Newfoundland, 269.
Revere, Paul, 4, 229, 241.
Revolutionary War, 194, 228.
Rhode Island (rōd ī′lănd), 224, 228, 232, 234, 235, 236, 240, 242; maps, 2, 29, 34, **225**, **238**.
Rice, 19, 44, 52, 86, 99, 110, 113, 125, 298; map, 132.
Richmond (rĭch′mŭnd), Virginia, 20, 147, 158, 170, 171; maps, 2, 29, **149**, **169**.
Riley, James Whitcomb, 218.
Rio Grande (rē′ō grän′dē), 17, 55, 59, 62, 100, 118, 120; map, 28, **280**.
Rio Grande Valley, Lower, 107, 108.
Rochester (rŏch′ĕs-tēr), New York, 5, 7, 198, 200; maps, 29, **177**, **191**.
Rock Creek Park, Washington, D. C., 172.
Rockford, Illinois, 220; maps, 29, **205**, **215**.
Rocky Mountain National Park, 68, 258.
Rocky Mountains, 12, 13, 56, 61, 66, 71, 72, 74, 78, 86, 99, 118, 145, 317, 321; maps, **60**, **319**.
Rome (rōm), New York, 5, 178; maps, **177**, **191**.
Roosevelt Dam, 17, 58.

INDEX 13

Roosevelt Lake, 58; map, **60**.
Roosevelt, President Franklin D., 239.
Roosevelt, Theodore, 295.
Roquefort cheese, 42.
Rosewood in Mexico, 283.
Rosin, 126, 156, 164.
Ross, Betsy, 229.
Rotation of crops, 83, 84.
Rubber: in Mexico, 279; in the West Indies, 298.
Rubber goods, 193, 203, 220, 242.
Russia (rŭsh'à), 99, 277.
Rutland (rŭt'lănd), Vermont, 236, 240; maps, **225, 238**.
Rye, 163, 206; map, 84.

Sacandaga River, 188.
Sacramento (săk-rà-měn'tō), California, 32, 46, 50; maps, 28, **37, 49**.
Sacramento River and Valley, 15, 16, 42, 44, 46, 56; map, **37**.
Saguenay (săg-ē-nā') River, 252; map, **249**.
Sahara (sà-hä'rà) Desert, 58.
Saint John, Canada, 247, 250, 251; maps, 2, **249**.
Saint John River and Valley, 250, 251.
Salem (sā'lĕm), Massachusetts, 228; maps, **225, 238**.
Salem, Oregon, 32, 42, 50; maps, 28, **37, 49**.
Salmon, 32, 45, 46, 48, 50, 232, 251, 260, 267, 272.
Salt, 47, 63, 114, 116, 117, 118, 170, 250.
Salt Lake City, Utah, 57, 74; maps, 28, **60, 73**.
Salt Lake Valley, 56.
Salton (sôl'tŭn) Sea, 44; maps, 28, **37**.
Salt River and Valley, 17, 58, 76.
Salvador (säl'và-dōr'), 294; map, **280**.
San Antonio (săn ăn-tō'nĭ-ō), Texas, 120; maps, 28, **103, 119**.
San Carlos (săn kär'lōs), Arizona, 61.
San Diego (săn dē-ā'gō), California, 1, 15, 17, 18, 45, 51, 52; maps, 2, 28, **37, 49**.
Sand dunes: in Death Valley and Mohave Desert, 47; in Indiana, 8, 9.
Sandusky (săn-dŭs'kĭ), Ohio, 8; maps, **205, 215**.
San Francisco (săn frăn-sĭs'kō), California, 13, 15, 16, 45, 46, 48, 50, 51, 296; maps, 2, 28, **37, 49**.
San Joaquin River and Valley, 42, 44, 56; map, **37**.
San Jose (hō-sā'), Costa Rica, 295; map, **281**.

San Juan (hwän') River, 294.
San Luis Potosi (sän lōō-ēs' pō-tō-sē'), Mexico, 285, 288; map, **280**.
San Pedro (săn pē'drō), Mexico, 285.
Santa Fe (săn'tà fā'), New Mexico, 57, 76; maps, 28, **60, 73**.
Santa Lucia (sän'tä lōō-sē'ä), 299; map, **281**.
Santiago (sän-tē-ä'gō), Cuba, 300; map, **281**.
Santo Domingo (sän'tō dō-mǐŋ'gō), Haiti, 300; map, **281**.
Saranac (săr'à-năk) Lake, 180; maps, **177, 191**.
Sardines, 45.
Sarnia (sär'nĭ-à), Canada, 256; maps, 2, **249**.
Saskatchewan (săs-kăch'ē-wŏn), 247, 257; maps, 28, **248**.
Saskatoon (săs-kà-tōōn'), Canada, 258; maps, 2, **248**.
Savannah (sà-văn'à), Georgia, 20, 166, 167; maps, 2, 29, **149, 169**.
Sawmills, 38, 48, 164, 186, 227, 228.
Scenery: in the Mountain States, 68; in New England, 236.
Schenectady (skĕ-nĕk'tà-dĭ), New York, 5, 196; maps, 29, **177, 191**.
School in Mexico, 288.
Schuylkill (skōōl'kĭl) River, 22; map, **177**.
Scioto (sĭ-ō'tō) River, 219; map, **205**.
Scotland (skŏt'lănd), 273.
Scranton (skrăn'tŭn), Pennsylvania, 187, 196; maps, 29, **177, 191**.
Seals, 266, 276.
Seaports: in Florida, 156; in the South Atlantic States, 150–166; in the West South Central States, 118.
Seasons in Central America, 292.
Sea trout, 135.
Seattle (sē-ăt''l), Washington, 1, 12, 13, 14, 32, 39, 42, 45, 48, 273; maps, 2, 28, **37, 49**.
Seekonk (sē'kŏŋk) River, 240.
Seminole (sĕm'ĭ-nōl) Indians, 152.
Seneca (sĕn'ē-kà) Lake, 179; map, **177**.
Sequoia (sē-kwoi'à) National Park, 34.
Seward (sū'àrd), Alaska, 273; map, **319**.
Sewing machines, 193, 221, 236.
Shad, 230.
Sheep, 12, 15, 40, 41, 54, 57, 67, 71, 74, 76, 78, 87, 114, 118, 134, 135, 162, 163, 184, 208, 234, 269; map, 71.

Shenandoah (shĕn-àn-dō'à) River and Valley, 612, 171; map, **149**.
Sherbrooke (shûr'brŏŏk), Canada, 255; map, **249**.
Shickshock (shĭk'shŏk) Hills, 251.
Shipbuilding, 228, 240, 242, 250, 251.
Shipping: in Mexico, 282; in Montreal, 254; in New England, 227; in North Central States, 93; in Vancouver, 260.
Shoes, 79, 214, 218, 224, 235, 284.
Shreveport (shrēv'pōrt), Louisiana, 116, 125; maps, 29, **103, 119**.
Shrimp, 107, 136, 153, 164.
Sierra Madre (sĭ-ĕr'à mä'drä) Mountains, 285, 289; maps, **280**, 319.
Sierra Nevada (nē-vä'dà) Mountains, 32, 50, 317; maps, **28, 319**.
Signal Hill, 269, 270.
Silk, 176, 193, 196, 220, 224, 228.
Silver: in Canada, 247, 256, 260; in Central America, 291, 294; in Cuba, 300; in Mexico, 283, 284, 285, 288; in Newfoundland, 268; in North America, 320; in the United States, 12, 13, 47, 57, 63, 64, 66, 74, 90.
Silverware, 236, 242.
Sioux (sōō) City, Iowa, 88, 96; maps, 29, **81, 94**.
Sioux Falls, South Dakota, 79, 95; maps, 29, **81, 94**.
Sioux Indians, 11.
Sioux River, 95.
Sisal (Henequen), 125, 282, 283, 298.
Sitka (sĭt'kà), Alaska, 274; map, **248**.
Ski-jumping in New England, 237.
Slate, 236.
Slater, Samuel, 234.
Smelting, 13, 17, 63, 64, 74, 97, 118, 288.
Smith, Captain John, 226.
Smithsonian Institution, Washington, D. C., 172.
Snake River, 61; maps, 28, **60**.
Snake River Desert, 54.
Soda, 47.
Sod houses on the Great Plains, 79.
Soo Canal, 204; map, **205**.
Sorghum, 86, 112.
Sorghum cane, 161.
South America, 19, 46, 125, 167, 194, 218, 245, 303–316.
South Atlantic States: 147–174, 175, 202, 223, 291; important products, 147; statistics, 147; maps, **149, 169**.
South Bend, Indiana, 8, 9, 214, 221; maps, 29, **205, 215**.

INDEX

South Carolina (kăr-ô-lī'nȧ), 20, 147, 156, 158, 159, 167, 168; maps, 29, 34, **149, 169**.
South Chicago (shĭ-kô'gō), 216.
South Dakota (dȧ-kō'tȧ), 12, 78, 79, 83, 87, 90, 95, 96, 101; maps, 28, 34, **81, 94**.
Southern Pacific Railway, 76.
South Platte River, 86; map, **60**.
South Pole, 323–324.
Soy beans, 134.
Spain (spān), 18, 262, 278, 293.
Spaniards, 76, 287, 293, 298.
Spanish mackerel, 135, 153.
Spanish Main, 291.
Spices, 167, 228.
Spinach, 108.
Spindle Top Oil Field, 116.
"Spirit of St. Louis," 18, 97, 172.
Split Rock Falls (Adirondack Mountains), 181.
Spokane (spō-kăn'), Washington, 13, 40, 320; maps, 2, 28, **37, 49**.
Spokane River, 40; map, **37**.
Sponge fisheries of Florida, 153, 154, 155.
Springfield (sprĭng'fēld), Illinois, 221; maps, 29, **205, 215**.
Springfield, Massachusetts, 3, 239, 241; maps, 29, **225, 238**.
Springfield, Ohio, 214; maps, 29, **205, 215**.
Spring Wheat Region, 83, 84, 85, 88, 95.
Squash, 26, 232.
St. Anthony's Falls, 12, 93.
St. Augustine, 153; maps, **149, 169**.
St. Croix River, 239; maps, **225, 238**.
St. Francis Valley, 254.
St. John's, Newfoundland, 262, 265, 268, 269, 270; maps, **249**, 319.
St. Johnsbury, Vermont, 242; maps, **225, 238**.
St. Johns River, 20, 156.
St. Joseph, Michigan, 88; maps, **205, 215**.
St. Lawrence River, 190, 251, 252, 253, 254, 262, 318; maps, **249**, 319.
St. Lawrence Valley, 180, 182.
St. Louis (lōō'ĭs), Missouri, 79, 88, 97, 118, 126, 127, 221; maps, 29, **81, 94**.
St. Louis River, 95.
St. Paul, Minnesota, 10, 11, 79, 88, 91, 93, 95, 126; maps, 2, 29, **81, 94**.
St. Paul's Inlet, 263.
St. Petersburg, Florida, 154, 155, 156; maps, **149, 169**.
St. Thomas, 302; map, **281**.

State Capitol of New York at Albany, 199.
State Capitol of Virginia at Richmond, 171.
State Forest Service of Maine, 228.
Staten Island, 190, 192; maps, **177, 191**.
Statue of Liberty, 244.
Steel, 8, 10, 212, 218, 220, 221, 250, 288.
Stock raising, 71, 74, 76, 258.
Stockyards, 10, 88, 95, 96, 118, 120.
Stone, 127, 224.
Stone Mountain, 21.
Storm King Mountain, 179.
Stovepipe Wells, Death Valley, 48.
Stowe, Harriet Beecher, 24.
Strait of Belle Isle, 262, 270; map, **249**.
Strait of Canso, 251.
Strait of Northumberland, 251.
Strait of Georgia, 260.
Strawberries, 44, 113, 132, 152, 162, 232.
Sudbury (sŭd'bẽr-ĭ), Ontario, 256; maps, 2, **249**.
Suez (sōō-ĕz') Canal, 295.
Sugar and sugar manufacturing and refining, 74, 76, 99, 108, 109, 125, 153, 192, 194, 196, 298, 300, 302; map, 108.
Sugar beets, 57, 61, 76, 84, 87, 108, 206; map, 108.
Sugar cane: in Cuba, 300; in Mexico, 279; in the United States, 19, 100, 109, 152; map, 108; in the West Indies, 297.
Sulphur, 88, 114, 116, 117, 288.
Sulphuric acid, 64.
Summer camps in New England, 239.
Sunnyside Hill, 63.
Superior, 93; maps, 81, 94, **205, 215**.
Supply crops, 83.
Supreme Court, United States Capitol, Washington, D. C., 173.
Susquehanna (sŭs-kwĕ-hăn'ȧ) River, 175, 176, 196, 198; maps, **177, 191**.
Susquehannocks, 176.
Swamps in Florida, 20, 151, 164.
Sweet potatoes, 86, 132, 160, 185.
Swine, 40, 74, 96, 112, 114, 118, 132, 134, 160, 184, 206, 207, 208, 269; map, 87.
Switzerland (swĭt'zẽr-lănd), 257, 260.
Sydney (sĭd'nĭ), Nova Scotia, 250, 251, 268; map, **249**.

Syracuse (sĭr'ȧ-kūs), New York, 5, 198, 200; maps, 29, **177, 191**.

Tacoma (tȧ-kō'mȧ), Washington, 15, 42, 45, 48; maps, 28, **37, 49**.
Tallahassee (tăl-ȧ-hăs'ê), Florida, 147; maps, 29, **149, 169**.
Tamiami Trail, 152.
Tampa (tăm'pȧ), Florida, 153, 156, 157; maps, 29, **149, 169**.
Tampa Bay, 157; maps, 29, **149, 169**.
Tampico (täm-pē'kō), Mexico, 279, 282, 284, 288; map, **280**.
Tangerines, 152.
Tanneries and Tanning, 186, 214, 218, 288; mineral and vegetable tanning, 186.
Tarpon (tär'pŏn) fishing, 106.
Tarpon Springs, Florida, 154, 155; map, **169**.
Tate (tāt), Georgia, 166.
Tea, 228.
Telephones on farms, 82.
Tennessee (tĕn-ĕ-sē'), 118, 126, 127, 128, 132, 133, 136, 137, 138, 140, 142, 143, 144, 148; maps, 29, 34, **131, 139**.
Tennessee River and Valley, 140, 143; maps, **131, 139**.
Terre Haute (tĕr'ē hōt'), Indiana, 221; maps, 29, **205, 215**.
Texas (tĕk'sȧs), 17, 19, 71, 100, 101, 104, 107, 110, 111, 112, 113, 114, 115, 116, 118, 120, 121, 130, 132, 134, 135, 193, 254, 278, 321; maps, 28, 34, **103, 119**.
Texas, Republic of, 19.
Texco (tĕks'cō), Mexico, 289.
Textiles, 127, 147, 176, 224, 235, 239, 242, 247.
Tidal bore, 245.
Timber, 32, 50, 57, 66, 93, 127, 142, 147, 166, 180, 202, 210, 224, 228.
Timber line, 66.
Tin, 196, 288.
Tin cans, 45, 50, 76.
Tobacco and tobacco manufacturing, 20, 26, 127, 132, 133, 135, 142, 147, 156, 158, 167, 168, 170, 184, 196, 224, 232, 233, 256, 284, 298, 300, 302, 318; map, 132.
Toledo (tȯ-lē'dō), Ohio, 6, 8, 206, 212, 220; maps, 2, 29, **205, 215**.
Tomatoes, 108, 132, 160, 167, 185, 232.
Tombigbee (tŏm-bĭg'bē) River, 19, 140; map, **131**.
Tonapah, Nevada, 64; maps, **60, 73**.

INDEX

Topeka (tŏ-pē′kȧ), Kansas, 79, 88, 89, 96; maps, 29, **81, 94**.
Toronto (tŏ-rŏn′tō), Canada, 247, 255, 256, 257; maps, 29, **249**, 319.
Tourists in Florida, 154.
Towns: in Alaska, 273; in Central America, 293, 294; in Mexico, 288; in the United States, 1, 8, 10, 20, 24, 66, 80, 88, 116, 158.
Trade winds in the West Indies, 297, 298.
Transcontinental Air Transport, 220.
Transportation: in Guatemala, 293; in Labrador, 272; in Mexico, 282, 284; in North America, 318; in the United States, 72, 126, 142, 152, 170, 202, 204, 212, 214, 220.
Trapping: in Canada, 260; in Labrador, 270.
Travel: ways of, 5; in Alaska, 274.
Trees: big trees in California, 34; cone-bearing, 136; cypress, 102, 104, 129, 164; deciduous, 136; Douglas fir, 35; elm and maple in New England, 230, 231; pine in Mexico, 283; pine, Southern, 100, 101, 136, 164; redwoods, 33, 39; Sitka spruce, 35; Western hemlock, 35; Western red cedar, 35.
Trenton (trĕn′tŭn), New Jersey, 22, 176, 193, 195; maps, 2, 29, **177, 191**.
Trick Falls, Glacier National Park, 69.
Trinidad (trĭn′ĭ-dăd), 299; map, **281**.
Trinity Cape, 252.
Tropic of Cancer, 297, 324.
Tropic of Capricorn, 324.
Trout, 232, 251, 257.
Troy (troi), New York, 196; maps, **177, 191**.
Truckee (trŭk′ē) River, 61.
Truck gardening and farming, 40, 92, 113, 132, 160, 162, 185, 186.
Tucson (tōō-sŏn′), Arizona, 17; maps, 2, 28, **60, 73**.
Tulsa (tŭl′sȧ), Oklahoma, 116, 122; maps, 29, **103, 119**.
Tuna, 45, 182.
Tung oil nuts, 153.
Tungsten, 47.
Turkeys, 114, 208.
Turnips, 86, 184, 232, 269.
Turpentine, 126, 156, 164.
Tuxpam (tōōs′päm), Mexico, 284; map, **280**.
Twain, Mark, 24.

Union Station, Washington, D. C., 172.
United Fruit Company, 291.
United States, 256, 257, 258, 261, 268, 273, 278, 283, 284, 288, 293, 294, 295, 296, 297, 300, 302; maps, 2, **28–29**, 34, 319.
United States, Our, 1–243.
United States and Canada, maps, **2**, 319.
United States Capitol, 20, 22, 23, 170, 173.
United States Department of Commerce, 172.
United States Military Academy, 196.
United States Naval Academy, 170.
United States Navy Yard: at Portsmouth, N. H., 240; at Philadelphia, 194; at Norfolk, Va., 167.
United States Treasury Building, Washington, D. C., 23, 172.
University of British Columbia, 260.
University of Toronto, 255.
Utah (ū′tô), 54, 56, 57, 62, 63, 64, 65, 66, 68, 72, 74; maps, 28, 34, **60, 73**.
Utica (ū′tĭ-kȧ), New York, 5, 198; maps, 29, **177, 191**.
Uxbridge (ŭks′brĭj), Massachusetts, 235; map, **238**.

Valley of Virginia, 162.
Vancouver (văn-kōō′vẽr), Canada, 247, 257, 258, 259, 260; maps, 2, **248**, 319.
Vancouver Island, 259, 260; maps, 37, 49, **248**, 319.
Vegetables, 30, 32, 42, 45, 50, 57, 58, 61, 62, 74, 86, 92, 108, 112, 113, 127, 132, 147, 152, 160, 162, 163, 167, 168, 170, 176, 184, 185, 186, 203, 206, 207, 208, 232, 245, 247, 260, 270, 273, 298.
Vera Cruz (vā′rä krōōs′), Mexico, 279, 282; map, **280**.
Vermont (vẽr-mŏnt′), 182, 223, 224, 231, 236, 239; maps, 29, 34, **225, 238**.
Vicksburg (vĭks′bûrg), Mississippi, 128, 129, 142; maps, 29, **131, 139**.
Victoria (vĭk-tō′rĭ-ȧ), Canada, 247, 260; maps, 2, 37, 49, **248**, 319.
Vineyards, 5, 6, 15, 185, 256.
Virginia (vẽr-jĭn′ĭ-ȧ), 147, 148, 150, 156, 158, 159, 160, 162, 164, 166, 167, 170, 226; maps, 29, 34, **149, 169**.
Virginia Beach, 167.
Virgin Islands, 302; map, **281**.
Volcanoes, 17, 273, 279, 291, 297.

Walla Walla (wŏl′ȧ wŏl′ȧ), Washington, 40; maps, **37, 49**.
Walla Walla Valley, 40.
Walrus, Alaska, 274.
Waltham (wôl′thăm), Massachusetts, 235; maps, **225, 238**.
Washing machines, 221.
Washington (wŏsh′ĭng-tŭn), 13, 32, 35, 40, 45, 46, 48, 210, 260, 321; maps, 28, 34, **37, 49**.
Washington, D. C., 20, 22, 23, 170, 172, 173; maps, 2, **149, 169**.
Washington, George, 20, 22, 165, 170.
Washington Monument, 20, 172.
Watches, 236, 242.
Waterbury (wô′tẽr-bĕr-ĭ), Connecticut, 236, 242; maps, **225, 238**.
Watermelons, 61, 132, 156, 160, 161.
Water power: in Canada, 252, 254, 256; in Labrador, 272; in Mexico, 279, 284, 285; in Newfoundland, 266, 268; in North America, 320; in the United States, 20, 34, 59, 93, 95, 137, 138, 142, 143, 148, 150, 168, 190, 198, 224, 235, 239, 321.
Watertown (wô′tẽr-toun), South Dakota, 95; maps, 29, **81, 94**.
Watkins (wŏt′kĭnz) Glen, New York, 179; map, **191**.
Weber Canyon, Utah, 72.
Weehawken (wē-hô′kĕn), New Jersey, 190; map, **191**.
Wenatchee (wē-năch′ē̇), Washington, 40; maps, **37, 49**.
Wenatchee Valley, 13, 40, 41.
West Indies, The, 19, 125, 150, 245, 292, 297–302; climate, 297; crops, 297–298; Cuba, 298, 300; Haiti, 300; Jamaica, 300; land of, 297; people, 298; Puerto Rico, 302; Virgin Islands, 302; map, **280–281**.
West North Central States, The, 78–98; important products, 79; statistics, 79; maps, **81, 94**.
West Point, 196, 199.
West Rutland, Vermont, 236.
West South Central States, The, 99–125; important products, 99; statistics, 99; maps, **103, 119**.
West Virginia (vẽr-jĭn′ĭ-ȧ), 147, 148, 162, 163, 166, 218; maps, 29, 34, **149, 169**.
Westward Movement, 27, 30.
Whaling, 229.
Wheat, 6, 12, 32, 40, 44, 48, 57, 62, 63, 74, 80, 83, 84, 85, 87, 88, 92, 93, 95, 96, 110, 113, 128, 140, 163, 167, 168, 184, 198, 206, 245, 247, 256, 257, 258, 283, 298; map, 83.

INDEX

Wheeling, 170.
Whitefish, 210.
White House, 20, 22, 23, 170, 172, 173.
White Mountains, 223, 224, 236; map, **225**.
White Sulphur Springs, West Virginia, 165.
Whitney, Eli, 112.
Whittemore, Amos, 235.
Whittier, John G., 234.
Wichita (wĭch'ĭ-tô), Kansas, 88, 96; maps, 29, **81, 94**.
Wigwams, 26.
Wilkes-Barre (wĭlks'bär-ĭ), Pennsylvania, 175, 187, 189, 196, 197; maps, 29, **177, 191**.
Willamette (wĭ-lăm'ĕt) River, 13, 14, 42, 45, 48, 56; map, **37**.
Willamette Valley, 15, 40, 42, 50.
Williamsport (wĭl'yȧmz-pōrt), Pennsylvania, 196; maps, **177, 191**.
Williams, Roger, 242.
Wilmington (wĭl'mĭng-tŭn), Delaware, 22, 147, 168; maps, **177, 191**.
Wilmington, North Carolina, 167; maps, 29, **149, 169**.
Wilson Dam, 143.
Winchester (wĭn'chĕs-tēr), Virginia, 162; maps, **149, 169**.
Wind Cave National Park, 90.
Windsor (wĭn'zēr). Canada, 216, 256; map, **249**.
Wine, 44.

Winnipeg (wĭn'ĭ-pĕg), Canada, 247, 257; maps, 2, **248**, 319.
Winston-Salem (wĭn'stŭn-sā'lĕm), North Carolina, 158; maps, 29, **149, 169**.
Winter in Montreal, 254.
Winter sports, 237, 239.
Winter wheat, 84, 97.
Winter wheat region, 83, 88, 96.
Winthrop, John, 226.
Wisconsin (wĭs-kŏn'sĭn), 10, 90, 93, 203, 204, 206, 207, 210, 211, 212, 213, 214, 217, 218; maps, 29, 34, **205, 215**.
Wizard Island, 33.
Wolves in Labrador, 270.
Wood pulp, 138, 148, 170, 186, 210, 224, 230, 247, 252, 254, 268, 272.
Woodsville, New Hampshire, 227; map, **238**.
Wool, 50, 57, 71, 76, 118, 208, 234.
Woolen goods, 97, 193, 235, 240.
Woolen mills, 50, 208, 235, 240.
Woonsocket (wōōn-sŏk'ĕt), Rhode Island, 242; maps, **225, 238**.
Worcester (wŏŏs'tēr), Massachusetts, 3, 236, 239; maps, 29, **225, 238**.
World War II, 45.
Wrangell (răŋ'gĕl), Alaska, 274.
Wright Field, Dayton, 220.
Wyoming (wĭ-ō'mĭng), 54, 56, 57, 62, 63, 64, 66, 71, 74, 76, 86, 87, 90; maps, 28, 34, **60, 73**.

Wyoming Valley, 175.

Yakima (yăk'ĭ-mȧ), Washington, 40; maps, **37, 49**.
Yakima Valley, 40.
Yale University, 242.
"Yankee Clippers," 228.
Yazoo (yăz'ōō) Basin, 128.
Yazoo-Mississippi Delta, 128.
Yazoo River, 128; map, **131**.
Yellowstone Falls, 68.
Yellowstone Lake, 68; map, **60**.
Yellowstone National Park, 68; map, **60**.
Yellowstone River, 12, 68; map, **60**.
Yonkers (yŏŋ'kērz), New York, 196; maps, **177, 191**.
Yosemite (yō-sĕm'ĭ-tē) Falls, 33.
Yosemite National Park, 34.
Youngstown (yŭngz'toun), Ohio, 218, 220, 221; maps, 29, **205, 215**.
Yucatan (yōō-kä-tän'), 125, 278, 283, 284, 292; map, **280**.
Yukon (yōō'kŏn), 247; map, **248**.
Yukon River, 273, 318; maps, **248**, 319.
Yuma (yōō'mȧ), Arizona, 17, 58, 59; maps, **60, 73**.

Zanesville (zānz'vĭl), Ohio, 213; maps, **205, 215**.
Zinc, 57, 63, 66, 74, 90, 97, 114, 188, 210, 211, 212, 256, 268, 300, 320.

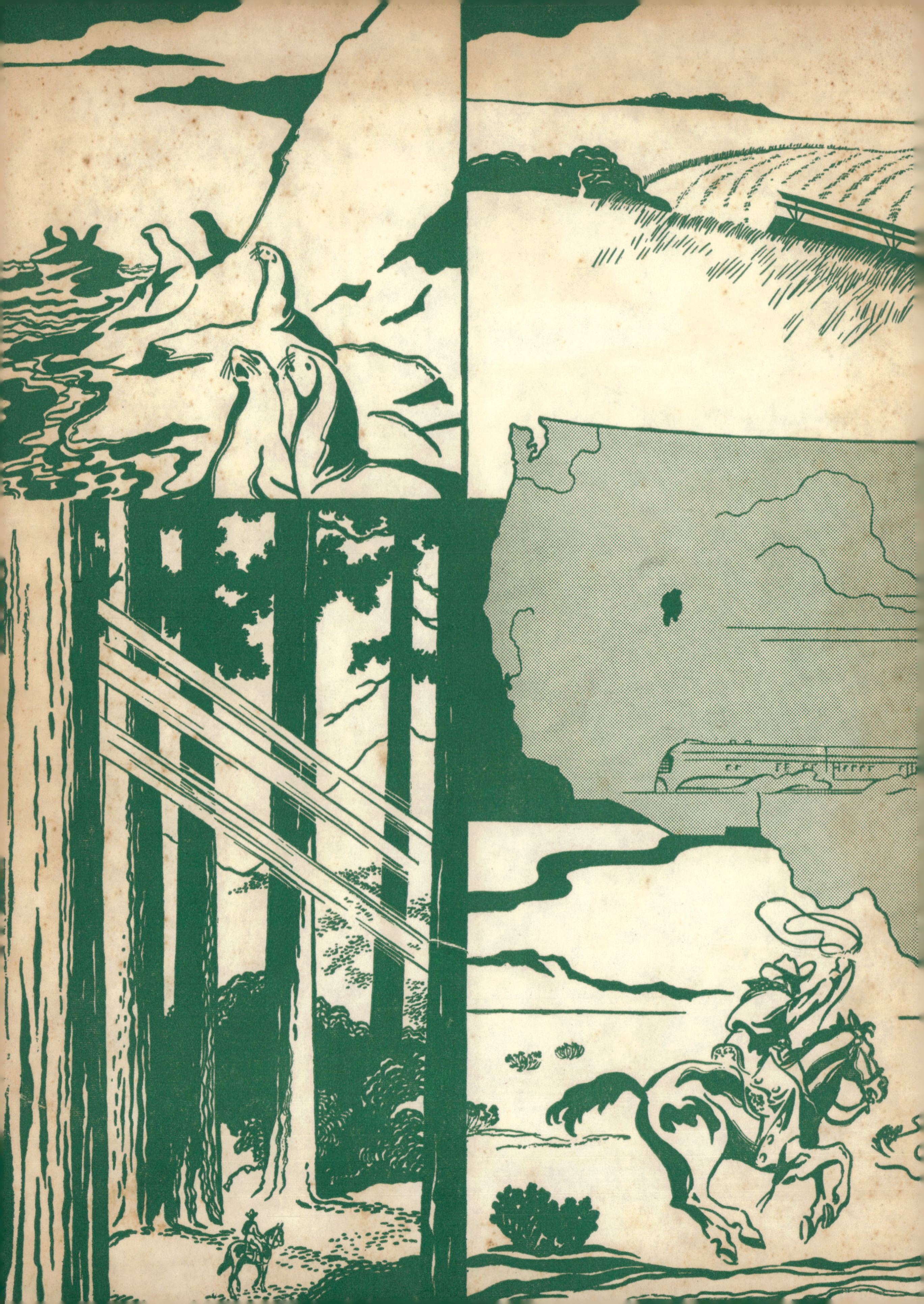